CRUCIBLE OF NATIONS

CRUCIBLE OF NATIONS

SCOTLAND FROM VIKING AGE TO MEDIEVAL KINGDOM

ADRIÁN MALDONADO

Published in 2021 by
NMS Enterprises Limited – Publishing
a division of NMS Enterprises Limited
National Museums Scotland
Chambers Street, Edinburgh EH1 1JF

Reprinted in 2024

Text and photographic images © National Museums Scotland 2021, 2024 (unless otherwise credited: see Acknowledgements page at the end of this book)

Format and additional material
© National Museums Scotland 2021, 2024

No part of this publication may be reproduced, stored in a retrieval system or transmitted in any form or by any means, electronic, mechanical, photocopying, recording or otherwise, without the prior written permission of the publisher.

The right of Adrián Maldonado to be identified as the author of this book has been asserted by him in accordance with the Copyright, Designs and Patents Act 1988.

British Library Cataloguing in Publication Data
A catalogue record for this book is available from the British Library.

ISBN: 978-1-910682-43-2

THE COVER
Cover illustration shows the Hunterston Brooch; NMS X.FC 8 (front and back views).

IMAGE CAPTIONS
page II: Silver bullion from the top layer of the Galloway Hoard.
page VII: Thistle brooch terminal fragment and other silver objects from the Skaill Hoard, Orkney.
page VIII: Silver pectoral cross from the Galloway Hoard.
page X: Top view of the lid of the vessel from the Galloway Hoard.
pages XVII and 212: Detail of a Trewhiddle-style disc-brooch from the Galloway Hoard.

Book design and cover by Mark Blackadder.
Printed and bound in Great Britain by Bell & Bain Ltd, Glasgow.

This product is made of material from well-managed FSC®-certified forests and other sources.

www.nms.ac.uk
www.glenmorangie.com

For a full listing of NMS Enterprises Limited – Publishing titles and related merchandise visit: www.nms.ac.uk/books

Contents

✶

FOREWORD by Dr Christopher Breward
NATIONAL MUSEUMS SCOTLAND   IX

FOREWORD by Thomas Moradpour
THE GLENMORANGIE COMPANY   XI

INTRODUCTION by Martin Goldberg
NATIONAL MUSEUMS SCOTLAND   XIII

CRUCIBLE OF NATIONS

CHAPTER ONE

Naming nations   3

CHAPTER TWO

An imperial age   25

CHAPTER THREE

Worlds of the dead   47

CHAPTER FOUR

Age of raids   73

CHAPTER FIVE

The serpent and thorn   101

CHAPTER SIX

A silver age   129

CHAPTER SEVEN

An animated world   161

CHAPTER EIGHT

An experimental age   189

Envoi   209

BIBLIOGRAPHY   213

INDEX   232

ACKNOWLEDGEMENTS   240

Foreword

Dr Christopher Breward
Director
NATIONAL MUSEUMS SCOTLAND

Crucible of Nations presents the findings of the latest phase of the long-standing relationship between National Museums Scotland and Glenmorangie, a partnership which has changed understandings of early medieval Scotland through innovative research into the national collections. Over the last three years, objects and evidence from the 9th–12th centuries have been reassessed and reconceptualised to address important questions about how the kingdom of Scotland emerged out of a multiplicity of earldoms, kingdoms and cultures, which were shaped by connections with the Anglo-Saxon world, Ireland and Scandinavia. This book traces the roots of what we today understand as Scotland, telling a compelling story of multilingualism and diversity not often associated with the medieval past, and demonstrating the connections that we can make to individual lived experience through the interrogation of material culture.

We are hugely grateful to Glenmorangie for their partnership and their support in realising this, the third in a trilogy of National Museums Scotland books about early medieval Scotland. Over more than a decade, our relationship has grown and deepened through our shared enthusiasm and ambition. *Crucible of Nations* is testimony to Glenmorangie's commitment to engaging with our national collections and stories with vision and imagination.

EDINBURGH 2021

Foreword

Thomas Moradpour
President and Chief Executive Officer
THE GLENMORANGIE COMPANY

We are proud to have inspired so much pioneering research into Scotland's early medieval history, since our collaboration with National Museums Scotland began in 2008. And we are particularly delighted to share *Crucible of Nations*, the third exceptional book celebrating the discoveries of The Glenmorangie Research Partnership.

Already our partnership has set the agenda for groundbreaking research into the early people of Scotland, and the pivotal transfer of power which accompanied the Romans' departure from Britain in the 5th century. Now *Crucible of Nations* reveals the impact of the vikings and the emergence of Scotland as a nation in the 12th century – told through the Museum's unrivalled collections.

Over the years, we have supported the work of archaeological research teams and artists on their mission to understand, interpret and present these collections to the wider world. We are honoured to have a share in the responsibility of telling (part of) Scotland's wonderful story for future generations.

As it takes us at least ten years to make our renowned single malt whisky, we perhaps appreciate more than most the precious commodity of time. Our partnership has allowed teams at National Museums Scotland to take the time to unpack extraordinary stories and to reveal new insights into Scotland's past – all brought to life in their inspiring galleries and in this illuminating publication.

EDINBURGH 2021

Introduction

Martin Goldberg
Principal Curator, Medieval Archaeology and History
NATIONAL MUSEUMS SCOTLAND

Horns blaring, hounds yelping, deer panting, the drum of horse's hooves galloping – the sounds of the hunt brought to life on an enormous stone slab. Above the hunt scene the endless meander in and out of interlace-decorated circles, symmetrical, rhythmic and infinite in their perfection, are understandable as art. The paired symbols at the top seem more abstract, but communicate a language now lost. The top symbol, like a lightning flash zig-zag breaking through abstract clouds, is part of a surrounding framework of twisting vine-scrolls, a Mediterranean plant, but populated by fantastic beasts. Below the hunt scene, an even more ancient art was used, with new levels of complexity – four fluid forms radiating out from the centre into a glory of interlocking triple spirals, scrolling out symmetrically to fill a perfect square, as if stretching to the four corners of the earth. Small triangles point in cardinal directions – north, south, east and west.

Despite the realism of the central scene, the sounds of the hunt never swirled around this stone. Instead it was the sound of a language from an ancient Mediterranean empire, singing a chant originally composed in the Holy Land of another continent. The life-size symbol of the cross that had dominated the front of the slab originated from those distant lands. The massive Hilton of Cadboll, Easter Ross, cross-slab is still a sight to behold, but in the past it was also part of a feast for the senses: the sound of Latin chants, the taste of continental wine, the smell of wax as the flicker of sputtering candles made those ancient designs and symbols dance.[1]

Originally over 3.5 metres high and 1.4 metres wide, the cross-slab provides a broad canvas in carefully dressed stone for a complex arrangement of icon, symbol and art. The precisely laid out design has been likened to an illuminated manuscript page rendered in stone, but we are missing the vibrant colour of the Book of Kells or the Lindisfarne Gospels. The cross-slab was probably created around the same time as these famous gospel books, during a high-point of artistic achievement in these islands in the 8th century AD (chapter 2). Between the 9th and 12th centuries these sacred books were curated in monasteries across Europe, treated like relics in their own right. The best archaeological evidence for the production of manuscripts

Opposite: Cross-slab of sandstone carved in relief from Hilton of Cadboll, Easter Ross, height 2340mm, NMS X.IB 189.

such as these in Scotland is nearby on the Fearn peninsula, at the monastery at Portmahomack, and it is from there the craftspeople who carved the Hilton of Cadboll cross-slab would have come. These artists were trained in design that is strikingly similar to the finest illuminated books.

Although the manuscripts produced at Portmahomack do not, as far as we know, survive, Scotland is incredibly rich in early Christian sculpture (chapter 7): and the Hilton of Cadboll cross-slab is one of the prime examples. The skill of the people carving stone on the Fearn peninsula in the 8th century was an achievement of international significance [2.14]. It is difficult to find comparable execution of detail and variety of ornament in stone carving elsewhere in contemporary Christendom.

When excavations at the chapel at Hilton of Cadboll discovered the broken base of the cross-slab in 2001, scientific dating evidence demonstrated it had been re-set here during the 12th century. This was 300–400 years after the slab was carved.[2]

Newly re-erected alongside a 12th-century chapel, the Hilton of Cadboll cross-slab probably would have seemed archaic in its decoration. It was as separated in time from its point of creation as the 17th century is from us today. How many of us now can interpret the intricate detail of a Baroque chapel? Similarly, how many 12th-century Christians on the Fearn peninsula would have understood all the elements of this 8th-century cross-slab? No one was carving this kind of sculpture any more in Scotland; the skill of masons in dressing stone for the glory of the Christian God was by then being invested in church architecture in new, continental fashions (chapter 8). The Christian cross design would still have been recognisable, but what must they have thought of the Pictish symbols on the reverse? Would anyone have understood them at this point, at least 300 years after they had fallen out of use (chapter 1)? The Picts may have disappeared from the landscape, but they had not completely disappeared from the scholarly imagination:

12th-century histories still told stories about the fate of the Picts and what it meant for the origins of the realm. They had, by this time, been reduced to stock characters destined to pave the way for their successors, the Scots, and this stereotyping of the past is in part responsible for our own poor understanding of these historical processes now.

Like the reuse of ancient *spolia* in medieval churches in Rome, what the 12th-century setting of the Hilton of Cadboll cross-slab tells us is that, centuries after it was carved, it still signalled the early Christian heritage of the community. It was a high point of achievement in what was now the distant past, something to be proud of and to cherish.

The cultural context that produced the Hilton of Cadboll cross-slab was very different to the time of its re-erection. What changes in society, in how people lived, had swirled around this stone during those centuries? Even though we do not know as much as we would like about the history of the Hilton of Cadboll stone between the 9th and 12th centuries, this book is a huge step towards filling in this gap.

BEGINNINGS AND ENDINGS

The years around AD 800 are often thought of as the beginning of the Viking Age, but it was also the beginning of an ending. Within a hundred years the kingdoms of the Picts were no longer mentioned in contemporary sources. With them went much more than just Pictish symbols. This century also represents an ending for the spiral art of interlocking triskeles and trumpet scrolls that survived in the lower square panel of the Hilton of Cadboll cross-slab.[3] These 'heritage motifs' are characteristic of what modern scholars have considered as 'Celtic' or 'Ultimate La Tène' art, with stylistic connections stretching back over a thousand years into European prehistory.[4] Why this style fell out of use for decorating stone, metal and manuscripts is as mysterious as the silence of our sources about the Picts. But the disappearance of the Pictish language at the same time seems more than a coincidence (chapter 1). It is a reminder of the fragility of cultural heritage, even when carved in stone.

Time and space are key issues here – much more so than in the previous two books produced by the Glenmorangie Research Project, a unique partnership initiated in 2008. This book has a tighter chronological framework than the first millennium of silver use covered in *Scotland's Early Silver: Transforming Roman Pay-offs to Pictish Treasures* (2017) and considers the varied landscapes and seascapes of Scotland in a more integrated way than the thematic and agenda-setting approach of *Early Medieval Scotland: Individuals, Communities and Ideas* (2012).[5] The three approaches in the subtitle of the latter publication were never intended to be comprehensive or prescriptive. They will be used throughout this book not as single chapter themes, but as part of the kaleidoscope of perspectives that the project has always advocated.[6] As with *Scotland's Early Silver*, this book is broadly chronological, but each chapter goes from events to processes and back again, reflecting on what material evidence can tell us about this period that historical documents cannot, and how these different records can be both complementary and contradictory.

The narrative (chapters 2, 8) starts and ends with 'long' centuries that de-emphasise events and show how material culture evidence is often better at demonstrating longer-term processes of change. What we think of as the 'Viking Age', with the 'Viking world' as its international context, is presented here as a series of overlapping 'Ages' and 'worlds' with different types of material culture chosen to illustrate them. Viking-age objects are traditionally assigned broad date ranges, but the approach in this book provides a greater sense that the 9th century is very different to the 11th. It considers Scotland's 'Viking world' in the context of regions usually left out of this discourse. Silver hoards in particular span these centuries, but the St Ninian's Isle Hoard, deposited in *c*.800, is a world away from the Burray Hoard, deposited in *c*.1000. Chapter 6 develops further the narrative begun at the end of *Scotland's Early Silver*, including the significance of 'opting out' of the hacksilver economy in some regions, and the slow emergence of a coinage economy (chapter 8). This provides a good example of how this book takes some different approaches, but also how it complements and connects to other parts of the Glenmorangie Research Project.

TIME AND SPACE

The geography of what we now call Scotland fundamentally affects how we interpret its history and the archaeological record. The modern boundaries of Scotland provide the usual frame to our historical picture, but this analogy should not be stretched too far back in time because Scotland's long and indented coastlines have always provided a means of contact and movement, and not necessarily to the closest neighbouring point of land. The line between Berwick and Carlisle which defines the modern land boundary is largely meaningless for the period under consideration in this book (chapter 8).

The fluctuating connections with other parts of Britain to the south and especially to Ireland have fundamentally shaped Scottish history, but new axes of contact with the world beyond these islands opened up at the beginning of our period that would change Scotland's history. Northern Britain has only had direct contact with Scandinavia and regular crossings to Norway for the last 1200 years. All previous sea connections to continental Europe began far to the south with different long-range systems developing up the Atlantic in the west or east towards the river systems emptying into the North Sea. These seascapes are of great importance across every age, but take on a fresh importance with direct connections to Scandinavia which were established for the first time from the 9th century. The way in which Viking raids (chapter 4) began at both Iona, Argyll and Lindisfarne, Northumberland, facing opposite directions but equally connected to the northern seaways, is emblematic of the reorientations of the centuries to come. Portmahomack was also subjected to a historically undocumented onslaught at this time, revealed through excavation. But the apocalyptic image of the Viking Age is somewhat tempered by the survival of the Hilton of Cadboll stone, along with Nigg and Shandwick elsewhere on the Fearn peninsula, still standing tall today.

Of course, carved stone monuments are designed to outlast their own time. Objects that do not often survive, such as those made from organic materials – wood, textile and leather – probably played a greater part in everyday life, meaning we are missing huge parts of the past.

The objects that do survive most readily, often made of harder materials such as metal and stone, give us a different view of time because of that longevity. These objects could play a part in multiple human lives – inherited, they could connect generations, taking with them genealogies and networks of human relations (chapters 3, 5). Objects are most often understood through particular moments in their lives – the day they were made, the time they were damaged and repaired, or the point at which they were committed to the ground. It is much harder to imagine the lives of people who lived with those objects all the days in between.

The focus of this book will be what we can learn from the things that have survived from this period, the objects people made, cherished and passed on, the things they consumed, destroyed, repaired and replaced. These people are the players acting against the backdrop of the geographical area we now call Scotland and the dramatic historical setting we call the Viking Age. While their historical records provide the usual script, there are always new stories to tell. In chapter 1, we will introduce those actors, their languages, and some of their names. But when so much of the historical script is missing and so many people who lived are voiceless to us, we must take advantage of the many stories contained in the objects themselves.[7] This book will look at what survives and put it centre stage – a richly illustrated material culture study that can provide some new answers to old questions and new questions to ask of previous certainties.

During the period AD 800–1200, the nation we now call Scotland began to take shape: it was not called this at the beginning of this period, and while at the end a significant area was being referred to as Scotland it was also not a finished project. There were regional kingdoms and various languages in 800 just as in 1200. What became Scotland was a product of the agency of Scots as much as the fluctuating fortunes of their neighbours. Multiple ideas of Scotland were coming into being among those neighbours and other developing national identities (chapters 1, 8). Artistic metaphors abound in trying to describe these complex cultural processes. The title of this book, *Crucible of Nations*, reflects this melting-pot of languages, objects and ideas, from which the medieval kingdom and ultimately the modern nation we call Scotland were moulded.

NOTES

1. Goldberg 2012, 160.
2. James et al. 2008.
3. Goldberg 2012, 151–4, 180–1.
4. Goldberg 2015a, 2015b.
5. Blackwell et al. 2017; Clarke et al. 2012.
6. Goldberg 2012, 206.
7. Clarke et al. 2012, XIX; Goldberg 2012, 203.

CRUCIBLE OF NATIONS

SCOTLAND FROM VIKING AGE TO MEDIEVAL KINGDOM

CHAPTER ONE
Naming nations

Despite appearances, this book is not actually about Scotland. That would be too limiting, because 'Scotland' is a term rarely used before the 12th-century period covered here. Even then, it referred to a kingdom which covered only part of the modern nation of Scotland. As late as the early 13th century, the term Scotland (in English) or *Scotia* (Latin) still referred to a territory that was north of the Forth–Clyde line, south of Moray and excluding much of the west coast.[1] Even when it exerted control beyond this core area, those lands were still referred to by name – for instance, Galloway and Cumbria in the southwest, and Northumbria or even just England in the southeast. From the 11th century, kings of Alba and later Scotland dominated much of the landmass north of the Tweed, and often well beyond, but the regions to the north and west remained outwith their reach. Argyll and the Inner Hebrides continued as a separate Lordship of the Isles throughout the medieval period, while much of the north, including the western isles, remained in the earldom of Orkney. So the political entity of Scotland did not yet exist in the 9th century; and by the end of the 12th it was only part of the story. We will continue to use the term as a geographical shorthand from here on in, as the collection in National Museums Scotland used to tell this story derives from its modern boundaries.

It is messy, then, to consider the north as a whole, but we believe this bigger story is worth telling precisely because of its diversity. The story of a 'crucible of nations' is not of any single people, much less a modern nation-state. It is about shared heritage and interaction, without ignoring these different voices. It is about shared experiences in the making. This story is valid to all its parts since, regardless of this variety of language and customs, they were joined by the networks which only material culture can reveal. This is a story not just of Scotland, but of the medieval kingdoms of England, Ireland, Isle of Man and Norway, and many others whose names are less well-known. It is a shared history of how all of these took shape, from a northern perspective.

In archaeology we do not dig any one time period: we lay out grids and trenches, then record faithfully regardless of what we find. The Museum's collections are rather like that – objects

Opposite: Reverse of the Hunterston Brooch, bearing Norse runic inscription on the hoop naming the owner *Malbriþa*, likely the Gaelic name Máel Brigte, Ayrshire, diameter 122 mm; NMS X.FC 8.

Figs 1.1a–b: Carved stone (and detail) bearing Pictish symbols and armed male figures, Brough of Birsay, Orkney, 8th or 9th century, height 217 cm; NMS X.IB 243.

from every aspect of Scotland's past, which we try to order and present in an engaging way. Often these objects are parcelled out into time periods and cultural groupings – Iron Age, Viking Age – to tell a story which is somewhat pre-determined. This book is an investigation which has never been attempted. It takes all of Scotland as its grid, and cuts an arbitrary sample trench through the 9th–12th centuries to investigate a period of rapid, dramatic change on a broad scale.

To embark on this journey, we still need to introduce the lay of the land, and the cast of characters. Because of the nature of archaeology, the focus is rarely on specific historical events, though we do have some people's names. A flying survey of the names and languages inscribed into the collections at National Museums Scotland will help to set the stage.

CRUCIBLE OF NATIONS

Figs 1.2a–b: *coordinate* by Simone ten Hompel, 2020; NMS X.2020.32; (below) detail of silver inset with silhouettes of early medieval silver objects on display.

THE GLENMORANGIE COMMISSION

The Glenmorangie Research Project has fostered creative approaches to Scotland's medieval past since its inception in 2008. The first phase of the project involved the creation of a wooden Pictish throne, an object which does not survive but is depicted on several carved stones of the 8th and 9th centuries. The second and third phases of the project took this approach further, with a broader set of craft commissions. We challenged modern craftspeople to recreate other objects that survive only in fragments – such as drinking-horns, leather satchels, bronze and iron handbells, and hacked Roman silver.[2]

For the fourth phase of the Glenmorangie Research Project we tried something new. Instead of a recreation or reconstruction of an archaeological object, we would approach a master craftsperson to respond to our collections through their medium in whatever form they chose. The Glenmorangie Commission was awarded to Simone ten Hompel. A metalsmith for over 45 years, Simone is one of the foremost craft artists and educators working in Britain. She is admired for her metalwork and sculptures which challenge how we see domestic objects.

Over a year of close collaboration, alongside Sarah Rothwell, Curator of Modern and Contemporary Design at National Museums Scotland, we opened our collections on and off display to Simone, who was particularly fascinated by our early medieval silver objects. She also travelled to Orkney to experience the landscapes of some of the Museum's most iconic collections, including the Skaill Hoard (chapter 6). In return, Simone took us into her workshop in London and taught us the basics of silversmithing in an eye-opening experience with other educators and students at the Glasgow School of Art.

Simone's response to this year immersed in early medieval metalwork was *coordinate*, a multimedia work of corten steel with inserts of silver and gold inlay. It represents an abstracted interpretation of Scotland's landmass, which explores Scotland's journey through time, its changing landscape, and the continual rediscovery of its past. *coordinate* was acquired into the permanent collection of National Museums Scotland in 2020 and is now on display in the 'Making and Creating' gallery in the National Museum of Scotland [Figs 1.2a–b].

AN EXPERIMENTAL AGE

Perhaps the single most important aspect of the landmass of Scotland at the turn of the millennium is the diversity of cultural landscapes that it contained. Regardless of what they may have called themselves, traces of many voices have come down to us in a variety of forms. In places like the southwest of Scotland it would not have been rare in our period to hear forms of British, Gaelic, Norse and English languages. Everyone has a mother tongue, but few people in this time could get by with one language alone.

Objects cannot prove the existence of an identity. The best way to attest to a group of self-identifying people is to have a testimony in their own words, but we have precious few texts surviving from the first millennium AD in Scotland. In the histories that do survive, we know people grouped themselves into broadly 'ethnic' categories: hence we have the *Historia ecclesiastica gentis Anglorum*, the ecclesiastical history of the Angles (written in Latin at Jarrow by Bede in *c*.730).

However, at the start of our period in the 9th century we begin to see evidence for history and literature being written down in the vernacular, i.e. the everyday spoken language of a place. Latin remained prestigious in learned circles, but had not been the spoken language anywhere in Britain for centuries.[3]

Perhaps the most famous examples of such vernacular sources relevant to our period are the Icelandic sagas, courtly tales of specific lineages and regions such as the *Orkneyinga Saga*, written down in 13th-century Iceland but compiled from oral tales in Old Norse gathered in Orkney from at least the 12th century.[4] Welsh, Irish and Old English literature, legal texts and histories burst onto the scene in this era like never before.[5] It is the first sign that something is changing in these centuries. None of the historical sources that survives is a complete and unsullied account of actual events, but taken together these will provide us with key names and dates.

From such documentary sources we can discern some of the main labels people used to describe themselves and others. Where Scotland is concerned, only in rare cases can we know the descriptors they used, since so few of our surviving sources date from before the 12th century. This is why all these descriptors used here, from Scotland to the Scots themselves, should be taken as shorthand for a much more complex reality on the ground.

Take the Picts for example. We have no single text or object where someone names themselves as a Pict [1.1a]. However, we have late Roman, Irish, British, English, and later Icelandic, accounts of Picts, so we can be confident this was a real term in common use.[6] But even in the absence of accounts in their own words, we know there were other, more specific labels used within the Pictish territories. The Irish annals and later Scottish historical texts refer to Fortriu, Orkney, Ce, Atholl and to other regional labels. The term 'Pict' was thus used of those who shared a language, but was not a straightforward ethnicity with which everyone north of the Forth automatically identified, and almost certainly had changing meanings from the 5th–9th centuries.[7] The kingdom of Fortriu based around the Moray Firth became dominant in the late 7th century, until the term became almost interchangeable with Pictland; yet a long-observed north–south divide began to harden by the end of the 9th century. The Picts and Fortriu famously 'disappear' from our sources by 900, and we begin to hear of a kingdom of Alba in central Scotland, a new kingdom of Moray in the north where Fortriu had been.

By contrast, for the Britons we have some evidence of a wider ethnic self-awareness in their own words, in the testimonies of St Patrick and Gildas since the 5th and 6th centuries respectively.[8] But the Britons also shape-shift in our period. From the 9th century, Welsh writers referred to themselves in Latin as *Britanni*, and their territories by the old Roman provincial title of *Britannia*, but in their own language they were

Cymry, meaning brethren or compatriots. In the 9th-century *Historia Brittonum* – a Latin history of the Britons written in northern Wales in *c*.830 – we see a keen awareness and acceptance of a kinship among the Britons of western and northern Britain. This effort to capture a pan-British identity was probably galvanised in opposition to the expanding power of the Mercian and Northumbrian kingdoms, which was threatening to sunder these ancient connections.[9] Old English sources in our period began to use the labels *Walh* or *Wealh* for Britons generally, a term used across the Germanic languages to denote both Latin and Celtic-speakers, but perhaps retaining a tinge of its pejorative meaning of 'subject peoples'.[10] From the 10th century, the vernacular term *Cymry* was also adopted by English-speakers in Northumbria as reflected in the term *Cumbra Lond*, Cumberland. As these northern regions were absorbed into the kingdoms of Scotland and England, the word *Cymry* settled into its use as a term mainly for Wales and the Welsh. Tellingly, the *Historia Brittonum* was translated into Gaelic in 11th-century Fife as the *Lebor Bretnach*, a sign of changing times in the north.[11]

The British and Pictish languages in this period were in steep decline in the north, but it is too simple to say that this was due to the expansion of a single Gaelic-speaking people. The *Scotti* were another people first mentioned in late Roman sources alongside the Picts, disparagingly for the most part, but by the early medieval period *Scotus* in Latin generally referred to any speaker of Gaelic. This is potentially confusing as it could refer to people anywhere from Ireland to the kingdom of Dál Riata in the west of Scotland, and by the 9th century increasingly by the Picts as well. This is why a 9th-century Irish scholar in Carolingian France was referred to as *John Scottus Eriugena*, John the Irish-born Gael, to distinguish him from Gaelic speakers in Britain.[12] Indeed, the collective noun *Goídil*, 'Gaelic-speakers', was only coined in the 9th century, in acknowledgement of the widening use of the language across nations.[13] In the sources composed in Ireland, people were more commonly described by the name of their kingdom, region or kindred, so neither 'Irish' nor 'Gael' is particularly useful except as a shorthand, and we can expect the same applies to the 'Scots' of northern Britain as well. Like the Pictish kingdom of Fortriu, and the British kingdom of Alt Clut, the kingdom of Dál Riata also disappears from our sources by the 10th century.[14] The term 'Gaelic', although a late coinage, will be used here for the sake of simplicity to describe the language and its speakers.

It is interesting to note that instead of the vernacular terms Alba or *Cymry*, it was the English words 'Scotland' and 'Wales' that became commonly used by the later medieval period.[15] We can only understand this in the context of the rise of a new entity in our period, *Englaland*, a kingdom made up of English-speaking realms.[16] Not long before, in the early 8th century, the historian Bede had delineated the considerable diversity among the current occupants of this land, including Angles, Saxons and Jutes among others, each belonging to kingdoms such as Bernicia, Deira and Mercia. It was rare and exceptional in his time for one king to rule over the rest. But in the century that was to follow, over-kingship became the norm under the powerful kings of Mercia. In the 9th century, Alfred of Wessex (r.871–99) would commission a new version of Bede's history, this time in Old English rather than Latin. Alfred also styled himself in new ways, as king of not just the English but *Angol-saxones*, or *Anglorum Saxonum rex*.[17]

Yet the emerging entity of *Englaland,* or the land of the *Angelcynn*, the Angles, defined in part by their shared language, was not a straightforward 'unification' of all the English-speaking peoples under powerful kings. *Englaland* did not include all the English-speaking realms, some of which remained in the hands of the kings of Alba.[18] Indeed, the Forth–Tyne zone effectively remained ethno-linguistically 'debatable land' through to the 13th century, variously claimed but remaining formally external to both *Scotia* and *Englaland*.[19]

There is now considerable debate over the term 'Anglo-Saxon', as it is a commonly used archaeological and historical label, but one which has also been used to foster a distorted view of the past since at least the 19th century.[20] The use of this double-barrelled identity has a complicated origin, but it was certainly one of the labels appearing in our sources as early as the 8th century, and promoted by Alfred in the 9th century. Again, as in the case of the Picts, this is no guarantee that anyone accepted the term 'Anglo-Saxon' as an identifier at the time. The historian Bede may have preferred the term *Angli* for his own people, but the contemporary Irish sources only ever refer to the Northumbrians by one word: *Saxan*.

It is not until later in the 10th century that we can begin to speak of an entity known as 'England', even as regional labels like 'Wessex' and 'Mercia' remained in use. So while we must strive to be specific in describing actors in this narrative, and use regional labels where possible, the material evidence only rarely allows us that luxury. It will not always be possible to avoid using catch-all terms for clarity. In this, 'Anglo-Saxon' is still preferable to English for periods before the later 10th century because, as with 'Scotland', the term 'England' is a specific historical construct emerging in the era we are describing; and in fact we will be able to trace its emergence in part through the objects discussed herein. The term 'English', like 'Gaelic', will be used here mainly to refer to the language and its speakers.

Other labels were themselves new coinages of this period, and few of them can be called 'ethnic' as much as locational. For instance, historians tend to use 'Bernicia' and 'Deira' to refer to the northern kingdoms of the English, but these terms are in fact used very rarely in our period. More commonly these areas and their people were given a locational term *Norþymbre*, the Northumbrians, those from north of the Humber, but there is every indication that this was a neologism of their turbulent era.[21] Indeed, the Irish sources never use this term, nor do they refer to *Angli* at all: instead, from their perspective the Northumbrians were only ever *Saxan*, Saxons, and sometimes northern Saxons.[22] The term *Norþymbrum* then is clearly only relevant for other English-speakers to the south. Both may well be exonyms, ethnic labels which are different from those used by the people themselves. It is worth reflecting on how many of our commonly used labels are similarly from an outside perspective. These examples should remind us that identities were never static, even within themselves, much less within the period we are describing where so much was changing.

The clearest new arrival in this period were the people we usually call 'the Vikings'. It will become clear throughout this book that the people we refer collectively to in this way were never a single, self-identifying 'race' or ethnicity. The term 'viking' itself is occupational, referring to seafarers and specifically seaborne pirates, and thus many historians choose to write it in lower-case when it is used at all. Its common use, like so many of our labels, is largely a creation of 19th-century and later scholarship. It appears only rarely in runic inscriptions from the 10th century onwards, and in the *Anglo-Saxon Chronicle* the word *wicinge* (pirate) is used only three times between 879 and 917; otherwise 'heathen', later 'Dane', were the most common terms for Scandinavians in England.[23] 'Viking' never appeared in the Irish sources, which instead used several different labels that included *Gaill* ('foreigners') or *Nordmanni* ('Northmen', interestingly a loanword from English), and later the common terms *Finngaill*, *Dubgaill* and *Gall-goídil* ('fair foreigners', 'dark foreigners' and 'Gaelic-foreigners'), which seem to be an expression of different kin-groups and political allegiances.[24]

By the 11th century we cannot seriously speak of 'vikings' anymore; the age of raids and overwintering camps was long gone, and we are instead dealing with a variety of terms used by modern historians and archaeologists to suggest a 'mixed', hybrid or otherwise 'othered' population – Hiberno-Norse,

Anglo-Scandinavian, Anglo-Danish, even Scotto-Norse. However, there is one term used in contemporary Irish sources that adopts the hyphenated form. The term of *Gall-goídil* ('foreigner-Gael') first appeared in the 850s, indicating that a collective had emerged which incorporated people of both Irish and Scandinavian descent. It became linked to a political group by the 10th century that made its own territorial claims in western and southern Scotland, eventually giving its name to the lordship of Galloway, but we should not expect that the 11th-century Galwegian identity was the same as those first described in Ireland over a century before.[25] Beyond this notable example, people were generally defined by their language, their location or the law they lived under.[26] The proliferation of double-barrelled terms in archaeological texts marks the limitations of the material culture to 'reveal' the identity of the user. It is a sign that archaeology, like identity itself, is messy, and never more so than in this period. That messiness is not something to avoid, but to explore as meaningful in itself.

And so we come back to the 'Scots' and 'Scotland'. Their story will be told in these pages in greater detail, but as we have seen these terms can be slippery. The 10th century saw the disappearance of Picts and Fortriu from our contemporary sources, and the emergence of a new kingdom referred to as Alba. Its subjects were referred to as *fir Alban*, the 'men of Alba'. Like all the other terms discussed above, the word is old but its application was new. It was the Gaelic word used for the landmass of Britain, adopted from a possible British/Pictish cognate *Albid*.[27] Its first appearance as a political entity, in what became known as the Chronicle of the Kings of Alba, was in a report of attacks on Dunkeld (Perthshire) and 'all of Alba' in 903. In 904, however, the same source reported a victory over vikings by the 'men of Fortriu'; while another source, the *Chronicum Scottorum*, reports an otherwise unknown Ead king of *Cruithentúath* (the Picts) killed by vikings in their raiding in Alba that same year.[28] The sense of political turmoil is palpable here. Thereafter, Alba referred exclusively to a northern kingdom ruled by Causantín mac Aéda (r.900–43) and his successors, and English sources soon also refer to the *Scottas* and *Scotia* as the people of this kingdom, rather than in the older generic sense of all Gaelic-speakers.[29]

The debate remains as to whether Alba was a 're-branding' of an essentially Pictish polity, or a more root-and-branch transformation.[30] There is no space to go into this complex debate here, but this much is clear. What we are seeing, in almost real time, is the transition from a label referring to a specific people, the Picts, or their main kingdom of Fortriu, to a *locational* term, Alba. This is actually part of a broader pattern in this period. We also begin to hear of kings of *Eriu*, Ireland, not just kings of specific lineages, at this time: this is partly because the territory of Ireland now contained more than just the Irish, but also because the nature of kingship was changing as well.[31] The appeal of Alba then was partly to do with the fact that it was different to a kingdom of just Picts. The former Pictish territories of the north were highly curtailed by the emergent earldom of Orkney which, at its greatest extent, covered the Hebrides in the west and as far as the Dornoch Firth in the east.[32] As Fortriu became the separate kingdom of Moray, the centre of gravity of what had once been the Pictish dominion was now in Perthshire and the Tay estuary, ruled by Gaelic-speakers. This required a new name because it did not straightforwardly resemble anything that had come before. As the kings of Alba continued to exert their dominance further south and west, the kingdom covered a multi-ethnic and multilingual territory consisting of Gaels, English, Britons, and in erstwhile alliance with the kings of Dublin. Alba, as a locational term, had a triple advantage: it retained an existing word already in circulation; it was not specific of any one ethnic or linguistic group; and in its invocation of the ancient word for Britain, it also signalled through its sense of history the imperial ambition of its kings.[33]

NAMING NATIONS

So while the Picts disappeared from our sources, they were in good company: so did the kingdoms of Bernicia, Dál Riata, Alt Clut, and several others in this period. Our mistake is in trying to see the early medieval past as a struggle between distinct peoples, who then 'mix' from a state of purity. It is a fantasy that comes from misreading our source material, and is then too often uncritically applied to the artefactual evidence. The size and shape of Scotland as it emerges in our sources towards the end of our period was by no means to be taken as a natural or foregone conclusion. King David I of Scotland (r.1124–53) spent his reign battling the lords of Galloway and the mormaers of Moray, while striking alliances with earls of Orkney and occupying northern England as far as the Tyne. While we always call him the king of Scotland today, at his death in 1153, in the Irish *Annals of Tigernach,* he was referred to as *rí Alban & Saxan,* 'the king of Alba and Northumbria'. Much of how we understand identity in our period depends on when – and where – our sources were composed.

In short, even our textual sources show how labelling collective people using contemporary sources can be fraught. It also brings home one of the most important themes of this book – of this period as *an experimental age,* where identity itself was in flux everywhere. The artefacts discussed here more often than not display the connections between people.

FROM PEOPLES TO PEOPLE

While the written sources may be problematic, they give us a sense of at least one of the irreducible elements of collective identity, which is language. Political allegiances come and go, but the connections of language precede and shape both ethnicities and kingdoms in the medieval period. The evidence for mother tongues and multilingualism provides the most eloquent expression of how early medieval history as the history of separate *peoples* has blinded us to more interesting stories about *people.*

Thankfully, these historical sources are not the only evidence for language in our period. The evidence from place-names is too complex to consider in detail here, but every grid-square of the map in Scotland contains these artefacts of the early medieval period, capturing the layering of voices over the centuries.[34] While there are few reliable written accounts from Scotland in the 9–12th centuries, ironically, perhaps, there is a rich seam of material evidence for literacy and multilingualism. We have artefacts inscribed with words and names that allow us to speak of individual people as much as peoples. These inscribed objects show us that several alphabets were used in our period. Contrary to ideas of a 'Dark Age', people were not just multilingual but potentially multiliterate. Most of these artefacts or inscriptions are difficult to date – some are too fragmentary to be deciphered – but nonetheless they are rare and precious snippets of language frozen in time.

The country is dotted with inscribed stones and other objects bearing evidence for the great variety of languages and scripts. What is striking is the range of alphabets represented: in the 5th–12th centuries there are as many as seven forms of writing found in what is now called Scotland: Latin script, Greek characters, Kufic from the Arabic world, ogham used for Celtic languages, runes for Germanic languages (two separate alphabets: the futhorc [7.3] used in England and in southern Scotland; and the Younger Futhark used in Viking-age Scandinavia [1.3], here typically referred to as Old Norse runes), and Pictish symbols.[35] Of these only one was not in active use within Scotland: Kufic only appears on imported dirham coins, of which, see chapter 6. Greek also had a limited symbolic function, mainly as Christograms on deluxe ecclesiastical products such as stone crosses and illuminated manuscripts, but there is evidence it was taught in insular monasteries.[36]

Latin was certainly heard in what is now called Scotland

Fig.1.3 (right): Polished bone implement with A-rune repeated three times, Westness farmstead, Rousay, Orkney; NMS X.1992.38.1.

Fig. 1.6 (below): Iron knife with bone handle inscribed with ogham, length 84mm; NMS X.GAA 252.

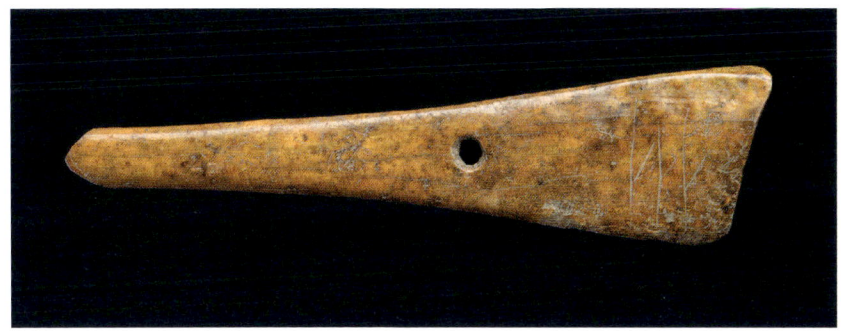

since at least the Roman invasions of the 1st century AD, leaving an important collection of Roman military and civic monuments with Latin letters. The only evidence of literacy on a non-Roman site so far is the tantalising survival of a pebble etched with the first few letters of the alphabet by an inhabitant of the hillfort of Traprain Law, East Lothian, probably in the early centuries AD.[37] After the Roman period, the earliest evidence for Latin literacy, and presumably spoken Latin, is from the remarkable series of inscribed stone monuments scattered across southern Scotland from Kirkmadrine in Galloway to the Cat Stane in Midlothian, which were a shortlived phenomenon of the mid-5th to early 7th centuries.[38] By the 9th century, evidence for Latin literacy was almost exclusively bound up with the Church – meaning it was taught to a privileged few rather than in general use – but memorials bearing Roman letters continued to be put up [1.4, 1.5].[39]

The dating of the Pictish symbols remains controversial, but their use certainly continued into the 9th century [1.1b].[40] As the symbols are not yet deciphered, we rely on two stones that have Latin inscriptions to discuss the end of the series. The Drosten Stone, St Vigeans, Angus, is a cross-slab bearing a small Pictish-language inscription in Latin letters that may contain the name of a Pictish king, Uoret, who reigned c.839–42.[41] The other inscription is on Custantín's Cross, Forteviot, Perthshire [2.1a]. This one certainly names a Pictish king, Custantín son of Uurguist (d.820), but uses no symbols.[42] Indeed, despite some virtuoso examples of possible 9th-century date from St Vigeans and Meigle, Perthshire, there are no symbols used in major royal monasteries at St Andrews, Dunkeld and Forteviot. This leads to the perception that the symbols were falling out of fashion by the early 9th century, but it may be instead that they were only suitable for specific arenas of aristocratic display.[43] The important point for the current discussion is that their demise was due to changes in political authority, not caused by invasions or population change.

The ogham alphabet is most strongly associated with Ireland, and was developed as early as the 2nd or 3rd century AD to capture the sounds of archaic Gaelic.[44] We know this because we can see the language developing into its later forms as spellings of commonly used words and names change over time. In Scotland, the earliest dated example is a knife-handle incised with ogham from the Broch of Gurness, Orkney [1.6], radiocarbon-dated to the 4th–6th century, showing it had reached northern Scotland by this early date. The 'Pictish' oghams are notoriously difficult to read, much less date, but there is good evidence they continued in use throughout our

NAMING NATIONS

Fig. 1.4: Latin inscription naming Jesus Christ on a fragment of cross-slab from Portmahomack, Easter Ross, height 480mm; NMS X.IB 286.

Fig. 1.5: Latin inscription naming the son of Medicius on a fragment of cross-slab from Lethnott, Angus, height 190mm; NMS X.IB 132.

period of study to capture both Gaelic and Pictish languages, and cannot be used as evidence for Irish migrants as much as maritime connections spanning from Ireland to Shetland well before the Viking Age.[45] A long period of use in various contexts is suggested by the wide geographical distribution of oghams, spanning the country from Lochnaw, Galloway, to Lunnasting, Shetland [1.12].

The ogham script certainly continued in use throughout the Viking Age, including in Orkney and Shetland. We have critical evidence of it being taught in the early medieval monastery at Inchmarnock in Bute, where slate tablets dated to the 8th century have examples of both Latin and ogham letters being taught, as well as support evidence for multi-script education in the monastic 'school'.[46] Ogham appears on two runic cross-slabs from the Isle of Man in the 10th century, and an 11th-century bilingual cross at Killalloe, Co. Clare, naming Thorgrim in both runes and ogham, which illustrates the multilingual world of the Irish Sea zone.[47]

The futhorc, the alphabet commonly called 'Anglo-Saxon' runes, was also in common use in southern Scotland as part of the English-speaking kingdom of Northumbria from as early as the 6th century to as late as the 12th century. We will see more evidence for it as far as Pictland later, showing that there is still much to be learned about its use. It appears both on memorial crosses as well as graffiti on personal objects, but it is still much rarer than ogham.

In the 9th century there is a new alphabetic arrival into Scotland, the Younger Futhark, most often referred to as Old Norse runes.[48] These are strongly linked to the northern isles and the Hebrides, with occasional outliers. While the futhorc seems to go out of use after the 9th century in Scotland, Norse runes continue to be used in a limited manner through the later medieval period. Despite their association with the Viking Age, it is in fact difficult to date the examples from Scotland; it may be that none is as early as the 9th century, and the majority are 11th century or later.[49] However, the earliest runic inscriptions from Britain and Ireland are found on bone, antler or wood objects, meaning there may be a phase of writing on personal objects in the Viking Age that remains archaeologically invisible in Orkney and Shetland.[50] This would help to explain some slight evidence for influences from runic writing which appear in the latest ogham inscriptions. There are no bilingual monuments in Orkney and Shetland, but there are other hints of interplay between scripts. Ogham did not traditionally make use of word separation, one of the reasons why fragmentary inscriptions can be difficult to read; but late ogham inscriptions begin to use it and it is possible this was inspired by runic conventions.[51] In fact Shetland may be one of the places where this interplay is happening: oghams from Bressay, Cunningsburgh and Lunnasting all use double dots as word separators, unique in the ogham corpus, which also appear in Norse runes (such as at Papil).[52] These ogham stones also bear other evidence for late use, including Norse names at Bressay (p. 20) and the use of special characters.[53]

OGHAM AND RUNE-CUTTERS IN THE NORTHERN ISLES

In light of the ongoing debate over Norse-Pictish relations in the northern isles, it would be helpful to see if and how ogham and Pictish symbols remained in use during or after the 9th century. There are only four places where Scandinavian runes appear on the same site as Pictish symbols (Birsay and Orphir in Orkney, Cunningsburgh in Shetland, and Monifieth in Angus). Only in the case of the lost bronze plaque from Monifieth do they appear on the same object; at the other three, the runes could be centuries later than the symbol stones, but were certainly still visible.[54] The symbol stone from Orphir was built into the walls of the same 12th-century church that also bore runic inscriptions.[55]

We now have the first empirical evidence for interaction among rune and ogham writers in the northern isles. There are four oghams and five runic inscriptions on the Brough of Birsay, with another ogham inscription from Buckquoy on the coast facing the Birsay islet.[56] These inscriptions can be set against a background of Pictish symbol stones from Brough of Birsay and Oxtro opposite. If we focus only on the inscriptions in stone, we can see that the corpus of oghams and runes in the Birsay area belong to a very particular monument type – slabs of naturally occurring Orkney flagstone with inscriptions on their narrow edge. Whatever the date of these inscriptions, they seem to form a related practice of writing names onto walls, something that occurs in at least two alphabets on the Brough of Birsay. The only other site where Pictish symbols, ogham and runes are found in the same locality is Cunningsburgh, and at least one of these oghams is of the 'late' or Viking-age type. A recent pilot

project assessing the 'handwriting' of the runes and oghams using high-resolution laser-scanning of the grooves of the letters from Birsay and Cunningsburgh, demonstrates that the Birsay runes and oghams were carved by several different hands, while the runes and oghams from Shetland are more alike than they are different.[57] Further work is required, but these results bear out what has long been suspected about the interplay between writing systems in this multilingual and colonial context [1.7–1.9].

Fig. 1.7 (opposite, above): Fragment of rune-inscribed stone with cross-shaped word separator, Aith's Voe, Cunningsburgh, Shetland; NMS X.IB 104.

Fig. 1.8 (opposite, below): Ogham-inscribed stone, Brough of Birsay, Orkney; NMS X.2015.27.

Fig. 1.9 (below): Laila Kitzler Åhfeldt, Swedish Heritage Board, and Henrik Zedig, Länsstyrelsen Västra Götaland, Sweden, laser-scanning inscribed stones on display, 2019. (Photograph by Neil Hanna)

AN ANIMATED WORLD

Perhaps the most important message that we can take from this body of evidence is that literacy was more widespread than we might think in early medieval Scotland. Contrary to the perception of the early medieval period, and specifically the Viking Age, as a benighted dark age of barbarism, the inscribed objects tell us that writing held considerable power. There are even instances where it was the presence of letters themselves, rather than a complete word, that was needed. For instance, a perforated bone-tool from the late Norse farmstead of Westness, Orkney, well polished from use, has a runic inscription consisting of just three graphs: 'AAA' [1.3]. In a similar vein are inscriptions which only have the first letters of an alphabet, such as a bear-tooth pendant from the Brough of Birsay reading only 'FUTHARK', which is the runic equivalent of writing 'ABCDEF' in Roman letters [7.2]. These 'meaningless' inscriptions demonstrate the power of writing as an act in itself. Our search for ethnic significance in our written objects may be blinding us to their real meaning: in this era, those with knowledge of letters held a kind of power that was not just about communicating or recording, but could even be amuletic or protective.[58] This is made explicit in the inscribed prayer on the St Ninian's Isle sword chape, but the inscription of just a personal name, or a simple description of the object, was about more than marking possession or ownership.[59] It was the recognition of the power of language in *an animated world*, where the letters and words themselves, once read or spoken, had the capacity to act.

This may be why, of all the early medieval inscriptions we have in Scotland, the vast majority likely record personal names. If the act of carving these in stone was for the name to be spoken aloud for future generations, then we can understand these not as records but as calls to action.

Before the 9th century, the most numerically dominant form of inscription in Scotland is Pictish symbols, of which there over 200 instances, with some notable exceptions mainly found north of the Forth and east of the Druimalban mountain range which traditionally formed the boundary between Dál Riata and Pictland.[60] As we saw above, the symbols were used over a long period of time, certainly as late as the 9th century. After this comes ogham, with some 48 examples recognised from Scotland to date; of these, only a handful are likely to be 9th century or later (pp 14–15). Ogham is used to capture Gaelic, British, Pictish and Norse names, as we will see below. In one case – a spindle-whorl from Buckquoy, Orkney – the object comes from a 9th-century 'Pictish' context, but has what appears to be a Gaelic sentence: *Benddact anim L'*, a prayer for the soul of 'L', another useful reminder that when vikings arrived in Orkney, they came into an already multilingual landscape, not just a 'Pictish' one.[61]

Objects inscribed in Latin are next, with some 43 examples, of which again only a handful are 9th-century or later, including the 9th-century crosses naming Pictish kings at Forteviot and St Vigeans (p.11). Latin, British, Pictish, Gaelic and English names are captured in Latin letters. For instance, several stones carry the Pictish names 'Ethernan' and 'Nectan', which may refer to saints by those names; a silver sword chape from St Ninian's Isle, Shetland, deposited *c.*800, captures the otherwise unattested Pictish name 'Resad' [2.12]; while from Angus there is a memorial cross inscribed 'FILII MEDICII', 'the son of Medicius', a Latin name [1.5].[62] Interestingly, in two cases one name is written twice on the same object, with slightly different spellings: 'Cuthgar'/'Huthgar', an Old English name at Ardwall, Kirkcudbrightshire, and 'Flann'/'Flaind', a Gaelic name on Iona.[63] Both are on cross-slabs from early monasteries where Latin book-hand was used to inscribe funerary memorials. These memorials may be capturing changes in pronunciation over the period of their use, providing further evidence for a context in which written names were supposed to be read aloud.

Old Norse runes appear on 24 sites across Scotland, totalling 56 individual inscriptions (33 from one single site, Maes Howe).[64] They almost exclusively capture Old Norse names, and are easily legible when preserved undamaged. Hence there is *Grímr* and *Thorbjorn* of Cunningsburgh [1.11], and from Kilbar, Barra, a wonderfully wrought cross has a monumental runic inscription along the back remembering *Thorgerth, Steinar's daughter* [3.26]. Female names are vanishingly rare in the ogham and Latin corpus of Scotland, so this is a sign that the social inclusivity of monumental inscriptions is changing in the period we are discussing.

In Orkney some runic inscriptions can be dated to the 11th and 12th century as they capture Latin names like *Philippus* (from Birsay) [see 1.10], possibly a cleric of the church there.[65] In one case from Naversdale near Orphir, a part of a Latin Christian prayer, the *Pater Noster*, was executed in runes. The 33 runic inscriptions from Maes Howe all seem to be from the mid-12th century and provide male and female Norse and Latin names.

Norse runes appear as early as the 10th century in the Irish Sea zone. In another famous case, Norse runes inform us that the last owner of the Hunterston Brooch, Ayrshire, was *Máel Brigte*, a common Gaelic name. The discovery of this boundary-crossing inscription from southwest Scotland seems to be an important eyewitness to the *Gall-goídil* rulers of this area from the 10th century, as we will discuss in chapter 6 (pp 145–6).

In contrast, Old English runes are restricted to a narrower area of Northumbria: only about a dozen are known to date. Five of these are from a single recent discovery, the Galloway Hoard, dating from the end of the 9th century.[66] These were short words (ED, BER, TIL, and one undeciphered) etched onto silver arm-rings. The words seem to be name elements, as one hacked silver arm-ring bears an indisputable full English name: Egbert. This is a groundbreaking discovery not only because of the small number of known futhorc inscriptions from Scotland, but because they appear on 'viking' objects, raising questions about the people who gathered and deposited behind our Viking-age hoards (chapter 4).

Other boundary-crossing inscriptions can be found in Shetland where, as mentioned above, there is considerable evidence for interaction among rune- and ogham-writers. Lunnasting is one of the ogham stones which bears late features, making it likely to be 9th-century or later, and one of many in Scotland with a version of the Pictish name Nechtan [1.12].[67] At Bressay, however, we see a period of multilingualism captured in stone [1.13 a–b]. Here we have a cross-slab, the Picts' preferred style of monument, with crosses of arcs and imagery inspired from illuminated manuscripts. Similar encircled crosses from Papil and Mail attest to a shared aesthetic among Shetland early Christian sites. Unlike Papil and Mail, however, there is no runic inscription from Bressay. Instead, the Bressay stone has a remarkable ogham inscription running down its narrow sides, one of the longest intelligible messages in the Scottish ogham corpus. One side reads, 'CRROSCC : NAHHTVVDDAddS : DATTRR : aNN'; the other, 'BENiSESMEQQDDRoANN'.[68]

The reading is, as always, up for debate, but the words and names are clearly legible as they use the word separating dots inspired by runic script. There is the word 'cross', loaned into Pictish from the Latin *crux*. The next word is a Celtic name, possibly Nectudad. The third word is *dattr*, which seems to be the Old Norse for 'daughter'; however, an ogham stone from Cunningsburgh contains the word 'DATTU[-]' which may suggest this is a Pictish word instead of a Norse one.

The final word on this side is the personal name 'An', which could be either Celtic or Germanic. The opposite side has no word separators, but clearly the same hand has carved both. The Irish word 'MEQQ', 'son of', is common enough that it allows this to be read as 'Benises son of Droan', both Celtic-language names, the first either Pictish or Irish, the second a male Irish name. The presence of Irish names is no surprise:

Fig. 1.10: Rune-inscribed stone bearing the name *Philippus*, from Brough of Birsay, Orkney; NMS X.IB 191.

Fig. 1.11: Rune-inscribed stone in memory of the commissioner's father, *Thorbjorn*, from Cunningsburgh, Shetland; NMS X.IB 103.

Fig. 1.12: Ogham-inscribed stone bearing Celtic-language personal names, from Lunnasting, Shetland; NMS X.IB 113.

Figs 1.13 a–b: Cross-slab depicting clerics, lions and other animals, with ogham inscriptions running vertically on both narrow edges, from Bressay, Shetland; NMS X.IB 109 (front and back views).

NAMING NATIONS

we have already seen it in the Buckquoy ogham spindle-whorl. In short, all the names might be Celtic, alongside a possible Norse word for 'daughter' and the Irish word for 'son', but in what looks like Pictish grammar. There is perhaps no clearer indication of the multilingual context of the northern isles as a cultural crossroads in this period.

If this does use the Norse word for 'daughter', it can be read as either 'The cross of Nectudad, daughter of An / Benises son of Droan' or 'The cross of Nectudad's daughter An / Benises son of Droan'. The unwritten link between the two sides may be taken to mean that it was carved in memory of, or commissioned by, Benises son of Droan. Either way we have a cross commissioned by or in memory of a woman who has a Celtic name, perhaps in a Norse-speaking milieu, using ogham script. None of the oghams from Scotland bears a female name, but several runic inscriptions do. The presence of female names would join others in runic inscriptions at Kilbar and Thurso.

However we read the inscription, the Bressay cross-slab tells us about the early Viking Age in Shetland. A date around *c*.900 has been suggested both on the nature of the inscription as on the art style. This stone has been discussed as a key piece of evidence for this transitional period, but many interpretations are possible.[69] Is Bressay showing us the last gasp of a Shetland Christian elite, who were in the process of 'going viking'? Or is it capturing Norse settlers marrying into local elite families? Whether this period of multilingualism was peaceful or not, this inscription seems to reveal something far from the traditional narrative of an aggressive 'pagan Norse' takeover of the isles. Runic inscriptions commemorating Gaelic and Norse-named individuals on the Isle of Man were also similarly found on cross-slabs, showing us that even in 'viking'-dominated contexts, Christianity and Celtic naming practices remained available avenues of expression, at least for the elite.[70] However we read it, Bressay and other stones tell us that women held some of the cards in these negotiations. It is also a sign that the Christian Church not only survived the age of raids, it received a new phase of elite patronage, as also attested by the runic cross-slabs from Inchmarnock, Kilbar, Thurso and Iona.[71] The relationship with Scandinavian settlers and Christianity will be returned to again in this book.

So while there are few bilingual objects from Scotland, there is fascinating evidence for bilingualism in the inscriptions. In many cases these are the only primary texts we have from this period for some regions. Like the Pictish names written in Latin on the Drosten Stone or the St Ninian's Isle chape, the alphabet does not determine the spoken language of the commemorand: the alphabet and other modes of communication are a form of technology, and context is everything in understanding them.

The key to the significance of the Bressay stone is that the familial relationships are captured in names which appear to be from different languages. In this light we can perhaps return to the imagery of the Bressay cross [1.13a–b], in which both sides feature clerics and beasts facing one another. The lions on one side open their mouths towards each other, while on the reverse a cleric appears to 'speak' a figure-of-eight to the other who 'speaks' to the cross. It may be that the multilingualism of this inscription (one side using runic-inspired word separation and Norse elements, the other in only Celtic names and words, and without word separation) is a deliberate theological message about the union of disparate families and languages under the cross.

SCOTLANDS? RETHINKING NATIONHOOD

This chapter serves as an introduction not just to the people whose material cultures we will be exploring, but also to some of the themes that we will return to throughout this book. The idea of the 9th and 12th centuries as *an experimental age* helps remind us these objects were not fully formed expressions of any one identity, but the tools and technologies by which these identities were being created. It helps turn our attention from seeking out evidence for differences between *peoples*, to the experiences of individual *people*, as far as the objects will allow us to do so. The objects used here were not static but animated, and we will see throughout this book numerous examples of the ways in which supposedly inanimate objects could have person-like (and even animal-like) qualities, even 'charisma'.[72] Finally, we are looking not simply at Scotland, a political entity specific to certain parts of northern Britain. The objects studied here will show the connections which took place even across linguistic and political boundaries.

The temptation after all this is to call Scotland a mosaic of peoples in the 9th to 12th centuries, but even this metaphor does not capture the way individuals interacted: mosaic tiles, after all, remain separate. Nor was it a melting-pot, where all voices were blended together, erasing what was unique to each perspective.

We may not be speaking of Scotland alone, but the connections between people as embodied by these objects tell us there is something unique about the experience of history in this part of northern Britain. Scotland's glens and straths direct movement from east to west, and its indented coastlines and islands invite interaction by sea. Yet its mountain ranges and micro-climates do create a sense of separate worlds – not one, but many *Scotlands*, even today. The metalsmith Simone ten Hompel (p. 5) likes to say that silver has many flavours, according to what metals it is alloyed with. We will hear a lot more about the power of silver in the Viking Age in the pages that follow. The alloying of metal, sometimes for colour and texture, sometimes for strength, sometimes simply to stretch out a short supply, seems a good guiding metaphor for how the layering of languages, and perhaps identities, created nations.

NOTES

1. Broun 2007, 7.
2. Clarke et al. 2012, 106–12; Maxwell et al. 2014: <https://www.nms.ac.uk/collections-research/our-research/featured-projects/early-medieval-scotland/bringing-the-past-to-life/> [accessed August 2021]
3. Smith 2013; Hall 2010.
4. Crawford 2013, 39–50; Jesch 2005.
5. Smith 2013.
6. Noble and Evans 2019, 10–20.
7. Woolf 2017.
8. Winterbottom 1978; Fraser 2013; Woolf 2020.
9. Charles-Edwards 2012, 437–40.
10. Pryce 2001.
11. Clancy 2000.
12. Woolf 2002.
13. Herbert 2000.
14. Sharpe 2000.
15. Woolf 2002.
16. Molyneaux 2015, 5–9.
17. Dumville 2017, 109; Molyneaux 2009.
18. Molyneaux 2015, 7–9.
19. Broun 2007; 2010; Dumville 2017; McGuigan 2015a.
20. Rambaran-Olm and Wade 2021; Wood 2019.
21. Rollason 2003, 107.
22. For example, *Annals of Ulster* (867) refers to the 'northern Saxons' in both the Latin, *rex Saxan Aquilonalium,* and Gaelic, *Saxanu Tuaiscert,* in reference to a battle between Northumbrians and vikings: McGuigan 2015b.
23. Downham 2009, 143.
24. Downham 2011; Etchingham 2014.
25. Clancy 2008; Jennings and Kruse 2009; Downham 2015.
26. Hadley 2002; Downham 2009.
27. Broun 2015b, 119, fn. 75; Dumville 2000.
28. Evans 2015, 152, fn. 102.
29. Woolf 2002.
30. Broun 2015b; Clancy 2010b; Charles-Edwards 2008.
31. Herbert 2000.
32. Crawford and Taylor 2003.
33. Evans 2015; Herbert 2000; cf. Howlett 2000.
34. Taylor 2002.
35. Pictish symbols are not universally accepted as a lexigraphical system, but for positive arguments see especially Samson 1992; Forsyth 1997; Lee et al. 2010.
36. Tilghman 2011; Lacey 2008.
37. NMS X.GV 968; Blackwell et al. 2017, 41.
38. Forsyth 2005.
39. Forsyth 2020.
40. Forsyth 1997; Noble et al. 2018.
41. Clancy 2017, 113, with alternative readings suggested.
42. Campbell and Driscoll 2020.
43. Goldberg 2012.
44. Stifter 2020; Swift 1997.
45. Forsyth 1996a.
46. Forsyth and Tedeschi 2008.
47. Barnes et al. 1997.
48. Barnes and Page 2006.
49. Freund 2020, 158–60.
50. Johnson 2020, 207–17.
51. Barnes and Page 2006, 92–3.
52. Forsyth 1996a, 225–6, 412.
53. *Ibid.*, 122–38.
54. Barnes and Page 2006.
55. Batey 2003.
56. Forsyth 2021; Barnes and Page 2006.
57. Maldonado et al. in preparation.
58. Johnson 2020, 97–100; 272–80.
59. Forsyth 2020.
60. Foster 2014.
61. Forsyth 1996b.
62. Forsyth 2020.
63. Thomas 1967; Fisher 2001, 129, no. 46.
64. Barnes 1994; Barnes and Page 2006.
65. Barnes and Page 2006, 170–2.
66. Goldberg and Davis 2021, 42–5.
67. Forsyth 1996a, 412.
68. *Ibid.*, 129–37.
69. See contrasting views in Smith 2001 and Bäcklund 2001.
70. Jesch 2015, 56–7.
71. Liestøl 1983.
72. Burström 2015; Vedeler 2018; Brunning 2019.

Below: Detail of the brooch-pin found in the woman and infant grave from Westness, Rousay, Orkney; NMS X.IL 728.

NAMING NATIONS

CHAPTER TWO

An imperial age

Coming off the A9 road toward Forteviot, west of Perth, one is hardly at a precipitous height. Yet the view from the Gask Ridge down to the River Earn is one of Scotland's finest. The green fields of Strathearn unfold with the ribbon of the Earn snaking off into the distance. It certainly feels like a royal vista.

Two thousand years ago, this landscape was under the watchful eye of Roman soldiers, as the Gask Ridge formed for a short while the northernmost Roman frontier.[1] The imprints of their signal stations and fortlets can still be seen just on the other side of the A9, and when the conditions are right the shadows of Roman temporary camps can be seen from the air. It was from this vantage point that an ambitious stone cross was set up in the early 9th century. It stood like a sentinel in this spot for over a thousand years until it was removed for conservation in 1998, and moved indoors to St Serf's Church, Dunning, in 2002.[2]

Opposite: Broken terminal of a silver penannular brooch with gold filigree panelled ornament and amber insets, Achavrole, Dunbeath, Caithness, length 72mm; NMS X.FC 9.

This cross looked far beyond just the Earn valley. On its west face a panel of interlaced doves are said to encode a reference to St Columba, known in his time as Colum Cille, the dove of the Church. Were a dove to fly due west from here, it would eventually reach Columba's monastery on Iona. It may seem like a world away now, but the valley of the Earn was one of the main thoroughfares connecting the Pictish realms to the kingdom of Dál Riata in the west, via Strath Fillan and Loch Awe. There is plenty of evidence that emissaries travelled frequently between the monastery and the royal seats of the Tay and Earn. It is even possible that the name 'Earn' derives from *Éirenn*, making Strathearn read something like 'Ireland's river valley'.[3] Despite the homage of the cross to St Columba, its shape was unlike the ringed high crosses which by now had become iconic of Iona. Instead, its form with double-curved arms and vine-scroll ornament looked south to the 'victory crosses' of Northumbria.[4] But the images on the cross were resolutely Pictish.

An armed man on horseback rides stoically beneath the cross, his armed retinue of spearmen lined up below. On the opposite face of the cross, as if 'behind' the rider, is a name incised in Latin letters which were only deciphered in 1995: *Custantin filius Fircus*, who must be the king recorded in the

Figs 2.1 a–b: Custantín's Cross, or Dupplin Cross, in original location, with the village of Forteviot, Perthshire, in the valley below, 1988; detail shows armed men on the shaft of the cross, below the horse and rider. ([a] Photograph courtesy of Professor Stephen Driscoll; [b] © Doug Simpson/Still Print)

Irish annals as *Custantín mac Fergusa, rex Fortreinn*. The cross has long been known simply as the Dupplin Cross, but we can now call it by its name: Custantín's Cross [Figs 2.1 a–b].[5]

By the time Custantín died in 820, he had seen the world change. He had been king of the Pictish kingdom of Fortriu since 789. It was rare for a king to sit on the throne for so long, but in his own lifetime King Offa and his successor Coenwulf had enjoyed Mercian dominance over the rest of the Anglo-Saxon kingdoms with reigns of several decades long. On the continent Charlemagne had done something even more ambitious: he had gone from a Frankish king to being crowned the first Roman emperor in the west since the 5th century. The heights of power attained by these men did not always survive them, but there must have been a sense that new forms of rulership (and subjecthood) were now available.

Custantín had also been given an imperial name. In contrast to the traditional royal names of his predecessors, his name evoked Constantine the Great, the Roman emperor who, according to legend, saw a vision of a cross in the sky before the Battle of the Milvian Bridge, leading him to victory. Shortly after this, Constantine issued the Edict of Milan in AD 313, ensuring the toleration of the Christian faith within the empire and his own legacy as a founder of Christendom. Perhaps more importantly, however, his was also the name taken by contemporary Roman emperors in Constantinople, like Constantine V who reigned 741–75.[6]

This remarkable Pictish ambition statement was a product of its time. The Pictish kingdom of Fortriu had grown expansive under Onuist map Vurguist (*c*.729–61), finally dominating ('smiting' is the word used in the contemporary Irish annals) its rivals of Dál Riata in the west, and cultivating allegiances with the powerful kings of Mercia.[7] His reign is noted in more English and Irish sources than many previous Pictish kings, so it is clear he had a real impact. It is at this time, in the mid- to late 8th century, that the monastery of Iona appears to have entered into a new golden age, producing masterpieces of

Fig. 2.2: Monolithic sandstone arch carved on one face with human figures, animals and a central damaged cross, early 9th century, Forteviot, Perthshire; NMS X.IB 36.

art and milestones in theology. In both stone and illuminated vellum, the influence of Pictish art styles in this golden age is unmistakable.[8] After his domination of Dál Riata, Onuist lavished his largesse on the Church in east and west, founding a church at Cennrighmonaid (later St Andrews), while also supporting the transformation of Iona into a major pilgrimage destination, a new Jerusalem with high crosses, multiple churches and streets paved in stone.[9]

As typically occurred, Onuist's death created a crisis of succession and a period of some instability, but in 789 his descendant Custantín took the throne. In AD 811, Custantín also took the kingship of the Scots for himself – the first king of the Picts who was also to be proclaimed king of Dál Riata.[10] After this he set out to establish a 'natural' authority for his family, which would hold onto the kingship until 839. One of his most potent strategies was to transform the ancient cult centre of Forteviot. His cross overlooking the site from the Gask Ridge was just one trace of this programme. The remarkable Forteviot Arch is another [2.2].

The entrance to National Museum of Scotland's 'Kingdom of the Scots' gallery is framed by the massive, monolithic Forteviot Arch. Long associated with the palace of Cináed mac Ailpín, who died there in 858, Forteviot has been seen as something new and different in the 9th century. It was a royal place but, unlike the remote fastnesses on hills and sea-cliffs of a previous era, it was an open settlement in the heart of one of Scotland's most fertile river valleys. The carved stone monuments there attest to a major stone-built church and perhaps a mausoleum. It shows the confidence, swagger even, of kings safe in their overlordship and with an eye towards the future. The historical records call it a *palacio*, a palace, evoking parallels with Carolingian royal complexes incorporating church and court, even if the Pictish version of a court would have looked very different.

The Arch is the last material trace of this powerful place. The art style links it to the cross which bears Custantín's name, and they were certainly part of the same programme. The large male figure on the left of the Arch is wrapped in classical drapery, with a drooping moustache that was positively Carolingian in scale. The moustache matches that of the armed rider and his retinue on Custantín's Cross, but on the Arch he bears a long staff in place of a spear. Unlike the similar toga-wearing figure on the St Andrews 'sarcophagus',[11] he is completely unarmed; and instead of lovingly detailed leather shoes the figure on the Forteviot Arch is barefoot. Below his feet is a long-horned bull and all signs indicate this is a king in Old Testament drag, perhaps Custantín as David the Good Shepherd himself, given related Davidian imagery on the cross. Two smaller figures bear similar staffs, their shorter but still prodigious moustaches identifying them as part of the warrior class, even subject kings. Unlike the larger figure's flowing curls and ponytail, the smaller figures are scrunched and hooded: are they subjects or

AN IMPERIAL AGE

hostages? Between them are the traces of a cross and a lamb, the *Agnus Dei*, at the apex of the Arch. It is a statement of Christian triumph, and potent royal propaganda. Certainly Custantín wanted to be remembered as a pious king. One of the few other things we know about his reign is that he founded a church at Dunkeld in honour of St Columba, the patron saint of Iona. The Arch is completely unique in Britain or Ireland and, if the large figure is the same as the rider on Custantín's Cross, these are portraits of a named person on a monumental scale – the first in Scotland since the Roman period.

The Christian triumphalism may seem somewhat ironic given what we know about the site of Forteviot. A series of excavations revealed this was anything but a 'new' place in AD 820.[12] The site of the medieval parish church and modern village had been enclosed by a large ditch, creating a promontory refuge overlooking the fields in every direction. The fields to south and west were revealed to be a major ceremonial landscape on a scale matched only on a handful of sites in Scotland. Multiple henges, cairns and a palisaded enclosure date back to the Neolithic with substantial reworking in the Bronze Age and Iron Age, with Roman artefacts showing it was still occupied into the first millennium.

From the 5th century, a remarkable new phase of activity began at the prehistoric complex at Forteviot. Burials in round and square mounds began to be made outside the prehistoric monuments, as if respecting them, or basking in their aura of antiquity. At the same time, massive pits were dug into the ancient henges themselves, as if searching for the source of their supernatural power. One Bronze-Age cist in a barrow mound was reopened in the 5th or 6th century, emptied of its prehistoric remains and replaced with an offering of burnt grain. This mound was also surrounded by large pits full of burnt grain, but no other evidence of feasting, settlement or manufacturing activity. These grain-pits represent events involving bonfires, dated by radiocarbon to the 5th–11th centuries. In the 7th or 8th century, one of these pits was filled with burnt grain and burnt human bone. Cremation was certainly not part of the usual burial repertoire of the Picts at this time, and may even have been actively frowned upon by the Church, but in the heightened festival atmosphere of the gatherings that took place here, these kinds of flirtations with prehistoric monuments were perhaps overlooked.

If all this sounds like the antithesis of Christian practice, it is now clear that this activity continued while the putative Forteviot palace/church and its related crosses were being put up. It means that there was no real problem marrying Christian cult with the ancient ceremonial gatherings and fire festivals taking place here. Custantín may even have led some of them. The depiction of him as a barefoot cattle-drover under the cross on the Arch may be a glimpse into an aspect of a procession, his entry into the sacred arena as a penitent, working both as a link to ancient inauguration rites as well as an allegory for leading his followers into Paradise. The aura of ancient tradition at Forteviot trumped any of our modern concerns with labelling things as 'Christian' or 'pagan'. Similarly elaborate kingship rituals are known from Irish inaugural sites like the Hill of Tara and the Rock of Cashel.[13] But we cannot call these deposits 'survivals' of a pagan era, because they seem to have been newly devised in a time by which Christianity had become irrevocably enmeshed with royal authority. Even elaborate statements of Christian faith such as the Pictish cross-slabs bear scenes from myth that were long seen as pagan 'survivals', but are more readily understandable as theological messages in a local idiom.[14] On one cross-slab from Forteviot, a wolf-like beast with a horn mauls a snake that is trying to ensnare him: this is one of many such creatures unique to Pictish Christian art, and we will meet this horned beast again later (chapter 5, p.122). Death was thought of as a battle with demons, which finds ample parallels from the theological literature of the day.[15]

Fig. 2.3: Silver and gold filigree penannular brooch terminal with amber inset from the Croy Hoard, length 44mm; NMS X.FC 13.

In this light, the sacrifice of grain in large bonfires around mounds can be read as a way of honouring or invoking the protection of the long-dead inhabitants of these mounds. The same can be said of the bonfire pits at Forteviot: they were innovations in a Christian context and, if not overseen by clergy, at least tolerated by them. If these were the accepted ways that kings were proclaimed, or their authority reaffirmed, in early medieval Scotland, the Church appears to have involved itself from an early date.

Custantín's successors continued to occupy the centre at Forteviot. Cináed mac Ailpín died at the *palacio* in 858, and any of the stone crosses, or more tantalisingly one of the late square barrows, may be marking his grave. But whatever the power of the ceremonies held at Forteviot, they did not outlive the 9th century. Archaeology allows us to see the invention of traditions at Forteviot with remarkable clarity, and shows that early medieval power and kingship was not timeless and conservative. It was being transformed, perhaps in a cataclysm of fire. This was an animated world where time itself was tangible – the past could be unearthed and remade, in exactly the same way as Old Testament imagery and local mythologies were remixed in relief on crosses throughout the country.

Like their contemporaries the Mercians and Franks, the kings of the Picts had hit their stride in the late 8th century. They had achieved a dominance over their neighbours which seemed built to last. Custantín and his successors seem to have controlled Britain north of the Forth, and were at least equal players with their British and Northumbrian neighbours to the south. Such confidence can be seen in the artistic achievements of the age, capturing the continental zeitgeist for all things Roman, without sacrificing the basis of their power in their sacred places and symbolic repertoire. True to his name, Custantín's ambitions were imperial, but empires do have a tendency to fall.

THE LONG EIGHTH CENTURY

What made the Pictish kingdom so powerful by the time of Custantín? Can we really believe it was simply down to the ambitions of a few powerful warlords? Surely there was more to ruling than the ability to throw epic festivals in the Perthshire countryside. To understand the 9th century we have to cast our gaze more widely. Archaeology is not always adequate for pinpointing historical events, much less historical figures. Instead its strength is in a longer-term view. One in particular seems to be apposite here, often called the 'long eighth century'.[16] Around the North Sea zone, the 8th century was a time of increased production, specialisation of labour, and monetisation.[17]

From a Scottish perspective, the 'long eighth century' is more visible through the increased production of fine metalwork and sculptured stones [2.3, 2.4], both indirect markers of increasing prosperity and centralisation of resources at royal villas and monasteries. We know that some monasteries, like Iona, were founded well before the 8th century, but they hardly register archaeologically until the 7th century – and it may be that our image of what a monastery looked like is bound up with the elaborate crosses and shrines of the 'long eighth century'.[18] Indeed, some of our best-known objects, from cross-

AN IMPERIAL AGE

Fig. 2.4: Cross-slab depicting mythical beasts locked in combat, late 7th or 8th century, Woodwray, Angus; NMS X.IB 202.

slabs in stone to brooches in gilt-silver, can often only be dated to AD 700–800, give or take a few decades at either end. And yet the monasteries, cemeteries and hillforts which grew to such great heights in this era seemed to peter out gradually during the early 9th century, as the nature of kingship and patronage changed. In short, the 8th century seems to have been a golden age for art and archaeology in the north, and to a certain extent the 9th century remains in its shadow.

The 'long eighth century' was a time of growing connections and widening networks. The aristocracies of the Scots, Picts, Britons and Northumbrians had long been entangled through intermarriage and fosterage practices by the time of the first viking raids. Imports of Mediterranean and continental vessels carrying wine, oil, spices and dyes in the 5th–7th centuries can be found from Whithorn in Galloway to Rhynie in Aberdeenshire, but only in limited quantities.[19] The spread of these exotic goods across kingdoms represent gift-giving networks from kings to their clients, the ritualised redistribution of royal favour that greased the wheels of early medieval politics. Even if the imports from those heady days were no longer flowing in by the 8th century, some of the power centres established in that time remained important into the start of the Viking Age because of the long-distance networks they opened up. We often call this a 'gift-giving society', but that is only part of the story.

Those exotic luxuries were largely confined to the west and southwest of Scotland. In the 'long eighth century', new opportunities for trade had begun to shift towards the North Sea zone. The best argument for the wide-ranging connections enjoyed by the eastern lowlands focuses on the firthlands at the mouth of the Great Glen. This has long been a crucial nodal point not only because of its favourable harbours and sandy landing-places. It is also one of the most direct routes from the east to the west coast, as well as providing maritime links to north and south. This area formed the core of the kingdom of Fortriu.[20]

There are growing hints that this favourable position was fuelled by long-distance maritime connections well before the Viking Age. The Picts are not always thought of as navigators on the same level as the Scots of Dál Riata or vikings of a later era, but given the prodigious naval forces commanded by the kings of the Picts going back at least to the 6th century, it is plausible that the promontory fort of Burghead looming over one of the major harbours of the Moray Firth was one of the major power centres of Fortriu. Just as the kingdom of Mercia flourished in the 8th century by taking advantage of both western and eastern trade routes,[21] the Pictish realm dominated by Fortriu was in a privileged position with access to the western seaways via the Great Glen. The excavations at Portmahomack

Fig. 2.5: Wooden paddle from a horizontal mill, Bankhead, Dalswinton, Dumfriesshire, length 393 mm; NMS X.PD 12.

turned up tantalising evidence of North Sea trade links in the form of a silver sceat.[22] Sceattas are early coins that were used in trade sites across the North Sea from England to Denmark in the late 7th and especially in the early 8th centuries. This is only the second one to be found in Scotland, the other being from the Anglo-Saxon settlement of Dunbar in East Lothian.[23]

In hindsight, this coin is less of an outlier than it looks. A study of Anglo-Saxon period finds from Scotland up to the 9th century shows the area between the Moray and Dornoch Firths is a notable cluster of imported finds from 600–900.[24] 'Hotspots' for imported material take in the promontory of Burghead [4.37], where notable examples include a 'Trewhiddle-style' 9th-century silver drinking-horn mount; the monastery and settlement site of Portmahomack; and the beach market and other waterfront trading centres at Culbin Sands and Clarkly Hill. Among the vessel glass, beads and coins found elsewhere in Scotland, the sceat from Portmahomack and a rare disc mount of 6th-/7th-century date from Dornoch stand out as unique, attesting to direct contact between Fortriu and the wider North Sea world.[25]

This of course begs the question of what goods were being produced in Scotland for shipment abroad (as gifts or commodities) to enable such contacts. One clue comes from Forteviot: the conspicuous sacrifice of grain in large pits shows that there was, in a sense, money to burn here. It all adds to a growing corpus of evidence, largely from development-led excavations, of grain-pits across eastern Scotland dated 8th–11th centuries, showing indirect evidence for agricultural expansion in the later first millennium.[26] Such grain was not necessarily being produced for export, but the expansion of agricultural capacity stands as a proxy for increasing wealth. The best evidence for this comes from across the country at Hoddom in Dumfriesshire, where the monastery incorporated a major grain-processing facility with evidence that it acted as a central place for the storage, drying and redistribution of surplus from the 7th–11th centuries.[27] Rare proof for the wider infrastructure this represented comes from the paddle of a horizontal mill from Dalswinton, Dumfriesshire, radiocarbon-dated to the 7th–9th centuries [2.5].[28] Among the earliest dated deposits from Portmahomack were grain-pits and kilns; and from the 9th century at least one of the workshop buildings was transformed into a kiln-barn.[29] Control of this source of wealth is what backed the introduction of master sculptors such as those who carved the deluxe classically inspired relief crosses found in numbers at Hoddom [2.6].

But the greatest source of wealth at Portmahomack came from a different kind of agriculture – their carefully managed herds [2.7]. From the 7th century, the workshops were producing calfskin for vellum, or manuscript parchment, in quantities for export. But this was only the highest-grade animal skin product being made here. Probably the most mundane but consistent source of wealth was leather and other cattle-hide products.[30] Other monasteries across Scotland show signs of craft specialisation at this time: Iona was producing leather goods such as decorated shoes; and even smaller sites such as Inchmarnock, Bute, had their own 'side hustle' in the production of black cannel-coal jewellery.[31] It is most interesting to see rare notices of 'Irish' ships (*Scottorum navis*) in contemporary Frankish sources, arriving into the Loire region with leather shoes and clothes.[32] Skin and hide products, butter and cheese, were the kinds of exports that northern Britain and Ireland were known for on the continent. Monasteries prob-

Fig. 2.6: Cross-shaft with haloed figures carved in relief, 8th or 9th century, Hoddom, Dumfriesshire; NMS X.IB 9.

Fig. 2.7: The 'Calf Stone', a panel of sandstone carved on one face depicting a bull, cow and calf, and possible lion, manticore and lamb, from Portmahomack, Easter Ross, width 775mm; NMS X.1999.27.11.

ably also gained control of grain-processing and redistribution from early on, if Hoddom is any indication. The early Irish texts use cattle as a standard unit of value, and later land assessment in northeastern Scotland was based on the productivity of various resources including grain, timber and peat.[33]

These fundamentals of the economy allowed for the kinds of elite trade and exchange we are more used to tracking in the archaeology of the period. The best evidence for trade in the era is in fact bound up in those very 'gifts', which we showcase as treasures in our Museum.[34] The gleaming brooches of silver and gold, set with amber and glass, are the products of a thriving system of long-distance exchange. Iron is relatively easily sourced in Scotland from bog-ore and iron-rich seepages, renewable resources generated by minerals slowly percolating through the natural biosphere.[35] But the lead, tin, copper, silver

Fig. 2.8 (right): Silver ingot from a 7th-century context on the hillfort of Clatchard Craig, Fife, length 73mm, weight 28.42g; NMS X.HHC 121.

Fig. 2.9 (below): Selection of stone ingot moulds, Brough of Birsay, Orkney, including (bottom, right) a mould of imported steatite, with eight matrices on four sides, length 145mm; NMS X.HB 577.

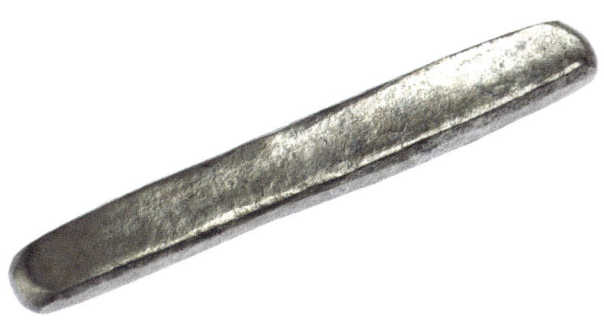

and gold in these brooches and pins that make up so much of the evidence for early medieval Scotland was rare or not consistently available.[36] Tin and possibly copper were imported from elsewhere since the Bronze Age; in early medieval Scotland, glass was always derived from recycled material brought in from outside; and amber was sourced from as far away as the Baltic through complicated trade routes in place for centuries. When we gaze upon these treasures in their showcases, we must appreciate just how difficult it was to acquire their basic components.

Previous studies of non-ferrous metalworking in early medieval Scotland have established that it only occurred on high-status sites like hillforts and monasteries, with few exceptions.[37] It seems to indicate that the supply of such metals, and the skills to work them, were heavily controlled by the elite. As such, the iconic brooches, pins, reliquaries and other treasures that we know were being crafted since the 5th century, could only have emerged from a background of supply of precious metals. These raw materials were sourced and redistributed in the elaborate ceremonies which took place at defended royal sites, as shown by the presence of ingot moulds for the casting of metal bars at hillforts like Dunadd, Argyll.[38]

There are many examples of stone moulds for casting bar- and disc-shaped ingots from across Scotland, increasingly from sites of 7th- and 8th-century metalworking activity, including recent excavations at King's Seat, Dunkeld, Perthshire, another royal centre.[39] It is not always possible to tell what metal was being made into ingots, but a silver ingot from the hillfort of Clatchard Craig, Fife, dated to the 7th century, joins evidence for the casting of large silver penannular brooches there [2.8].[40] Several bronze ingots are known from early medieval craft-working sites in Ireland, but so far in Scotland these are mainly unstratified finds from metal-detecting.[41]

As we will see in chapter 6, silver ingots have been noted as one of the hallmarks of the Viking Age, where huge quantities of them were deposited in well-dated hoards. Stratified finds of complete silver and bronze ingots show the concept pre-dated the Viking Age, and ingot moulds date back at least to Roman Newstead and Traprain Law in the southeast.[42] What sets the Viking-age ingots apart is the evidence for hacking and hammering, characteristic of the later bullion economy (chapter 6) [2.10].[43] Four stone ingot moulds from the monastery of Whithorn pre-dated the Viking-age layers and at least one of them was used to cast a rare gold ingot found intact.[44] At least ten stone moulds are from the Brough of Birsay, clearly coming from both 'Pictish' and 'viking' layers, where copper-alloys and silver were both detected [2.9].[45] At the monastery of Portmahomack, in contrast, five stone ingot moulds were all from the Viking-age phase (pp 38–40).[46]

Bar-shaped ingots are not the only or necessarily the most effective way to prepare metal for a metalworker. The chopping and hacking of ingots for the crucible always introduces the potential for loss of material. Instead the bar ingot is designed

Fig. 2.10 (left): Silver ingots. (left) Whitmuirhaugh, near Sprouston, Scottish Borders, length 35 mm, weight 10.6 g, NMS X.2005.6; (right) fragment, from Branxholme, Scottish Borders, length 15.5 mm, weight 9.47 g, NMS X.2016.30.

Fig. 2.11 (below): Silver penannular brooch, Clunie, Perthshire, diameter 116 mm; NMS X.FC 176.

THE WEALTH OF THE MONASTERIES

By the 8th century there was less and less separation between the archaeological signature of a monastery or a secular power centre: monasteries were power centres as much as centres of learning, and royal halls and hillforts both incorporate aspects of Christian ritual.[48] To have power in this age meant being favoured by God, who in turn protected the faithful. It is inherent in the Christian messages and symbolism inscribed into weapons and protective gear, such as the sword chape from St Ninian's Isle, Shetland [2.12], which bears a prayer to the Holy Spirit.[49] Whether producing finished objects or processing bulk foodstuffs, the pre-Viking monasteries of Scotland and elsewhere were economic powerhouses, even where they do not include evidence for coins, ingot moulds or balance scales.[50] The monasteries were very wealthy by the time the vikings came, and the Northumbrian churchmen Bede and Alcuin famously admonished abbots, bishops and kings alike for over-indulgence in such luxuries.

for ease of trade and transport [2.10]. The fact that bronze and silver ingots are rare in Scotland only shows that hoarding such wealth was not yet the end goal, rather the production of the elite goods which truly symbolised power. There is some sense that by the 9th century at least, there was an understanding of standard units of assessment of silver and gold in Ireland and Scotland.[47] In short, the widespread use of ingots is a sign of an economy based on the exchange of raw materials, and more work is needed on the origins of these networks, and whether this material was only exchanged as tribute in a gift-giving system [2.11].

All this begs the question of the role of the monasteries in the wider economic transformations of the later first millennium AD. Founding a monastery also meant accessing lines of correspondence extending from Ireland to Rome, gifting and receiving saints' relics, altar vessels, vestments and other liturgical accoutrements, and establishing supply-lines for commodities like wine, incense and oil.[51] While austere anchorites and wandering ascetics were certainly one aspect of early Christianity in the north, the major monasteries were centres of production and consumption deeply entangled with secular and royal politics.

Some of the most precious commodities that are known to have moved from Britain to the continent in the 8th century were gospel books, including famous examples like the *Codex Amiatinus*, sent from Monkwearmouth-Jarrow to Rome by Bishop Ceolfrith in AD 716.[52] Several missionary campaigns

CRUCIBLE OF NATIONS

were mounted from Ireland and England to the continent from the 7th century onwards. The missions to Frisia and Germany in the early 8th century are particularly well-documented, and one of the recurring themes in the surviving correspondence of these missions was the gifting of books, relics and other necessary field-gear for the foundation of new churches.[53] The influence of insular art, including inputs from northern Britain and Ireland, in the great illuminated gospels of their day, becomes especially clear in missionary centres with links to these islands. It has been argued that Portmahomack was one of the places supplying material to the missionary hub at Echternach, for instance, while excavations at both Iona and Portmahomack provided evidence for the manufacture of glass studs of the kind that were used on altar plate found in Ireland, such as the Ardagh Chalice and the Derrynaflan Paten.[54] The debris from these workshops includes offcuts and scrap that are notoriously difficult to piece together, but also provide examples of object types like reliquary shrines, pendant crosses and decorated items that no longer survive [2.13].[55]

There is more at stake here than point-scoring over who produced which manuscript or chalice. If we are arguing that the kingdoms of northern Britain were more fully integrated in the socio-economics of the 'long eighth century', we need to remember what this means in a wider context. Turning to the well-established landscape archaeology of England and Ireland at this time, it means a gradual process of increased agricultural production and more specialised settlement types. It means increased centralisation of cereal-processing through the establishment of mills, as has been proposed at Hoddom, Iona and Portmahomack [2.5]; and increased participation in long-distance networks of exchange. Power in this era flowed from control over land and participation in trade as much as military prowess.[56] The wealth of the monastery and the power of the kingdom were proportional, and both flowed from the exploitation of natural and human resources.

The story of other sources of wealth will be picked up in chapter 6, but it is worth stating here that in the north, where there were no established emporia for regulated trade, the monasteries were the closest thing to such centres of production, trade and redistribution.[57] There is also no getting away from the reality that the increased production of this age was powered in part by unfree labour – whether enslaved people obtained through the constant warfare of expansionist kingdoms, or labour exploited by the lay brethren of monasteries in exchange for spiritual access.[58] The role of slavery in the

Fig. 2.12 (left): Silver-gilt scabbard chape, with inscription invoking the Holy Spirit and the Pictish name Resad, width 81 mm; NMS X.FC 282.

Fig. 2.13 (right): Fragment of a stone cross bearing trumpet-scroll ornament from Portmahomack, Easter Ross; NMS X.IB 130.

AN IMPERIAL AGE

creation of wealth in this period is a theme we will return to later, but for now it is worth stressing that the long shadow of forced labour accompanies every economic boom in this era, and long pre-dates the Viking Age.[59] The basis for certain aspects of what we consider to be the 'viking' economy, then, were in part learned from existing insular practices.

WHEN DID THE VIKING AGE BEGIN?

So just how wealthy were the monasteries at the dawn of the Viking Age? There are tantalising clues in the Northumbrian evidence that may shed some light on the kinds of goods that were available in northern Britain more generally. Among the relics buried with St Cuthbert when his remains were translated into a decorated coffin in AD 698 were a silver-plated wooden altar, pocket gospel book with decorated leather cover and a liturgical comb of elephant ivory.[60] The Northumbrian monk Bede famously left an account of his possessions before he died in 735, stipulating that his personal stash of pepper, incense and 'napkins' (probably a liturgical cloth) be shared out among his brethren.[61] At the end of the 8th century we get some glimpses of the kinds of rich gifts being exchanged between Britain and the continent in the letters of Alcuin of York, one of the leading intellectuals of his day, who had been sent as an ambassador to the Carolingian court and who became part of Charlemagne's inner circle as a spiritual adviser. In a letter to the monks of Whithorn in 790, he thanks them for a poem on the miracles of St Ninian by sending an altar cloth of silk.[62] But Alcuin was less accepting of personal embellishment, and a recurring theme of many of his later letters to the clergy in England is to avoid luxurious dress and lay fashions, singling out especially silk robes, colourful garments, finger-rings and, in one case, 'ostentatious belts'.[63]

Alcuin's letters also give us a unique perspective on the tumultuous first years of raids.[64] The Viking Age in Britain is most often taken to start at 793 with the infamous raid of the monastery of Lindisfarne, the head Church of Northumbria. It is customary to say that this event sent shockwaves right across Europe, and Alcuin certainly appeared particularly concerned about it in several letters that were sent at the time. He again took the opportunity to warn Abbot Hygbald and his monks against ostentatious dress, probably not the words of solidarity they wanted to hear from colleagues in France. But perhaps the most striking letter is one addressed to Aethelred I of Northumbria in which Alcuin accused the king not just of 'wasteful clothing', but of adopting the 'pagan way of cutting hair and beards'.[65] He makes it clear that this was the same style as those pagans who had just attacked Lindisfarne. Alcuin had been back in Northumbria from 790–3 and could feasibly have noticed the king sporting his new style. Had he also witnessed some of these pagans?

Our sources for this period are notoriously incomplete, but we can glimpse the appearance of Scandinavian raiders in England before Lindisfarne.[66] The first we can be sure of was not in northern Britain, but in Portland, Dorset, in the kingdom of Wessex. In 789 the *Anglo-Saxon Chronicle* reports the arrival of three ships of 'Danes', who killed the king's reeve when he rode out to them. There are further tantalising hints of undocumented raids along the Kent coastline in the 790s from other evidence including, again, the letters of Alcuin.

A recent reassessment of the archaeological evidence for the earliest viking raids explains the significance of this activity appearing first in the English Channel zone.[67] The seaways of southern and eastern England were buzzing with merchant ships through the 8th century with the rise of the regulated markets known as *wics*. These were coastal settlements that had grown up around harbours to take advantage of the booming trade opportunities across the North Sea zone. From the middle of the 8th century, a generation or more before the traditional start of the Viking Age, we begin to see the regular participation of Norse merchants through the arrival of goods from the far north into the major markets like Ribe in modern-day Denmark.[68] Probably the bulk of these goods were in the form of organic material such as furs, which would not leave much of an archaeological footprint. Of the inorganic goods that still survive, some of the most distinctive are the whetstones of fine-grained schist which are only sourced from quarries in Norway. Hundreds have been identified from layers dated 705–850 at Ribe, with the greatest number coming specifically from contexts dated 760–800. Of these, the vast majority are now confirmed to have come from quarries in Trøndelag, a journey of roughly 1100 kilometres by sea.[69]

This joins growing evidence that what we call the 'Viking Age' began as the growing entanglement of Scandinavian seafarers in the burgeoning maritime trade opportunities across the North Sea and the Baltic. A spectacular find of two mass burials of young men armed to the teeth in large ships in Salme, Estonia, has now been dated to *c*.750. These men were shown through stable isotope analysis to have originated from Sweden, and it is suggested they were part of a mission to secure access to trade routes from the east with links to the royal court of the Svear at Helgö.[70] This can be seen as the dramatic opening to the defining phenomenon of the Viking Age: the establishment of eastern routes to Central Asia, Byzantium and the Islamic world. The silk, pepper and incense arriving in Bede's England had probably come from overland routes increasingly monopolised by the Frankish kingdoms. By the end of the century we are in a new world awash with exotic silks from the east, much to Alcuin's dismay. The story of the coming century was one of increasingly bold efforts of Scandinavians to break into and monopolise this burgeoning market. The appearance of Scandinavian ships out in the English Channel from at least the late 780s forces us to put the first raid at Lindisfarne in a much longer context. The inspiration for Aethelred's 'pagan' hairstyle and beard must remain a mystery, but all this should raise new questions about how much the raiders of Lindisfarne knew before AD 793.

MONASTERIES AND THE START OF THE VIKING AGE

The significance of the western seaways to the history of Christianity is well established. The stereotype of the 'celtic' hermit clinging to the edge of a cliff on the Atlantic coast has driven the study of early Christianity in Scotland since the earliest days of the discipline. The search for 'desert places' in the sea was an active pursuit for some in the early monastic movement in Ireland, as well as in Scotland. In the process, monks appear to have encountered Iceland and the Faroe Islands as much as a century before the start of the Viking Age.[71] These were not one-way suicide missions, as they are romantically characterised; their discoveries were dutifully reported back, along with observations of solar and climatic patterns for the advancement of science.[72] It has even been suggested that one of the most precious gifts appropriated by the early viking navigators was knowledge of the sea-roads.[73]

We will show later in this book how major monasteries facing the western seaways, like Iona and Whithorn, were not abandoned in the face of viking raids, but found new ways to flourish as the Hebrides began to be known as the *Innse Gall*, the islands of the foreigners, and the Irish Sea became a 'viking lake'. With the tantalising find of continental silver sceattas at Portmahomack and Dunbar, a royal villa and monastery, we can at least begin the process of bringing northern Britain into the ferment of the North Sea trade even before the Viking Age. That these early monasteries survived to a certain extent into the period of Scandinavian settlement in the northern and western isles can be demonstrated through the frequent use of place-names in *papar-*, a loan-word from Gaelic into Old Norse probably denoting a term used to describe an anchorite, but latterly applied to island sites with monastic settlements by later Norse-speakers.[74] There are about 30 places which retain such names, from Pabbay, south of Barra, to Papil on Unst, the northernmost island of Shetland.[75] In contrast to the old-fashioned impression, fuelled by the 13th-century Icelandic sagas, that the *papar* were frail hermits on the edge of the world, the name is also used of major monastic settlements like Papil, Shetland, and Papa Westray, Orkney, both with evidence of continued occupation and patronage under Norse-speaking lords.

Thus, the story of pagan viking animus toward the insular monasteries needs some recalibration. The wandering of the shrine of St Cuthbert is a case in point. According to a late account compiled in Durham, the keepers of the relics of St Cuthbert at Lindisfarne were forced to flee from viking attacks in 875; they attempted to transport them to Ireland before travelling to Whithorn, ending up at Chester-le-Street and eventually Durham itself. This is usually taken as an example of the hazards of an island monastery in the age of raids, but an earlier account in the 10th century does not mention viking raids in 875, nor even the first fateful raid in 793, despite how catastrophic it seemed to Alcuin at the time.[76] In reality, sculpture continued to be produced on Lindisfarne through to the 10th and 11th centuries, and the 'migration' of the community may have been retrospectively synchronised with 875 as the year the 'Great Army' came north.[77] Another way to read this is that the shrine of Cuthbert remained on Lindisfarne for a century or longer after the raid in 793, and indeed we know that a monastery continued to exist here because it was raided in 893, 941 and 1061 – in two of those cases by kings of Scots rather than vikings![78]

But the ultimate outcome was, of course, disruption to our sources covering the monasteries of the north, creating the issues the community of Durham tried to paper over in the 12th century. Indeed, it is the silences in our sources that are most interesting: does this indicate the absence of raids, the result of communication lines severed by raids, or is it only a matter of which kingdom's records survive best? In Scotland, we must be alive to all these possibilities. For instance, much more is heard about raids in Iona and Dunkeld, precisely because these are where the contemporary chronicles were being kept. But even then there are surprising gaps, including the foundation date of Dunkeld itself, which remains unclear. What must have been a catastrophic raid occurred at Dunkeld in 878, because the Irish annals record the relics of Columba arriving in Ireland to 'escape the foreigners'.[79] Yet there is no record of any specific attack in Scotland that year, though the annals cannot be expected to be a complete account. If we turn to the southwest, we are even more in the dark: if Whithorn's diocese survived the Viking Age, we certainly lost track of the names of its leaders after Beadwulf (appointed 791). Similarly, we only have one possible name of an abbot of Hoddom, Wulfheard (789–96?), the recipient of a letter from Alcuin written 789–96, and this was only recognised very recently.[80]

If we stick only to historical sources we lose sight of events in many parts of Scotland after the 9th century. In the northeast we have precious few recorded events, and only when they involve the activities of the ruling dynasties of Alba after 900. Yet we know it is an area of considerable investment, at least according to the number, quality and ambition of the early medieval sculpture surviving from here, before and after 800 (pp 178–81). The early viking raids that must have occurred in these areas went undocumented. Despite the wealth and significance of Portmahomack, mentioned several times already, our historical sources are completely absent as to its very existence. Excavation has only revealed evidence of Viking-age conflagrations in rare cases – including at Portmahomack.[81]

The burning event at Portmahomack [see 2.14a–e] was apparently catastrophic for the site. A scorched-earth layer

Figs 2.14a–e: Fragments of deluxe cross-slabs, possibly destroyed in a raid on Portmahomack, Easter Ross; (from a–e) NMS X.IB 280A, 280, 285, 131, 190 (not to scale).

AN IMPERIAL AGE

covered the entirety of the northern workshops, and there was evidence for the smashing up and re-using of early Christian crosses as hard standing directly over the burning horizon. The site was not abandoned but changed in use. Now, instead of producing vellum for manuscripts and fine church-plate decorated with glass studs, the workshop was given over to more secular pursuits. Buckles and other dress items were now being cast in bronze. Several ingot moulds show that silver and other metals were being melted down into bars for transport. Other moulds for unique objects seem to be for weights, another indication that the function of the site had turned toward mercantile activity. In the main cemetery under the later medieval church, burials continued but slowed to a crawl, suggesting a major reduction of the clerical staff; two burials dated to the 9th–11th century show evidence of blade wounds to the head, one being fatal. None of this proves a viking raid, of course, but a sophisticated dating programme strongly suggests that the burning event occurred between 780–810, at the very opening of the traditional age of raids in the north. However, fires could have happened by accident – a burning layer alone would not prove the site was attacked. All the evidence put together adds up to more than the sum of its parts.

In other words, it seems that, despite being missed out by history, this major monastery of Fortriu was on the front lines, in the same way as Iona and Lindisfarne. Yet despite this striking evidence, raids on monasteries were not always disastrous. The real lack of archaeological evidence for such a catastrophic event almost anywhere else strongly suggests that whatever happened here was exceptional, and might even be seen as a raid gone wrong. But other explanations are possible.

VIKING PANIC

With the limited range of historical sources available for northern Britain, it is not really surprising that the first viking raids attract so much attention. News of attacks on Lindisfarne and Iona in particular spread fast, evoking emotive responses from colleagues in continental monasteries. There is no denying the violence that accompanied some of these early raids. The following are the entries in the contemporary Irish annals which deal with attacks on the monastery of Iona alone:

AD 795: Ravaging of Iona of Colum Cille.
802: Iona of Colum Cille was burned by the heathens.
806: The community of Iona, to the number of 68, was killed by the heathens.
825: Violent death of Blathmac son of Flann at the hands of the heathens in Iona of Colum Cille.[82]

Not only was Iona raided first in Scotland, it was raided often. Iona and Lindisfarne were the leading churches in Dál Riata and Northumbria respectively, and enjoyed close links going back to the foundation of the latter by monks of the former in the 7th century. Because of the selective coverage of the annals, it is clear the raids that are documented are only the tip of the iceberg. Archaeology should be in a position to turn up more evidence of such 'burnings' and massacres. In over a century of excavations on Iona, no certain evidence of these raids has emerged. Another puzzle is that while Iona was raided repeatedly, no attack on Lindisfarne was recorded for another century. Yet the notion of 'viking panic' is pervasive as an explanation for historical and archaeological change in this period.[83]

The apparent dearth of archaeological evidence for Viking-age raids on monasteries is not unique to Scotland, but in fact consistent across Britain and Ireland. Despite the image of constant burnings and slayings given by the contemporary

Fig. 2.15: The 'Hostage Stone', sketch on slate depicting a possible viking raid, from Inchmarnock, Bute, length 180mm; NMS X 2012.27.

texts, in most cases the point of a raid was not to destroy but to extract and leave enough behind to extract again at some future date. Indeed that is precisely what the Iona entries show us. Unlike the trope of a monastery irreversibly destroyed by vikings which we see so frequently in histories of the age, it is clear that Columba (or Colum Cille) continued to be venerated at Iona, and there is evidence for abbots, bishops and other high-ranking clergy present on the island throughout our period of study.[84] As with Lindisfarne, further raids (as late as 986) indicate that a community worth raiding remained. Another lesser-known fact about the attack on Lindisfarne is that it resulted in the taking of captives, not just outright massacre. In Alcuin's second letter to Bishop Hygbald, he pledges to reach out to Charlemagne for help in negotiating the release of the 'youths' taken in this raid. It shows that the leaders of the warband were potentially in diplomatic contact with kings, or that ransom was the aim to begin with.[85]

Why raid a monastery? The answer usually amounts to the search for portable wealth in the shape of jewelled reliquaries and altar plate, with shades of a generalised pagan antipathy toward Christianity depending on the author. More recently, it has become clear that the taking of hostages either for ransom or for selling into slavery was likely much more lucrative than anything to be gained from the relatively small amounts of precious metal used in ecclesiastical metalwork.[86] It has even been suggested that viking attacks took place at or near feast days, to make sure of the best chance of capturing the most number of people.[87] Reliquaries and other treasures are sometimes recorded as being carried off, and we know that some were bought back, so keeping a reliquary intact would have been a good investment, despite the few references to the 'breaking' of shrines in the contemporary annals.[88] The 'Hostage Stone' from Inchmarnock, possibly a child's doodle on a slate, seems to capture the moment a hostage, and maybe a reliquary along with him, were taken away by raiders [2.15].

Even the character of these early raids is now in question. Rather than hit-and-run raids, it is possible that overwintering of warbands and fleets had occurred since the earliest raids on Lindisfarne (793) and *Donemutha* (794).[89] The taking of cattle 'tribute' in Ireland in 798 is also indicative of more than just coastal piracy: this was not portable wealth, but tells us about the need to feed a large army, as well as the capacity to do more than hide out on ships.[90] As early as 807 we begin to hear of raids inland in Ireland.[91] By 810 a fleet of 200 Danish ships attacked Frisia and placed them under tribute.[92] A step-change in the nature and quantity of raids in Ireland also began in the 830s, with a fleet of 120 ships descending on the Liffey and the Boyne in what is clearly an invasion, no longer (if it ever was) for random plunder.[93]

This all reveals that from the very start of the Viking Age, raids involved negotiations, diplomatic embassies, perhaps formal treaties. It helps us to understand viking raids better, not just as bolts from the blue by an uncontacted alien race, and places these raids in the longer, pre-Viking context of violence and warfare in Britain, Ireland and the Carolingian world.

From Ireland to the continent, raiding, plunder, the taking of hostages and the payment of tribute were facts of life in the pre-Viking as well as the Viking-age Christian kingdoms. Several authors have detailed the centrality of tributary relationships to the Frankish kings, even to the extent of raiding rival

AN IMPERIAL AGE

churches.⁹⁴ What is different about the early viking raids is that they came from a 'third party', as it were. That is, they came from outside the established structure of political rivals and, in some cases it seems, they also went further than honour or social mores would allow: the enslavement of monastic brethren, and the sale of Christians to non-Christians, may have been 'red lines' that raiders did not cross. It is also clear, though rarely explicit, that sexual violence against women, and the castration of young boys, were unwelcome innovations of the age.⁹⁵

However, violence against churches was not an innovation of the Viking Age. There is a notorious episode of 619 in which St Donnan was burned, along with 150 of his brethren, on the Isle of Eigg; and later in the 7th century Adomnán, ninth abbot of Iona, mentions the 'persecution' of churches by rival kindreds of the Dál Riata.⁹⁶ Adomnán also led the famous effort to exempt churches and their clergy from violence as non-combatants. The *Cáin Adomnáin* or the *Lex innocentium*, 'Law of the Innocents', was promulgated at the Synod of Birr, Co. Offaly, in 697, notably also signed by the king of the Picts. However, although this may have helped to keep the peace for a while, as monasteries grew more reliant on royal patronage the line between secular and ecclesiastical politics was increasingly blurred. By the late 8th century, in the context of intense competition for the over-kingship of Ireland, rival kindreds upped the stakes until, in the 760s, their monasteries began to be drawn into proxy wars.⁹⁷ The 770s and '80s would see an explosion of church-burnings and battles between monastic communities. In fact, while raids on churches did increase after 800, there were more church-burnings in Ireland reported in 750–800 than 800–50.⁹⁸ In 804, another law was passed asserting that monastic brethren were exempt from being drafted into military service, which says a great deal about the situation by then.⁹⁹

Back to northern Britain, the 780s was a similar period of factionalism among the Picts after a period of united rule, with as many as three kings of the Picts and another of Dál Riata at any given time. Custantín came to power in 789 after a 'battle between the Picts', as the Irish annals reported it; he was the fifth named king of the Picts in just the last decade.¹⁰⁰ But his rivals were still at large and it was not until 811 that he would defeat the last of them for control of both Dál Riata and all Pictland. As noted at the opening of this chapter, his monuments at Forteviot speak of confidence and imperial ambition by the time of his death in 820.

If the situation was tense among the Picts, being a king of Northumbria had by the late 8th century become a dead-end job, with compulsory redundancies by assassination a common occurrence. Even those kings who made it out alive were deposed by councils of ealdormen, lay nobles who seemed to gain increasing control in the Anglo-Saxon kingdoms over the coming centuries. One in particular, named Sicga, was said to have murdered the king in 788 and then died himself in mysterious circumstances in 793. Despite this chequered career he was still buried at Lindisfarne, so he presumably had some pull with his pagan-bearded king, Aethelred I. The overall sense is one of unrest and unsavoury dealings.

Why is this significant for us here? The pattern which emerges over the long term, before, during and after 793, is that attacks on churches went hand-in-hand with periods of internecine strife.¹⁰¹ The case has even been made for possible Pictish involvement in the first raid on Lindisfarne.¹⁰² In this respect it is worth remembering Custantín did not take over Dál Riata until 811, after which point there were no raids on Iona until 825, five years after his death. Did Custantín come to an agreement with the first viking raiders to hit his rivals where it hurt the most? If so, we can see the conflagration at Portmahomack, dated 780–810, with new eyes. While we are drawn, like moths to a flame, to a viking raid as our explanation, it is not the only one available from our sources.¹⁰³

One final remarkable discovery can be mentioned here. In the cemetery of the early monastery of Portmahomack, stable isotope analysis of bones and teeth was able to determine whether people buried here were born locally or travelled from afar.[104] What they found, from all periods assessed, was a high level of mobility. One individual from the monastic cemetery, a male aged 18–25, dated to AD 670–880, came from a place with an older geology than anything near Portmahomack, and a colder climate than the vast majority of Britain. While an origin in the Scottish highlands is a remote possibility, it was suggested that Scandinavia was a better fit. Only one other individual from the Portmahomack cemetery, this time from a definite post-800 context, had a similar northern origin. This latter individual died from lethal blade wounds to the head. Was a viking raider buried among the monks? Or did the monastic community have dealings with Scandinavians before the supposed raid in the early 9th century?

The suddenness of the Viking Age is in some ways more apparent than real. The disruption of the available historical source material is undeniable, and the nature of record-keeping for northern Britain seems to narrow down to a few major sources, but there are several ways to interpret gaps in the source material.[105] Many of the ways we date our objects are bound up in the assumption of a break around the early 800s. Rather than marking a drastic change, the appearance of 'intrusive' materials and practices that we call the 'Viking Age' are surprisingly piecemeal and scattered during these early decades.[106] After this short foray into the historical evidence, we will see how archaeology can weigh in on these debates.

CUSTANTÍN'S DEATHBED CONFESSIONS

As Custantín lay dying in AD 820, his legacy enshrined in stone monuments at Forteviot, how would he have reflected on the state of his kingdom? Over the last three decades, he had reigned in the age of the first viking raids. Custantín's Cross at Forteviot seems to encode a message of support for the Columban federation of churches, and indeed he may even have founded its primary eastern daughter house at Dunkeld. Was this an act of penance after allowing attacks on it before he became king over Dál Riata in 811? We should consider the possibility that his hand was forced by the threat of the fleets amassing in the North Sea zone by the late 8th century. One likely scenario is that he came to an agreement to broker the peace within his realm – one that involved giving the raiders land in the northern parts of his realm, or at least guarantees of safe passage.[107] The raid on Portmahomack may have been part of this process – unless it was part of the internecine strife that pre-dated his reign.

Historical speculation aside, all of this helps to complicate our stories of the Viking Age. This is no bad thing as long as it helps us to devise new and more sustainable interpretations from our fragmented evidence. Crucially it introduces a major theme running through this book: that the Viking Age involved more than 'vikings', and that the people and activities we label this way included more than Scandinavians. It reintroduces all our stock characters – be they Picts, vikings, Gaels, Britons or Northumbrians – as knowledgeable actors with agency and something to gain, not just everything to lose.

NOTES

1. Wooliscroft 2002.
2. Ewart et al. 2008.
3. Clancy 2010a.
4. Carver 2019, 529–34.
5. Campbell and Driscoll 2020; Goldberg 2012, 170–4.
6. Fraser 2009, 362.
7. Fraser 2009, 303–5; Woolf 2001.
8. Henderson and Henderson 2004.
9. Campbell and Maldonado 2020.
10. Campbell and Driscoll 2020, 210.
11. Foster (ed.) 1998.
12. Campbell and Driscoll 2020; Brophy and Noble 2020.
13. Newman 2007; Gleeson 2019.
14. Goldberg 2012.
15. Thompson 2004; Whitworth 2020.
16. Moreland 2000; McKerracher 2018.
17. Maddicot 2005; Metcalf 2007; O'Sullivan et al. 2014, 213–4.
18. Maldonado 2016; Carver et al. 2016; Clarke 2012.
19. Campbell 2007.
20. Noble and Evans 2019, 14–20.
21. Maddicot 2005.
22. Porcupine type Series E from the Low Countries, dated AD715–35: Carver et al. 2016, Digest 6.2, p. D84.
23. Blackburn 2000.
24. Blackwell 2018, 129–32.
25. See also discussions of North Sea contacts in Strachan et al. 2019.
26. *Ibid.*, 142–3.
27. Lowe 2006.
28. Maxwell 1956; AA-29705, 1310 BP +/- 55, AD644–877 at 95% probability.
29. Carver et al. 2016, 276.
30. *Ibid.*, 226–8.
31. Barber 1981; Hunter 2008a.
32. O'Sullivan et al. 2014, 265–6.
33. Kelly 2000; Ross 2019.
34. Clarke et al. 2012.
35. Coleman and Photos-Jones 2008, 14–15.
36. Blackwell et al. 2017.
37. Heald 2011; Campbell and Heald 2007.
38. Lane and Campbell 2000.
39. C MacIver, pers. comm.
40. Close-Brooks 1986.
41. Youngs 1989, no. 150; e.g. Crock Cleuch, Scottish Borders, TT 39/02; Baleshare, North Uist, TT 86/06.
42. Shiels and Campbell 2011, 67–9; Burley 1958.
43. Graham-Campbell 2009, 198–9.
44. Hill 1997, 400–2; 115–17.
45. Curle 1982; Heald 2005.
46. Carver et al. 2016, 216 for an emphasis on silver-working; 271, 274 for the ingots.
47. Swift 2013; Etchingham and Swift 2004.
48. Clarke 2012.
49. Forsyth 2020.
50. Ó Carragáin 2014; Carver 2019, 648–54.
51. Geary 1994, 195–200; McCormick 2001, 704–19.
52. Breay and Story 2018.
53. Wood 2001.
54. Henderson and Henderson 2004, 215–6; Carver et al. 2016, 217–8; Reece 1981, 23–5.
55. Campbell et al. 2019; Carver et al. 2016, 211, illustration 5.6.19.
56. Compare Pickles 2020.
57. Carver et al. 2016, 339–340.
58. Maddicott 2005; Crabtree 2010.
59. McCormick 2001, 2002; Pelteret 1995.
60. Webster and Backhouse 1991, nos 98–100; Lasko 1956.
61. Heisey 2011.
62. Clancy 2001, 4.
63. Garver 2018.
64. Downham 2017, 2–3.
65. Garver 2018, 220.
66. Downham 2017.
67. Griffiths 2019.
68. Baug et al. 2019; Price 2020.
69. Baug et al. 2019.
70. Price et al. 2016.
71. Charles-Edwards 2000, 586–7; note the earliest evidence of

human occupation of the Faroe Islands now pre-dates the monastic movement: Church et al. 2013.

72. Dumville 1997, 5–7.
73. Dumville 2002, Heen-Pettersen 2019.
74. MacDonald 2002.
75. Fisher 2002.
76. Cross 2017.
77. McGuigan 2015a, 68.
78. Petts 2017.
79. Dumville 1997, 19–22; Broun 1997a, 121–2.
80. Parker 2012.
81. Carver et al. 2016.
82. Kruse 2013, 20.
83. Ellis 2021.
84. Herbert 1988; Clancy 2003; Maldonado et al. 2021.
85. Downham 2017, 2; cf. Etchingham 2021.
86. Lucas 1967; Smyth 1999; Etchingham 2021.
87. Smyth 1999, 21.
88. Downham 2017, 11; Etchingham 1996, 35–47.
89. Woolf 2007, 45, 64.
90. Downham 2004, 75.
91. Charles-Edwards 2000, 588.
92. Downham 2017, 3–4.
93. Stout 2017, 139–42.
94. Lund 1989; Coupland 2014.
95. Dumville 1997, 9–10; Valante 2013.
96. Fraser 2009, 342–4.
97. Charles-Edwards 2000, 594–5.
98. Etchingham 1996, figs 3–4, 11–12; Stout 2017, 111–14.
99. Clancy 2003, 220.
100. Fraser 2009, 328–9.
101. Stout 2017, 111–14, 139–40; Clancy 2011; Charles-Edwards 2000, 589.
102. Woolf 2007, 55–7.
103. Griffiths 2019.
104. Carver et al. 2016, Digest 4.4, D34–40.
105. For example, Evans 2017.
106. Griffiths 2019.
107. Woolf 2007, 56–7.

CHAPTER THREE
Worlds of the dead

Our view of the 9th–12th centuries is largely filtered through the worlds of the dead. Many of the names of historical figures in the annals come only from their obituaries. A large proportion of all the archaeological evidence we have for clothing, dress items, weapons and tools comes from the remarkable series of furnished graves (more than 200 in the latest estimates) which dot the coastlines of the north and west.[1] In other parts of Scotland, carved stone grave-markers and crosses are often the only material evidence for these centuries. Our vision of life in early medieval Scotland comes mainly through their hope for an afterlife.

Just as a funeral might capture an idealised portrait of the deceased, we have to be conscious of both the medium as well as the message. To understand why we have the objects we have, we need to know why people were buried with or without grave-goods, in ships, under mounds, in an anonymous heap of stones or within the shadow of a church. For instance, an iron sickle can tell us about food production, metalworking technology, natural resources or something of the economics of the time. But if we overlook the fact that we have almost no early medieval sickles except those found in Viking-age graves, we are missing a crucial part of what objects meant to people at this time.[2] The furnished 'pagan' graves of the 9th and 10th centuries ironically provide a unique window on insular artefacts as much as Scandinavian material culture. This chapter will step aside from the historical narrative and instead introduce the critical evidence for life that only the world of the dead can provide.

The evidence for burial in Scotland in this period is remarkably scattered and regionalised. At the opening of the 9th century, we are in a phase where it becomes increasingly difficult to see the dead. Outwith the 'viking' burials we will discuss below, there are vanishingly few dated burials. Thus we have only rare glimpses into burial practices at this time of rapid change. What we have are, generally speaking, rather anonymous 'flat' graves, not marked on the surface in ways that survive archaeologically, with no grave-goods, facing east. This could be said of burial from the 5th century onwards in Scotland: often they are only recognisable as early medieval through radiocarbon-dating.[3]

Opposite: Detail of the lower guard of an iron sword hilt with silver and copper-alloy inlay, from a male-gendered grave (10), Westness, Rousay, Orkney; NMS X.1997.247.

In contrast to this are the numerous 'pagan' or 'Norse' graves, mainly to be found in the northern and western isles, which characterise the 9th and 10th centuries. Whether they are always the burials of 'pagans' or 'Norse' is a question we still need to answer, but they are the most unambiguous evidence of a social practice imported from abroad in the 9th and 10th centuries. A full new study of these graves is long awaited, so in this chapter we can take the chance to focus on a few key examples and the stories they have to offer.

But before we cast 'Christian' and 'viking' burial as mutually exclusive visions of death in this era, we should stress the considerable evidence for diversity everywhere and the amount of overlap.[4] It is also clear that these ostentatious graves, 'Norse' or otherwise, must only represent a small fraction of the population. Their limited numbers and restricted demographic representation (mostly adult men and women) means they do not even represent a significant proportion of the population, and perhaps not even a very representative form of the contemporary view of death and the afterlife. As we will discuss in chapter 7, these centuries saw the establishment of numerous family chapels, and later parish churches, as part of the wider process in which the Church became increasingly central to everyday medieval life. The carved stone grave-markers which became more common attest to changing attitudes to the worlds of the dead – one in which more individuals were commemorated with public memorials, where the dead were 'present' in new ways.

All of these changes have to be seen in the wider context of evolving Christian attitudes towards the soul and the afterlife. Even though the concept of Purgatory, a middle place between Heaven and Hell, was still taking shape in these centuries, a number of inscribed grave monuments ask for prayers in the name of the dead. There is a wealth of Old English literature describing attacks by demons and other creatures after death, requiring protections such as a grave cover with the sign of the cross, burial in consecrated ground, and preservation of the cadaver in innovative ways which appear archaeologically.[5]

Increased anxieties over the fate of the soul show that corporeal death was only the start of a long journey. This long predates the Viking Age, with the 'majestic rider' motif on Pictish sculpture perhaps capturing a specific version of this from the 8th century onwards.[6] The concept of death as a journey finds numerous cross-cultural parallels of course, but most notably with ship and boat burials of Scandinavia.[7] These join other evidence, archaeological and literary, for the conception of afterlife journeys in Old Norse mythology.[8] The mounds and cairns created by such ostentatious burials would have generated their own stories and myths for as long as they stood. The same can be said of Pictish barrows and funerary monuments.[9]

In chapter 2 we saw that the kings of the Picts were establishing an imperial image at one of their major royal centres at Forteviot, and this involved ostentatious and novel forms of commemorating the dead. They may not have been buried with masses of grave-goods here, but the funerary ritual could be complex, involving lots of material culture not left in the grave itself. Burial in this period is therefore not so much a spectrum from lots of grave-goods to no grave-goods. It is instead a diversity of ways of transforming the memory of the living to the worlds of the dead, which was achieved using material culture.[10]

WIELDING TIME, ASSEMBLING SPACE

One thing which emerges clearly from the burial record is the clear patterning of burial rituals across vast areas. Among furnished 'viking' burials, only certain classes of objects were acceptable, and these tended to be strongly 'gendered' into male and female assemblages. Alongside these graves there are several unfurnished inhumations as well, showing that not all participants in these new funerary landscapes were required to be buried in this way. For instance, while Orkney and Shetland were the focus of Scandinavian settlement, they did not have the same approach to 'pagan' burial. Orkney hosts the densest concentration of furnished burials in Britain or Ireland outside the town of Dublin itself.[11] In Shetland, by contrast, there are perhaps 13 furnished burials, whereas there are at least 40 furnished alongside several unfurnished graves known from just two Orkney cemeteries of Pierowall, Westray, and Westness, Rousay, alone.[12] And some of these Shetland graves are represented by a single object, unlike the full sets of weapons in burial chambers known from Westness in Orkney.[13] Likewise, boat burials are seen as some of the most iconic 'viking' graves, but not a single one is known from Ireland. These are the first indications that the 'pagan Norse' burial form was only deployed in specific circumstances.

Material culture in the early medieval period is so often attributed 'ethnic' significance that it is all too easy for these labels to slip, as if by osmosis, onto the corpse. Instead, the best way to understand any early medieval grave is in the way it manipulates places and objects in the process of memorialising the dead. To get there we have to look at the process of assembling a grave, and the way that time and space were folded into each one.[14] There are lots of things that need to be assembled for any grave – including family and community members, each of whom brought their own memories, stories and other social entanglements with the deceased. In the case of furnished graves, some of the objects may have come along with these people as part of the funerary ritual. This might help to explain the jarring concurrence of local and imported objects, items which look brand new and those which bear signs of generations of use, in constructions that were new and elaborate, but often in areas of pre-Viking and even prehistoric evidence for settlement.

It is clear that one of the primary purposes of the ostentatious furnished 'pagan Norse' grave was that of land-taking. In Norway, burial mounds could be used almost like charters, proof that one's ancestors held the land and it was passed down to their heirs.[15] Spectacular examples, such as the boat burials of Scar, Kiloran Bay and Ardnamurchan, have created an image of Viking-age graves as isolated mounds far from settlement. However, these highly symbolic monuments played multiple roles in a largely maritime context, where they took on great vistas and were meant to be seen from a long way even at sea.[16] It is also true that furnished burials rarely came in large groups: just a handful of sites can be called 'cemeteries', perhaps only Westness, Pierowall, Machrins, Cnip and Reay. Many of our sites have been discovered in less than careful circumstances before modern excavation and recording, and the dispersed pattern of finds may be more apparent than real. One good example is the Machrins, Colonsay, site, now an area of sand dunes partially obscured by a golf course and airstrip. There are only a few well-excavated graves from here, but the overall spread of finds show that there were several graves, not all furnished, from the machair.[17] These cemeteries aside, the overall picture is that an elaborately furnished burial was a statement that did not often need to be repeated.

Land-claims were often effected through an ostentatious funerary ritual, but also in the careful selection of the place of burial. The placement of graves in ancient monuments, such as the ruined broch mounds which dot the northern isles and Caithness, was a common occurrence – an appropriation of a kind of ancestral status within a local context. The funeral was a theatre of memory, one that involved an audience of survivors and mourners who remain invisible to us – except through the arrangement of the corpse and the selection of grave-goods.[18] The funeral may only have been witnessed by a select few, but barrows and other monuments were means of communicating to the future by connecting with the past.

A good example is the Broch of Gurness, Orkney – today

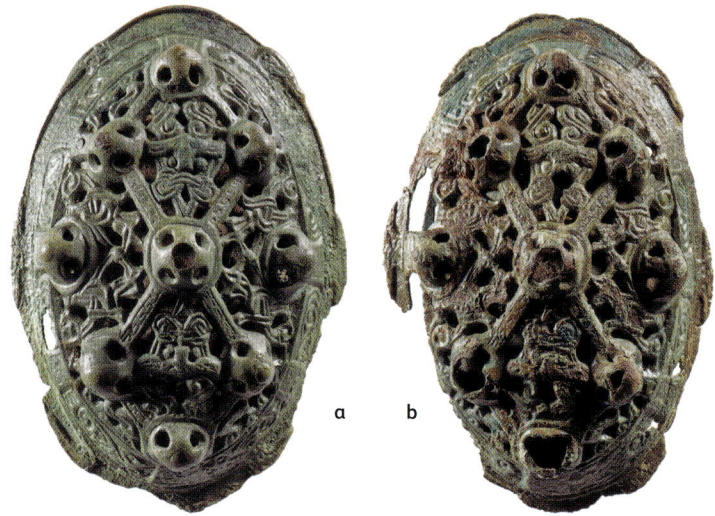

Figs 3.1a–d: Grave-goods from a female burial at the Broch of Gurness: (a, b) a pair of oval brooches, NMS X.GAA 220.1–2; (c) an iron sickle-blade, NMS X.GAA 263; (d) an iron neck-ring with pendant in the form of a Thor's Hammer, NMS X.GAA 264.

one of the most striking ruins of this kind of Iron-Age stone tower, surrounded by a 'village' of outbuildings of stone and a great enclosure ditch. In the 9th and 10th centuries, the site would have looked like a large, overgrown rubble mound with traces of later drystone structures, a prominent local landmark with a wide view over the Eynhallow Sound.[19] The ruins were reused for what seems like a number of burials or settlement activity, given stray finds of objects such as shield bosses and pins; but the only intact, excavated grave was that of a woman wearing the traditional Scandinavian female costume of oval brooches at the shoulders, a rare iron necklet, an iron sickle and a knife [Figs 3.1a–d].[20] She was also buried in a long cist, facing east, both aspects of local 'Christian' burial, and her grave would have been overshadowed by the ruins around it. Yet the reuse of the mound, which seems to have remained a busy place in the Viking Age, was made to communicate a claim to territory in a way that spoke to the past as much as the future, to a diverse audience which may have included Christians.

In addition to the practicalities of visibility, there is a rich mythological and supernatural component to the act of burying the dead in mounds, something we can only glimpse from later Old Norse sagas and poetry.[21] Less often considered is the Irish and Old English literature on death, the afterlife and barrow mounds in particular, which surely have something to add to our understanding of these funerary monuments in an insular context. As we saw at Forteviot, the Picts had their own attitudes to barrows and cairns, even if the stories they told around these have been lost to time. But in Alba as in Ireland, earthen mounds, old and new, were used for royal rituals of inauguration and the promulgation of laws.[22] Barrows in the Old English tradition were 'inhabited' by the dead, but into the Christian era they were also the abode of demons and other creatures.[23] In Scotland, England and beyond, mounds remained in use as gathering-places, outdoor law courts, gallows and other places of assembly and authority.[24]

As we will see below, the funerary attire in these graves often included long-lived heirlooms, brooches and other items sometimes generations old before they were 'laid to rest' alongside the dead. In one striking example, a belt-fitting decorated in the 8th-century 'Vendel' art style of Scandinavian origin was found in the area of Loch Seaforth at the traditional boundary between the 'isles' of Lewis and Harris [3.2]. This must pre-date the arrival of Scandinavian settlers to the Hebrides, but the rivet

Fig. 3.2: Gilt-bronze buckle-plate of 'Vendel-type', Ath Linne, Loch Seaforth, Lewis, 8th century, length 47mm; NMS X.2006.4.

punched through in a repair tells us this had been refashioned in some way and was old by the time it was deposited here, possibly in a grave.[25]

The burial of the dead was always a purposeful deposition, and can best be understood as a process of enabling remembering and forgetting of aspects of the deceased. Communities accomplished this by assembling a space for the deceased and their commemoration, and by wielding time with the use of meaningful objects. It must have worked: we are still talking about these episodes more than a thousand years later, even if their names are lost to us.

FAMILY MATTERS

Given the monumentality of some furnished graves, it is easy to think that burial mounds were only raised for the benefit of future travellers to see, but they were first and foremost funerals arranged on behalf of well-known members of the community by their survivors. As we will see, we need to be able to read the emotion in these deposits to understand them. Yet it is also true that a large proportion of these graves contain weapons of war and the character they portray seems more aggressive than mournful. The inclusion of swords, axes, spears and shields with individuals sexed as biologically male has led to the widespread use of the term 'warrior burial' for these deposits. But it is clear these graves follow a set of widely shared conventions, meaning that, to a certain extent, the grave-goods were dictated by tradition and by rules about how men and women should be buried, more than an accurate representation of an individual's actual belongings.

Only in a few cases has there been decent enough preservation of bone to test whether men buried with weapons were warriors in life [3.3]. One study of Scandinavian skeletal assemblages demonstrated that violent trauma was surprisingly rare in Viking-age cemeteries.[26] A detailed osteological study of the skeletons at the cemetery of Westness, Rousay, Orkney, showed that two men buried in boat graves with weapons had indeed lived hard lives. They were the tallest in the cemetery by some margin, but they had also died as the oldest males in the cemetery at the relatively advanced age of 45–60 years.[27] Grave 11 is one of only two graves in Britain or Ireland with a 'complete' set of weapons, meaning sword, shield, spear, axe and a quiver of arrows.[28] The men in graves 11 and 34 had developed arthritis – unsurprising given their age. They both also had several chipped teeth, with evidence for abrasion of the incisors reminiscent of tooth-filing practices detected elsewhere in Viking-age Scandinavia.[29] Both had bone deformities in their hands or feet likely caused by healed injuries. Intriguingly, one of them (grave 34) had arrowheads in several places about the skeleton, including one in the rib-cage: but as there was no mark on any bone it is not possible to prove, as the osteologist suggested, that this man died in a flurry of arrows.[30] It is more likely these men were 'retired' after a lifetime of fighting and were commemorated with displays of weaponry and ostentatious use of boat chambers alongside their family members [3.4].

At Westness then, two men had led a fighting life but lived long enough to be part of a settlement with its own cemetery at

Westness.[31] We can also dimly perceive the nature of this settlement. The Norse-style longhouse from Swandro, on the opposite end of the bay from the cemetery, seemed to post-date the main use of the cemetery, but recent excavations have turned up a midden layer in a reused prehistoric chambered cairn, including fish-bone and a coin of Eanred, king of Northumbria (810–40); this joins an older find of a stamped silver finger-ring of 10th-century type [3.5].[32] Such finds reveal a more ephemeral form of occupation here contemporary with the Westness cemetery, before the construction of the longhouse in the 10th or 11th century.

It is the family component that may be the critical factor in the weapon graves at Westness. Of the certain boat burials from Scotland, only Kiloran Bay on Colonsay, Fetlar on Shetland, and Ardnamurchan on the mainland opposite Mull, were

Fig. 3.3 (left): Reconstruction of an oval, stone-lined grave from Westness, Rousay, Orkney, as displayed in the 'Early People' gallery, National Museum of Scotland.

Fig. 3.4 (right, above): Iron shield boss, NMS X.IL 199, iron axe-head, NMS X.IL 200, and spearhead, NMS X.IL 201, from a grave at Pierowall, Westray, Orkney.

Fig. 3.5 (right, below): Stamped silver ring from Swandro, near Westness, Rousay, Orkney, 10th century, diameter 20mm; NMS X.HD 748.

single graves.³³ In the case of Fetlar, the boat burial was for a single woman. The remaining examples are all from cemeteries – Westness, Rousay; Pierowall, Orkney; Machrins, Colonsay – or have multiple individuals buried in them – Scar, Sanday; Carn a' Bharraich, Oronsay. In the latter two they include both men and women and, in the case of Scar, a child;³⁴ in fact, half of the individuals interred in boats in Scotland were women. The boat burials are often stereotyped as classic warrior graves, but in Scotland at least they seem to relate to established settlements of the later 9th and 10th centuries, and may be better understood as akin to later Scots 'lairs', set up and maintained by a family, not just a raider or merchant passing through.

It is important to remember the immense cost and value of a seafaring vessel – there is evidence that ships were often jointly owned rather than being the 'possession' of one person, and the retirement of a ship affected not only one person but a crew and, potentially, a community.³⁵ The 'sacrifice' of a ship would have been a decision not taken lightly, and would have acquired a much broader cosmological significance for the community present at the funeral and those living with the monument in subsequent generations. From an anthropological perspective, this could be seen as a fertility deposit, but this is rarely the way we discuss boat graves in the Viking Age.³⁶ The metaphorical aspect of a boat-sacrifice seems particularly apt at Westness, a settler cemetery established amidst an existing Pictish burial ground, in which many of the new graves were either boat burials or in boat-shaped mounds. While these new graves certainly overshadowed the existing burials, which seem to have been marked by upright stones, they did not disturb them; indeed, according to the radiocarbon-dating, some of the 'Pictish' burials in unfurnished long cists may have continued to be made alongside the boat and pit graves here.³⁷ The audience for these repeated displays was one which added to, rather than displaced, existing funerary rites in a mixed community of settlers and locals, but also has an air of competitive display about it, suggesting that the cemetery was used by more than a single family. To add another layer to the 'identity politics' here, isotope analysis demonstrates that at least one of the women buried in this 'pagan' manner was of insular origin (p. 61). The competition for status and legitimacy among incomers and locals was not just among Norse migrants, but also migrants of insular origin.³⁸

THESE ARE NOT VIKING SWORDS

Just as boats cannot be seen as simple 'possessions' in the Viking Age, the swords of this era can tell us a great deal about the interconnectedness of the things we so bluntly associate with a 'viking' identity. In all but a handful of cases in Scotland, Viking-age swords only come down to us as grave-goods. This means that, however they were used in life, we can only perceive them through the perspective of funerary offerings. It also indicates that the surviving swords are overwhelmingly from a very restricted part of the country, primarily its northern and western islands and coastal zones.

The latest published study counts 34–36 reliable accounts of 'viking swords' from Scotland, of which 30 certainly came from graves.³⁹ To these we can now add two new finds – one that comes from a boat grave in Ardnamurchan and one from a male weapon burial under a rectangular cairn in Mayback, Papa Westray.⁴⁰ It is worth noting that non-funerary swords are all from areas outside the Scandinavian-controlled north and west and, along with recent metal-detected pommels, most are of types which post-date the furnished burial phase of roughly 850–950.⁴¹

Why were swords so strongly associated with graves? For one thing, a sword of good iron was a valuable and expensive object – one not casually lost. They were also more than just commodities. Several studies have shown that early medieval weapons, and swords in particular, could have names, histories, personalities, and were strongly imbued with the character of those who owned and gifted them.[42] Other weapons held symbolic significance – axes could be decorated with inlaid silver, oaths could be sworn on shield bosses. These were not inanimate objects, but had an animated quality about them, even a character of their own. This was not specific to a pagan Norse perspective either and is a phenomenon observed well into the Christian era in Britain and beyond.[43]

A good percentage of the Viking-age swords which come down to us were in fact made outside Scandinavia. Demand for Frankish steel was one of the engines that initially drew Scandinavians into the North Sea trade zone, to the extent that Carolingian kings tried to ban the sale of weapons to pagans in the north.[44] There are numerous examples of Frankish blades being fitted with new hilts of Scandinavian fashion. The value of these swords went beyond the quality of their steel, into what they signalled for the wearer. In particular, foreign swords – whether won in battle, received as gifts, or bought on the open market – conferred considerable status on their owners.[45] Older swords, handed down over generations, were also highly valued due to the histories they had accrued.[46]

Frankish and Anglo-Saxon swords became fashionable in graves of the 9th and 10th centuries, and one recent study has identified dozens of insular swords from Viking-age graves in Norway.[47] In fact, the styles that we now routinely call 'viking swords' consist of either those made outside Scandinavia, or imitations made in Scandinavia. Swords which are difficult to fit into a particular style may be evidence for production outside the main manufacturing centres. Some styles may have been associated with a single workshop, and there were even famous 'brands' of blade that displayed the maker's name and inspired forgeries.[48]

It turns out it is very hard to define a 'viking sword' at all, and the term hinders more than it helps. A century has passed since Jan Petersen established a widely influential sword typology for Norway in *De Norsk Vikingesverd* (1919). It remains a classic example of object typology, impressive in scope and allowing for patterns of use to be detected within and outwith Scandinavia. However, its types are based on only one part of the sword – the hilt – and the variations often come down to what seem today to be minor, and functionally insignificant, differences in the curve of the hilt-guard or the shape of the pommel. The typology worked well enough to be retained as a shorthand today, but it can be quite subjective: two different scholars might classify a sword differently using the same system.

Let us return to the swords from Scotland and see how they fit into these broader patterns. In the latest published study, at least 10 of 34 swords from Scotland were classified as Petersen's Type H.[49] Type H also happens to be the most popular sword type across Scandinavia, so for starters we can say that Viking-age burials in Scotland fit into the mainstream of their day. For instance, all four swords from the famous cemetery of Westness, Rousay, Orkney (including an antiquarian find from Swandro nearby [3.6a–b]) are of Type H. These are often, but not always, decorated with a distinctive pattern of alternating strips of copper-alloy and silver, creating a mesmerising and multicolour visual effect when they catch the light. At least according to those selected as grave-goods, it is the Type H that was most often used, and so we are on the safest ground calling these 'viking swords' simply based on their prevalence in Scandinavia and the wider Norse-speaking diaspora.

Of the remaining swords from Scotland which could be classified, 14 belong to a wide range of other types. One kind in particular captures the issues with the terminology of 'viking swords'. This is the famous sword hilt from a grave at Kildonnan, Isle of Eigg, classified as Type D [3.7]. It has been used as an icon for the Viking Age beyond Scotland and belongs to a wider category of 'prestige swords' with ornate decoration and extravagant use of precious metal.[50] The Eigg hilt has rare inlaid

Figs 3.6 a–b (left and middle): Sword hilt from Swandro, Rousay, likely from a grave at Westness; detail (middle) shows row of cast copper-alloy wolf-head mounts facing toward the grip; NMS X.IL 191.

Fig. 3.7 (bottom): Sword hilt of bronze inlaid with silver, Kildonnan, Isle of Eigg, length 190 mm; NMS X.IL 157.

silver, gold and bronze decoration which is difficult to parallel anywhere in Europe. There remains some debate over whether these were Frankish-made or Frankish-inspired Scandinavian hilts. It is probably safest to say it is both and neither at once. Elaborate gilded hilts of this type derive from Frankish types pre-dating the Viking Age – these were used by Carolingian emperors themselves into the 9th century, as can be observed in manuscript portraits of Charles the Bald.[51] The popularity of this style is reflected in imitations made in Scandinavia which, even if originally a Frankish type, may have quickly become associated with the highest levels of 'viking' aristocracy and was particular popular in Viking-age Ireland.[52] The same can be said of Type H hilts, ultimately of Frankish inspiration. Frankish smiths eventually would have started to make products directly for the booming Scandinavian market; and, as Scandinavian workshops were established, a diverse array of experts would have populated them. The swords would then be used by a class of highly mobile warriors who travelled for their careers, and who valued a foreign – or at least foreign-looking – sword. Assigning ethnic labels to these intentionally international objects is a fallacy.

Of the other sword-types identified in Scotland so far, we have examples of styles popular in Anglo-Saxon England, Denmark and Germany, alongside styles that were likely made in Norway. Some are very difficult to classify at all: the sword from Gorton, Strathspey [3.8], for example, has been classified as either Type Y, P or L over the years, and it is possible here that we have a sword which is hard to identify on purpose – that is, a merging of different types, maybe even executed in an insular workshop.[53] In a world of competitive display, a blending of styles showed knowledge of various fashions, and was another strategy to get ahead.

In truth, the biggest limitation with all our typologies is that the medium is the message. The very small percentage of people who were given furnished graves were those whose

Fig. 3.8: Double-edged iron sword with decorated pommel from Gorton, Strathspey, overall length 883 mm; NMS X.LA 1.

mourners could afford the sacrifice of those expensive, bleeding-edge(!) examples of blacksmithing technology.[54] These were almost certainly the land-takers themselves, new owners, some of them probably newly wealthy, requiring to show their status in a time of rapid change. If a sword was needed, then only a memorable sword would do. Sword-burials, like all such ostentatious furnished graves discussed here, are thus part of the means that land was claimed and inherited in this period, not the way every male could expect to be commemorated.

As a badge of status the swords used in such graves might invoke not just where they came from, but where they were going – referencing the continental and insular elites whose parties they were crashing. A 'viking' identity may not be the main thing these prestige objects were signalling – or rather, what we think of as 'viking identity' was more complicated and included the desire to adopt foreign fashions.[55] A boat grave from Machrins, Colonsay, may suggest a 'pagan Norse' identity on the surface, but among the grave-goods was a penannular brooch with parallels in the St Ninian's Isle Hoard, Shetland, as well as a Type L sword of a kind used in Viking-age Britain, emphasising the wide horizons of a highly mobile seafarer.[56]

So overall our definition of a 'viking sword' really depends on what we mean. If this refers to a sword made in Scandinavia or by Scandinavians in the 9th–11th centuries, we are rather missing the point, and in any case may never be able to prove this. If we mean swords that are intended to signal a distinct Scandinavian identity, then some of our most famous swords are not 'viking swords' at all. They were exotic even to vikings, and only became 'viking' to us because of their frequent use as grave-goods.

The reality is that what made a sword meaningful was its relationships: to its maker, to its owner, to mourners at a funeral, to the places it had travelled, the battles it had waged and, of course, to the swords of other notable warriors, Scandinavian or otherwise. In this sense, swords could be conspicuously hybrid – not an expression of any specific ethnicity, but the creation of a new identity that was proudly transnational. If we disagree over the exact typology of a sword, that is not the fault of the sword but ours for trying to impose such reductive labels. It is a pattern replicated in many other aspects of the Viking Age.

WEAPONS AND BECOMING MALE

This discussion of boats and swords has taken us away from the fact that what we are discussing are emotionally charged funeral celebrations. The best example of how such prestige objects were actually used comes from the 'Balnakeil boy'.[57] A

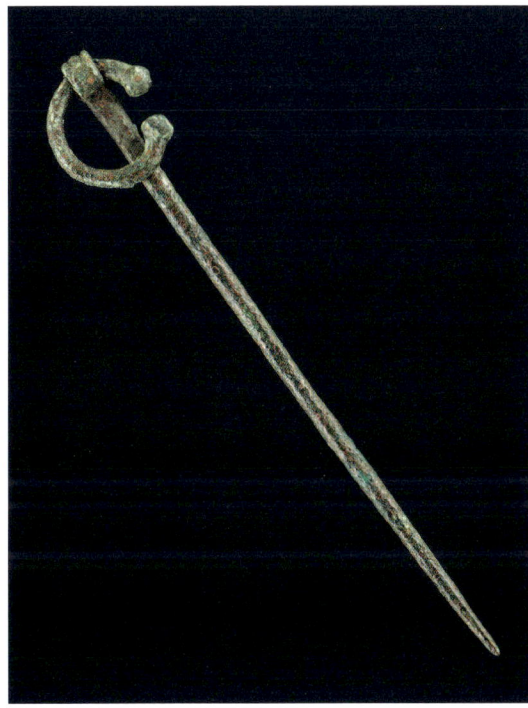

Fig. 3.9: Brooch-pin from a grave at Balnakeil, Durness, Sutherland, length 140mm; NMS X.1992.22.6.

youth of around 13 years, presumed male from the nature of the assemblage, was buried in a sandy shoreline in Durness on the north coastline of the Scottish mainland.[58] In the simple pit grave was an impressive suite of adult-sized weapons the youth could scarcely have wielded at his age, among other grave-goods of more ambiguous gendered significance [3.9]. However, there were teenagers among the 'warband' of decapitated soldiers of the Ridgeway Hill, Dorset, and it has been suggested that the concept of adulthood may have begun as early as twelve according to later Scandinavian textual evidence.[59] The osteological report at Balnakeil also noted that his right arm was enlarged, as if he had undertaken physical exertion of developing limbs – in other words, he may have begun his weapons training.[60] The weapons in this grave could feasibly have belonged to him – that is, he may have been already considered a 'man'.

But he was not necessarily expected to be able to wield these weapons in an afterlife. As with several other swords in Viking-age Scandinavian graves, his was deliberately broken, in this case by cutting off its tip, then placing the broken sword back into the scabbard.[61] At Balnakeil, the burial deposit can be seen perhaps as an invocation of an aspired, but foreclosed, future as the member of a warband. The weapons here would not necessarily have been the boy's 'possessions', but rather those of the family, as 'intergenerational objects'.[62] These weapons could have been promised by the family or warband or, alternatively ,'earned' in the struggle that caused his early death. It could then be seen as a form of inheritance, or a completely fabricated, desired future – in neither way a straightforward 'possession' of the person in the grave.

There is a metaphorical and interpretive potential in the act of breaking a valuable sword as a reflection of a life cut short too soon, but this is not exclusive to the burials of adolescents. This is a rare example of the ritual 'killing' of iron weapons that occurs in Viking-age graves.[63] In Viking-age Dublin and Woodstown, Co. Waterford, there are several examples that include five bent swords, nine broken swords, two bent spearheads, and eight dented shield bosses.[64] In Scotland there are a number of broken swords, but their corroded state often makes it difficult to determine how many were broken before burial. More demonstrably ritualised are the damaged shield bosses. In one of the boat burials at Westness (grave 11), the shield boss had been dented at least three times with a blunt, oblong object, perhaps the butt of an axe rather than a blade.[65] In another boat burial at Kiloran Bay, Colonsay, the shield boss has preserved mineralised textile showing it was carefully wrapped before burial. The wrapping clearly goes over the rim of the boss and into the interior, meaning it had been detached from its board and 'shrouded' [3.12].

Fig. 3.10 (right): Tinned-bronze sheet mounts from a grave at Ballinaby, Isle of Islay; NMS X.IL 142–144.

Fig. 3.11 (below): Conical mount of bronze from a grave at Machrins, Colonsay, height 21mm; NMS X.IL 797.

BREAKING DOWN SHIELD WALLS

While there are countless works published on swords, much less attention has been paid to shields, a key part of the Viking-age weapon set, at least according to how frequently they appear in the insular corpus of graves. As with swords, shield bosses are rarely found outside a funerary context. Despite being lower-value materials (wood and iron), it seems that they were rarely lost.

The bulk of the shield will always be lost to time – wood rarely survives in the acid soils of Scotland, leaving only the hard iron of the boss. The shield board itself, however, was a broad canvas that may have communicated key aspects of the war-band or individual's identity.[66] Indeed, it seems they could have done so in Pictish contexts too, given the different ornamentation on shields, like those depicted on the Birsay stone [1.1a].

In the wider Irish Sea zone, including notable examples from Arran and Colonsay, the conical form of the shield bosses derive from Anglo-Saxon types, an interesting example of hybridisation within an emerging Hiberno-Norse warrior culture.[67] There are also variations in how shields of various types were used: all the Scandinavian imports found in Dublin graves were dented or otherwise damaged, probably as part of the funerary ritual, as compared to only two of the 'Dublin type'.[68]

The Viking-age graves of Scotland also give us two potentially rare examples of decorated shields. The embossed (repoussé) sheet-bronze mounts from Ballinaby, Islay [3.10] are enigmatic. They bear an uncanny resemblance to the Pictish symbol known as the double disc, but the only other example of such plaques comes from another Viking-age grave from Dublin.[69] The repoussé technique is almost unknown in Scandinavia in this period and these are likely to have been produced by insular metalworkers, probably in Dublin. Such objects remain enigmatic, but their use as shield mounts or box mounts has been proposed. Interestingly they appear to have been found

in the female-gendered grave from Ballinaby, although there are issues with the attribution of these antiquarian finds.[70]

The other possible decorative shield is represented by a single tiny object: a conical mount with rivet holes for attaching to a sturdy wooden object, from an antiquarian excavation of a grave at Machrins, Colonsay [3.11]. These objects are extremely rare, but another was found in Dublin, and four from Woodstown, Co. Waterford.[71] Rare finds from Birka and Hedeby have been interpreted as decorative helmet mounts, but no evidence of helmets has yet been found in any insular Viking-age grave.[72] These objects are intriguing glimpses of the kinds of objects that were born out of the early Viking-age blend of styles in the seaways linking the Irish Sea and the Hebrides. Rather than cultural signposts, shields may instead be 'inter-cultural ... symbols of contact and change'.[73]

Fig. 3.12 (right). Shield boss showing mineralised textile, Kiloran Bay; NMS X.IL 762.

Figs 3.13 a–b (middle and bottom): Sword hilt showing traces of yarn-bound hilt, textile-wrapping and straw-bedding, from a grave at Balnakeil, Durness, Sutherland; NMS X.1992.22.1. Detail (bottom) shows straw and organic material mineralised to the Balnakeil sword scabbard.

Why go through the trouble of 'killing' weapons? As they were acquired at specific stages in one's life, they were used to 'bestow' a male gender and adulthood. At Balnakeil the 'killed' sword was wrapped carefully in textile, shrouded perhaps like the body of the person itself, as we saw with the Kiloran Bay shield boss [3.12].[74] The insular brooch-pin [3.9] discovered in this grave was found low on the skeleton alongside the boy's left thigh, not on the chest as would be expected if it were worn, indicating it had been used instead as a shroud-pin. Textiles so rarely survive in graves that it is easy to forget just how valuable they were in their own right: the wrapping of objects, let alone the cadaver, was an act of considerable sacrifice [3.13a].[75]

The remarkable preservation of this grave under the sand dunes of Sutherland also reveals parts of the funerary ritual that is lost from the typical grave in Scotland's acid soils. The corroded iron of the sword helped preserve organic materials around it. These show that the cadaver was laid on its right side on a bed of straw and feathers – to make it look as if they were asleep perhaps. Another adolescent of the Viking Age at Crow Taing, Sanday, Orkney, buried only with a knife leaving their gender ambiguous, was positioned in the same way, with arms and hands placed as if curled up in bed.[76] In the context of the death of a child at the cusp of adulthood, this could easily be seen as a way of mitigating the pain of unimaginable loss, one final act of parental care.

Regardless of the concept of ownership, which we will never be able to quantify at this distance, this burial would have represented a real sacrifice of more than just valuable objects by the survivors. These different aspects of the funerary ritual would have heightened what was already an emotional event. If the weapon set was a kind of inheritance, leaving it in the grave and killing the sword was definitively removing it from circulation. The funeral would have been a public display of a surviving family member or other leader discharging their duty

WORLDS OF THE DEAD

Fig. 3.14 (left): Iron shield boss from a grave at Balnakeil, diameter 130mm; NMS X.1992.22.2.

Fig. 3.15 (right): 'King-piece' of bone, from a set of *hnefatafl* playing-pieces in an oval grave from Westness, Rousay, Orkney, height 23mm; NMS X.1997.1031.1.

to continue providing protection for the community and to secure their collective future even with this loss. The disruption of the normal social order, wherein the boy would have grown into his arms-bearing status, was ameliorated by the public performance of continuity, in a way that has been shown to be a commonly occurring aspect of mortuary celebrations in gift-giving societies.[77]

Over the body of the Balnakeil youth was a shield and a spear. The shield [3.14] appears to have been placed over the head, another protective act perhaps, but one seen in many other adult burials with shields. Straw was also found above the shield boss, indicating the grave was backfilled with this material before the final closure. This would not only preserve the integrity of the grave deposit, it would also help to close the grave, searing in the mind the final glimpse of the funerary tableau before it was covered over. Through the highly memorable and emotionally charged funerary ritual, the child may have been arrayed so that the last memory was of him as an adult man.

Another male-gendered inclusion in this grave was the set of bone playing-pieces. These were undecorated and pegged for use on a gaming board. A similar set of plain gaming-pieces was found alongside the weapons of a male in an oval cist grave from Westness [3.15]. In the latter case, the gaming-pieces included a single larger piece, which indicates this was for the game *hnefatafl*, widely attested in Viking-age male graves.[78] However, there are some ambiguous objects in this grave that may give us pause about how we assign gender to entire burial assemblages. While the weapons were the most prominent offerings, the grave also included a needle-tidy alongside other tools making up a 'sewing kit'. Such tools are almost exclusively associated with female graves in this period. But if children's small fingers were useful in crafts like sewing, the needle-tidy may instead be a marker of age rather than gender; or perhaps his mother's gift, a token of the work they did together in the past. If there is an identity ascribed to the child through this process, it was not a normative male or female gender, but the youth's life in the context of their lived past and desired future. To call this a male grave is thus not telling the complete story, as it is a deposit which is in the act of generating an ancestral, family identity to an individual who left no descendants. To call this a 'warrior' grave rather diminishes the richness of this funeral as an act of creation, laden with emotion.

Balnakeil is admittedly an anomaly – no other juveniles were buried with weapons in Viking-age Scotland, if we exclude the knife (a common tool) from Crow Taing. But the questions raised here can be applied to any grave dressed and furnished with objects. They may be possessions, but whose? The deceased is only one option. The family or wider kin-group is another. A badge of office is another, in which case the objects can be seen as dually belonging to the dead and their patron, whether lord, family member, or a brother-in-arms. In an animated world, personhood included the dead and any objects buried with them. If such belongings were shared between the dead and the living, neither the person nor the objects in the grave were completely 'dead' – they continued to work for and on behalf of the living. This was a memorial to a family as much as an individual. There are lessons here for any furnished grave, child or adult, male or female.

Fig. 3.16: Oval brooches and beaded necklace from a woman's grave at Cnip, Lewis; NMS X.IL 799–844.

ISOTOPES, MOBILITY, DIET AND DNA

A scientific technique known as stable isotope analysis has transformed our knowledge of Viking-age graves in Scotland. It is a biomolecular analysis that looks at the isotopes of elements which get absorbed into human bone and teeth. The isotopes of carbon and nitrogen absorbed into our bones form an index of the kinds of foods we eat, whether marine or terrestrial. Other elements, like strontium and oxygen, are absorbed through drinking water from specific geological landscapes. Teeth form at different stages in our lifetime, so strontium and oxygen from primary teeth like molars can act as a sort of geological 'fingerprint' of where one was born, and can be compared with teeth and bones which formed later in life.

Stable isotope analysis of Viking-age burials pinpointed a 'fish event horizon' in Scotland – a point in which marine foods went from a negligible portion of people's diets to a major component.[79] This seems to occur mainly in the 9th–11th centuries across northern and western Scotland, and coincides with other archaeological evidence for fish-bone and fishing-equipment introduced on Viking-age settlements in these areas. But a diet high in fish was not observed for everyone; for instance, males from Westness had high marine intake, while women, even those buried in a 'pagan' manner, had less. Evidence for increased marine consumption is thus linked to the Viking Age in Scotland, but this is not uniformly the case across the wider Viking-age settlements.[80]

Strontium and oxygen stable isotope analysis, which allows us to trace mobility during one's lifetime, has been carried out on fewer Viking-age individuals so far, but the results are very interesting. One study compared isotope signatures for individuals from the cemeteries of Westness, Orkney, and Cnip, Lewis.[81] At Westness, two 'viking' males from weapon graves had isotopic signatures, which suggested an origin in Norway; the unfurnished and female furnished burials were all of insular origin.

However, there is a twist. Most of the 'Pictish' individuals were local, while the 'viking' woman (grave 5, buried crouched with a penannular brooch, sickle, spindle-whorls and reaping-hook) was from northeastern Ireland or eastern Scotland. At Cnip, a richly furnished female wearing oval brooches [3.16] was similarly found to be possibly from eastern Scotland or northern England. Two other individuals, a male and female, from Cnip, with few or no grave-goods, were also deemed insular, but not from the western or northern isles. There is uncertainty here, but the main point is that they were settlers – not Scandinavians, but not locals either.

It is also clear that mobility went both ways, or rather that people were highly mobile and in all directions.[82] Other 'viking' women – including one from Adwick-le-Street, Yorkshire, and one buried in Iceland – have possible Scottish origins according to stable isotope analysis.[83] The image that appears from the limited data available is of an age of high mobility, in which people buried as 'vikings' can be seen to be incomers, but from other parts of Britain or Ireland more often than first-generation Scandinavian migrants. Only further genetic analysis could rule out or confirm Scandinavian heritage, but it is interesting that in the few sequences published so far, individuals from Viking-age Orkney at Newark Bay and Buckquoy were also found to be of insular rather than Scandinavian heritage.[84]

Fig. 3.17: Oval brooch of brass from a grave at Pierowall, Westray, Orkney; NMS X.IL 197.

THE FUTURE IS FEMALE

This discussion of death in the Viking Age has thus far largely concerned male graves, but it is perhaps the female-gendered graves that tell the richest story of the period. This is especially true, if the isotopic evidence is any indication (p. 61), that many of the female graves were of insular-born women. This story is not just about the 'Norse' in Scotland. By looking at the commemorations of women before, during and after the Viking Age, the period begins to look more like a revolution of how power was claimed and wielded by women, not just 'warriors', in a period of social change.

Some of the most well-furnished graves of the Viking Age were those of women.[85] There are women buried as queens in ships; as merchants with the tools of their trade; and occasionally as warriors with weapon sets.[86] Yet they are still most often described in relation to men, particularly in their role as wives. The myriad ways women were commemorated can only be introduced here, but we will continue to explore it over the following chapters.

Viking-age graves with numerous grave-goods are often described as 'rich'. Despite generations of archaeologists who remind us that the dead do not bury themselves, these assemblages are often treated as reflecting the wealth of the deceased. This is based on two assumptions: that the objects in the grave were possessions of the deceased; and the concept of wealth in the 9th–10th century can be measured through the accumulation of material goods. The first assumption has already been dealt with in detail above. The second requires more work. We cannot assume objects had 'value' in a way measurable by the weight of precious metal or the distance travelled. On the other hand, we do know that materials of exotic origin were highly prized and are most often found in female-gendered graves.

The most obvious imports are the Scandinavian oval brooches (to be discussed more fully in chapter 5). These were largely made of base metals – almost exclusively brass – which allowed them to be mass-produced in the workshops of towns like Ribe. There is evidence some were gilded or inlaid with silver wire; and brass itself was rare in pre-Viking Scotland, so it is hard to judge just how 'precious' they would have seemed at the time. In any case, their ubiquity in Viking-age female-gendered graves shows that they were a potent symbol here and across the Norse diaspora. Their value was not just in the material or the distance travelled, but as a key to the form of dress which, in a funerary context, helped create the notion of a diaspora itself. This is an emotionally charged kind of value, difficult to measure yet clearly shared across wide areas.

Yet the use of oval brooches is not ubiquitous among women who were buried in Viking-age Scotland. For instance, as many as six furnished burials from Pierowall, Westray, Orkney, included oval brooches [3.17].[87] In contrast, only one of the women buried in Westness, Rousay, Orkney, wore them. It has been suggested that oval brooches in a Scottish context were restricted to younger women of child-bearing age, and this might have some influence on the distribution.[88]

The woman in Westness, who had been buried with oval brooches, captures the essence of Scotland's Viking Age in a single grave. It is one of the most elaborate in Scotland, according to the number and range of objects found within it [3.18]. Swords and other objects have been ploughed up along the Rousay coastline since at least the 19th century, but it was

CRUCIBLE OF NATIONS

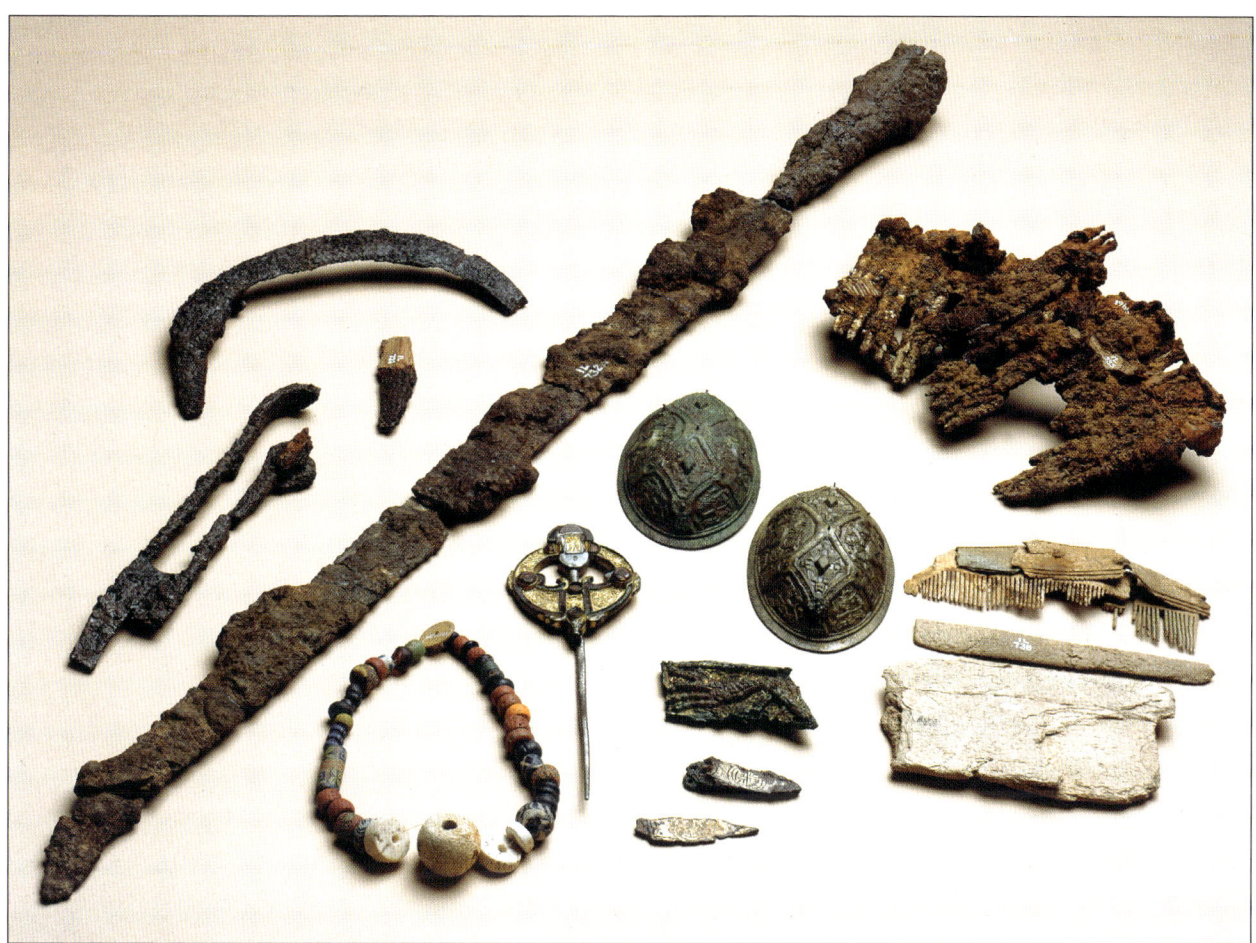

only when the local farmer was burying a dead cow in 1963 that an intact grave was encountered (although the burial of the animal did destroy much of the context). The objects were sent to the National Museum of Antiquities of Scotland for identification and a rescue excavation followed.[89]

The picture that emerged was of an elaborate double grave for an adult woman and a newborn infant. The oval brooches, even out of context, already tell us that the woman was dressed in the typical Scandinavian-style burial costume. A collection of 39 beads of glass and other materials presumably came from a necklace strung between the two oval brooches [3.19]. The beads were a collection from Irish, Anglo-Saxon, Frankish and Frisian sources, along with Baltic amber, and rare bone and stone beads of unknown origin.[90] Over her dress she would have been wrapped in a shawl or cloak fastened with a 'third brooch', another aspect of Scandinavian fashion. In this case it was made from a hacked fragment of an insular Christian shrine or book cover, modified with a catch-pin to make it into a brooch [7.16]. The object had been cut down to just one corner of the original design, depicting a wolf or lion: if the latter, then it likely represented the symbol of Mark the Evangelist. This would have been a distinct message to anyone who had previously witnessed such sacred objects, that their power had been broken, or appropriated for personal use.

Fig. 3.18: Selection of objects from a female-gendered grave assemblage excavated in 1963 at Westness, Rousay, Orkney; National Museums Scotland.

Fig. 3.19 (left): String of 39 glass, paste, bone and stone beads, Westness, Rousay, Orkney (1963); NMS X.IL 740.

Fig. 3.20 (left, below): The Westness Brooch, a hinged brooch-pin of silver with gold filigree, red glass and amber insets, overall length 175 mm, Westness, Rousay, Orkney (1963); NMS X.IL 728.

Figs 3.21 (below): Pair of Northumbrian-style strap-ends, Westness, Rousay, Orkney (1963), length 50–52 mm; NMS X.IL 731 A–B.

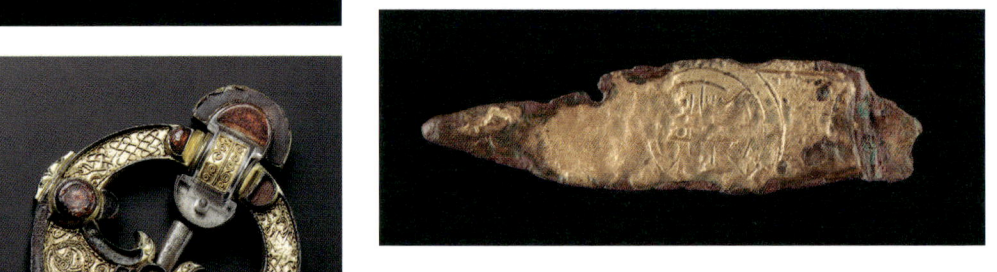

Certainly the most famous object from this grave was the Westness Brooch, the finest example of a gilt-silver brooch-pin yet found from Britain or Ireland [3.20] (see also pp 115–18). In the 8th-century context it was made, this gilt-silver brooch-pin could only have been worn by those of the highest status. It is notable that it was not fragmented but preserved as an heirloom for at least a century before it was left in this grave.[91] And it is not certain whether it was worn by the woman in the grave, or added as a graveside offering (there is no evidence of a box or purse for keeping it in). If worn, the brooch-pin would have been used to fasten a cloak or other outer garment. This would have obscured the items underneath, with interesting implications for the image being presented at various points, or for different audiences, at the funeral.

The assemblage included a matching pair of Class A2 Northumbrian copper-alloy strap-ends with cruciform ornament [3.21]. Anglo-Saxon strap-ends are almost non-existent in the Norse-controlled parts of Scotland or Ireland, but com-

Fig. 3.22 (left): Iron reaping-hook or sickle from a female grave (5), Westness, Rousay, Orkney, length 155 cm; NMS X.1997.???.

Fig. 3.23 (right): Iron ploughshare from a male boat grave (11), Westness, Rousay, Orkney, length 160 mm; NMS X.1997.233.

monly found elsewhere in Viking-age northern Britain.[92] It is a rare glimpse of a fashion adopted from the Northumbrian world here in Orkney, maybe hinting at the origin of some of the women of this community. The small iron knife is generally seen as a personal item, but the Type 5 antler-comb of Norse type is a kind that may be reserved for funerary display in Scotland and Ireland.[93]

If worn by the deceased, the brooch-pin, strap-ends, comb and beads suggest a combination of Scandinavian, Irish/Scottish and Northumbrian dress styles, made from raw materials assembled from across northwest Europe; and in the wolf/lion brooch, worn near the heart, a new kind of object in between worlds. In short, between these dress-fasteners and other 'personal' objects, we have an elegant snapshot of the age of raids in a single grave.

But the grave had more than just dress items. It also included a wide array of tools, less photogenic today after a millennium of corrosion, but which would have been more visible in the funerary tableau when complete with their organic handles. Many of these could be seen as 'possessions' of the woman, or perhaps the symbols of a woman's responsibilities according to her status.[94] Many of them relate to the preparation of textiles. Textile production tools are commonplace in 'wealthy' female graves, including boat burials from Scar, Sanday, to Vinjum, Sogn og Fjordane, Norway. The Westness burial also included an iron 'weaving sword' for beating the weft of an upright loom; two iron heckles for combing flax fibres for the preparation of linen; a pair of iron shears; and a bone-needle.[95] The production of linen was minimal in Scotland before the Viking Age.

A plaque of cetacean bone is now thought to be a rubbing-bone for smoothing textiles.[96] If so, this is an insular type of object, used in Scotland since the Iron Age, and may indicate continuity of weaving traditions into the Viking Age.[97] The iron weaving sword is almost certainly an introduction from Scandinavia, an object laden with metaphorical potential as a woman's equivalent of some of the most iconic male grave-goods of the time.[98] Iron weaving swords were used to make tighter weaves out of coarser threads, for instance in the production of sailcloth.[99] An example from the boat grave in Scar, Sanday, was broken before burial, perhaps an echo of the ritual 'killing' of swords as at Balnakiel (p. 57).

The inclusion of weaving tools in the Westness woman's grave represents various stages in the creation of textile from the production of thread, to the loom, to the final preparation of cloth. In a way they also represent an entire landscape, telling us about the rural economy local to Westness, in contrast to the wide horizons represented by the dress items.[100] To this we can add the iron sickle, a type of tool found in three male and two female graves at Westness [3.22]. This was a further stand-in for the wealth of the land and to the sustenance of the community this family was responsible for maintaining – and again found in some of the 'wealthiest' graves. It has been noted that the elderly woman in the boat grave at Scar was unlikely to have participated in the harvest herself, but was perhaps responsible for its production and distribution; in this sense, the inclusion of sickles is another proclamation of landowner status.[101] The inclusion of a sickle and ploughshare [3.23] along with a set of weapons in boat grave 11 drives home the point that these were the aspirations of a settled community. A large copper-alloy bowl, heavily damaged and corroded, was also found in the 1963 woman's grave, likely originally for a kind of food offering. These tools, dress items and other objects together created an image of the world in microcosm, near and far, an image of continuity in a time of loss to a community.

This grave was thus highly elaborate in terms of the types of objects included, as well as the uniqueness of others such as the Westness Brooch. As far as could be reconstructed, the grave was a subterranean chamber of sorts, made of stacked stone slabs. If this were the case, it was different to all the other graves from Westness that would be excavated subsequently, such as the 'oval graves' and pits walled and floored with flagstones [3.3]. It was certainly more elaborate than any of the other female-gendered graves from this site. So was it a reflection of one woman with a higher status than the others?

To discuss this solely as a reflection of 'wealth' would be to miss one last crucial clue to the context of this funeral. Perhaps the single most important inclusion in the grave was the body of a newborn infant. The bones were barely formed, and it is apparent that the child and mother had died in childbirth.

This is not the only Viking-age cemetery in Scotland to include infants, but it is rare.[102] Perhaps the most elaborate treatment was received by the infants buried at St Ninian's Isle, Shetland, in a 'cairn complex' consisting of six adjoining stone cists. Two of the compartments were marked with simple, cross-marked stones. Their ages ranged from newborn to 2.5 years, and they were all radiocarbon-dated to the 9th–10th centuries.[103] The visibility of infants at all, let alone with occasional grave-goods and more elaborate forms of commemoration, seems to set Scotland apart from other areas in the Viking-age Norse orbit. It is a shame that we cannot know for certain whether any of the items in the disturbed Westness grave from 1963 were associated with the infant.

But we now understand this better as a memorial to a mother and newborn who died in tragic circumstances. She was in her twenties or early thirties according to osteological analysis. The mix of insular, Scandinavian and continental material in the grave may have been symbolic of her own biography, or the story of the newly constituted community. Rather than simply understand these objects as an index of 'wealth', other variables including age, gender, status and lifecycle contributed to the structure of the funerary deposit.[104] It is worth restating that the funerary costume chosen for the individuals in these cemeteries was not a statement of biological descent, or reflective of the deceased's own possessions in every case, but selected by the mourners according to the socio-economic status they aspired to; and, as we have seen for the Westness female and the Balnakeil youth, certainly informed by the circumstances of their death. In no small part these assemblages were structured as an outpouring of emotion, especially heightened for those lost too soon, or those whose deaths would be most disruptive to the future of the community.[105]

SANCTUARY

This chapter so far has dwelt on one of the most compelling phenomena of the age, the 'pagan Norse' form of burial. However, we have now seen that at a number of sites some people were buried in ways often read as 'Christian': in long cists, the prevailing grave-form in pre-Viking Orkney and Shetland, facing east, and with few or no grave-goods. Even at Westness, it is clear that burial in unfurnished long cists, facing east, continued during and after the fashion for boat graves and oval graves. Are we seeing 'tolerance' for different religious beliefs? Two cultural populations sharing the same burial space?

It is worth noting that, according to stable isotope analysis, some of those buried in the 'Christian' manner at Westness

had the highest marine protein in their diet – in one case, even higher than the two men buried in boats. In other words, it is likely this cemetery was used by a diverse group of people rather than a single community. The implications are that choosing the site of Westness for a cemetery was no accident: it was a continuation of the local place of burial. The new arrivals, Norse and insular, could apply the new 'Norse' form of burial when needed, but could also continue to bury in the local manner as well. Continuity of an explicitly Christian burial place was also noted above at St Ninian's Isle, Shetland. In fact, in the northern isles, the Viking-age occupants retained the long-cist burial form far longer than elsewhere in Scotland, where it had been largely abandoned after the 7th century.[106]

Another intriguing aspect of Viking-age burial can take us beyond the northern and western isles. Many furnished burials are found in or near Christian churchyards. This challenges our concept of 'pagan' burial practices.

There is actually more evidence of dressed or furnished burial from church sites in Scotland than of attacks on churches. One study estimated that a quarter of all insular viking burials were associated with churches, or sites that eventually became churches.[107] Such evidence from churchyards includes stray finds that are highly likely to have come from furnished burials: an axe from St Ola's, Whiteness, Shetland; decorated insular copper-alloy belt-fittings from St Ronan's Church, Iona [3.24], and Ashaig, Skye; Viking-age combs from Mail, Cunningsburgh, and North Berwick, East Lothian.[108] Excavated examples from within or near church sites include weapon burials from Auldhame, East Lothian [3.25] and Kirkcudbright, Dumfries and Galloway; as well as burials with grave-goods at Barhobble and Whithorn, both in Wigtonshire, and at Newark Bay, Orkney.[109] In addition to these examples, there are several interesting associations, including a number of male weapon burials that seem to ring the enclosure of the early monastery of Kildonnan on the Isle of Eigg. Many fascinating

Fig. 3.24 (left): Fragment of copper-alloy decorated strap-fitting from St Ronan's Church, Iona, 10th century, length 50 mm; NMS X.1996.299. (Image by Heather Christie)

Fig. 3.25 (right): Decorated copper-alloy 'horse-tack' belt-fitting from a 10th-century male grave, Auldhame, East Lothian. (Image by E Campbell)

Fig. 3.26 (left): Cross-slab of garnet metapelite with a Norse runic inscription on reverse in memory of Thorgerth, daughter of Steinar, from Kilbar, Barra; NMS X.IB 102.

Fig. 3.27 (below): Fragment of cross-head of schistose slate inscribed with incomplete dedicatory inscription in Norse runes, Inchmarnock, Bute, width 210mm; NMS X.IB 93.

interpretations have been offered for these, from mercenaries in the employ of the Church, to acts of penance.[110] The simplest explanation is that these were forms of appropriating or continuing local burial places under new management, as argued above for Westness.[111] The location of Viking-age burials in Ireland in places with pre-existing ecclesiastical activity is also suggestive of church burial as a form of land-taking.[112] This need not have been a peaceful act, as demonstrated by the remarkable burials of members of the Great Army warband in the churchyard of Repton, Derbyshire.[113]

By the 10th century, Christian faith and affiliation became important variables. Thanks to runic inscriptions on crosses from Barra [3.26], Iona, and Inchmarnock [3.27], Bute, we are aware that Norse-speakers were buried as Christians from at least the 10th century (chapter 1). There is also a growing series of dressed burials from ecclesiastical cemeteries from 10th-century northwest England and the Isle of Man which suggest this was less 'pagan' than we have been led to assume.[114] The quality and rarity of objects found in the 10th-century burials at Carlisle Cathedral speak to competitive display among the elite rather than ethnic signalling.[115] However, some amount of group affiliation is still possible: recurring items in these later ecclesiastical burials are decorated belts of possible Dublin manufacture, now found from Workington, Cumbria, to Auldhame, East Lothian, to Iona and Skye in the Hebrides.[116]

And this is only to focus on furnished burials. The majority of burials in ecclesiastical sites were not furnished in this way, so we might be missing a silent majority of people when discussing Viking-age burial thus. As runic-inscribed crosses show, there were other ways of claiming land and competing for status beyond conspicuous offerings of valuable objects in the grave.[117] And if furnished burial is not always a 'pagan' statement, how should we think about sacred Christian metalwork deposited in graves across the viking diaspora? We will return to these issues later.

CONCLUSIONS

As ostentatious as the oval and boat-shaped cists of the Westness graves were, they are not simply to be understood as markers of power over the local population. Indeed, the Viking-age cemeteries of Scotland are singularly concerned with what might be called ancestral landscapes. In the case of Westness, the 'pagan' burials are a short phase of a long-lived cemetery. Radiocarbon dates show that burials in 'Christian' long cists at Westness both pre- and post-date the furnished graves. It is not a case of two ethnic groups living side-by-side, each according to their own funerary customs. It is as if some people were buried in different 'time zones' to others: some in the long-term, locally grounded long-cist tradition, others communicating with other areas far beyond those shores.[118] Both are to be included in 'Viking-age' deathways. As we have noted, there are people of insular, but non-local, origins among the 'viking' graves. There are also people in long cists which date to the Viking Age and whose bones and teeth betray a diet higher in seafood characteristic of the Viking-age diet. Whether they saw themselves as pagan or Christian, Norse, Pictish or Irish, their form of burial is not telling us these stories, because that is not what these formal deposits were about. Instead, they represent the emotionally charged transformation of the living member of a community into a venerated ancestor who will lie restfully in the grave. They achieved this through the kind of material culture that we coldly classify into categories like tools, weapons and dress items. They only become 'ethnic' statements to people like us, centuries later, who have forgotten their names and replace them with new ones like 'viking' and 'Pict'.

The example of the Westness cemetery shows that even the highly militarised ritual of burial in boats and with weapons could be seen as statements of authority and legitimacy, even of family and inheritance. We also should not discount the strong emotive aspect of the complex, drawn-out displays that such graves represent. Regardless of the intended audience, these performances drew together a complex mix of mythological and supernatural understandings of ships and burial mounds, and ensured that a new form of memory, even a mythology, would emerge around them.[119]

But there is also no denying that 'pagan viking' burial does stand out in its time. It is a practice that was rooted in a Scandinavian form of dwelling in an inhabited landscape that was transplanted to these shores. It was able to take root here because it fulfilled a need to justify changes of land tenure and, to a great extent, the growing power imbalance that tipped heavily in favour of those who were plugged into the new maritime economy (chapter 6). Some amount of social rupture has to be behind these changes. The question then is why it is so hard to observe that rupture in any other form of archaeology of the 9th century.[120] As we will see in the next chapters, the shifts in settlement, diet and economy really begin to manifest archaeologically in the 10th century and onwards. The 'viking' burials precede these changes, as if they are in the process of heralding a great change, not proof that it had taken place. It is as if they are aspirations to a certain kind of world. These burials were not showing us the world as it was, but as it was being re-made. And that is the key to understanding them.

Nowhere is this creation of a new 'world' more visible than in the incorporation of existing landscapes of burial – including Christian churchyards – into the sacred topography of the settler class. Crucially, this settler class was not all incomers from Scandinavia. In the next chapters we will discuss just how much the appropriation of insular objects – including shrines, reliquaries, horse-gear, brooches and pins – acted to foster these changes.

NOTES

1. Paterson and Stanford 2020; Graham-Campbell 2021.
2. The only early medieval sickles in National Museums Scotland not from graves are two from Viking-age middens at Jarlshof, Shetland, NMS X.HSA 917–918: Hamilton 1956, 128, pl. XXIII.
3. Maldonado 2013.
4. Buckberry and Cherryson 2010; O'Brien 2021.
5. Thompson 2004; Buckberry and Cherryson 2010.
6. Goldberg 2012.
7. Nordeide 2016.
8. Lindow and Andren 2020, 912–6; Price 2010.
9. Hall 2014.
10. Williams 2006.
11. Graham-Campbell 2003b, 129.
12. Latest estimate of furnished graves from Shetland and Pierowall as given in Graham-Campbell 2021, 274.
13. Stummann Hansen 2000, 89.
14. Compare Harris et al. 2017.
15. Skre 2001, 10–11.
16. Harrison 2007; Macleod 2015a.
17. Becket and Batey 2014.
18. Rundkvist and Williams 2008.
19. McLeod 2015b, 10.
20. Hedges 1987.
21. Price 2010.
22. Driscoll 2004b; Warner 2004.
23. Semple 2013.
24. O'Grady 2008; Sanmark 2017, 219–27; Semple and Sanmark 2013.
25. C. Paterson, pers. comm.
26. Arcini 2018, 60–4.
27. Sellevold 1999.
28. Harrison 2016, 305; the other is Kiloran Bay, Graham-Campbell and Batey 1998, 150; Harrison and Ó Floinn 2014, 284–5. There were surely examples from heavily disturbed graves in Dublin as well.
29. Compare Arcini 2018, 73–83; Loe et al. 2014, 63–4.
30. Harrison and Ó Floinn 2014, 129 notes that arrows were rare in Dublin graves but always found singly about the grave, not bundled in quivers, which is also the case in the majority of examples in Kaupang. This speaks to a funerary ritual involving arrows, rather than specific inclusions of arrows as weapon sets; cf. Paterson et al 2014, 159.
31. Kaland 1973, 1993.
32. Canmore ID 2169; Bond et al. 2017; Graham-Campbell 1995, 161.
33. Graham-Campbell and Batey 1998; Batey 2016; Harris et al. 2017.
34. Owen and Dalland 1999.
35. Price 2010; Jesch 2001; Westerdahl 2008, 2016.
36. Larsson 2007, 287–98.
37. Sellevold 1999.
38. Compare McGuire 2019, 17.
39. Żabiński 2007.
40. Harris et al. 2017; Dunbar and Paton 2018.
41. Non-funerary swords: Gorton, Strathspey, NMS X.LA 1; Mein River, Torbeckhill, Dumfriesshire, NMS X.IL 340; and Harviestoun, Clackmannanshire, NMS Q.L.1972.1; sword pommels only are from Abington, South Lanarkshire, NMS X.2009.11; Aberlady, East Lothian, NMS X.2001.16; and Bonchester Bridge, Scottish Borders, NMS X.2016.51.
42. Brunning 2019.
43. Sayer et al. 2019.
44. Solberg 1991; McCormick 2001, 732.
45. Dobat 2015.
46. Sayer et al. 2019, 544–6; Brunning 2019.
47. Mikkelsen 2019, appendix Q.
48. Peirce 2002, 7–10.
49. Żabiński 2007.
50. Peirce 2002, 42–5.
51. Willemsen 2021.
52. Harrison and Ó Floinn 2014, 78–9.
53. A possibility suggested by C. Paterson, pers. comm.
54. Harrison 2016, 310–16.
55. For example, Dobat 2015.
56. Anderson 1907, 441; Grieg 1940, 197.
57. Batey and Paterson 2013.
58. The individual is part of a wider genetic study which will confirm biological sex: A. Sheridan, pers. comm.

59. Loe et al. 2014; McGuire 2019, 17; Hadley and Hemer 2011.
60. Batey and Paterson 2013, 636–7.
61. *Ibid.*, 640–1.
62. Klevnäs 2016, 470.
63. Aannestad 2018.
64. Harrison and Ó Floinn 2014, 273–7, table 8.
65. S. Harrison, pers. comm.; NMS X.1997.251.
66. Harrison 2016, 307.
67. Harrison 2000.
68. Harrison and Ó Floinn 2014, 273–7.
69. *Ibid.*, 127–8.
70. S. Harrison, pers. comm.
71. Russell and Hurley 2014, 164–5; Harrison and Ó Floinn 2014, 128–9.
72. Holmquist Olausson and Petrovski 2007; Kalmring 2014.
73. Harrison 2000, 76.
74. Batey and Paterson 2013, 634.
75. Øye 2015.
76. Dunbar and Roy 2018.
77. Metcalf and Huntington 1991.
78. Hall 2016, 440–4.
79. Barrett and Richards 2004.
80. Müldner 2016.
81. Montgomery et al. 2014.
82. Hadley and Hemer 2011.
83. Speed and Walton Rogers 2004; Hayeur Smith et al. 2019.
84. Margaryan et al. 2020.
85. Harrison 2008; McGuire 2009.
86. Stalsberg 1991; Dommasnes 1991; McLeod 2011; Price et al. 2019.
87. Thorsteinsson 1968.
88. McGuire 2009, 262–3.
89. Archaeologist Audrey Henshall took the call-out; the cemetery was subsequently excavated by Sigrid Kaland; the site is currently being written up for publication by Caroline Paterson.
90. Hickey 2014; C. Paterson, pers. comm.
91. Stevenson 1989.
92. Thomas 2000.
93. Ashby 2009.
94. Owen and Dalland 1999, 143–4; Øye 2015, 7.
95. McGuire 2009, 214.
96. Owen and Dalland 1999, 83.
97. Hallen 1995, 222; Anderson 1873, 560–1; cf. Stirling and Milek 2015.
98. Gordon 1990; Brunning 2019.
99. Øye 2015, 5.
100. Compare Cartwright 2014.
101. McGuire 2009, 179.
102. Sellevold 1999, 7; McGuire 2019, 15.
103. Barrowman 2011, 111–12.
104. McGuire 2009.
105. H. Williams 2007a; Halsall 2010, 281.
106. Compare Hedges 1980.
107. Harrison 2007, 176–8.
108. St Ola's: Barrett et al. 2000, 12. Iona and Ashaig: Paterson and Stanford 2020; Campbell et al. 2019. Mail: Watt 1993, 106. North Berwick: Hall and Bowler 1998; cf. Higgitt 1995.
109. Auldhame: Crone et al. 2016. Kirkcudbright: Scott 1983. Barhobble: Cormack 1995. Whithorn: Hill 1997. Newark Bay: Barrett et al. 2000, 12.
110. McLeod 2015a; Crone et al. 2016, 170.
111. Compare Harrison 2007.
112. Harrison and Ó Floinn 2014, 246–8.
113. Jarman et al. 2018; Biddle and Kjølbye-Biddle 1992.
114. Halsall 2000.
115. Compare McCarthy et al. 2014.
116. Paterson and Stanford 2020; it is also possible the Iona example was made locally: Campbell et al. 2019, 313.
117. Compare Hadley 2008.
118. Svanberg 2003, 190–1; 201–3.
119. Price 2010; Williams 2006, 172–5.
120. Griffiths 2019.

CHAPTER FOUR
Age of raids

The monastery of Iona was the first site to be attacked by viking raiders in AD795. Yet after the tragedies weathered over subsequent raids, the monastery managed to bounce back. The relics of Columba remained intact, as the Irish annals report that Indrechtach, the abbot of Iona, travelled to Ireland with them in 849. For all that we stereotype the early 9th century as an apocalyptic time of constant raids in which no coastal monastery was safe, it is clear that in fact for many of the wealthy large monasteries, life went on. Indrechtach must have felt secure enough to travel again in 854 when he decided to go on pilgrimage to Rome. It was a grave mistake. The Irish annals report he was killed on his way there by pirates – not Scandinavians, but 'Saxon robbers'.[1] A shrine of a shadowy 'Indract' at Glastonbury Abbey, Somerset, was first noted in the 12th century, but given its pride of place by the altar it is likely this was indeed the martyred abbot of Iona, perhaps providing a clue to the location of his killing.[2] One imagines he travelled laden with gifts, which he may not have parted with easily. It is another reminder it is not only Scandinavians who could go 'viking' in this age of raids – and another reason why the word should be spelled in lower-case, as it refers to a kind of activity not an ethnic label.

Patchy as they are, our surviving contemporary sources for the earliest viking raids report the taking of people, cattle and, of course, portable wealth. There is copious evidence for these events in the form of objects found far from the place they were made, and in very different circumstances than their intended function. Can we identify what was taken, how much, and from where? These questions are frustratingly hard to answer with certainty.

It is less often asked why the Scandinavian vikings went to so much trouble. Was it really worth all the long journeys, and the risk of death or maiming, to bring back trinkets of bronze with microscopic amounts of gold applied to the surface?[3] The previous chapters set the stage for more well-informed actors on both the Scandinavian and insular sides in these events. We can now turn to the archaeology and see what it can and cannot tell us if we take a look with fresh eyes.

By the end of the 9th century the bulk of the surviving material culture in Scotland was coming from the islands. Orkney,

---

Opposite: Composite silver pendant encasing a damaged glass bead, with coin of Coenwulf of Mercia (d.821), Galloway Hoard, NMS X.2018.12.71.5.

Fig. 4.1: Ladle of beaten bronze with concentric circle ornament in the bowl, from a woman's grave at Ballinaby, Isle of Islay, length 445 mm; NMS X.IL 147.

Shetland and the Hebrides were revitalised in what we call the Viking Age in a way that has rather sucked the oxygen out of the room for everywhere else in Scotland. In what seems like a blink of an eye, the eastern heartlands of Moray and Strathearn go from the imperial ambitions of the last kings of the Picts (chapter 2), to a curious hiatus where carved stones bearing symbols are no longer being erected, while burial grounds and hillforts appear to be abandoned. The vikings often carry the blame for what looks like a distinct break in the archaeological record for much of eastern and lowland Scotland, but some of these changes were a long time coming.

Rather than marking a sudden, drastic change, it is now clear that the changes of the Viking Age were remarkably gradual. The archaeology of settlement is no longer as simple as a picture of Scandinavian culture transplanted into an alien setting. Even the 'Norse' burials have more of the 'insular' to them than is usually appreciated (chapter 3). The story of the Viking Age is often the narrative of what was lost: territory, lives, dynasties. But from the perspective of the objects themselves, the overall picture that emerges of this age of raids, roughly 800–950, is not subtractive but illuminating. One way to read graves and hoards with insular objects is that they shine a light on the sacred matter and dress accessories of the Christian world in a way we would otherwise not be able to see [Fig. 4.1]. These objects can be reassembled to tell part of the earlier story of the insular kingdoms, but ultimately they tell a different one: not an afterlife, but a new lease of life in a world of expanded horizons.

DISAPPEARING ACTS

The story of the 9th and early 10th centuries, often called the 'early Viking Age', is one of huge historical importance to the emergence of what became the kingdoms of Scotland and England. In the usual royal-centric approach to history, we see a shift from the earliest raids on coastal monasteries like Iona to organised military campaigns against the halls of power. In 839 the annals record a disastrous defeat of a combined force of Picts and Scots by a Scandinavian army – a pitched battle, not a raid, as several kings and their family members are named. This was the full-scale toppling of a regime, and was a turning-point in Scottish history.[4] It would not be the last: another apparent occupation of the Pictish kingdoms occurs in AD 866; a four-month siege of Dumbarton Rock in 870 ends the British kingdom of Alt Clut; a campaign in 875 concludes with the death of one of the last kings of the Picts; and another slaying of a king in 900 marks the first use of the title 'king of Alba' in our sources.

These events have to be understood in the context of a change in the nature of 'viking' activity across Britain, Ireland and Frankia in this period. As noted in chapter 2, the earliest raids were likely enmeshed in local politics from the start, but from the 830s and '40s the first permanent settlements are established in Ireland and, crucially, we get the first documented alliances between vikings and insular kings. In 838, the Britons of western Cornwall joined forces with a viking fleet to fight back the expansion of the kings of Wessex, our first unequivocal evidence for an insular allegiance with viking warbands.[5] In 841, a Danish warband was granted the island of Walcheren in Frisia in return for military support for the Frankish kings.[6] The extraordinary campaigns of the 'Great Army' in England from 865–78 succeeded in toppling the kingdoms of Mercia, Northumbria and East Anglia, and ended in a treaty between Alfred of Wessex and Guthrum, establishing the Danelaw. Each of these treaties and alliances involved assurances including Christian baptism, massive payments of tribute, sometimes even arranged marriages.[7] In short, from very early in the 9th century, the activities of 'vikings' were as political as they were profitable and cannot be seen as the product of a completely external or foreign agency.

We can stay in the world of kings and their battles briefly to make a few bigger points. Just as it is very difficult to distinguish insular and Scandinavian actors by archaeology alone, the historical sources are not as straightforward as they seem. In Scotland we get an interesting series of attacks on monasteries in the middle of the 9th century, but only some of them by vikings. An unlocated battle in 839 between unnamed 'gentiles' (pagans or vikings) and the Picts resulted in so many royal deaths that it caused a succession crisis, of which the eventual beneficiary was the famous Cináed mac Ailpín (r. 842–58). Viking military activity only continued to ramp up in his reign, with an undated campaign of *Danari* – Danes – who 'wasted Pictavia to Clunie and Dunkeld'.[8] This is the first evidence that viking armies had reached important royal centres far inland in northern Britain.

But it was not only Scandinavian warbands who tried to test the mettle of the upstart new king of Fortriu. The Britons were said to have burnt Dunblane, presumably meaning an early monastery there. Cináed was also said to have burned Dunbar in East Lothian and attacked the monastery of Melrose in the Borders. As occurred in Ireland since the 8th century, wars of succession had spilled over into violence on rival churches (chapter 2). Cináed would die peacefully in 858 at his *palacio* at Forteviot, a sure sign of continuity with the power centre established by his predecessor Custantín before 820 [2.2]. Cináed even named one of his sons Custantín, or Constantín mac Cináeda (d. *c.*875), in a show of continuity, manufactured or otherwise. As with any other king of his age, this stability was won through violence, sometimes against the sacred places of rivals.

All the while, the permanent settlement of vikings in Britain and Ireland continued apace. In 847, 'Northmen' reportedly gained control of 'all the islands around Ireland', presumably meaning at least the Inner Hebrides, part of Dál Riata and thus within the scope of the term 'Ireland'.[9] It has been argued that this event is a Scottish equivalent to the establishment of permanent camps in Ireland in the 830s and '40s, and a likely starting-point for the dating of any 'viking' burials in the Hebrides. It is less well recorded how they came to gain control: though we assume it was by force, it could also have been by treaty or other negotiation to keep the peace.

Another fateful change relevant to Scotland comes in 853. In that year, conflict between different Scandinavian factions in Ireland culminated with the arrival of Óláfr (Amlaib in Irish sources) who, with his brother Ívarr (Imar in Irish sources) and their descendants, would become major players in the years to come.[10] They were distinguished from other Scandinavians in Ireland, who in 853 were referred to for the first time as *Gall-goídil* ('foreigner-Gaels') who were allied to the Irish king Mael Sechnaill against the armies of Óláfr/Amlaib. This new coinage indicates that by this point 'vikings' is too vague a term to capture the people we are discussing here. By the time we get to the Great Army, we are talking about a diverse, multinational, rotating cast of characters including Danes, Frisians and likely some amount of insular adherents. Ívarr is listed as one of its many leaders; and the siege of Dumbarton in 870, carried out by Ívarr and Óláfr, must be understood in the context of the movements of the Great Army.[11]

These military campaigns led to political machinations that re-drew the map of Britain in the 9th century. By the year 900, we are not just talking about the disappearance of the Picts; we are also witnessing the end of the British kingdom of Alt Clut, the Gaelic-speaking realm of Dál Riata, the sundering of the Northumbrian kingdoms and the establishment of new entities in their wake. Seen in this light, the 'end of the Picts' is

just one of many regime changes that would shape the emerging kingdoms of Scotland, Ireland, England and Wales. However, the fragmentation of the former Pictish realms was the only one that also resulted in the disappearance of a language, a reminder that political machinations can lead to tragic cultural impacts off the battlefield.

INVISIBLE VIKINGS IN THE NORTHERN ISLES

The historical sources thus only really concern the inner circle of the literate classes and their patrons, and even at this level they remain scattershot in terms of events in northern Britain. It is natural to assume that archaeology would usefully fill in these gaps, but so much depends on visibility, and the most visible archaeology for this period still remains firmly within those elite circles: power centres, monasteries and monumental burials. Thankfully excavations on settlements provide a wider set of materials to consider. When this is all drawn together, it is striking how little seems to relate to the kings and battles of the above historical resources.[12]

There has always been some vagueness around the archaeology of the earliest Viking Age. Insular objects are difficult to date given the long-lived styles used (chapters 5, 7). As for the Scandinavian material, the temptation has long been to draw their dating as if by gravitational pull toward the start of the Viking Age around *c.*800. It was assumed that the earliest raids of the 790s must have been mounted from a base within Britain, and it seemed natural to assume it must have been on the nearest landing-places from Norway, in Shetland and Orkney. A recent reassessment of the earliest insular finds from furnished graves in Norway posits that the taste for insular sacred metalwork was gained through trade expeditions in the late 8th century, providing some context for the reports of Scandinavians in the English Channel before the raid on Lindisfarne in 793.[13] The earliest contacts with Scandinavia may have been attempts to break into the markets of the southern shores of the North Sea, not to colonise the northern isles.[14]

As discussed in chapter 3, it appears that the majority of 'viking' burials fall within the broad range of *c.*850–950, for which there is a plausible historical context for a settlement of the Hebrides in the late 840s noted above. Whatever the richly furnished graves of men and women were hoping to achieve, it is something that did not happen immediately after the first raids. Burial ought to be thought of as an aspect of settlement. It is one of many ways in which our expectation that 'vikings' acted a certain way – a way which should be visible archaeologically from the moment Scandinavians set foot in Scotland – has not been borne out.

Perhaps the most intensive archaeological work – and scholarly debate – has been on the settlements of the Viking Age. As with the burial evidence, the 'Norse' layers of these sites

Fig. 4.2 (opposite): Stone with drawings or doodles of animals and possibly boat prows, Jarlshof, Shetland, length 169 mm; NMS X.HSA 794.

Figs 4.3 and 4.4 (opposite): The large assemblage of graffiti on slates from Jarlshof, Shetland, begins in the pre-Viking era. The distinctive curled hair of the figure from Jarlshof, NMS X.HSA 793, matches those in Pictish carvings, such as the figure from Burness, Orkney, NMS X.IB 201.

Figs 4.5a–d (below): 'Viking' finds from Jarlshof, Shetland, now known to be of 11th–12th century date: (a) bone-pins of beast-head, thistle and axe-head types, NMS X.HSA 3, 4, 2, 12, 8, 7; (b) silver ring-money arm-ring, NMS X.HSA 995 A; (c) crutch-headed, stirrup ringed pin, length 89 mm, NMS X.HSA 846; open-work pendant, likely from a horse-harness, 43 mm diameter, NMS X.HSA 4396.

were customarily dated in sequences beginning c.800. The most influential of these was the early publications of finds from the remarkable site of Jarlshof, Shetland. The romanticisation of this site began even earlier than the first excavations. The area was previously known only as Sumburgh, and the ruins of the 16th-century tower house were referred to as 'de Laird's Hoose' at the time the novelist and antiquarian Sir Walter Scott toured the islands in the 19th century. Inspired by the partially sand-inundated ruins, Scott re-fashioned it into the fictitious pile of 'Yarlshof', a pseudo-Norse rendering of 'laird's hoose', when he wrote his 1822 novel *The Pirate* – and the name has become attached to the site ever since.[15]

Excavations took place at the eroding settlement of Jarlshof from the 1930s onward, but the finds from the Viking Age were conditioned by historical expectations that the Norse settlement and construction of longhouses began immediately at the turn of the 9th century. Many objects from Jarlshof, assumed to be early viking, are now recognised as either pre-Viking (such as the famous incised slates [4.2–4.4]) – or more often from centuries later.[16] To take only finds assigned to the 'Parent Farmstead', there are objects that we now know are certainly late 10th- and 11th-century.[17] These include the animal-headed bone-pins with long, straight shanks; a silver arm-ring, a development of the mid-10th century onward; and bronze ringed pins of crutch-head type [4.5a–c].[18] An open-work pendant is now recognised as an 11th-century type with a cluster of finds in the Low Countries [4.5d].[19] The coins from Shetland are only late 10th century and onwards, and Jarlshof is no exception.[20] In general, the finds from Jarlshof do not tell us much about the early Viking Age.

Another iconic site often characterised as emblematic of the early Viking Age in Orkney is the Brough of Birsay. Unlike Jarlshof, Birsay has benefited from much more extensive con-

AGE OF RAIDS

Fig. 4.6 (right): Fragments of an Anglo-Saxon gilt-bronze disc mount with animal and foliaceous interlaced ornament, Brough of Birsay, NMS X.HB 450, reconstructed using a line-drawing of a mount from a woman's grave at Hillesøy, Tromsø, Norway, diameter 89 mm. (Norges arktiske universitetsmuseum Ts4052)

Fig. 4.7 (below): Double-sided antler-comb of insular type from 'Lower Norse Horizon' at Brough of Birsay, length 153 mm; NMS X.HB 200.

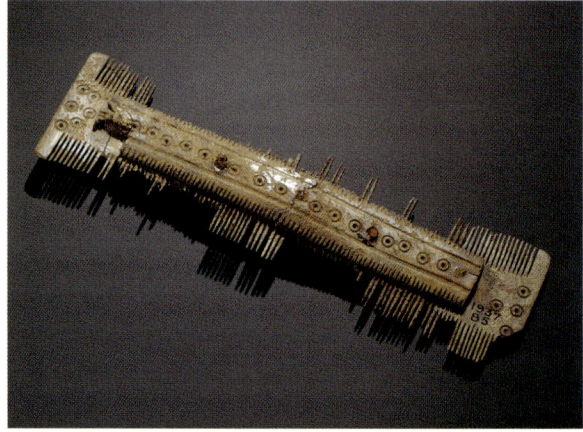

trolled excavations in the post-war era which have established a long sequence of occupation from before, during and after the early Viking Age.[21] However, the stratigraphy was just as complicated and finds were sorted into notional Lower, Middle and Later Norse 'horizons', with an underlying 'Pictish' horizon ending at the notional date of 800.[22] However, 'Pictish' finds were discovered throughout the 'Norse' layers too, and there are reasons to believe that the early metalworking phase extended past 800. Another difficulty is that the royal Pictish settlement of Birsay had already established an international set of connections for elite exchange before the start of the Viking Age, so exotic imports found there could have come via these diplomatic links and not viking raids [4.6].[23] Birsay remains an indispensable eyewitness to the entirety of the Pictish to viking transition in Orkney, but the chronology of its most famous finds is difficult to rely on.

Later excavations of settlement sites in Orkney have revealed why these sequences are difficult to date by house type or artefact typology alone. A site at Buckquoy, across the sound from Birsay, has inspired decades-long debates on the nature of the settlement. A 'Pictish' cellular structure was seen to contain insular and Norse types of bone- and antler-combs side-by-side, as indeed did Birsay itself [4.7], suggesting a period of Norse and 'native' interaction. The discovery of a spindle-whorl incised with an ogham message in Gaelic tells us that we should not see the inhabitants of pre-Viking Orkney as simply 'Picts' either.[24] In the latest reading of this site it is possible that an existing structure was modified in the 9th century, giving a hybrid stone structure with 'Pictish' cellular elements and 'Norse'-style long hearth: the sequence ends with a male weapon grave inserted into the abandoned structure, helpfully dated by a clipped silver coin of Edmund (940–46).[25] Similar coin-dated 9th-century phases of use of Pictish and earlier prehistoric structures in Orkney at Saevar Howe and Swandro, Rousay, attest to a period of cohabitation, or at least co-option of existing settlements, within the 9th and early 10th centuries.[26] This is now proven by well-dated sequences in Orkney (Pool, Sanday) and Shetland (Old Scatness).[27] The dating of longhouses more generally across Scotland is complicated by ephemeral turf-built sequences which are nearly invisible to archaeologists. However, in general these are a century or more later than the earliest raids: 10th century if not the 11th in the best-dated examples from Shetland and the western isles.[28]

The evidence from Orkney and Shetland instead shows continuous occupation of indigenous settlement structures

Fig. 4.8: Pair of gilt-bronze hinged-strap mounts from a house-shaped reliquary shrine, converted into shoulder brooches, from a boat grave at Carn a' Bharraich, Oronsay, length 70mm; NMS X.FC 183–184.

until the 10th century. It means that other stray finds of dress items, combs, weapons and steatite vessels need no longer be drawn inexorably to AD 800, and there are now several classes of object that fit better under a 10th century, sometimes even a post-AD 1000, settlement framework. The image of the northern isles as a 'forward operating base' (in the terminology of the modern army), cannot credibly be produced from archaeological evidence alone; in its stead we can see a much more interesting phase of cohabitation, in which monasteries and certain power centres remained in use while new settlements were established. A highly mobile, multi-ethnic population connected by maritime networks that already extended to Pictland, England and Ireland, now included avenues to Scandinavia and eventually the North Atlantic. This evidence shows Orkney and Shetland to be in an ideal position to take advantage of the expanding horizons of the 9th century; over time they became a critical hub at the centre of the Scandinavian diaspora.

THE ARCHAEOLOGY OF LOOTING

For all the attacks on monasteries and pitched battles involving viking armies recorded in the early 9th century, archaeological evidence for them remains elusive. The events of just one day can rarely be spotted in an excavation where centuries are represented by thin layers of soil. We noted in chapter 2 the limited archaeological evidence for the burning of churches, despite historical records of repeated attacks.

That said, there is a wealth of evidence (as it were) for the plunder and destruction of ecclesiastical metalwork at this time. Of the 16 earliest graves containing insular material in Norway, four contained fragments of house-shaped reliquary shrines.[29] These distinctive caskets were used in Ireland and Scotland to transport saints' relics in the 7th–9th centuries and may have been suspended and worn by clerics while away from the church. It is possible that this is the object depicted as being carried by the bearded 'captive' on a doodle on a slate from the early monastery of Inchmarnock, Bute – perhaps an eye-witness account of a viking raid [2.15]. The hinged-straps of a house-shaped reliquary were found reused as a pair of shoulder brooches on a woman in a boat grave from Carn a' Bharraich, Oronsay [4.8]. Not all of them were hacked up for the crucible: a complete house-shaped reliquary from a boat burial in Melhus, Trøndelag, had been placed in a wooden box next to the woman's body.[30]

Some striking examples of how such sacred objects were treated show the range of the evidence. While there is little direct archaeological evidence for the several documented raids on Iona, several objects with artistic parallels to Iona have been identified among the corpus of insular objects found abroad. One of them, an ornate bronze crosier head discovered in the royal hall site of Helgö ('holy island'), Uppland, Sweden [4.9],

Fig. 4.9: Insular volute crosier head of bronze with glass and enamel settings, found in Helgö, Uppland, Sweden. (© Ola Myrin, The Swedish History Museum/SHM [CC BY])

has been identified as likely made on Iona.[31] It was found in a hall site with other exotic goods including a Coptic bronze ladle and a bronze statuette of the Buddha from the Indian subcontinent. This assemblage, it has been argued, relates to what must have been an impressive trophy-collection or, alternatively, a sort of 'gallery' of religious objects from the ends of the known world, at this royal cult place.[32]

A different fate met a matching set of D-shaped finials with very similar ornament to the Helgö crosier. Two of them went via private collections to the museum of St Germain-en-Laye near Paris. A third matching object came from the elaborate mid-9th century grave of the 'Gausel Queen', Rogaland, one of the wealthiest in Norway, with other insular objects including a complete set of gilt-bronze horse-harness gear and a hanging-bowl which has close links to the art of Iona.[33] The D-shaped mounts from St Germain and Gausel must have come from the same object, interpreted as the butterfly-shaped gable finials of an elaborate and unique metalwork tomb-shrine – perhaps the shrine of St Columba himself.[34] That these were ripped apart and dispersed suggests utter devastation and heartbreak for the community of Iona. But, as we have seen, the community persevered even after this, with the relics of St Columba still present on the island throughout the 9th century and beyond.[35]

These are extraordinary instances of famous shrines and relics being fragmented and dispersed, but also the range of decorated insular metal objects that were reused in this way is staggering. There is probably more evidence for insular shrines and reliquaries from Viking-age graves in Scandinavia than survives in the museums of Britain or Ireland.[36] The fragmentation began as soon as the objects were plundered. The most graphic demonstration of this is the so-called 'Shanmullagh Hoard', an assemblage of over 400 non-ferrous metal fragments including hacked up ecclesiastical material, dress accessories and lead weights, found when dredging the River Blackwater in Co. Armagh. It was argued that the bulk of these finds represents a single deposit, perhaps the result of a one-off raid of Armagh such as those documented in 895 or 921.[37] If so, royal monasteries in Ireland were still very wealthy a century after the start of the viking raids. Whether this represents the combined scrap of a metalworker or material being prepared for sale, it shows the reduction of insular metalwork for repurposing was still a lucrative pursuit a century after the first raids.

There is a little-known find from Scotland that may relate to a similar impulse. In the late 19th century, a group of about 50 parcels of embossed copper-sheet were found eroding from a drain in the moorland near Corrie Loch, deep in the uplands of Dumfriesshire. They include five concave bosses of bronze and very fine embossed sheets of gilt-copper bearing vine-scroll, egg-and-dart border patterns, and a figural scene. This suggests at least two different objects: a wooden processional or altar cross with metal mounts, and a possible ornamented book cover incorporating the scene of a frontal figure with elaborate hairstyle, in classical drapery, holding a book.[38] The vine-scroll and repoussé technique used suggest 8th-century Northumbrian manufacture, but the dismantling of the object, folding into small parcels and final deposition in a bog, suggest something far beyond the intended liturgical function of these objects. Could this be a sacrifice of similar kinds of hacked up ecclesiastical objects represented in the Shanmullagh Hoard?

Why go through so much trouble to hack up this metalwork into unrecognisable bits, rather than retaining the complete object? Decorated objects were repurposed as insets in lead weights, as seen in the Shanmullagh Hoard, but the Corrie Loch sheets seem too fragile for this kind of reuse. A secondary trade in scrap-metal is also a possibility – as is now well attested from the Great Army camp of Torksey, Lincolnshire.[39] The sheets of copper, the basis of alloys like bronze and brass, have been a precious source of raw material.

Less practical interpretations may exist. The fragments of insular metalwork found in Viking-age graves are often fashioned into brooches and pins. A major study of this material from Scandinavia (195 objects in total) found that ecclesiastical material was by far the most common (72% of all finds), followed by harness-gear (19%) and belts (9%).[40] Three-quarters of the ecclesiastical objects had certainly been reworked or modified in some way. Out of 118 graves with such material, 83% (68) were female. Were these 'trophies' raided by men and gifted to their wives? This has led to theories of raiding for 'bridewealth', where a presumed shortage of women in Norway created increased competition for men to seek their fortunes in the form of riches plundered from far-off locations, in order to afford to enter a marriage contract.[41] The question that remains is why, when the bullion value of these objects was so low, these objects carried such value.

A more recent analysis of the earliest insular finds from Scandinavia has confirmed they are coming almost exclusively to northern and western Norway from around *c*.800, alongside exotic Frankish and other goods obtained in the early markets of Denmark and Frisia.[42] It is further evidence that this taste for foreign luxuries was present from the earliest Viking age and may be considered a defining characteristic. In chapter 2 (pp 36–7), we noted that trade links with North Sea markets introduced a taste for exotic foreign goods in rural Norway. It was through contacts made on these journeys that northern navigators encountered insular traders and those with knowledge of the western seaways. The finds of insular shrine fragments and bowls alongside Frankish swords and exotica from the east obtained on these journeys, show that the opening of sea-roads to the west was part of a longer-term prestige economy based on competitive display. These objects, whether in silver or less precious metals, held a prestige value greater than their raw materials; but access to such materials also gave one considerable sway in a gift-giving economy [4.10–4.12].[43]

This approach suggests that these items, however small or unrecognisable, were distinct enough from existing Norwegian material culture as to be prized as visual tokens of successful journeys to the ends of the known world, mastery of the elements, access to cutting-edge naval technologies, as well as military prowess and the brotherhood of the warband.[44] But the objects in question were not just any random curios: they were powerful materials like saints' relics, brooches, altar gear and high-status dress items. Over time, the insular finds may have acquired specific cultural resonances within Norway (which we will explore with regard to brooches and pins in chapter 5). But as with so much of the material culture of the age, the overwhelming number of them come from graves, and we can only really understand the value these objects had as agents in funerary display and the grieving process (chapter 3). The graves that included these objects were almost exclusively for women rather than men, and their role as badges of status or protective amulets in a specifically funerary context cannot be dismissed (see chapter 7).[45]

Fig. 4.10: Fragment of gilt-bronze mount with inhabited vine-scroll and egg-and-dart ornament, Monkhouse Green, Stromness, Orkney, length 44.5mm, NMS X.FA 44.

Fig. 4.11: Unprovenanced mount in the shape of a penannular brooch with added quatrefoil settings and traces of gilding, maximum width 50mm; NMS X.FC 244.

Fig. 4.12: Cruciform mount of gilt copper-alloy, likely from a horse-harness, 'West of Scotland', width across arms 65mm; NMS X.IL 362.

HOARDING THE PAST

Given the copious evidence for looting, especially of sacred objects, represented by material in viking graves, it has long been assumed that the vikings caused a new kind of terror among the Christian communities of Britain and Ireland. This putative phenomenon, which we can call 'viking panic', has in fact been used as an explanation for historical events and archaeological activity for a millennium. Stereotypical 'viking' actors have been written into ecclesiastical histories and saints' biographies since the 10th century to patch up missing documents, gaps in the record, and changes of administration.[46] Like Celts, Goths and other 'barbarians' before them, viking raiders quickly became stock characters in the drama of European history and still are. The stereotype has been adopted by nationalist and less savoury historical movements in modern times. The way we use the term 'viking' itself is a completely modern invention.[47]

In archaeological terms, 'viking panic' has been used to explain an uptick in hoarding activity beginning in c.800. In Scotland, hoards across the first millennium AD tended to be of silver objects, but given new, early dates for some notable Pictish silver hoards, we are now left with a gap in the 7th and 8th centuries where there were very few hoards deposited in Scotland.[48] When hoarding began again around the 9th century, it was a different world. The hoards of the 9th century seem so eclectic when compared to what came before, that the only plausible explanation was 'viking panic', of stashing valuables in a hurry. The best example of this is the silver hoard from St Ninian's Isle, Shetland [4.13].[49] Bowls, brooches and other silver implements were placed in a wooden box and secreted under a cross-marked stone in a church. There was no damage to the silver objects other than the ravages of time; nor were there the coins or ingots of later bullion hoards. They do not look like the fruits of a raid, so much as the pooled wealth of a community, paralleled by later hoards in Ireland containing brooches alongside ecclesiastical metalwork.[50]

Several 'Pictish hoards' across Scotland dated to the 9th century may be the product of increased anxiety over portable wealth in an age of raids. However, the problem is that most are dated by the style of their objects: they are deemed 'Pictish' or 'native' hoards only because they do not contain Scandinavian material or the hacked silver bullion characteristic of 9th- to 11th-century deposits from the North Atlantic to the

Fig. 4.13. The St Ninian's Isle Hoard, Shetland, deposited c.800.

secret place, but carefully deposited in the floor near the east end of the early chapel: in all likelihood, right beside where the altar would have stood. This was an offering of silver regalia made to the church or its patron saint by the local grandees. The date of *c*.800 is based in part on the style of the metalwork, and partly to do with the notion of 'viking panic'. The Norwegian larch or spruce wood of the box may in fact be driftwood from North America; as outlandish as it seems, this was also one of the most common species identified in the charcoal from elsewhere on this site.[51]

The St Ninian's Isle Hoard stands at the cusp of a remarkable period of deposition that takes place all across Britain and Ireland over the next two centuries. Can all these be explained as 'viking panic'? And can we discern between 'security' hoards and other kinds of offerings or sacrifices – the votive or ritual deposits better known from prehistoric archaeology?

There are some notable collections of material from Scotland found in various poorly recorded contexts that are frustrating in that they no longer represent complete assemblages. These hoards were often found by field labourers cutting peat, digging drains, building rail lines and other heavy labour, which meant that the objects would only have been recognised after they had been damaged. Precious metals were often sold for scrap. Other objects too fragmented to be recognisable were not always offered to museums – or not accepted by them. The Crieff, Perthshire, mounts are a famous example [4.14], an ornate matching pair of chip-carved, silver-gilt mounts, one with a distinctive bust of a human head easily matched on a number of horse-harness mounts of presumed Irish or Scottish manufacture.[52] However, the fineness of these ornaments, and the surviving setting of what appears to be very rare rock crystal in one of them, means they may originally have come from an early Christian reliquary or book cover. They were certainly reused at some point, suffering wear and some damage, making it likely they were repurposed.[53] This points to probable

Baltic (chapter 6). The line between 'late Pictish' or 'native' and 'Norse' hoards is in fact rather blurry, and it is worth questioning the framework itself with a few key examples.

There are several reasons to quibble with the 'viking panic' theory of the St Ninian's Isle Hoard, particularly as the objects seem to have been gathered and placed with great care in a box of what appears to have been imported Scandinavian wood. For a long time it was believed the cross-slab marking the hoard was face-down, so that it would only look like a paving slab from above, but the original photographs prove this was not the case. In the latest reading, the hoard was not 'hidden' in a

Fig. 4.14 (left): Gilt-bronze chip-carved mounts with amber and rock-crystal insets found near Crieff, Perthshire, maximum widths 55 mm; NMS X.FC 3–4.

Fig. 4.15 (below): Copper-alloy harness-fitting donated along with the Crieff mounts, with D-shaped loop, diameter 32 mm; NMS H.TXB 94.

Viking-age looting and modification of ecclesiastical objects for secular use. The main evidence comes from careful archival research. These famous mounts are displayed alone, but they were actually found with other bronze-fittings, only one of which survives. Described as a buckle [4.15], it may instead be a harness-loop, perhaps from the very bridle-fittings the mounts came from. It is one of many stray finds of decorated equestrian gear from the period. Was this a hoard now lost, or perhaps even a disturbed furnished burial from deep inland in Perthshire?

A hoard of at least nine objects from Rogart, Sutherland, now survives as six objects scattered across several museum collections. They include penannular brooches of silver alongside lesser-value bronze objects that are not so well-known.[54] Included were a pair of Northumbrian copper-alloy strap-ends of a rare type dated late 8th–9th century.[55] Such strap-ends are most often found in Viking-age context in Scotland [3.21].[56] Among the brooches is the one that is usually referred to as 'the' Rogart Brooch [4.16 (left)], the largest and most elaborate of the Pictish penannular series discussed in chapter 5 (p. 111). The terminals of this brooch feature birds seeming to 'drink' from a central gemstone. Less elaborate versions of the same motif appear in all the Scottish brooch-hoards that are discussed here, including several from the St Ninian's Isle Hoard, and it may be they were deposited at similar times.

The motif of 'drinking' birds appears on another elaborate brooch from Clunie in Perthshire [4.17]. The area of Loch Clunie, with its medieval motte and possible crannog, was probably a power centre of the 9th and 10th centuries.[57] Three penannular brooches have now been found here, including a remarkable cast-silver type of likely 7th-century make, and a fragment of terminal from a 9th-century deluxe brooch with gold filigree ornament and a large setting for a gemstone.[58] It is highly likely that these three were part of a single, dispersed hoard – if so, the date of the latest object suggests an early Viking-age deposition. It is not possible, although tantalising, to connect it with the raids as far as 'Dunkeld and Clunie' in the reign of Cináed mac Ailpín, and it is known there were other campaigns in Dunkeld or Atholl in at least 875, 878 and 903. Clunie and Rogart belong to a group of poorly dated brooch-deposits which include an undamaged 9th-century brooch from the prehistoric ringfort of Aldclune in Perthshire, as well as an intriguing collection of penannular brooches and other objects, from Croy near Inverness, discussed in more detail below (pp 92–7).[59]

The poor recording of some of these antiquarian finds means that in many cases we are not even sure of what we are discussing. One find from Orkney captures the ambiguities. While ploughing over the small gravel hillock known as the Knowe of Moan, a short cist was encountered with a number

of glass beads inside. Further exploration by local children turned up a total of 64 beads of glass and amber, along with a chip-carved insular mount in the shape of a cross, and a bronze spoon.[60] Enquiries made thereafter revealed that beads were found both inside and outside the cist, and the metal objects probably all from outside the cist. Despite these difficulties, it has been presumed to be a Viking-age cremation. Its location in a possible reused prehistoric mound may lend credence to the burial interpretation.[61] However, this could also be understood as a cache of beads and other valuable items – similar bead-hoards are known from Hillswick in Shetland, as well as elsewhere in Scandinavia; and beads were among the finds of other mixed hoards including Croy, Galloway and the lost Burgar Hoard.[62]

Fig. 4.16 (above): Two penannular brooches from a hoard at Rogart, Sutherland: (left) silver brooch with gilt imitation chip-carved panels of interlace and bird-head mounts, diameter 120 mm, NMS X.FC 2; and (right) silver with gilt chip-carved interlace terminals, diameter 77.5 mm, NMS X.FC 1–2.

Fig. 4.17 (left): Terminal of a silver penannular brooch, set with gold filigree and three bird-head mounts facing a central red glass stud, from near Clunie Castle, Perthshire; NMS X.FC 177.

AGE OF RAIDS

Fig. 4.18: The lidded silver-gilt vessel from the Galloway Hoard before conservation, showing layers of textile wrapping, height 100mm. (AOC Archaeology © Historic Environment Scotland)

THE GALLOWAY HOARD

In 2014 the collection of objects known as the Galloway Hoard was discovered at Balmaghie, Kirkcudbrightshire. Its multiple parcels of silver ingots and arm-rings [6.3] made it easy to place it initially in the mainstream of 'viking' hoards of the late 9th to early 10th centuries. The Trewhiddle-style pectoral cross, with intact silver chain wrapped around it, was an astounding discovery, but complete dress items were a common find in these hoards, and the art style itself was named after another famous silver hoard of this time found in Cornwall.[63] The intact silver-gilt vessel [4.18] found in the richer deposit underneath the first parcel of silver objects was matched in two hoards in Yorkshire.[64] The bundle of arm-rings (p.132) and gold objects in the lower deposit showed that the objects in the hoard were exceptional examples of known object types. But the truly unique quality of the Galloway Hoard was in the contents of the vessel [4.19], glimpsed only in X-rays at first, and the amount of rare organic material like textile, leather and cord, which hardly ever survive intact.

After a brief investigation of the site and a major fund-raising appeal to secure it for the nation, conservation began at National Museums Scotland that would change fundamentally the story of the hoard.[65] Runic inscriptions in the Anglo-Saxon futhorc on four of the arm-rings were joined by a fifth on a clipped and folded arm-ring from the surrounding ploughsoil (p. 17), the latter providing the only complete name, Egbert. While the stamped arm-rings in the upper and lower silver parcels are characteristic of the Irish Sea zone (AD 880–930), the names and words inscribed in runes showed that it was not only Norse-speaking vikings who used and hoarded silver bullion. These inscriptions were matched by the largely English character of the material in the vessel, including nielloed silver disc and quatrefoil brooches, a silver-mounted rock-crystal ball and objects of various materials decorated with gold filligree. Only a bossed penannular brooch and a distinctive twisted-cable glass bead could be linked to Irish workshops. The area where the hoard was found was still part of the English-speaking kingdom of Northumbria around AD 900, though links across the Irish Sea would become increasingly apparent during the Viking Age. The contents of the hoard capture the pivotal and multilingual context of the wider Irish Sea area.

Indeed, the 'Hoard' is perhaps more like several hoards in one, each capturing a different experience of the age of raids. There are parcels of silver that seem fresh from the workshop, arm-rings decorated but never worn as jewellery. Some of the arm-rings and ingots were already hacked, a sign they had been used as a form of currency (chapter 6). The pectoral cross was in remarkably good condition, although it was missing what must have been an impressive central setting. The objects in the vessel were of much more diverse origins. The only coin in the hoard was decades old by the time it was deposited: a silver penny of Coenwulf of Mercia (died 821) perforated for use as a composite pendant (p.72). The silver-mounted ball and gold-mounted rock-crystal vessel must have been imported from outside of

Fig. 4.19: Selection of items packed inside the silver-gilt vessel in the Galloway Hoard, National Museums Scotland.

Europe, and both appear to be much older than their decorated mounts. The glass beads are also well-worn, and the silver vessel itself has been suggested as having a Central Asian origin, as might some of the silk. Other inclusions, such as two dirt balls bearing flecks of gold and bone, are less materially precious, but instead point to another kind of spiritual value – perhaps relics of the saints gathered from distant lands.

From an archaeological perspective, the Galloway Hoard acts as a bridge between eras: the hacksilver and bullion parcels look forward to the large silver hoards of the 10th century (chapter 6), while the complete objects and the coin reused as a mount are characteristic of the 9th-century hoards discussed in this chapter. It has also forced a re-think of the existing hoards from the south-west, and the historical circumstances of their deposition, beyond the usual viking raids on churches. As the age of raids became the age of silver, the nature of hoarding itself seems to change.

THE GREAT ARMY RIDES NORTH

The short historical sketch at the start of this chapter emphasised that the invasion of the Great Army was more than just something that took place in England. The events of the 860s and '70s in England were inextricably linked to events in Ireland, Frankia and, of course, Scotland. The sack of Dumbarton in 870, resulting in the break-up of the once-powerful kingdom of Alt Clut, and the defeat of the Picts at the Battle of Dollar in 875, which caused the death of Causantín mac Cináeda, were both led by members of the Great Army.

In the last few years, a number of archaeological projects have transformed our ability to track the movement of the Great Army across England, identifying specific winter camps as attested in the historical sources, even potentially identifying buried individuals.[66] There is now an 'archaeological footprint' of the Great Army which is being used successfully to pinpoint new, undocumented sites. This adds to existing research on the nature and make-up of the Great Army, which has complicated our image of it and raised new questions about just how much we can really treat it as a single, coherent 'army' as well as a diverse and multi-ethnic set of warbands.[67]

A rich seam of material dated to the late 9th century in Scotland can provide some proxy evidence for the momentous events which led to the establishment of the Danelaw and the recalibration of alliances and social ties across the kingdoms of the north. It cannot be a coincidence that the events of the 870s also led to a hiatus in our sources for Scotland, after which we no longer hear of Picts or Fortriu, but a new entity called Alba. What lessons might there be in looking at the Great Army from a northern perspective?

Two hoards in particular – the Talnotrie Hoard from Galloway and the Croy Hoard from near Inverness – are both dated by coin to the late 9th century. These hoards have elements typical of the early Viking Age, including silver coins

Fig. 4.20 (right): The Talnotrie Hoard, from Kirkcudbrightshire, deposited c.875; National Museums Scotland.

Fig. 4.21 (below): Silver coins including four pennies of Burgred of Mercia (d.874), one Carolingian denier of Louis the Pious (d.840), and fragments of two Abbasid dirhams, from the Talnotrie Hoard, Kirkcudbrightshire; NMS H.C18464–67.

from well out of their area of circulation, and other fragmented objects which have the look of looted material. But they also have complete objects of local or otherwise insular origin, which makes it impossible to determine the identity of the owner(s) or their intentions in stashing them away.

The Talnotrie Hoard [4.20] contains complete Northumbrian and Mercian silver dress items and coins, as well as hacked metal including gold offcuts, which has led to its interpretation as a stash of a travelling jeweller.[68] Other materials less easy to interpret this way are the lignite ring and three stone spindle-whorls, but some of these objects were damaged in retrieval and some may be intrusive: the lignite ring has been identified as a Bronze-Age dress-fastener.[69] A recent reassessment of artefacts relating to the Great Army argues that the metal content of the hoard fits well within its archaeological 'footprint', including the juxtaposition of Mercian issues with exotic coins of the Carolingian king Louis the Pious, an Abbasid dirham from the Baghdad Caliphate and an unidentified fragment of another, along with a decorated lead weight typical of market sites and viking encampments such as Torksey and Cottam.[70] This kind of weight capped with a fragment of reused insular metalwork is another sign of the Viking-age bullion economy that was turbo-charged within the Great Army camps.[71] There is even a plausible material connection to the Great Army: in 874/5, Healfdane's warband was said to have gone raiding in Pictland and Strathclyde, fitting in with the proposed date of deposition of Talnotrie.[72]

It is worth going through the hoard in detail to see if this Great Army connection holds up. There are ten coins of Northumbrian and Mercian mints, although as Galloway was part of Northumbria since the 8th century some of these can be seen as part of the local currency, or at least material that was readily accessible. Concentrations of 9th-century Anglo-Saxon coins in Galloway show that supply-lines were maintained.[73] A lost styca hoard with a 'silver crucifix', perhaps similar to the cruciform ornament found at Talnotrie or the pectoral cross from the Galloway Hoard, was found in the Lochar Moss near Caerlaverock, Dumfriesshire, and may be broadly contemporary.[74] The recurring inclusion of cruciform elements seems to link these hoards together. Given these and other metal-detected finds from across the region, we are safely within the Northumbrian cultural sphere.

The Arabic dirhams and fragment of Carolingian silver coin from Talnotrie are altogether more exotic [4.21]. Dirhams, the currency of the Islamic Caliphate, were imported into Britain

Fig. 4.22 (left): Two inset lead weights from Dumfriesshire: (left) Gulluberry, Kirkton, weight 31.22 g, DUMFM.2009.38, (right) Lochmaben, weight 152.55 g, ANNMS:2013.4. (Courtesy of Dumfries and Galloway Council Museums Service; image © National Museums Scotland)

Fig. 4.23 (right): Lead weight inset with reused chip-carved insular mount, Talnotrie Hoard, Kirkcudbrightshire, diameter 25 mm, weight 88.18 g; NMS X.FC 198.

Fig. 4.24 (below): Silver arm-ring with stamped ornament, Blackerne, Kirkcudbrightshire, diameter 43 mm; NMS X.EQ 95.

and Ireland beginning in the late 9th century and are the subject of a later discussion. Suffice to say their fragmented state shows they did not make it to Talnotrie as recognised standard currency, but for their weight in silver. The Great Army's role in the importation of Islamic coined silver is now greatly reinforced by the metal-detected assemblage from Torksey; until then, Talnotrie represented the second-earliest datable appearance of a dirham from anywhere in Britain, after the Croydon Hoard (c.872) which has clear historical links to the overwintering of the Great Army in London in 871/2.[75] The dirhams were as heavily fragmented as the similarly exotic Louis the Pious denier. Another similarly clipped fragment of a Louis the Pious silver coin was found along with a complete coin of Aethelred II of Northumbria (dated c.841–4) by metal-detecting near the site of Hoddom, Dumfriesshire [4.29].[76] Are we seeing the footprints of the Great Army on its way north?

As intriguing as this might be, more recent finds of Viking-age material culture across the southwest of Scotland make Talnotrie less of an 'intrusion' which can only be explained by the extraordinary historical personage of the Great Army. The early dirhams remain unique in Galloway, joined only by one unidentified example from Stevenston Sands, Ayrshire.[77] There are now a handful of other insular decorated lead weights from the region attesting to a wider usage than previously thought.[78] One is from Kirkton, along a major corridor of the Nith valley; while one from Lochmaben, in the neighbouring Annan valley, even has a similar cruciform ornament to the objects from Talnotrie [4.22, 4.23]. These join finds of possible 'viking' burials at Carronbridge and Wamphray, further up the Nith and Annan valleys respectively.[79] In addition, stray finds of silver arm-rings are known from Blackerne, Kirkcudbrightshire [4.24], and near Gretna, whilst a stamped gold ring from Tundergarth is the only one of its kind in Scotland – all of these likely relate to the late 9th or early 10th century.[80] Such finds reinforce the case for the presence of people connected to the wider Irish Sea trade zone far from the usual coastal concentrations of viking market activity. The massive size of the Lochmaben weight in particular, 152.55g, compared to the smaller weights used in the Great Army camps, is a good indication of the size of transactions being carried out here. They were likely used for goods in bulk, whether foodstuffs from the fertile river valleys, livestock or human chattel. Indeed, the decorated lead weights tend to be heavy, including the Talnotrie example at 88.18g and one at 58g from Whithorn. A metrological study of this small but significant group of weights has yet to be carried out, but it does not yet look as though they all conform to any single weight standard. Even determining the metrology of these weights would not reveal the ethnicity of their users as it is increasingly found that collections of lead weights, like those from the Great Army site of Cottam, have occasional

Fig. 4.25 (right): Globular pinhead, hollow metal core with copper-alloy outer layer, divided into quadrants, bearing triquetra scrolls of filigree work, diameter 25 mm, Talnotrie Hoard, Kirkcudbrightshire; NMS X.FC 199.

Figs 4.26 a–b (below): Pierced silver penny of Burgred of Mercia (852–74), moneyer Diga, pierced and retaining a fragment of silver mount, Talnotrie Hoard, Kirkcudbrightshire; H.C18464.

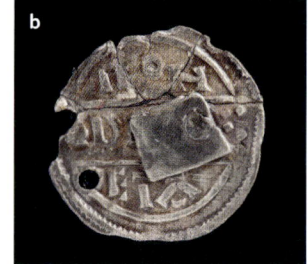

outliers that show the presence of users working across different weight standards.[81] The eclectic mixture of materials in the Talnotrie Hoard would fit into this general snapshot of a nimble, opportunistic approach to measuring value in a time of high mobility and before the establishment of widely agreed transnational standards.

If this is a jeweller's hoard, it is one well-connected to the burgeoning trade system being established between viking-controlled Dublin and York. While Talnotrie is often left out of the wider narrative of 'viking' hoards in Scotland, the finds of contemporary Trewhiddle-style and other complete ornaments in the Galloway Hoard [4.19] has forced a new look at the context of Viking-age finds in the region.[82] As will become clear, the ethnicity of the 'owner' (or 'owners', better yet 'depositors') is impossible to prove, and in any case it pales into insignificance when compared to what can be learned from the act of hoarding itself.

The Talnotrie Hoard was deposited in an upland moss and only discovered while cutting peat. It joins a wider series of early medieval metalwork deposits in the upland mosses of the southwest, including the hacked fragments from Corrie Loch (pp 80–81), the Monybuie, Kirkcudbrightshire, bronze handbell casing, and the Stidriggs, Dumfriesshire, iron tool hoard, radiocarbon-dated to the 8th–10th centuries.[83] To this we might also join the lost Lochar Moss hoard, although this one is in a low-lying context outside Dumfries. All these could date to the Viking Age, demonstrating that Talnotrie fits into a local pattern of deposition.

The debate over the depositors of the Talnotrie Hoard hinges not just on the coins, but on the enigmatic globular pinhead, which was compared to another one in silver filigree from a female grave from Ballinaby, Isle of Islay.[84] Both are superficially similar but come from separate, if overlapping, distributions in the 9th-/10th-century North Sea zone. Highly elaborate filigree pins began to appear in Hedeby, north Germany, and Dorestad, Netherlands, by the 9th century, soon becoming fashionable in England. Pins and beads incorporating hollow balls of silver ornamented with filigree appear in wealthy graves in southern Scandinavian market towns like Birka and Hedeby into the 10th century.[85] Some of these began to filter back to Britain through the Irish Sea trade zone as hacksilver: one crushed example survives in the Cuerdale Hoard, Lancashire (deposited 905–10), while some related finds have been discovered in contemporary silver hoards in Ireland.[86] The Ballinaby pin represents the southern Scandinavian variant and likely dates the grave to the early 10th century.[87] The Talnotrie pinhead [4.25] is part of an insular variant which seems to pre-date the southern Scandinavian series. Their distribution is strongly linked to East Anglia and probably represents some of the early Anglo-Scandinavian contacts noted in other forms of jewellery in this area.[88] The Talnotrie example remains an outlier, being of an otherwise unattested form divided into quadrants, with an outer 'skin' of copper-alloy – so while it remains fascinating, it cannot strictly tell us much more about the depositor of the hoard.

Another anomaly, largely overlooked in previous discussions, is that one of the silver pennies of Burgred of Mercia

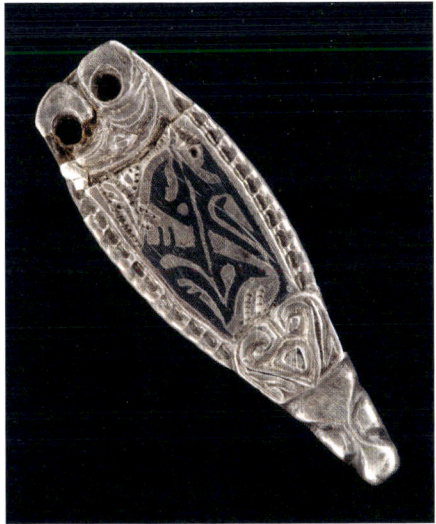 

Fig. 4.27 (left). Strap-end of Class A1, silver with backward biting animal in niello, from the Talnotrie Hoard, Kirkcudbrightshire, length 41mm; NMS X.FC 200.

Fig. 4.28 (right): Detail of finger-ring of gold with backward-biting beast on the bezel, diameter 25mm, found near Selkirk, Scottish Borders; NMS Q.L.1993.1.

(852–74) was pierced as if to be mounted or suspended [4.26 a–b]. This example appears to have had at least three 'lives' before it was deposited here: from a mint, perhaps in London, to a double-perforation at one end, similar to those in Viking-age coin-pendant necklaces, which seems to have broken or been torn off. This required a third perforation to be made at the opposite end of the coin, either as a patch-up job or for wearing in a different way; the silver rivet and plate used to secure it partly survives.

It is striking that one of the only other coins of Burgred from Scotland, at Saevar Howe near Birsay, Orkney, is also pierced. This one is closely datable to 866–8.[89] Piercing is a recurring feature of Anglo-Saxon coins from Scotland. Two stycas from the Kiloran Bay, Colonsay, burial are pierced centrally, in a way that suggests use as coin-weights.[90] But the modified coin from Talnotrie has certainly been used as a pendant, and the others with two perforations at opposite ends may well have been displayed in this way. In a context where traders had to move between coin-using and coinless economies, coin-weights and coin-pendants could be a way of advertising one's access to quality silver or long-distance networks.

The Talnotrie Hoard also incorporates more distinctively Anglo-Saxon material culture, aside from its coins.[91] The silver strap-end and silver linked-pins are both rare in Scotland. We have already seen similar strap-ends from Rogart above, but the silver and niello of Talnotrie [4.27] makes it a particularly fine example of the northern class.[92] Another example of Trewhiddle-style ornament in southern Scotland is a fine gold and niello finger-ring found near Selkirk in the Scottish Borders, of roughly the same period as the Talnotrie Hoard [4.28].[93] Importantly, these objects were not nicked or hacked, and may be saying more about local fashions in Northumbrian Galloway than being used simply for their weight in silver. The pins, the lead weight and the four-pointed mount from this hoard all share the same cruciform motif. This makes it more likely to be a purposeful group of objects than an itinerant 'jeweller's hoard'.[94]

Perhaps rather than positing a Great Army as the explanation for the Talnotrie Hoard, it is now more interesting to consider that people in Northumbrian Scotland had ties to the Great Army trade zone. The record of Healfdane's army raiding in the north in 874 mentioned Strathclyde and Pictland – neither being an apt description for Galloway.

The Talnotrie Hoard may not relate directly to the events of 874, but in 875 we have a better idea of where the army went. The location of the Battle of Dollar indicates that the Great Army, like any number of armies before and after, would have crossed the Forth at or near the Fords of Frew close to Stirling, and then headed toward the Perthshire royal centres, potentially Forteviot and certainly Dunkeld. It is worth pausing here to consider the impact metal-detected finds may have already made in this regard. There are scatters of Northumbrian and Hiberno-Norse finds across this region, and it has been suggested that finds of Viking-age date, such as insular metalwork

AGE OF RAIDS

Fig. 4.29 (left, above): Incomplete Carolingian silver denier of Louis the Pious (Class 2, AD819–22), struck at Pavia, Italy, part of the assemblage from Hoddom, Dumfriesshire; NMS X.1999.29.195.

Fig. 4.30 (right): Copper-alloy pin with damaged racquet-shaped head and ring-and-dot decoration, Blackhill House, Caputh, Perthshire, length 63mm; NMS X.FC 234.

Fig. 4.31 (left, below): Faceted bead of carnelian, from Coldingham Priory, Scottish Borders, width 8.5mm; NMS X.2014.280.1.

modified into harness-mounts, cluster on major roadways, allowing us to trace overland routes.[95] Elements of the Great Army 'footprint' may include a rare kind of polyhedral copper-alloy weight, previously unknown from Scotland, from Cowie, Stirlingshire, just before the fords over the Forth.[96] Similar 'cubo-octahedral' weights were introduced to England by the Great Army in the 870s, with 99 examples now recorded from the winter camp of Torksey alone.[97] However, these tend to be decorated with dots and are very small, weighing 4g or below, whereas the Cowie one is plain and weighs 24.58g. Rare heavier versions of cubo-octahedrals do exist, however, and the weight of Cowie corresponds precisely with the 'lighter' Scandinavian *øre* unit of *c*.24.59g used by lead weights from the Danelaw site of Cottam B, Yorkshire.[98] The Cowie weight may simply be a bespoke northern adaptation, adopting the polyhedral form of a regulated weight.

After winning the Battle of Dollar, Healfdane's army pursued the Pictish king Constantín mac Cináeda as far as Atholl, where he was killed. Viking armies had previously penetrated as far as Dunkeld and Clunie in the reign of Cináed mac Ailpín, 'all Pictland' in 866 and Dunkeld again in 878. There are intriguing glimpses of 9th-century Northumbrian finds which may be linked to these episodes. From Caputh near Clunie there is a racquet-headed pin of a type hardly found in Scotland but very common in Mercia and Northumbria [4.30], including the Danelaw phase of the Yorkshire site of Cottam B.[99] On the main route through Atholl, near the modern A9 road, there are rare Northumbrian silver Class A strap-ends of the 9th century at both Stanley and Logierait, with parallels from the Rogart Hoard mentioned above.[100] Less distinctive of the Great Army 'footprint' is a scatter of remarkable finds which have been considered odd outliers, but may potentially be explained by the movements of an army with Northumbrian, Danish and Irish links. Moving from south to north, these include the gold ring from near Selkirk discussed previously; a carnelian bead recognised during the research for this book from Coldingham in the Scottish Borders [4.31]; the lost gold neck-ring from Braidwood Fort, Midlothian;[101] the Irish-style brooch-pin from Dunipace, Falkirk [5.21]; and from Clunie itself there is the possible hoard of penannular brooches [4.17], which may relate to a period of stress caused by these raids, bearing in mind earlier raids. It will never be possible to link such stray finds to specific historical events, but they must all be seen in the context of the documented overland raids from 839–900.

This brings us to the other collection of exotic materials known as the Croy Hoard [4.32] from near Inverness, a mixed-material hoard like Talnotrie, deposited after AD845 based on the mint date of its coins.[102] The site is between Inverness and Burghead, in the heartlands of the kingdom of Fortriu. The hoard consists of complete and fragmented objects, coins, beads and a balance beam from a set of scales, the kind of object that in Scotland is often a calling-card of the Viking Age [6.16, 6.17]. Yet there are no dirhams, and the fragmented state of the silver objects may be from the circumstances of recovery rather than purposeful hacking for a bullion economy. Like Talnotrie, this hoard falls into the cracks of early medieval Scottish archaeology – too 'viking' for Pictish studies, too 'Pictish' for viking studies. This has left it relatively unknown, despite holding the key to understanding the northern experience of this momentous stage of insular history.

Fig. 4.32: The Croy Hoard, near Inverness, deposited after c.850: (second from left) a portion of ribbon-like ornament of silver wire knitted in the trichinopoly technique, length 152mm, NMS X.FC 25; (right, below) two pierced silver coins of Coenwulf of Mercia (796–821), NMS X.FC 24–23.

AGE OF RAIDS

The Croy Hoard contains a nearly complete penannular brooch of early 9th-century type (only missing its pin), joined by fragments of two other penannular brooches of comparable date, and a small group of glass and amber beads. Like the Talnotrie Hoard, one prehistoric find has crept in: a fragment of an Iron-Age yellow spiral bead with numerous local parallels. A ribbon-like ornament made of fine knitted silver wire, cut off at both ends, is considered to be an insular dress ornament with parallels from later silver hoards [4.32].[103] Another silver hoard from Cornwall at Trewhiddle (deposited c.868) had a chain-like ornament of fine silver wire, one end of which was tied to a glass bead. The beads of amber, an exotic material likely imported from the Baltic, would have had semi-precious value on their own. Two silver coins of Coenwulf of Mercia (796–821) and Aeðelwulf of Wessex (838–58)[104] provide the dating evidence. These have travelled a long way out of their usual circulation, and are pierced twice each, as if for mounting [4.32]. (We have already encountered similar perforations on a coin from the Talnotrie Hoard.) There was a widespread use of coins for display in northern Scotland: they were more than just bullion, tokens of monetary value. In the same way as Trewhiddle and Talnotrie, this hoard contains little or no diagnostic 'viking' (as in Scandinavian) material, but fits in with other eclectic assemblages of insular and imported material from the late 9th century.

Even though the coins were demonetised and used as jewellery, the presence of the beam of a balance scale may indicate there was an economic motive for collecting this group of objects. Balance scales will be part of a wider discussion of the changing Viking-age economy (chapter 6), but it is worth pausing on this object. Most Viking-age balance scales have folding arms for ease of transport. However, some early types, like the balance from a boat grave at Kiloran Bay, Colonsay, have a single, rigid beam, known as a fixed-beam balance [6.16]. The zoomorphic elements at the ends of the Croy balance are rare among insular finds: two from viking Dublin have similar ornaments, one from a folding balance and one from a fixed-beam.[105] A set of balance scales from Ronaldsway, Isle of Man, have outward-facing bird heads at the ends of the fixed-beam, drawing parallels with the bird-head suspension ring from a balance found at Meols on the Wirral, opposite the Isle of Man.[106] A damaged folding balance with similar bird-shaped suspension rings was found in a cist on the Isle of Gigha, off the coast of Kintyre in Argyll.[107] Decorated balances such as these, with tinned-bronze scale pans, have been associated with insular workshops, with several notable examples found in Scandinavian graves.[108]

But none of these balances forms an exact parallel for the Croy balance beam [4.33]. In fact, the closest parallel is from a boat grave in Haug, Verdal, Trondelag [4.34].[109] Like Croy and Kiloran Bay, this is a fixed-beam balance rather than the more common folding type. Haug, Croy and Ronaldsway [4.35] are the only examples with a flat-bar construction, setting them apart from the majority of examples with round-sectioned arms, and all three are smaller than their counterparts at Dublin and Kiloran Bay. Only Haug and Croy have back-turned beasts as finials. The animal heads of the Haug and Croy balances have numerous insular parallels, most notably in the end-beasts of various house-shaped portable reliquaries.[110] This supports an insular origin for this rare form. The Ronaldsway deposit cannot be closely dated, while the Haug boat grave is dated only 800–900, so the coin evidence from Croy is the best dating evidence for the group.

Another aspect that connects these three balances is that they are not quite equal-armed, as a reliable balance should be. Ronaldsway had 24 notches cut into one arm, while Croy and Haug have 20 notches each. This would upset the balance of the arms. These notches indicate that the balances were used in a different way, as a specific form of balance called a 'steelyard'. These use a pendant counterweight which was moved

Fig. 4.33: Damaged balance beam of copper-alloy with inward-looking animal-head terminal, notches cut into one side for use as a steelyard, from the Croy Hoard, length 114mm; NMS X.FC 15.

Fig. 4.34: Fixed-beam balance scale modified for use as a steelyard, with zoomorphic terminals, Haug, Verdal, Norway, length 118mm. (Photo: Åge Hojem, NTNU University Museum. CC BY-SA 4.0)

Fig. 4.35: Fixed-beam balance scale modified for use as a steelyard, with zoomorphic terminals, Ronaldsway, Isle of Man, length 90mm. (© Manx Museum)

across the notches to weigh out pre-determined units, and the Ronaldsway balance retained its plumb-bob lead counterweight. Steelyards of rather different form were used in Roman Britain and remained in use in the Byzantine east, but generally do not reappear in the west until the 12th century.[111] The Croy balance thus seems to have been a shortlived experiment in the early development of the insular forms of balance scales that did not catch on.

Croy and Talnotrie have been called metalworkers' hoards, and it is notable that the Haug grave also had smithing tools including hammer and tongs. Smithing tools and balance scales appear together in a grave in Dublin, where the tools are clearly for non-ferrous metalworking rather than blacksmithing.[112] It may be that these balances had a specialist role linked to weighing out specific quantities of metal. We will return to this in chapter 6.

There is one more aspect of the Croy balance to consider. In the course of researching these objects for the current project, a runic inscription was discovered on the 'reverse' of the balance beam [4.36]. Like the runic inscription on the arm-rings of the Galloway Hoard, this is in Anglo-Saxon futhorc, not Old Norse runes. The message appears to be very simple: possibly just 'weigher'.[113] This is currently the most northerly instance of Anglo-Saxon runes in Britain, which raises several new questions about the nature of this hoard and its depositor. Like the Talnotrie Hoard, the Croy Hoard is a mixture of local and Anglo-Saxon material. The balance beam links it to the Irish Sea–Danelaw trade zone; the coins are the kind found in Great Army linked hoards; the runes show the participation of Anglo-Saxons in connecting the north to the emerging hacksilver economy (pp 86–7). The absence of dirhams and lack of lead weights from the northeast of Scotland suggests that we are not seeing the full 'footprint' of the Great Army, but the unusual nature of the balance beam from Croy means we should not expect to find the same kinds of objects in this area.

The perforation of coins is another link between these hoards. The only other coin of Coenwulf of Mercia from Scotland is the one pierced for use as a composite bead pendant in the Galloway Hoard, deposited decades after it was minted (p. 86).[114] It is tempting to push the date of the Croy Hoard into the late 9th century, given its parallels to the Talnotrie

Fig. 4.36: Detail of runic inscription on the back of the balance beam from the Croy Hoard; NMS X.FC 15.

and Galloway Hoards. But if we return to the wider evidence for long-distance contacts in northeast Scotland, these finds become part of a longer story of communication between Fortriu and the Anglo-Saxon kingdoms (chapter 2).

The presence of Anglo-Saxon coins and runes here in the heartland of Fortriu is not as unprecedented as it seems. The harbours of the Moray and Dornoch firths afforded opportunities for maritime trade even before the Viking Age. At some point in the 9th century, the occupants of the Pictish power centre of Burghead, a short sail along the coast from Croy, obtained a rare Trewhiddle-style drinking-horn or blast-horn, surviving only as the silver mount around the rim [4.37].[115] It had for a long time seemed like an extreme outlier, leading to suggestions it could only have been brought here by 'viking intervention',[116] yet it is equally plausible it was brought here as a gift from a southern emissary. It is not the only such item from Burghead. In 1861 the Society of Antiquaries of Scotland acquired a coin of Alfred of Wessex (871–99) from Burghead, notably pierced in two places; while excavations at Burghead by the University of Aberdeen in 2017 obtained another early penny of Alfred.[117] Both coins, found more than a century and a half apart, were pierced in two places, just like those from Talnotrie and Croy, and the two from Burghead remain the only Alfred pennies from Scotland. These pierced coins also join an imitation gold solidus of Louis the Pious found near Elgin, a common forgery of a kind we now know was being made in England among other places, including in the Great Army winter camp at Torksey.[118] Like the others, this one was also pierced in the same distinctive way, at two opposed ends.

How are we to explain this concentration of exotic finds? The coin issues and Trewhiddle-style metalwork are certainly reminiscent of the kinds of materials being hoarded in the 860s and '70s in southern and midland England.[119] But these objects are mixed with locally sourced Pictish material in the Croy Hoard; and the coins were not necessarily circulating, but were being displayed as dress accessories. Are we seeing another Great Army warband this far north, or were local people proudly displaying tokens obtained further south? The Anglo-Saxon runic inscription on the Croy Hoard balance beam suggests there is no need for Danish raiders to have brought this material north at all.

The coins may hold the answer. Three 'viking' burials in Scotland have coins with similar date ranges – all have been linked to the archaeological 'footprint' of the Great Army. Primary among these is the Kiloran Bay, Colonsay, boat grave, which has a set of balance scales, lead weights and two pierced Northumbrian stycas. Stycas of Wessex and Northumbria are also found in graves at Midross, near Luss, Loch Lomond, and the cremation burial at Kingscross Point, Arran.[120] A final pierced coin of Burgred of Mercia (dated 866–8) comes from the reused broch of Saevar Howe, Orkney.[121] One of the coins from Midross, of Aethelred I of Wessex (dated c.871), was also pierced like the ones discussed here; as were the coins from Kiloran Bay, Burghead, Elgin, Saevar Howe, and the Galloway Hoard

CRUCIBLE OF NATIONS

Fig 4.37: Silver rim-mount for a drinking-horn or blast-horn, from Burghead, Moray, diameter 75mm; NMS X.IL 214.

coin-pendant. The display of coins this way seems to be specific to the north, outside coin-using areas. Rather than tracing the footsteps of Great Army warbands, we are seeing a distinctively northern response to new kinds of wealth generated in the turmoil of the Great Army years. The Galloway and Croy Hoards bear Anglo-Saxon runic inscriptions, while the Kiloran Bay boat burial has close links to Dublin in its weapons and balance scales. They are like shockwaves or echoes of the dramatic events of the 860s and '70s, reverberating through neighbouring kingdoms.

GOING VIKING

These are just a glimpse into the kinds of objects that we know were the product of raiding activity in the 9th century. Perhaps the biggest surprises are how gradual the Norse 'takeover' of Orkney and Shetland seems to have been, and how much of the material from graves and hoards in Scotland is insular rather than Scandinavian. The hoards of the period are almost impossible to categorise as either 'viking' or 'native', and it is clear we now need to revisit a lot of assumptions about even the most well-studied assemblages. The discovery of an Anglo-Saxon runic inscription on the steelyard balance beam from the Croy Hoard, and patterns of deposition along overland route-ways, shows just how much is still up for grabs if we direct new attention to old finds.

Talnotrie and Croy, as with several of the stray finds noted above, are more striking not for their contents, but for their appearance in areas with no known Scandinavian settlement. This might suggest they are a product of the times, and not a particular cultural context. It is possible that the 'oddness' of these deposits is in fact our emerging awareness of people of insular origin participating in the economic changes brought by the viking invasions, or responding to these historical circumstances in locally specific ways. The appearance of pierced coins from Galloway to Orkney makes it less likely that they involved a single group of people as much as a similar economic impulse to display access to new forms of wealth. The artefacts reveal much greater involvement of actors across Scotland in events better recorded elsewhere in Britain and Ireland than previously considered. These finds beg serious questions about more than just how to find 'vikings', but about those we are calling 'vikings' in the first place – and perhaps those who stood to benefit from these fast-moving changes.

Another message coming out of this loud and clear is the sheer amount of wealth moving around in the north, in the form of silver and gold dress accessories, exotic goods such as those from the Galloway Hoard and, overall, the momentous first taste of Arabic silver as seen at Talnotrie. The repeated incursions into Pictland across the 9th-century show that the northern kingdoms were themselves highly prized. Only by considering the age of raids across the north as a whole do these connections begin to appear.

NOTES

1. Clancy 2004.
2. Lapidge 1982.
3. Lucas 1967.
4. The following is based on Woolf 2007, unless specified.
5. Lund 1989, 50.
6. See now also IJssennagger 2017.
7. Abrams 2020.
8. Woolf 2007, 101–2.
9. *Ibid.*, 351.
10. Downham 2007.
11. Hadley and Richards 2021, 42–4.
12. Compare Clarke et al. 2012, XI–XX.
13. Heen-Pettersen 2019.
14. Griffiths 2019.
15. Hamilton 1956, 6.
16. O'Meadhra 1993; Graham-Campbell et al. 2019.
17. Hamilton 1956, 106–32.
18. Bone-pins: Graham-Campbell 1980, 60. Ringed pins: Fanning 1994. Arm-rings: Graham-Campbell 1995.
19. Deckers 2012.
20. Metcalf 1995.
21. Morris and Barrowman 2021.
22. Curle 1982.
23. Blackwell 2018, 133–6.
24. Forsyth 1996b.
25. Ritchie 1979; cf. Griffiths 2019, 7.
26. Hedges 1983; Bond et al. 2017.
27. Dockrill et al. 2010; Hunter et al. 2007.
28. Stummann Hansen 2000.
29. Heen-Pettersen 2019, table 1.
30. Heen-Pettersen and Murray 2018.
31. Kruse 2013; cf. Murray 2015, 101, who argues for a provenance in the northern half of Ireland.
32. Androshchuk 2007; Staecker 2009.
33. Bakka 1965, 39–40; Youngs 1989, no. 138; Henderson and Henderson 2004, 120.
34. Kruse 2013.
35. Jennings 1998; Clancy 2011; Maldonado et al. 2021.
36. Wamers 1983, 1985.
37. Bourke 2010, 33.
38. Wegner 2006; Webster and Backhouse 1991, no. 135; National Museums Scotland (NMS) X.FC 179; compare to Wamers 1987 and Bell et al. 1990.
39. Hadley and Richards 2016, 47–9.
40. Wamers 1985, 41–2.
41. Barrett 2010; Raffield et al. 2017; cf. Jesch 2015, 107–8.
42. Heen-Pettersen 2019.
43. Sindbæk 2011a; Sheehan 2013.
44. Ashby 2015.
45. Glørstad 2012.
46. Cross 2017; Ellis 2021.
47. Svanberg 2003; Jesch 2015, 4–8.
48. Blackwell et al. 2017, 127–30.
49. Barrowman 2011; Clarke et al. 2012; Small et al. 1973.
50. Youngs 1989, nos 124–7.
51. Fragments were identified upon its discovery but have since been lost: Graham-Campbell 2003a, 25–7; Barrowman 2011, 146–7.
52. Youngs 2001.
53. Spearman 1993, 136–9.
54. One on display in Dunrobin Museum, Sutherland; a terminal of a second is in the Ashmolean Museum, AN1927.127.
55. Small et al. 1973, 82, Ashmolean Museum AN1927.124 and AN1927.124.
56. Class A2b, Thomas 2000, 226; a pair in the 1963 grave at Westness, Rousay; another from Reay, highly likely to have come from a grave: Blackwell 2018, 132, 183. Two further finds from Perthshire are discussed on page 92.
57. Hall et al. 1998.
58. NMS X.FC 177; NMS X.FC 176; NMS X.1993.7.
59. Graham-Campbell 1987a, 255–7.
60. Cursiter 1887; the finds are now in the Hunterian Museum, B.1914.524, B.1914.864-6. The mount NMS X.FC 244, illustrated above, has been associated with Knowe of Moan, but it was not in any account of that find, and was in fact registered in 1936 with the note: 'Locality unknown. Has been in the museum for very many years but never registered.'
61. McLeod 2015a ('Legitimation through association').

62. O'Sullivan 2015, 82; Graham-Campbell 1987a.
63. Webster and Backhouse 1991, no. 246.
64. Ager 2020.
65. Goldberg and Davis 2021.
66. Hadley and Richards 2021; Jarman et al. 2018.
67. Richards 2004; McLeod 2011; Raffield 2016.
68. Maxwell 1913; Graham-Campbell 1995, 3–4.
69. F. Hunter, pers. comm.
70. Hadley and Richards 2018.
71. Haldenby and Kershaw 2014.
72. The latest dated coin is 852–74; Graham-Campbell 1995, 4.
73. Blackwell 2018, 111–16; Griffiths 2014.
74. Graham-Campbell 1995, 4–5.
75. Brooks and Graham-Campbell 1986 [reprinted 2000].
76. Lowe 2006, 133–4; NMS X.1999.29.195.
77. NMS H.C9681; Graham-Campbell and Batey 1998, 98.
78. Hill 1997, 392–3.
79. Owen and Welander 1995; Blackwell 2018, 213.
80. Graham-Campbell 1995, 157–8.
81. Haldenby and Kershaw 2014, 117.
82. Graham-Campbell 2020, 458.
83. Monybuie: Eeles and Clouston 1967; Stidriggs: Dumfries Museum, DUMFM: 1989.2.1-20; Leahy 2013; Canmore ID 89407; information from Joanne Turner.
84. NMS X.IL 145.
85. Kalmring 2017.
86. Graham-Campbell 2011a, 121–2.
87. Compare Kershaw 2013, 148, 153.
88. Ross 1991, 339–47; Kershaw 2013.
89. Hedges 1983, 93.
90. Williams 1999, 26–7.
91. Webster and Backhouse 1991, no. 248.
92. Blackwell 2018, 167–9.
93. Webster and Backhouse 1991, no. 203.
94. Blackwell 2018, 169.
95. Blackwell 2018; Buchanan 2012; Hall 2007.
96. Dunblane Museum, width 16mm, TT 177/15.
97. Hadley and Richards 2018, 3.
98. Haldenby and Kershaw 2014, 115–17.
99. Haldenby and Richards 2009.
100. TT 01/15; TT 11/15.
101. Graham-Campbell 1995, 153–4.
102. Graham-Campbell 1995, 3; Anderson 1876; Ross 1886.
103. Graham-Campbell 2011a, 123–4; 1:1,086, pl. 51.
104. Harrison and Ó Floinn 2014, 172–4.
105. Skinner and Bruce Mitford 1940; Megaw 1940; Griffiths et al. 2007, 70.
106. Hunterian Museum GLAHM:A.188/1; Bryce 1913.
107. Harrison and Ó Floinn 2014, 172–4.
108. Farbregd 1974.
109. Compare Campbell et al. 2019; Blackwell 2011; Megaw 1940; Armstrong 1922.
110. Morrisson 2012; Kyhlberg 1975.
111. Harrison and Ó Floinn 2014, 164–6.
112. D. Parsons, pers. comm.
113. Goldberg and Davis 2021, 80.
114. Graham-Campbell 1973.
115. Webster and Backhouse 1991, no. 247.
116. Noble and Sveinbjarnarson 2018: 134–5.
117. Blackburn 2007; Hadley and Richards 2016; Lyons and MacKay 2008.
118. Brooks and Graham-Campbell 2000.
119. Hadley and Richards 2018, 15.
120. Midross: Buchanan 2012, 115. Kingscross Point: Balfour 1909; Williams 1999, 28.
121. Hedges 1983, 84, 93, fig. 14.

CHAPTER FIVE

The serpent and thorn

After the high historical drama of kingdoms rising and falling, we come back down to earth to look for the individuals who lived through these momentous times, or at least shadows and traces of them, through their material culture. We will never know their names, but nothing is more personal than the clothes that people wore. Cloth and hides rarely survive, but this period is rich with metal dress-fasteners and accessories that give us a sense of how people presented themselves. Metal dress accessories were once the province only of the elite, but this era of urban workshops and thriving markets increased production to scales that were not seen before in the early medieval period. If we imagine that each dress item stands for an individual who once lived, we can now see a much bigger cast of characters than ever before – more than the historical record could ever name. Fashions also moved quickly in this period and took hold over great distances, with many new ideas introduced from Scandinavia, Ireland and beyond. But through all of these changes, two trends persisted – the serpent, protective beasts embedded in the design of many dress items; and the thorn, an emphasis on the fastening implement which speared through fabric [Fig. 5.1].

MORE THAN A FASHION

We need to understand early medieval dress items differently from the way we look at clothing today. Materials had distinctive properties and value systems of their own, as defined primarily by the long and eventful trajectory of silver in Scotland.[1] Pins and brooches, like swords and other objects already discussed, had life stories and held memories.[2] They connected more than just layers of fabric – they connected people, sometimes across generations. Even in a time of rapidly increased production of dress items, such as in the 9th–12th centuries, every pin, brooch and belt-fitting was still handmade, each finished product unique. The value of an object was not merely in the amount of materials, but in the craftsmanship behind it, its journey from the maker's hands to yours, and all the people and places these stages entailed. The art in, and of, these

Opposite: Detail of bronze trefoil brooch, with 'Borre-style' ornament, from a woman's grave at Clibberswick, Unst, Shetland; NMS X.IL 224.

Fig. 5.1 (below): Detail of zoomorphic ornament in gold filigree on the cusp of the Hunterston Brooch, Ayrshire; NMS X.FC 8, detail of brooch hoop.

Fig. 5.2 (above): Beast-headed bone-pin from Kerrera, Argyll, length 100mm; NMS X.FC 303.

Fig. 5.3 (below): Detail of wolf-head attachment loop on the head of the Westness Brooch, found in the woman and infant grave from Westness, Rousay, Orkney (1963); NMS X.IL 728.

objects was not merely ornament. The writhing beasts and interlace patterns on dress items and other objects had agency – the capacity to act and intervene, on the wearer and viewer alike.

Art styles and patterns had heritage and pedigrees of their own, and 'copies' or 'imitations' were not seen as derivative or inferior, but a continuing conversation with that heritage.[3] What we see as 'art styles' were in fact carefully curated traditions, full of meaning and memory. In a real way, the animals and fantastical hybrid creatures depicted in metal and stone acted to guard, protect, even threaten.[4] Endless loops of interlace could ensnare demonic forces. There were different forms of beasts and abstract ornament used across insular and Scandinavian art styles, but there are enough broad commonalities in how they were deployed – beast-heads 'guarding' terminals and openings, interlace and other abstract ornament covering surfaces, geometric patterns for borders and frames – to suggest that there were cross-cultural parallels in how 'art' was understood.

We can also tell from the words used for dress items that they were understood in ways that are wonderfully animated.[5] There were several words used for brooch in Old Irish, mainly *delg*, meaning thorn. *Duillend*, meaning leaf, was a word used for the blade of a spear, and also for the pin of a brooch. A glossary written in the 10th century shows that different forms of brooch were referred to with loan-words from other languages. There were brooches called *briar*, from Old English *brēr* for bramble, probably again in reference to its thorns; and *cataid*, from a Pictish word describing the action of turning the pin of the brooch to fasten the garment underneath, specific to the penannular brooch. A variation on this, *cartait*, may come from the Old Norse pronunciation of a Pictish word, which is interesting in light of the Hiberno-Norse boom in new penannular brooches and other hybrid objects described below.[6] These examples show that brooches in particular carried with them certain kinds of cultural memory, even when used in different contexts.

Another indication that dress-fasteners had an animated quality to them was the use of beast-heads as terminals (zoomorphic in the jargon of archaeologists). There is a long history of using animal, or animal-like, motifs at the head of a pin [5.2] or the terminals of dress-fasteners like brooches, rings and armlets [5.3]. The beasts are not always recognisable from nature, nor do they always look naturalistic, but features like eyes and snouts can be deduced. These zoomorphic forms began as serpents or dragon-like heads at the end of a long pin, at the ends of spiralled coils, or facing one another across the gap of a penannular brooch.[7] The convention of zoomorphic brooches became implicit in their design over time, regardless of whether a recognisable beast was depicted.[8]

The 9th–12th centuries saw an explosion of evidence for personal dress items in Scotland in comparison to that which came before. Brooches remained largely the province of the elite, but metal pins now came to the fore in great numbers over wide areas. For the first time probably since the end of the Roman period, markets appeared across Scotland, fuelled by the influx of a new, rather foreign concept: money (see chapter 6). More people could adopt the dress of the elite by sporting new metal dress-fasteners, which in turn were produced by the hundreds to meet the demand. The surface of the brooch, which for so long had carried zoomorphic imagery, was ceded to the functional capacity of the thorn; but upon closer inspection, the serpent was still there – only lying in wait.

Fig. 5.4 (right): Antler-comb of Ashby Type 5, Westness, Rousay, Orkney (5), length 182 mm; NMS X.1997.767.

Fig. 5.5 (below): Tweezers formed from a single strip of bronze folded into a trefoil head, with segment of wire-loop surviving in one arm showing it was carried as a toilet set, Brough of Birsay, Orkney, length 57 mm; NMS X.HB 431.

BODY POLITICS

The turn of the millennium saw great changes in the perception of the body itself. As discussed in chapter 2, the Forteviot Arch [2.2] and Custantín's Cross [2.1a] may be the first 'portraits' of a named individual from Scotland, in contrast to the depictions of generic riders, warriors or biblical figures from Pictish sculpture up to this point. The changes in burial practice that emerged in Christian monasteries of the immediate pre-Viking period, but remained very influential in this period, were forms of commemoration that were intended to preserve the integrity of the body after death, including recumbent, body-sized grave-markers and 'head boxes'.[9] These changes reveal a growing concern with the process of bodily transformation in the grave and how it affected the fate of the soul.[10]

In tandem with these processes, we also see a rise in the production of tools for refining personal appearance, in particular antler- and bone-combs. These are prominent finds at pre-Viking sites in Scotland and were supplemented by an influx of new continental and Scandinavian combs from the 9th century onwards.[11] Combs are most often studied as signals of Norse migration and acculturation, but we should not lose sight of what they tell us about bodily appearance and hygiene in this period. We noted previously (pp 36, 37) that Alcuin and contemporary churchmen were particularly concerned with hairstyles and facial hair at the dawn of the first viking raids, and they distinguished 'heathen' from acceptable styles. These anxieties over bodily politics were not new to the Viking Age: just a few years before the first raid on Lindisfarne, a papal legate to Northumbria was appalled at the way some were dressing, including the 'heathen' practice of tattooing, likely adopted from the neighbouring (Christian) Picts.[12]

The changing styles of comb from the classic 'Pictish' forms of high-backed or double-sided types to long single-sided 'composite' ones [5.4] may reveal changing fashions for both men and women. The finds of such combs side-by-side in 9th-century contexts such as Birsay and Buckquoy suggest there was much interchange and inspiration to be gained from increasing contact, not only between insular and Scandinavian worlds, but also wider contacts across the North Sea zone.[13]

There is also some evidence for changing hygienic practices, in the form of tweezers and related toilet items. Rare examples from sites like Birsay [5.5] and Freswick indicate that more attention was being paid to the management of facial hair and grooming generally, and there is evidence for their use and manufacture in Viking-age Dublin.[14] Combs deposited in graves open up a raft of questions relating to how the body was prepared in a funerary context,[15] but also tell us that such practices could be more than 'fashions'. It has been observed, for instance, that all combs used as Viking-age grave-goods in Britain and Ireland were imported Scandinavian types, despite the clear evidence that insular combs were still in use.[16] Just as Alcuin's anxieties reveal, bodily appearance could be heavily political and ritualised. In this respect, the clothes worn on the body reveal landscapes of conflict as much as fashion choices.

Fig. 5.6: Group of objects from a woman's grave at Ballinaby, Isle of Islay; NMS X.IL 137–155.

WEAVING IDENTITY

We have already discussed how the production of textiles was significant enough to be represented in some of the most elaborate female-gendered graves [5.6]. A cluster of needles in the grave of the 'Balnakeil boy' hints at the association of young people in the process as well. Textile production was a domestic necessity, but in an age of trade it could also be a pathway to wealth, as will be discussed later (chapter 6). However, the textiles themselves only rarely survive. In most cases we must rely on proxy evidence for them in the form of the tools used, which, as we have seen, are largely filtered through the lens of the funerary assemblage. That is, we do not have a complete snapshot of the tools available and how they were used, but rather the graves provide a selection of items suitable for creating an ancestral identity for the deceased.

These funerary assemblages already tell us that something had changed by the late 9th century. There were tools never seen before in these islands, like iron weaving swords and heckles for combing flax [3.18]. Archaeological excavations also reveal that the production of flax was accelerated during this period, meaning that linen was increasingly used, a fabric rare in pre-Viking Scotland.[17] In addition to new kinds of dress-fasteners from Scandinavia noted in female graves, it is clear that some people at least were dressing in different ways.

Most of our evidence for clothing is in the form of the dress-fasteners and other accessories which survive relatively well in the ground. Many of these objects are found in place in the grave so that we have a good idea of how they were worn. But unlike weaving tools, we also have a relative abundance of dress-fasteners from outside of graves. These stray finds from metal-detecting activity, alongside finds of dress items in hoards, give us a more rounded view of contemporary fashions. Stray finds may have little archaeological context, but together they can give us an indication of where people adopted such fashions. Finds from hoards give us a different sense of how these objects were valued.

While the discussion below will by necessity focus on the metal pins, brooches and buckles which survive best, in every case we must keep in mind that these objects fastened textiles, fabrics and leather which were the more immediately visible communicators of identity and status. One type of object allows us to visualise both, although only for a small, if significant, group of people in northern and western Scotland.

WOMEN OF A CERTAIN AGE

Our period is defined by widening horizons, with shared items of material culture, language and literature which allow us to describe what has been called a Scandinavian 'diaspora' stretching west from Scandinavia, Britain and Ireland, to Iceland and

Fig. 5.7: Oval brooch from Ballinaby, Isle of Islay, length 112 mm; NMS X.IL 215.

Greenland, and east around the Baltic littoral and into Russia.[18] The striking aspect of this phenomenon is how much of it is communicated specifically through objects used by women.[19] In chapter 3, we noted how the use of certain kinds of grave-goods, especially weapons, could be used not just to 'reflect' the identity of the deceased, but actively to create a new identity for them as ancestral guarantors of land-claims for a settler community without written charters. Dress items were used in the same way, and never more frequently than the oval brooches so typical of the Viking-age female-gendered burial costume [5.7].

Oval brooches have traditionally been used as an index for Norse settlement. It is easy to see why: they are very different to any insular form of dress-fasteners and are instantly recognisable as a Scandinavian type that first appeared in Scotland in the 9th century. Indeed, the first acquisition of unambiguous grave-goods from a Viking-age burial by the Society of Antiquaries of Scotland was a pair of oval brooches from the burial at Castletown, Caithness, in 1787, and more would soon follow.[20] One of the earliest works of archaeological typology produced by the Keeper of the National Museum of Antiquities of Scotland, Joseph Anderson, in 1874, was on 'relics of the Viking Period of the Northmen in Scotland', of which nearly a quarter was devoted to oval brooches.[21] They are icons of the Viking Age – history in a half-shell.

But as often happens with icons, we see them as obvious in some way and forget to think more critically about them. In Scotland, they show that women came over from Norway and perhaps retained a 'Norse' culture by using such objects. We have noted individuals of insular origin (based on biomolecular analysis) amongst those buried in a 'Scandinavian' manner, so we can already question this aspect of identity relating to oval brooches (p. 62). Another important point is that they are always imports from Norway. This type of dress-fastener was being produced in the market town of Ribe, in what is now southern Denmark, early in the 8th century; in fact, it is only types dated from the late 8th century onwards that begin to appear in Norse graves.[22] In other words, they were just another of the myriad influences and ideas picked up from the first forays of Norse merchants into the emporia of the North Sea trade zone. They quickly began to be manufactured across Scandinavia and developed distinct regional types; manufacturing is attested in Birka, Hedeby and Kaupang.[23] From c.850 there is a step-change in production, where one type of oval brooch began to be produced in multiple workshops and became the most common type across Scandinavia.[24] The oval brooch is not some timeless symbol of Norse identity: it was a relatively new fashion, and its social significance was developing at home and abroad at the very same time.

Recent studies of oval brooches add texture to their broad Scandinavian attribution – the majority are found in Norway and Sweden, and seem to have gone out of fashion sooner in Denmark. Among the western settlements, Scotland has the most – 62 compared to 49 in Iceland, 19 in Ireland, and 15 in England.[25] This concentration in Scotland is significant, but there are good explanations for lower numbers elsewhere: Iceland was settled later; England had more input from Denmark where oval brooches were less frequently worn; and in Ireland burials are concentrated in Dublin.[26] The examples from Dublin are mainly of earlier forms and so, whatever their social function was, it seems to have ended sooner there than in the rural settlements of the Scottish north and west. In contrast,

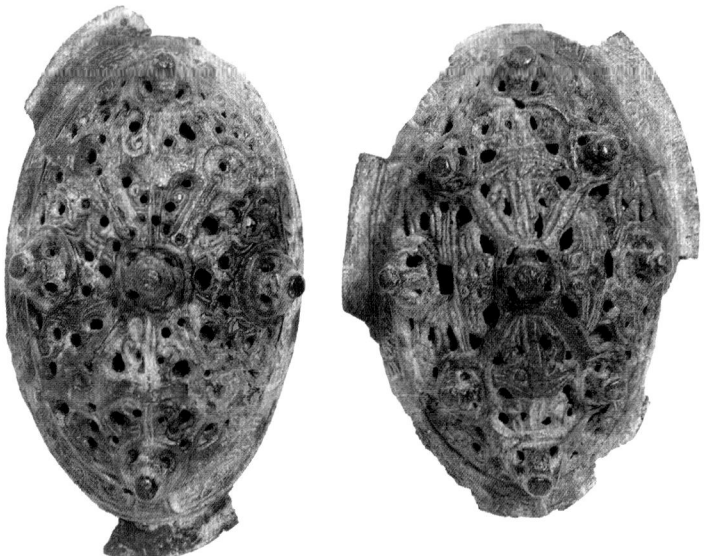

Figs 5.8: Mismatched pair of oval brooches from Langhills, Westerseat, Caithness, length c.80 mm; NMS X.IL 217–218

those from England are generally later, and while oval brooch use was very rare overall (as few as five graves, the rest being stray finds), it appears to be more of a 10th-century phenomenon rather than a sign of 'primary' Viking-age settlement.[27]

Given the evidence discussed in chapter 3 that furnished burials played a specific role in establishing land-claims in a time before written charters, we can see oval brooch burials in a similar light. A strong suggestion from these examples is that the use of oval brooches in funerary costume was determined not only by the biography of the woman in the grave, but the need of a community to mark the foundation of a settlement, or the establishment of a new household. As raids and land-taking became settlement expansion, they need not always refer us to the beginning of the Viking Age, nor to incomers specifically from Scandinavia, but to people of Scandinavian heritage moving across the diaspora.

We can break this down still further for Scotland. The 62 known oval brooches in Scotland come from 28 sites. In Orkney the oval brooches were strongly associated with the cemetery of Pierowall, where they were found in six graves; as many as in the viking market town of Dublin despite the far higher number of graves there overall.[28] Pierowall alone has more than the five from Shetland, three of which are from Unst. As discussed previously (p.62), at the other Orkney cemetery of Westness only one woman was laid to rest with oval brooches. The Broch of Gurness woman wore the only brooch pair from the Orkney mainland, despite a wealth of evidence for furnished graves and Viking-age settlement. The remaining sites correlate broadly to the regions of known Scandinavian settlement, but not its intensity; there is a scatter across the Hebrides, with none on Colonsay despite a concentration of furnished graves, and four on Islay where there is little other evidence of Viking-age structures. The use of oval brooches must be seen as specific to an as yet uncertain set of variables and not a simple index of settlement.

It is notable that some are mismatched pairs [5.8], which indicate that it was not always possible to obtain or to replace them. There is also considerable evidence for use-wear and for repair, suggesting they were kept for a long time before being deposited in the grave – so they cannot be used straightforwardly to date the arrival of a migrant.[29] This also shows that they were treated as valuable heirlooms: they need not only have retained a 'memory' of a distant homeland, as much as the tales told of the fateful migration event itself that loom large in any family with immigrant roots. These must also be joined with the emotional weight of an object, passed from mother to daughter or daughter-in-law, and perhaps worn by multiple generations, alongside that family's claims to landed status in these multifaceted funerary events.

And here is where we can see the social role these jewellery items performed. It has been noted that the overt references to female anatomy evoked by the pair of oval brooches is a sign of their role in projecting (and protecting) a woman's fertility, and that they may have been worn by women of specifically married status.[30] We must remember that gender as a socially constructed phenomenon is strongly tied to both age and status, and the projection of attributes of 'womanhood' is associated with specific points in the lifecycle. It has been noted that the most elaborately gendered funerary assemblages for women in Scotland were for women of child-bearing age; and therefore the use of oval brooches, with their fertility symbolism, was most

Figs 5.9: Oval brooches from a boat grave at Carn a' Bharraich, Oronsay, showing mineralised textile adhering to the pin, length 90mm; NMS X.IL 329–330.

appropriate for women of specific ages, in addition to marital status and social standing.[31]

It is likely that some oval brooches were handed down through the female line, perhaps as bridal gifts even to women not of Scandinavian descent. This would help explain why they tend to be found with woman of child-bearing age: women who had received them from the generation before, but had died perhaps before they could pass them on. If so, then they do speak to the movement and mobility of Scandinavian traditions of inheritance and gender-roles, but will only in some cases point to first-generation migrants, or to women of Scandinavian origin. They evoked powerful memories, but their use over long periods of time means we cannot assume these were always memories of a Scandinavian homeland. If they were also in some way amuletic or protective during the period of child-rearing, this would only have added to their emotive effect, but not in the way we usually think. As objects worn by women of a certain age and status in life, they also evoked memories made in these islands as well.

The other fascinating thing about these brooches is that their placement on the body means we can reconstruct the form of dress they were used to fasten. The paired oval brooch was designed to link the straps of a pinafore-like dress which would have slipped over a full-length tunic or shift. Their pins pierced the fabric of the dress, resting on the undergarment as well as any shawl or cloak worn over the shoulders. As such, they were in contact with all three layers of clothing and, as the body decomposed, a microenvironment can form in which the corroding metal allowed for the mineralisation and preservation of these textiles. In the right conditions, oval brooches preserve fragments of organic material which would otherwise have been lost entirely [5.9]. In one case in Hyrt, Hordaland, textiles remained on both the inner and outer sides of the brooch, allowing for the identification of a blue-dyed inner linen garment, a dark blue-green layer presumably indicating the strap-dress, and a finely woven diamond twill wool of dark blue covering the oval brooches entirely.[32] Recent analysis of a woman's grave in Ketilsstaðir, Iceland, found as many as five different textiles used, including an undergarment of linen (white if undyed), which must have been imported into Iceland as flax was not grown there. The dress over this was of various kinds of wool sourced locally, the main body being dyed blue with strips of recycled or applied bands of different weaves. Blue was the colour of choice for women, at least in funerary costumes, as attested widely in surviving textiles from graves.[33] Textiles like these have survived less well in Scotland, but an intriguing example comes from the woman's grave from Cnip, Lewis. Attached to the oval brooches were traces of as many as four different fabrics, and loose fragments of linen and possibly silk were found. At least one of the brooches was also covered with fabric, again suggesting that these inner garments were often obscured by an outer cloak or shroud.[34]

As such, oval brooches did not operate in a vacuum, and much more work is still needed on the textiles they fastened to see what they can tell us about clothing in the Scottish experience of the Viking Age. But there is something we can say with more certainty. What is striking about the female burial costume, in Scotland and Norway alike, is how frequently the oval brooch was combined with an insular dress-fastener – whether a belt, ringed pin, or both. That includes all instances at Pierowall, which shows that the female burial costume had been 'hybridised' already by the time it became visible here. Just as brooch burial must have changed its meaning from the 8th–10th centuries, it would certainly have been adapted to local circumstances in different ways.

The pins most likely wrapped the body in a cloak or even a shroud – in either scenario the oval brooches were no longer visible on the cadaver, so we may have over-emphasised their distinctiveness in an archaeological context, at the expense of understanding the intimacy of these objects to the women who used them and handed them down. The appearance in Scotland of both early and late variants of oval brooch clearly reveals continued contact with Scandinavian fashions after the initial period of settlement. It is as important as ever to emphasise that the passengers of the sailing vessels we imagine when we think of the Viking Age included women and children as well as armed men. And finally, if their links to fertility and marital status were the crucial factors, then we must add another twist – oval brooches are not symbolic of all women, but specifically of mothers and mothers-to-be. In other words, oval brooches moved through the diaspora not as a token of generic 'viking' identity, but in ways specific to the experience of motherhood in a Viking-age context.

THE THORN

In a time before zips, buttons and multiple sizes off-the-peg, dress-fasteners were essential. A simple bone-peg or toggle can hold cloth together, but in the European Iron Age pins became increasingly elaborate and decorative and, with the impetus of the Roman world, the brooch, a more decorative and elaborate pin-based fastener, grew in popularity. By the late Roman and early medieval periods, brooches of various styles began to be used not just as functional objects, but as badges of status and affiliation.[35] As so often happens throughout history, mundane and everyday items sometimes get singled out as having deeper, ritualised significance.

In northern and western Britain and Ireland, a distinctive type of dress-fastener called the penannular brooch had become an expression of power by the early medieval period.[36] These horseshoe-shaped hoops have a sliding-pin attached, and with the pin inserted through layers of cloth and out again one of the terminals can be slid under the emerging point of the pin, bracing the fabric in place. These brooches have a long history that extends back to the Roman period, and their continued use and development here for centuries thereafter gives them a fascinating pedigree which we cannot spend more time on here.[37] By the 7th and 8th centuries, brooches were being made in well-guarded forts and crannogs, and given as gifts which tied giver and receiver together.[38] They entered into early Irish law codes as ways of measuring status, where the weight of silver and gold, or the colour and style of brooch used, were governed by a strict honour code.[39] They were more than a fashion choice – wearing a certain kind of brooch was a declaration of certain rights and privileges. If it was handed down or gifted on to another recipient, these social ties were remembered and communicated, adding to the 'biography' of the object.[40]

In addition to interpersonal relationships, these heavily regulated objects in turn tell us about the places where such laws and honour codes applied. Their form does not simplistically dictate an ethnic identity, but as they moved through the world on the body or as gifts they created both communal and individual identities. They were alive with power and agency.

The symbolic capacity of penannular brooches was massive for such small objects. Images of them can be found rendered in stone in Pictish and Irish sculpture of the time, worn by lords, clerics, saints, even by Jesus Christ and the Virgin Mary.[41] But symbolic versions of penannular brooches circulated in other

ways. In Ireland and western Scotland, what has been defined by modern scholars as a 'pseudo-penannular' brooch became fashionable in the 8th century. The clue is in the name – these look like penannular brooches but the terminals had expanded to the point where there was no gap between them, rendering them virtually non-functional, or at least not as penannular brooches. In some cases, such as the Tara Brooch, they require a secondary chain or other fastener to work.[42] Some, like the Breadalbane Brooch, have been modified back to a penannular form and may have been reversible, to allow the wearer to communicate different messages about their identity depending on where they found themselves.[43] Some examples, like the Hunterston Brooch [5.10], became very large indeed, as if to make more use of the space for intricate ornament, and perhaps to be seen by a larger audience. These prestige brooches were so cumbersome they may only rarely have been worn and instead were meant to be displayed, gifted or handled some other way: the object used as a token or symbol in itself.[44] Given their lavish use of gold, amber and a mastery of fine metalworking craftsmanship, they were likely used by royalty or by high-ranking clergy, but fundamentally as symbolic, as much a badge of office as a fastener. Even though these developments occurred before the start of the Viking Age, the concept of the prestige display brooch would continue to be significant in the centuries to come. We know these items were still in circulation into the Viking Age because the Hunterston Brooch had Norse runes incised on its reverse in the 10th century (pp145–6).

The most common types of penannular brooches in Scotland can be seen in the St Ninian's Isle Hoard, which included twelve examples deposited in a Shetland chapel early in the 9th century (chapter 4). Eleven of them are roughly the same size and shape, but with variations in the form of the terminals. Most have circular terminals with three or four projecting lobes, but others have expanded triangular and square-shaped terminals, with one distinctive type terminating in beast-heads facing one another across the gap. The use of gold and silver on these brooches indicates they were also used for display, but considerable evidence for wear shows this display was in the context of use as dress-fasteners. This may explain why so many of them outside hoards have come down to us in a fragmented or broken state.

In addition to these, a much larger 'panelled brooch' from St Ninian's Isle has expanded triangular terminals, with deeply

Fig. 5.10 (left): Hunterston Brooch, Ayrshire, diameter 122mm; NMS X.FC 8.

Fig. 5.11 (right): Detail of the terminals of a penannular brooch from the St Ninian's Isle Hoard, Shetland, showing animal heads facing towards a central setting; NMS FC 284.

Fig. 5.12: Terminals of a penannular brooch from the hoard from Rogart, Sutherland, showing bird heads facing towards a central setting: NMS X.FC 2.

recessed compartments which contain beds of chip-carved interlace. It is a purposefully exaggerated version of the others and may even have been a 'display' brooch, used for ceremonial occasions as suggested for the Hunterston Brooch. Regardless, it shares enough design features with the smaller silver brooches to suggest it belongs to the same workshop. In particular, a close look at its terminals shows the central gem-setting, now empty, was surrounded by four bird-like creatures, each of which faces inwards toward the inset. This motif appears explicitly on three other brooches from the hoard and may be implicit from the position of bosses on several others [5.11].[45] In one case, the inward-facing birds in the terminals are joined by birds facing towards a gem in the cartouche at the apex of the hoop; in another, the hoop ends in profile bird heads seemingly pecking at the central glass-setting, while three duck-like heads face outwards, away from the setting, as if guarding it.[46]

The motif of creatures 'drinking' is also found on a silver spoon from the same hoard, but is rendered in its most accomplished form in other penannular brooches from across the country. The filigree-decorated brooch from Clunie, Perthshire, of a similar size to the St Ninian's Isle brooches but more elaborate in its ornamentation, has three duck-like heads pointing in towards central settings of red glass in each terminal [4.17]. The largest brooch from the hoard from Rogart, Sutherland, uses separately cast bird heads modelled in the round, four on each terminal and two in the cartouche of the hoop [5.12]. The bird heads again seem to 'drink' from the central settings of red glass, but they are themselves larger and more prominent than the setting itself. A mould for casting just such a bird head was discovered on the Brough of Birsay, Orkney, so we know at least one place where these could have been made, even if the brooch moulds that survive from Birsay were in general smaller and simpler than the ones being discussed here.[47] The Rogart Brooch is also cast in a design reminiscent of the largest panelled brooch from St Ninian's Isle, with chip-carved gilt beds of interlace in deep recessed compartments. It may be that these belonged to the highest echelons of Pictish aristocracy, or perhaps clergy given their potential Christian symbolism.[48] It is interesting that all these surviving examples may have come from hoards (pp 83–5). Possibly by the time of their deposition, they had shifted in value from gifts with the potential for building further social relationships to a simpler form of transferable wealth.[49] Perhaps the social function they once served had been made obsolete in the time or place they were deposited. Much depends on when that occurred, and by whose hands.

As we have seen, the hoards containing these brooches are difficult to date and have been discussed as a Pictish phenomenon.[50] It is striking then that the brooches in these hoards are similar to the kinds of insular penannular brooches that were deposited in Viking-age graves: in Scotland these include examples from Westness; Machrins, Colonsay [5.13]; and Carronbridge, Dumfriesshire.[51] The Westness and Machrins examples are copper-alloy brooches from well-known cemeteries; Carronbridge is a silver brooch from what appears to be a

Fig. 5.13 (above): Bronze penannular brooch from a grave at Machrins, Colonsay, diameter 54 mm; NMS X.FC 189.

Fig. 5.14 (below): Pseudo-penannular brooch of gilt copper-alloy with glass-settings, with connecting-bar removed and pin replaced with 'Pictish' fold-over type, from Pierowall, Westray, Orkney, diameter 76 mm; NMS X.IL 198.

single, isolated grave. Of these, the expanded triangular terminals of Westness, Rousay, are a common type; while those from Machrins and from Carronbridge have clear parallels to the St Ninian's Isle and related series.[52]

In addition to these, a series of related insular brooches found in Viking-age Scotland are worth a mention here.[53] The brooches from Pierowall [5.14] and Westness [3.20] are two of the most elaborate from Scotland, and were used in a context of ostentatious, competitive display in large cemeteries.

The Viking-age use of insular brooches in Scotland is indicative of a much wider phenomenon. A recent study identified 16 complete or fragmented insular brooches in Viking-age graves in Norway.[54] Of these, 15 were from female-gendered graves, unlike their more ambiguous gendered function in an insular context (see opposite page). All but two of the Norwegian examples were deposited intact, like the Scottish examples. That so few were hacked and repurposed show they were valued as functional objects and not for their often negligible weight in precious metal or their constituent parts. Notably, they cluster in western Norway, mainly Rogaland and Sogn og Fjordane, areas with the majority of early Viking-age insular finds and thus closely linked to the earliest raids of Britain and Ireland.[55] These patterns reveal the immediate effect, and perhaps some of the cause, of those earliest forays abroad.[56]

Fig. 5.15: Bronze trefoil brooch from a woman's grave at Clibberswick, Unst, Shetland, length 40mm; NMS X.IL 224.

THE GENDER OF THE BROOCH

Given the way they were depicted in stone sculpture, it seems that both men and women wore penannular brooches in pre-Viking insular contexts. This contrasts with the social function of jewellery in Scandinavian contexts, where dress items used in funerary contexts were strongly gendered. Exceptions are insular brooches and brooch-pins, which in Norway were first introduced as imports in the 9th century, soon spawning local imitations. These early imports are almost exclusively found in female-gendered grave assemblages. This contrasts with their use in Scotland itself, where insular brooches and brooch-pins are found in both male and female Viking-age furnished graves, perhaps more similar to the way they were used in an insular context.

But once imitation penannular brooches and brooch-pins began to be made in Norway, they were now to be found in both male and female graves, while certain types in the 10th century were almost exclusively used in male graves.[57] Thus the use of the insular-derived brooch-type seemed to 'swap' its gendered attribution when its provenance changed from exotic import to badge of status in a local context. In effect, the insular brooch brought along with it notions of authority and power, effecting social change in Scandinavia.[58]

Another instance of such gender-swapping objects comes in the form of trefoil brooches. These objects were originally inspired by the distinctive trefoil mounts on Carolingian sword belts, as depicted in 9th-century gospel books.[59] They were one of many exotic styles adopted as dress items in the Viking Age, with evidence for the manufacture of trefoil-shaped brooches in the market town of Hedeby. For a shortlived moment, they remained 'masculine', appearing in a small number of male-gendered graves, but they quickly and permanently became one of the most typical female 'third brooch' dress-fasteners in Norway and Denmark from the late 9th into the 10th century.[60]

Despite their popularity in Scandinavia, in an insular context they appear to have been more strongly associated with southern fashions, appearing in numbers in England, but in only two cases in Scotland, from Pierowall and Clibberswick [5.15], Unst, Shetland.[61] Only the latter survives, one of the clearest instances of 'Borre-style' ornament in Scotland, from a woman's funerary costume along with a pair of oval brooches. These objects are a reminder that even traditionally 'Norse' concepts of dress and gender were evolving even as they were used across the diaspora.

THE SERPENT AND THORN

Fig. 5.16: Silver penannular brooch from St Ninian's Isle, Shetland, diameter 75 mm; NMS X.FC 286.

A number of insular brooches in Norway may have come from Pictland. A silver brooch from a possible female grave in Hålen, Sogndal, bears the outward-facing animal heads seen in a brooch from St Ninian's Isle [5.16]. The motif on Hålen is almost identical to a lost brooch from Banchory Ternan, Aberdeenshire, where the interstices between the bird heads form a neat cross made of fine interlace.[62] This type of brooch is also found far outside of Scotland, from Viking-age York to Ireland, and another example from a male grave in Norway.[63] It tells us that brooches of the kind stashed away in St Ninian's Isle are an important glimpse into the sorts of objects more widely available, and crucially still in circulation at least as late as the occupation of York in the late 9th century.

There are interesting differences in the way that insular brooches were used in Scottish Viking-age graves and elsewhere. In Norway and Ireland they tend to be ornate silver-gilt brooches, whereas in Scotland they are more often copper-alloy. An example from Kilmainham, Dublin, is a deluxe version of those found in silver and copper-alloy at St Ninian's Isle and Machrins. Along with the ornate silver-gilt brooch-pin from Westness,[64] this shows that some of the finest examples were taken out of circulation, often far from home, for use in Viking-age funerary display.

At the other end of the scale, the copper-alloy brooches tend to be smaller than their Scottish counterparts. It is precisely these smaller, base-metal types that were being produced at the Brough of Birsay, according to the clay moulds and one extant example.[65] These small, copper-alloy brooches were less likely than the elaborate silver examples to have been kept for long periods of time as heirlooms. It raises the possibility that the 'Pictish' workshop extended into the Viking Age, and was producing brooches fashionable among both Picts and Norse.

Some of the finest insular penannular brooches come from hoards, including some notable finds from Ireland. One with very little known provenance is the 'Dalriada' or Loughan, Co. Derry, brooch, the only penannular brooch made of solid gold.[66] The almost calligraphic 'beasts' on the reverse can be linked with those on the reverse of a complete gilt copper-alloy penannular brooch from Børøyna, Rogaland [5.17].[67] Both were at least made under 'heavy Pictish influence', with clear parallels to the stippled zoomorphic ornament on the St Ninian's Isle silver bowls and the Monymusk Reliquary.[68] Insular brooches are almost always called 'Irish' in the catalogues of Scandinavian museums, but we should allow for more input from Pictish workshops.

It is rather a fool's errand to try to pinpoint where such items were made as they were clearly highly mobile – as were the craftworkers behind them – and their design was purposefully 'insular' in the sense of art styles shared among northern Britain, Ireland and Wales. Yet there is some sense that brooches were worn differently as they moved through different regions. For example, the Pierowall brooch shares several design features with the Børøyna brooch; but it originally included a connecting-bar across the terminals to render it pseudo-penannular.[69]

Fig. 5.17 (left): Gilt copper-alloy panelled penannular brooch from a grave in Børøyna, Rogaland, diameter 94mm. (© Terje Tveit – Museum of Archaeology, University of Stavanger)

Fig. 5.18 (below): Gilt copper-alloy pseudo-penannular brooch modified by removing the connecting-bar to make it penannular, Isle of Mull, diameter 114mm; NMS X.FC 5.

them valuable.[72] They retained this power well into the Viking Age, as we will see further below, when brooches grew to ludicrous sizes of silver hoop in a context of competitive display in the 10th century.

MICROCOSMS

The symbolic capacity of the brooch-hoop was considerable. While brooches like Hunterston [5.10] were blown up to display more intricate ornament, others were being miniaturised [5.20], a different kind of artistic achievement. Some brooches were effectively just pins with brooch-shaped heads, where the hoop did little if anything to actually fasten the fabric and instead could be given over to decorative treatment. As often as not, this ornament was in the shape of a miniaturised brooch of recognisable type. Such 'brooch-pins' are often found in Ireland, strongly associated with crannogs, artificial lake settlements that were the seats of power and display at the start of the Viking Age.[73] At Ervey, Co. Meath, a silver penannular brooch with circular terminals was found near a brooch-pin of the same shape, but in miniature.[74] As so many are stray finds, brooch-pins are difficult to date, but they were certainly still in circulation by the time of the Viking Age, as illustrated by examples from graves.[75]

The Westness Brooch, the discovery of which in 1963 precipitated the excavation of a major Viking-age cemetery (see chapter 3), is perhaps the finest extant example of the type [3.20]. It has been described as a miniaturised version of the Hunterston/Tara type of pseudo-penannular brooch, and must have been made in the same craft tradition, if not the same workshop.[76] For the class of people entitled to wear brooches of silver, gold and amber, the intricacy of their brooches required ever more elaborate and likely ritualised processes of attachment: the Tara Brooch (Bettystown, Co. Meath) was uniquely

The bar was at some point filed off, changing it into a penannular brooch before it was deposited in a grave at Pierowall. This modification of pseudo-penannulars to make them more amenable to fashions in northern and western Britain can be observed in a number of Scottish finds, including the Breadalbane Brooch and the Mull Brooch [5.18] – neither, sadly, with precise provenance.[70] It shows the frequency with which these brooches moved around, with their mobility accelerated still further once they became desired objects in the Viking Age.

As such, the insular brooch, whether made of base-metal or covered in gold and amber, was a symbol that was loaded with meaning and social (if not literal) currency beyond its material worth. The chip-carving, settings and intricate ornamentation add to the visual splendour of what in St Ninian's Isle were of lower quality metal (sometimes less than 50% silver).[71] It was the social relations these brooches embodied that made

THE SERPENT AND THORN

Fig. 5.19: Damaged head of a copper-alloy brooch-pin with two missing insets, from a boat grave at Carn a' Bharraich, Oronsay, diameter 44.5 mm; NMS X.FC 185.

fitted with a knitted silver chain rather than a cord. Brooch-pins were often fitted with loops extending from the head to allow a cord to be tied to the pin, helping to fasten them. On the Westness Brooch, a snarling wolf-head protruding from the head acted as an attachment loop [5.3]. One must imagine this was a rather cumbersome form of dress-fastener, but then so was the Hunterston Brooch. As small as they were, their surfaces were used for complex Christological iconography, revealing to us that they were meant for close-up interaction by knowledgeable actors, perhaps high-ranking clergy as much as aristocracy.[77] They were microcosms of the concept of the brooch, a symbol cultivated for centuries as the emblem of power and authority.

Brooch-pins come in many forms, from gilt-silver at one end of the spectrum to simple cast bronze at the other. While most were likely made in base-metal, they visually cite more elaborate brooches and those 'copies' retained a version of their power. The brooch-pin is in truth a slippery category containing hinged brooches like the Westness Brooch as well as simpler ones like the brass pin worn by a male in Westness grave 2 [5.20 (centre), 3.3].[78] Its style is of two beast-heads forming terminals of the hoop, joined together by a panel of interlace, with a precise parallel from the 9th- to 10th-century material from the River Blackwater in Northern Ireland.[79] The animal head that projects from the hoop is not perforated and could not be used for the attachment of a cord, similar to the corresponding wolf-head of the Westness Brooch. In effect, this brooch contains references not only to the kinds of beast-head terminals of brooches used in northern Scotland (to be discussed below), it also appears to reference the form of more elaborate brooch-pins than itself. It is a copy of a copy. As the example from Westness was deposited in one of the most elaborate male burials on this site, we should not dismiss it as any less meaningful for being a facsimile. Another example found on Vallay, North Uist, has a plain head with non-functional spur in the same place as the Westness wolf-head [5.20 (far right)].[80] In effect, this type of brooch-pin references not only penannular brooches, but also other brooch-pins. These pins operated on many levels beyond dress-fasteners.

This in turn means we should not dismiss the Westness Brooch from the 1963 woman's grave as mere 'loot'. Given the insular origin of at least some of the men and women of this cemetery (chapter 3), we must allow the possibility that the display of this brooch was understood as affording a specific authority or status. It is equally possible that the Westness woman or her family held that brooch as a token of their status. Its deposition as part of her funerary costume could then be seen as a powerful statement of their rights and privileges as insular aristocracy, as much as the Scandinavian oval brooches and her elaborate grave offerings signalled their privileged position in 'Norse' circles.

The Westness Brooch stands at the head of a series of brooch-pins of silver, amber and other fine ornament. The only close parallel from Scotland is a silver brooch-pin with amber insets from Dunipace in Falkirk [5.21].[81] In chapter 4 (pp 91–2), this was floated as possibly relating to the movement of a

branch of the Great Army through the area in the late 9th century. It shares design features with other brooch-pins from Ireland, with the void enclosed by the hoop filled with gem-settings, a feature specific to brooch-pins which never occurs in full-size brooches.[82] The only other parallel of this type from Scotland has no clear provenance, but was purchased in Glasgow, making it possibly another find from the central belt like Dunipace [5.22]. A provenance from Glasgow itself would not be so unlikely, given the Great Army-assisted siege of Dumbarton Rock in 870 and subsequent transformation of Govan in

Fig. 5.20 (left): Selection of brooch-pins: (top row, from left), 'purchased in Glasgow', NMS X.FC 11; Ireland, NMS X.FD 4; (bottom row, from left) Ireland, NMS X.FD 6 and 5; Westness, Rousay, Orkney (2), length 118.6 mm, NMS X.1997.1028; Balnakeil, Durness, Sutherland, NMS X.1992.22.6; and Cul na Muice, Vallay, North Uist, NMS Q.L.1961.16.

Fig. 5.21 (right, above): Brooch-pin of gilt-silver, set with amber, found near Dunipace, Stirlingshire, length 113 mm; NMS X.FC 10.

Fig. 5.22 (right, below): Detail of brooch-pin of copper-alloy from the Bell Collection, 'purchased in Glasgow'; NMS X.FC 11.

THE SERPENT AND THORN

Glasgow into a royal mausoleum.[83] This brooch-pin is not in silver like Westness and Dunipace, but its expanded triangular terminals, semi-circular setting at the top of the hoop, and animal-like creatures protruding from the outer ring of the hoop, again recall miniature pseudo-penannular heads like the Westness Brooch. We will return to the Strathclyde area in chapter 6 to explore the aftermath of 870.

The brooch-pin is quite a rare form of dress-fastener in Scotland, but overlaps with a much larger class of ringed pins. Even more than the oval brooch, the ringed pin became the calling card of the Viking Age in Ireland and Scotland [5.23]. Like the brooch-pin they originated in Ireland long before the 9th century. The type consists of a long pin with a freely swivelling ring attached at one end. The pin would pierce the fabric and a cord tied to the ring would be wound around the shaft of the pin to help secure it.[84] The ring was usually undecorated, but rare forms such as the knobbed ringed pin fall somewhere between the ringed pin and brooch-pin classifications [5.24, 5.25]. Early forms appear in crannog sites in Ireland, but it was in Viking-age Dublin where production went into overdrive. The manufacturing techniques used seem to be fully within the Irish mainstream, and it is argued that Irish metalworkers were brought to the newly founded trading settlement to supply the relatively cheap form of dress item. In effect, the Dublin vikings adopted a local form of dress almost immediately.

In a major study, 263 ringed pins were identified in Dublin alone, a third of all known examples in Europe, including 60 from Scotland.[85] More recent work suggests there are as many as three times those now known from Dublin and, at the time of writing, in Scotland there are now up to 128 of these pins.[86] Recent finds have tended to cluster in eastern and southern Scotland, outside the areas of Scandinavian settlement, which partly reflects the bias of metal-detecting activity, but also suggests a heretofore unsuspected eastern fashion in line with trends in Ireland.[87]

It was also very quickly adopted into Scandinavian forms of dress. These pins are relatively cheap and easy to produce in large numbers, so their presence in graves cannot be explained straightforwardly as 'loot' or as ostentatious display. They do not carry the same visual citations of brooches as the brooch-pins. The early loop-headed types often carry no ornament, and even the more decorated polyhedral-headed [5.26] types so commonly found in Dublin, and kidney-ringed types [8.21], would need to have been seen up close. As such, their presence is mainly indicative of the textile items they would have fastened. Essentially, with brooch-pins and penannular brooches of insular type, they are the archaeological remnant of the cloak and evidence for the adoption of insular forms of outerwear as much as objects of desire in themselves.[88]

The best example of how they came to be incorporated into 'viking' fashions is from the cemetery of Pierowall, already mentioned several times above for its notable mix of dress items. All six graves which had oval brooches paired them with a metal pin, presumably to fasten an outer cloak, and in five of these cases it was specifically reported as a ringed pin.[89] In fact, about a third of all finds of oval brooches in Scotland were used with ringed pins, brooch-pins or related insular fasteners.[90] This forces us to rethink what we know about the 'viking' style of dress altogether, as insular items quickly seem to have taken over the position of the outer 'third brooch'.[91]

Interestingly, the use of ringed pins in Viking-age graves is more frequent in Scotland than in Ireland, where the pins were likely being made.[92] This is partly to do with the overall longer-lived habit for dressed burial here. But given the high numbers of ringed pins now known from Scotland, and no longer confined to the northern and western isles, there is a case to be made for the ringed pin as being more important in the Scottish experience of the Viking Age – a possibility we will return to below.

Fig. 5.23: Selection of loop-headed ringed pins from Scotland; National Museums Scotland.

Fig. 5.24: Rare form of knobbed ringed pin, Roslin, Midlothian, length 150mm; NMS X.2014.7.

Fig. 5.25: Knobbed ringed pin from a boat grave at Carn a' Bharraich, Oronsay, length 135mm; NMS X.IL 331.

Fig. 5.26: Selection of polyhedral-headed ringed pins, Scotland, 10th century; National Museums Scotland.

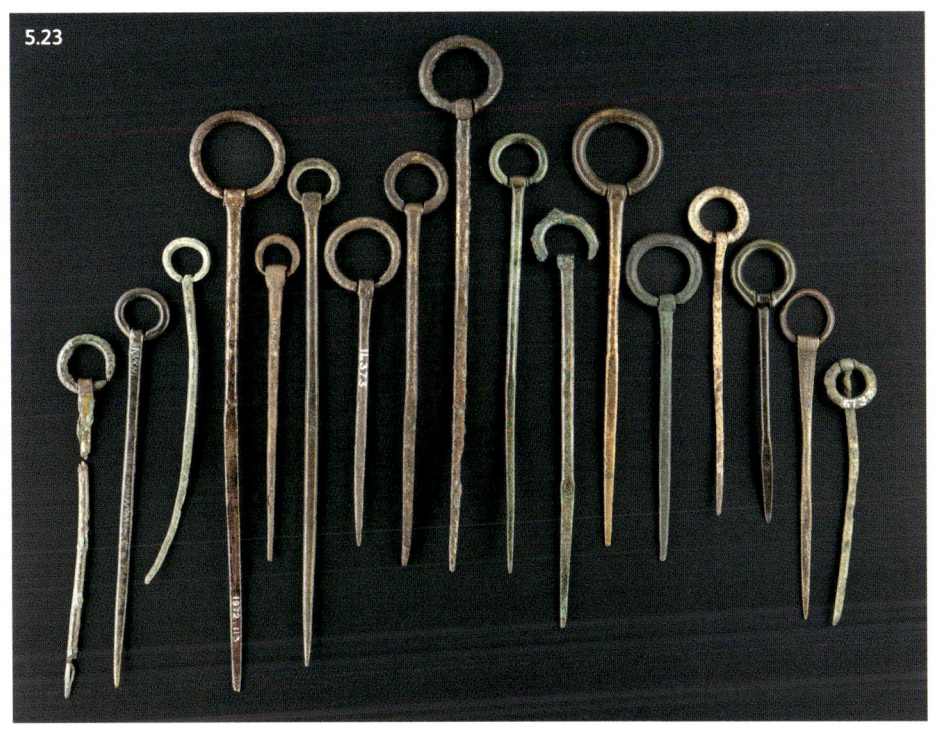

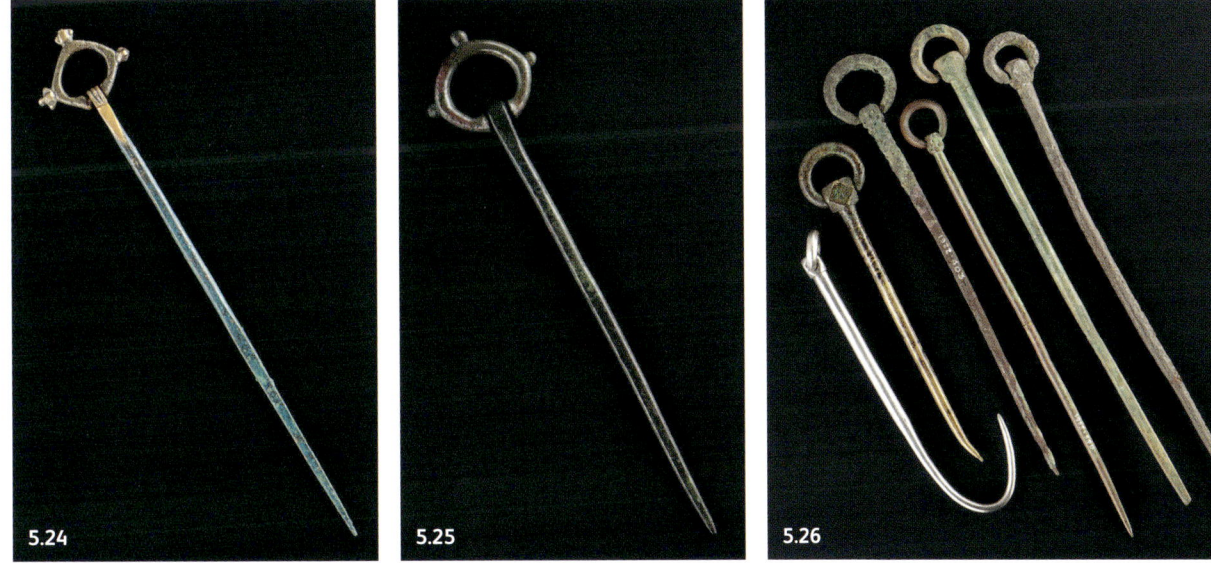

THE SERPENT AND THORN

Fig. 5.27 (above): Bronze stud decorated with yellow enamel, length 13 mm, Freswick, Caithness; NMS X.FC 256.

Fig. 5.28 (below): Copper-alloy buckle, length 117 mm, NMS X.IL 853, with matching strap-end, length 93 mm, NMS X.IL 854.1, and ringed pin, length 122 mm, NMS X.IL 852, from a woman's grave, Cnip, Lewis.

EQUESTRIAN FASHION: BELTS FOR HORSES AND HUMANS

An interesting side-effect of having furnished graves is that they provide us with a glimpse into kinds of objects which only show up rarely in settlement contexts. Before dressed burials appear in Scotland, our knowledge of dress styles comes mainly from the portrayals of human figures on Pictish cross-slabs and related Christian monuments.[93] These tell us that clerics and kings wore decorated leather shoes, full-length robes with hoods for clerics and belted tunics for men. Yet before the furnished burial tradition, we have almost no evidence for the use of belts in Scotland. It is only from the mid-9th century that belts become visible to us, but even then they are mainly through examples of equestrian rather than human fashion.

In the 9th century we get complete horse-harness sets from burials across the insular and Scandinavian worlds, some still worn by the horse. Horse-gear has been found in graves of both men and women. In Scotland, the most complete set comes from Kiloran Bay, Colonsay, in which decorated mounts and strap-fittings were in the central chamber of a boat grave along with iron weapons and other furnishings.[94] They were not in this case worn by the horse, the skeleton of which was found in the prow or stern of the boat, outside the stone-lined chamber.

In other graves the horse was buried 'dressed' as well. The woman from Rogaland known as the 'Gausel Queen' was buried bedecked in a wealth of insular and Scandinavian objects. At her feet was the head of a horse, still bearing its spectacular gilt-bronze harness-fittings. This is a recurring pattern in male and female graves in Scandinavia, including the now famous Birka warrior woman.[95] In the case of Gausel, the ornaments are certainly of insular make, and possibly Pictish, bearing Christian imagery.[96] In more than half of all cases, a single piece of a harness-fitting was reused and modified into a brooch, similar

CRUCIBLE OF NATIONS

120

to the way reliquaries were fragmented and repurposed (chapter 7) [5.27].[97] There are good reasons to believe that such ornate fittings were not just for display, but afforded supernatural protection for the animal and, by extension, its rider.[98] The possibility some of these bridle-fittings, including the set from Kiloran Bay, were made in ecclesiastical workshops, and were perhaps used by high-ranking clergy, may help us understand why they were prized even as modified objects.[99] Related buckles, such as one from a male-gendered grave at Kildonnan, Isle of Eigg, have hollow cavities that may even have held relics inspired by the belt-shrines and carrying straps of insular reliquaries.[100] It is likely the objects were ascribed, or retained – a kind of amuletic quality in a pagan context.

This brings us back to the belts. Belt-buckles and ornamented strap-fittings are almost all found in Viking-age graves in Scotland. Most of them are of insular make and often, like the horse-fittings, bear cruciform motifs. One particular type of belt-fitting consists of a strip of bronze sheet folded over a strap of leather and secured in place with a row of domed rivets. These have been likened to horse-tack belts, and examples from a male grave from Auldhame, East Lothian [3.25], and a female grave from Cnip, Lewis [5.28], may be derived from earlier horse-harness mounts – human fashion imitating horse fashion.[101] The Cnip female wore a similar belt-set in combination with oval brooches, a beaded necklace and a ringed pin, in a revealing merger of insular and Scandinavian dress that primarily occurs in the zone of Hiberno-Norse settlement.[102]

RETURN OF THE SERPENT

Complete insular metal dress-fasteners are an important but numerically quite small proportion of surviving Viking-age accessories. But they must have had an impact because, before long, variants of these dress items began to be made in Scandinavia. Indeed, penannular brooches, brooch-pins and ringed pins put together are second only to oval brooches for the most common dress items in Scandinavian Viking-age grave-goods.[103] The ringed-pin, of imported or Scandinavian variant type, became so ubiquitous that one example even made it to the North American site of L'Anse-aux-Meadows in Newfoundland.[104]

Before the start of the Viking Age there was no tradition of using annular or penannular brooches in Norway. By the 10th century, a few different variants had appeared. Some of the earliest were simple copies of insular dress-fasteners. Three such objects – a ringed pin, brooch-pin and penannular brooch – were found in the boat-grave cemetery at Gulli, Vestfold. These could easily be mistaken for common types seen in Scotland and Ireland, but all seem to have been made locally: the ringed pin is of 'Vestfold-type', a local variation on the Irish ringed pin; the brooch-pin is similar to one from Carn a' Bharraich, Oronsay [5.19]; and the penannular brooch has lobed terminals of St Ninian's Isle type.[105] The first two came from female-gendered chamber graves of the late 9th century; the penannular brooch from a male-gendered boat grave.

The Scandinavian 'imitations' soon became variants suited to local tastes.[106] There are examples of insular-looking penannular brooches with expanded triangular terminals, but bearing Scandinavian 'Borre-style' art. In eastern Scandinavia, there are virtually no insular pins, but elaborate Baltic-inspired brooches and brooch-pins are used. As far as they had developed, the insular ancestry of the latter can be seen clearly as echoes of earlier design features, including spectacle-like circular terminals, and an animal-head boss protruding below.[107]

Fig. 5.29 (right): Silver penannular brooch with beast-head terminals, St Ninian's Isle, Shetland, diameter 71mm; NMS X.FC 295.

Fig. 5.30 (below): Damaged penannular brooch of copper-alloy and traces of silvering, with beast-head terminals, Freswick Links, Caithness, diameter 51mm; NMS X.IL 559.

The penannular brooch form in particular was highly influential in the Viking Age. The production of brooches at this time went from a highly exclusive royal prerogative in the pre-Viking era to a broad array of types. We have already seen that ornate silver-gilt brooches like those from the St Ninian's Isle Hoard, Shetland, were only rarely found in graves. More often than not, the brooches in graves tend to be smaller and of copper-alloy, so we might propose that the first viking raids disrupted the production of ornate silver brooches of St Ninian's Isle type. Yet some clearly remained in circulation, as seen from the late 9th century in the Croy Hoard, even if by then they were being hacked to pieces. The smaller, cheaper copper-alloy variants, like those produced on the Brough of Birsay, remained in use and were incorporated into the Scandinavian-style costume – as we see from burial assemblages.

There is one type of brooch in particular that must have remained circulating in the 9th century because of the imitations it inspired. One of the St Ninian's Isle brooches had a distinctive pair of terminals shaped like horned beasts with teeth bared [5.29]. A closely related but smaller brooch of copper-alloy, which originally had been silvered on its surface to make it look more like the St Ninian's Isle type, came from Freswick Links, Caithness [5.30]. It is clearly a copy of the St Ninian's Isle beast-terminals with similar curls emanating from the mouth, and a prominent horn: though on the Freswick brooch, instead of bared teeth the mouth was left open. The beast depicted on these brooches may be specific to the Pictish bestiary – one of the wide array of hybrid Pictish monsters that are a speciality of their stone sculpture, in this case a horned beast with sharp teeth.[108] On a deluxe cross-slab from the monastery of Portmahomack, another horned 'dragon' with a serpent-tail licks the cross through bared fangs.[109] What is most distinctive about the Pictish style of beasts is their shape-shifting form – alongside realistic animals drawn from life, there were creatures not identifiable as wolves, lions, dragons or serpents, but bearing attributes of several at once. The iconic type is, of course, the 'Pictish beast' itself, a commonly used symbol representing a dolphin-like horned creature. Another beast with wolf-like attributes, clawed feet and a large horn is locked in combat with a serpent on a cross-slab from Forteviot.[110] The beasts on the St Ninian's Isle chapes have porpoise-like mouths, but sharp predator's teeth and scaly backs. Horse-headed, fish-tailed beasts abound in northern Pictish sculpture, with one from Jarlshof sparking years of debate as to whether it was a Pictish hippocamp or a Viking-age dragon [7.38].[111]

Brooches with confronted beast-heads were a northern

Fig. 5.31 (right): Figurine of a lion with spiral ornamented hip joints and curled mane, copper-alloy with tinned surface, from a male grave at Islandbridge (1866C), Dublin. (Reproduced by kind permission of the National Museum of Ireland)

Fig. 5.32 (below): Penannular brooch of tinned copper-alloy with beast-head terminals, Ferkingstad, Karmøy, Rogaland, diameter 59mm. (© Terje Tveit – Museum of Archaeology, University of Stavanger)

iteration of the penannular brooch series. Penannular brooches had sported animal-shaped terminals since the Roman Iron Age, but by the 8th century the animal heads had gone into hiding, represented in abstract form only.[112] The examples from St Ninian's Isle and Freswick brought the beasts back in a big way, with a distinctively 'Pictish' spin on an old trope. We know they were being made in the north thanks to a clay mould for one from the Brough of Birsay workshop, although it is of rather different form, lashing tongues through sharp teeth, as seen in the Portmahomack 'dragon' stone and one of the St Ninian's Isle silver chapes.[113] Two more examples in silver have been found by metal-detecting activity, interestingly both in Fife, although in both cases they were fragmented and may be evidence for the use of hacksilver as a form of currency.[114]

While the St Ninian's Isle brooches and chapes were stashed in the church, the examples from Freswick and Fife show that others remained in circulation, as did one more notable find. A striking bronze figurine of a lion was found in one of the most elaborate male assemblages from the Islandbridge complex of graves in viking Dublin [5.31].[115] The lion's spiral hip joints and its curled mane are reminiscent of creatures in sculpture from Pictland and Iona. The tongue lashing out from between sharp teeth, similar to that on the St Ninian's Isle chape, make it likely to have been taken from a reliquary or a related object from a workshop in northern Scotland. Its form has distinct parallels to the 'dragon' from Portmahomack, but is perhaps closest in the style of its mane and its snarling maw to the lion from a reliquary or book-shrine, clipped and reused as a brooch in the Westness (1963) grave (see pp 51–53) [7.16].

Once variants of insular penannular brooches and brooch-pins began to be made in Norway, the confronted beast terminals were among the first to appear [5.32].[116] These were demonstrably modelled on the St Ninian's Isle/Freswick types of confronted beasts, with the lashing tongues of the St Ninian's Isle chape and the Brough of Birsay brooch mould. The Norse imitations do not have the horn of the beasts from Portmahomack, Freswick and St Ninian's Isle, and there are other features such as the ring-and-dot ornament of the Norse variants which set them apart.

The snarling creatures of Pictish art seem to have struck a chord with Scandinavian tastes. A Scandinavian class of Viking-age carved whalebone plaques shows that they often bore a motif of confronted beasts very similar to those on Pictish brooches; the example from a boat grave in Scar, Sanday, in

Fig. 5.33: Whalebone plaque decorated with beast-heads and fret pattern, from a boat grave at Scar, Sanday, Orkney, maximum width 210 mm. (Courtesy of Orkney Museum)

Orkney, is particularly interesting as the beasts here also have horns that are reminiscent of the Pictish creatures [5.33].[117] Another close parallel comes from the Baltic dragon-head dress-pins, a likely 10th-century series of distinctive dress-fasteners that appear mainly in southern and eastern Scandinavian market towns, including Birka and Hedeby: these pins bear many similarities to the earlier Norse and Pictish beast-head terminals.[118] Rather than claiming a direct inspiration from insular metalwork, it is more likely that these are 'false friends', related motifs with fortuitous parallels. In other words, despite the stylistic differences between insular and Scandinavian art styles, this was one point of similarity that shone through, perhaps because of shared meaning or protective function, and so they became fertile ground for variants in the centuries to come.

AGE OF VARIANTS

Despite what might appear as a cumbersome way of securing clothing, the idiosyncratic insular ringed pin developed into the calling-card of the Viking Age when the trading outpost of Dublin was established. A core part of the new town was a metalworking zone populated with insular craftspeople, whether attracted by new patrons or forcefully relocated to supply the new settlement. This process has several parallels and precedents. As noted in chapter 2, this is precisely what occurred perhaps a generation earlier, on a much smaller scale, at the Pictish monastery of Portmahomack. There the craftworkers were retained, but put to work to create dress items and weights for trade. Similarly the reuse of brooches such as those made at the Brough of Birsay in Viking-age graves should make us rethink the date of this 'Pictish' workshop: the kinds of zoomorphic terminals and 'tabbed objects' being created there were of the same type as those being made in the Portmahomack trade-town phase and are potentially contemporary developments in this primary interface period. If we can link these three workshop sites to post-raid reorganisations, then it appears that the raiders were not just smashing and grabbing – they wanted to control the means of production.

Penannular brooches and brooch-pins were adopted by incoming raiders and settlers soon after the start of the Viking Age: first as 'loot' or trophies of raids, and then as new variants made in Dublin and Scandinavia alike. The 'lives' of these object types then took an interesting divergence. The wearing of penannular brooches began to wane in much of Scotland after the 9th century. Heirlooms such as the Westness brooch-pin continued to be found in graves, or in chopped-up fragments such as those in the Croy Hoard. That is, they were still in circulation, but were used and deposited in new ways. It is not clear how long penannular brooches continued to be made in Scotland.

From the 870s onwards we begin to see new sources of silver flowing into Britain and Ireland, as will be discussed in chapter 6. It spurred a burst of innovation in both the insular and Scandinavian worlds, resulting in new kinds of penannular brooches bearing a blend of art styles and design [5.33] that heralded the aesthetic of the century to come: a new silver age had arrived. The penannular brooch form morphed into a way of showing off this new abundance of silver, with increasingly

Fig. 5.34 (right): Silver bossed penannular brooch from Ireland, diameter 91 mm. (© The Trustees of the British Museum)

Fig. 5.35 (middle): Ball-type brooch of copper-alloy with tinned surface, from a male-gendered grave at Kildonnan, Isle of Eigg, diameter 64 mm; NMS X.IL 163.

Fig. 5.36 (bottom): Baluster-headed silver pin of 'Vestfold type' from a boat grave at Kiloran Bay, Colonsay, length 117 mm; NMS X.IL 784.

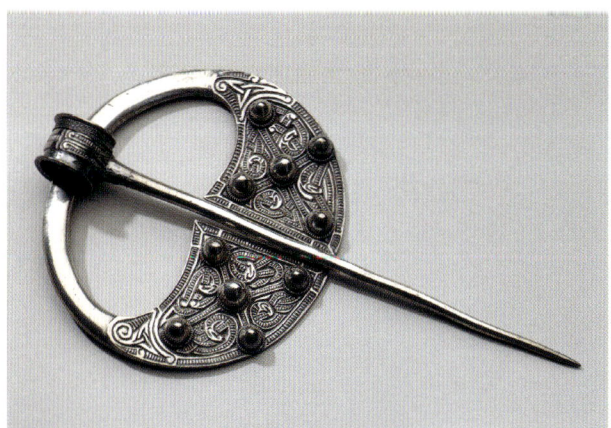

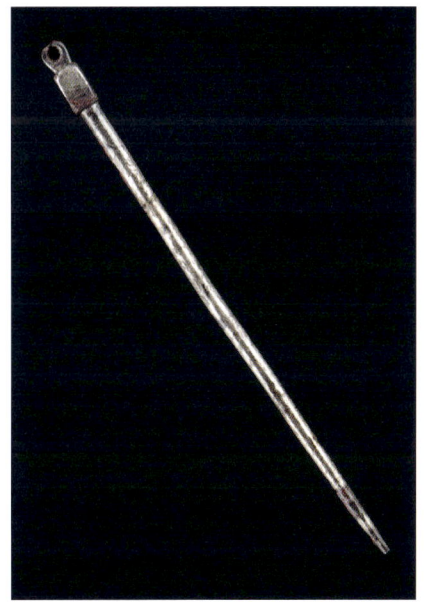

larger versions with longer pins more ostentatious than useful. The famous thistle and ball-type brooches that show up in hoards of the 10th century grew out of a rather obscure variant of penannular brooch which was unique to Ireland.[119] Variants were made in the Irish Sea zone and Norway, showing the movement of objects and ideas going in both directions. Several forms of Scandinavian-made ringed pins and brooches are found in both Britain and Ireland: a sign of continued contact after the age of raids. For instance, a ball-type penannular brooch of tinned bronze, giving it the appearance of silver, came from a male-gendered grave on Eigg [5.35], while Norse-made ringed pins appear across Britain and Ireland [5.36]. These fashions were born of, and used throughout, the diaspora.

To end where we began, oval brooches are so often taken as evidence for the presence of Scandinavian migrants, yet the movement of insular brooches and pins in the opposite direction is seen mainly as the product of looting. We must keep in mind that the use of insular brooches in Norway may represent more than just stolen goods, but also the movement of insular women, and they did not all have to be slaves, much less 'trophy wives'. Marriage alliances could be high-level political manoeuvres. The classes of people who could wear objects like silver-gilt brooches and brooch-pins would have been powerful movers in an insular context and we should instead think of these women as influential actors. Certainly the dress-fasteners they wore made a significant impact abroad and were quickly incorporated as status symbols, even jumping across gender for the Viking-age class of *nouveau-riche* merchant-warrior males.[120] Their power came from showing knowledge of, and access to, riches across the sea. During the early medieval period, dress items were more than mere fashion – they were alive with power.

NOTES

1. Blackwell et al. 2017.
2. Clarke et al. 2012, XIX.
3. Goldberg 2015b.
4. Blackwell 2011; Dickinson 2005.
5. Etchingham and Swift 2004.
6. Isaac 2005; with thanks to G Rhys for discussion.
7. Kilbride-Jones 1980, 5–11; Newman and Burke 2011, 207–9.
8. Blackwell 2011; Whitfield 2014.
9. Maldonado 2011, 263–4.
10. Thompson 2004; Williams 2016.
11. Ashby 2009.
12. Fraser 2009, 335.
13. Curle 1982; Ritchie 1979.
14. Wallace 2015, 346.
15. H. Williams 2007b.
16. Ashby 2009, 14.
17. Bond and Hunter 1988.
18. Jesch 2015.
19. For example, Kershaw 2013.
20. Graham-Campbell 2005, 210.
21. Anderson 1874.
22. Sindbæk 2011b.
23. Harrison and Ó Floinn 2014, 133–4; cf. Sindbæk 2014, 182–5; with thanks to Caroline Paterson for discussion.
24. Petersen's Type 37, or P37; Sindbæk 2011b, 419.
25. Norstein 2020, 41.
26. Kershaw 2013, 226–7; Harrison and Ó Floinn 2014, 132–3.
27. Norstein 2020, 47; Paterson et al. 2014, 154–5.
28. Thorsteinsson 1968; Harrison and Ó Floinn 2014, 132–3.
29. Norstein 2020, 48–68.
30. Hayeur Smith 2004, 72–3; 74–5.
31. McGuire 2009, 262–3.
32. Øye 2015, 19, figs 1.7–1.9.
33. Hayeur Smith et al. 2019.
34. Welander et al. 1987, 165–8.
35. Halsall 2010; Martin 2015.
36. Nieke 1993.
37. Kilbride-Jones 1980.
38. Lane and Campbell 2000; Close-Brooks 1986.
39. Swift and Etchingham 2004.
40. Brunning 2020, 101.
41. Goldberg 2012; Trench-Jellicoe 2000.
42. Whitfield 2001.
43. Brunning 2020.
44. Blackwell 2012, 19–22.
45. National Museums Scotland (NMS) X.FC 287, X.FC 289, X.FC 291; cf. NMS X.FC 288, X.FC 290.
46. NMS X.FC 289; NMS X.FC 286.
47. Curle 1982, 95.
48. Henderson and Henderson 2004, 102.
49. Owen and Welander 1995, 767; cf. Swift and Etchingham 2004.
50. Graham-Campbell 1987a.
51. Westness: Grave 5, a female in an oval cist, unregistered in NMS. Machrins: a male-gendered boat grave, Anderson 1907, 441. Carronbridge: a male-gendered grave, Dumfries Museum 1995.1.100, Owen and Welander 1995.
52. Compare Small et al. 1973.
53. Pierowall: Grieg 1940, 94, fig. 53b. Carn a' Bharraich: female in a boat grave, Anderson 1907, 439. Westness: female in stone-lined chamber grave, Stevenson 1989.
54. Glørstad 2012, table 1.
55. Compare Heen-Pettersen and Murray 2018; Heen-Pettersen 2019.
56. Ashby 2015.
57. Glørstad 2012, 34–6.
58. *Ibid.*, 39.
59. Willemsen 2021, 110–11.
60. Kershaw 2013, 172.
61. Graham-Campbell and Batey 1998, 133, 154; cf. Paterson 1997.
62. Small et al. 1973, 93; pl. XL; Stuart 1867, lxxxiii, pl. 13.
63. York Coppergate: Mainman and Rogers 2000, 2570. Ballynagloch, Co. Antrim: Youngs 1989, no. 85; Veø Prestegaard, Møre og Romsdal, B1471, in Small et al. 1973 as Veøy. See also recent finds reported to the Portable Antiquities Scheme including Lincolnshire Market Rasen, NLM4501.
64. Harrison and Ó Floinn 2014, 148–9.
65. Curle 1982, 95.
66. Youngs 1989, no. 83; Ryan 2004.

67. Discussed in Small et al. 1973, 129–30 and elsewhere as Bergøy; found with a copper-alloy arm-ring and a buckle.
68. Youngs 1989, 90; Ryan 2004, 120.
69. Small et al. 1973, 87–8.
70. Youngs 1989, nos 72 and 75, British Museum 1919,1218.1 and NMS X.FC 5 respectively; Brunning 2020.
71. Blackwell et al. 2017, 127.
72. Swift and Etchingham 2004.
73. Armstrong 1922, figs 2–3.
74. Lucas et al. 1960, no. 77, fig. 27; no. 70, fig. 29.
75. Armstrong 1922, fig. 3, no. 4; Steinforth 2018, 86, fig. 3b; Grieve 1914.
76. Stevenson 1989.
77. Blackwell 2011; Ryan 2011.
78. Confirmed as brass by scientific analysis, meaning it was most likely made in one of the Viking-age trade towns whose workshops specialised in this metal, perhaps Dublin: Eremin et al. 2002.
79. Blackwell 2011; Bourke 2010, no. 290, fig. 34.
80. Compare Bourke 2010, no. 285, fig. 31.
81. Youngs 1989, no. 90.
82. Armstrong 1922, fig. 3, no. 1.
83. Driscoll 2004a; Driscoll 2016.
84. Fanning 1994.
85. Fanning 1994, 1; Fanning 1983.
86. Wallace 2015, 285–7 for Dublin; author's count for Scotland.
87. Buchanan 2012, 121–3.
88. Burström 2015, 36.
89. Thorsteinsson 1968.
90. Norstein 2020.
91. Graham-Campbell and Batey 1998, 150.
92. Harrison and Ó Floinn 2014, 155–7.
93. Ritchie 2005.
94. Graham-Campbell and Batey 1998, 120; Paterson and Stanford 2020, 88–9.
95. Price et al. 2019.
96. Oma 2018; Stevenson 1985, 235.
97. Wamers 1985, 41.
98. Oma 2018; cf. Nicolay 2007, 225–35; Bourke 2003.
99. Paterson and Stanford 2020, 90.
100. *Ibid.*, 92.
101. Crone et al. 2016, 60–2; Paterson and Stanford 2020, 90–1.
102. Paterson et al. 2014, 76; Norstein 2020, 91; Paterson and Stanford 2020, 92.
103. Graham-Campbell 1987b.
104. Fanning 1994, 34.
105. Aannestad 2014, 40–2.
106. Graham-Campbell 1987b; 2011b.
107. Graham-Campbell 1984.
108. Henderson 1996.
109. Carver et al. 2016, illus. 5.3.13.
110. Campbell and Driscoll 2020, figs 8.9, 8.10.
111. Graham-Campbell et al. 2018.
112. Blackwell 2011.
113. Curle 1982, 27; confronted beast-heads with bared teeth or lashing tongues are frequently depicted on Pictish cross-slabs, for instance on the reverse of the Dunfallandy stone, Canmore ID 26295, and the recently discovered 'Conan Stone', Wester Logie, Ross, Canmore ID 12865.
114. Crail, TT 101/06, Buchanan 2012, 113; Lindores, TT 34/19.
115. Harrison and Ó Floinn 2014, 204–6, 464.
116. Graham-Campbell 2011b.
117. Isaksen 2012; Owen and Dalland 1999.
118. Kalmring and Holmquist 2018.
119. Graham-Campbell 1983.
120. Glørstad 2012.

CHAPTER SIX
A silver age

The kingdoms of northern Britain were rich prizes – and early targets – for seaborne raiders. The spread of elaborate, ostentatious burials which left their mark across the landscape have been used to tell a story of invasions and migrations. A closer look at the objects, rituals and people involved in these deposits now seem less about a 'viking' identity than the competition for land and the power that came with it.

But what was so valuable and desirable about northern Britain? It depends on when in the 9th–12th centuries that we look. The aim of viking raiders was initially to extract: portable wealth, slaves, the 'glittering prizes' used to bolster status in Scandinavia.[1] By the start of the 10th century, the game had changed in Scotland. The historical record tells us that besieging forts and effecting regime change in military campaigns which lasted years at a time was now the main goal. It was obviously worthwhile because, with the occupation of territories from established power centres it became easier to control trade and economic production. New forms of wealth and ways to get ahead had opened up that were not available at the dawn of the age of raids in 795, nor even in 865 when the Great Army arrived in England. New horizons now beckoned: the diaspora had expanded out to the North Atlantic after the colonisation of Iceland in the 870s. At the same time, a great wave of silver from the east began to crash over these islands.[2]

It is also clear only some parts of what is now Scotland participated in the new silver economy. While large amounts of cut silver objects (hacksilver), ingots and foreign coins were hoarded in the western and northern territories in areas of Scandinavian control, there are no surviving 10th-century silver hoards in the kingdom of Alba. Yet the kings of Alba remained major players, with their power consolidated in the richest agricultural territories of the eastern lowlands.[3] Over time, power shifted inexorably away from the isles and into those eastern lowlands, where the kings of Scots would eventually be based (see chapter 8). But the power of the kings of Alba shows there were several ways of prospering in this period that did not involve the exchange of standardised weights of precious metals.

Turning to how people made a living is important because it takes us into the home in ways we could not otherwise do

Opposite: Detail of serpent-like terminals from the silver arm-ring bundle within the Galloway Hoard; NMS X.2018.12.72.

6.1a b c

when the focus is on the battles and wealthy graves of the elite. Instead of following kings around, thinking about the economy helps us focus on daily life, food, shelter, livelihoods, getting by. It will help us answer the question of why the vikings came to Scotland, but also what Scotland contributed to the Viking Age.

IMPORTING SILVER

In chapter 4, we noted the appearance of a silver coin with Kufic script (known as a dirham) from the Talnotrie Hoard [Figs 4.20, 4.21, 6.1a–c]. This coin and others help to date the hoard to about AD 875. It is also the earliest Scottish find of its type, and one of the first of many dirhams from the Islamic world that had begun to flow into Britain and Ireland. To understand how such coins travelled thousands of miles to reach these shores, we have to consider Britain's place at one corner of a vast global story.

While western kings were in the arduous process of centralising ever-greater territories over the course of the 8th and 9th centuries, the Roman empire had continued to flourish in the east. We may not have mentioned Byzantium very often in this narrative, but the people in our story were well aware of it. A Pictish king even adopted the Byzantine imperial name Constantine, the first of four who would bear that name between 789 and 997 (chapter 2). The records of Carolingian trade routes and the flow of exotic goods like silk and pepper documented in Britain since the 8th century, all reveal continuing contact between Byzantium and the west, which only intensified in the Viking Age. In some perspectives, the Viking-age trade zone was a sideshow to much larger socio-economic forces operating in Eurasia at the end of the first millennium.[4]

It was long thought that the rise of Islam from the mid-7th century had sundered trade links across the Mediterranean, but this is no longer the case.[5] The great cities of the Abbasid caliphs, especially Baghdad, had grown into centres of commerce, learning and art. Their influence can be detected in the west even before the silver dirhams began to flow in. The weight and quality of Islamic dinars and dirhams were closely regulated and became known more widely as reliable sources of precious metal. Most famously, Offa of Mercia issued gold dinars with Kufic script in direct imitation of the coins of Abbasid caliph al-Mansur for his annual tribute payments to the pope.[6] Offa was imitating the highest-quality gold coinage available at the time for these ceremonial transactions.

It was silver rather than gold, however, which became the standard unit of account in the centuries to come. The processing of silver and lead ores in Melle in western France accelerated so intensively from the late 7th century that pollution has been detected in ice cores from the Alps 600km away, peaking in the early Carolingian period.[7] There are sources of silver within Britain as well; and while evidence for their exploitation in this period is still being investigated, it is clear the Anglo-Saxon kingdoms were still heavily reliant on Frankish and continental silver through the 9th century.[8] A silver 'crash' resulted from the eye-watering tribute payments of English kings to the invading Great Army, leading to such extreme debasement that by the start of Alfred's reign in 871 the coins of Wessex had 'lost all credibility'.[9] Meanwhile, the first silver dirhams were beginning to arrive: there are only three in the Croydon Hoard, London, deposited c.872, but fragments of at least 124 have now been identified in the Great Army winter camp of Torksey, Lincolnshire, should there be any doubt as to who was importing and using them.[10]

Figs 6.1a–c (opposite): Silver dirhams: (a) of Nasr II bin Ahmad, Samanid, minted in Tashkent, 921–2 (309 AH), from the Storr Hoard, Skye, NMS H.C9687; (b) of the time of Al-Mustakfi as Imam al-Haqq, with Abu Hasan Muhammad, minted at Baghdad, 945–6 (334 AH), from the Skaill Hoard, Orkney, NMS H.C9713; and (c) fragment only, 10th century (early 4th century AH), from Stevenston Sands, Ayrshire, NMS H.C9681.

Fig. 6.2 (right): Two pierced dirhams from the Storr Hoard, Skye: (left) Ismail, 899–900, Samarkand (286 AH), NMS H.C9693: (right) Nasr II, 940–1, Tashkent (308–28 AH), NMS H.C9690.

During the period of the first viking raids in Britain, Scandinavians had been busy expanding into eastern trade routes. The Rus', as they came to be known, were a diverse confederation of peoples, including Slavonic and Norse-speakers, who took control of the major riverine and overland routes connecting the Baltic Sea to the Byzantine and Islamic empires, via the Volga and other rivers of Russia and Ukraine.[11] In doing so, they created a northern 'back door' to the eastern Mediterranean, the Silk Roads of Central Asia, and to new sources of silver.

About half a million silver dirhams from this period are known from hoards across Europe, Africa and Asia, and c.80% of those come from Europe alone.[12] This visibility outside the area of production can be explained by the habit of hoarding and depositing vast numbers of such coins, among other silver objects, in northern regions. The Baltic island of Gotland seems to have been the major import/export hub for the silver trade between the east and west, where there are an estimated 65,500 dirhams from hundreds of hoards.[13]

How many of these dirhams made it as far as Scotland?[14] The earliest examples are from the Talnotrie Hoard, where two dirhams were highly fragmented, rendering them barely recognisable. Like the cut fragments from Torksey, these were used as hacksilver and not for their face value as coins. Similarly damaged stray finds of dirhams come from Stevenston Sands, Ayrshire, likely a beach-market site, and South Uist, relating to known Scandinavian settlement on the island.[15] And a silver hoard from Machrie, Islay (deposited c.970), also included dirhams but they have not survived. The rest come from two hacksilver hoards, each containing 19 dirhams, at Storr Rock, Skye (deposited c.935–40), and Skaill, Sandwick, Orkney (deposited c.960–80).

What sets the Storr Rock dirhams apart is their fine condition – they are intact. Of the other dirhams from Scotland, only one from Skaill is intact, whereas on Skye all but three are complete, despite some being half a century old by the time of deposition. The date profile of the Skaill and Storr dirhams is very similar, of issues dating 895–946 and largely of the same mints, such that they belong to the same silver stock despite being deposited a generation apart. This could explain why the older coins were more heavily used by the time of the Skaill Hoard.[16] However, two of the Storr Rock dirhams are pierced, as if worn as pendants, indicating they had circulated in different ways before being deposited in this hoard [6.2]. Exotic coins had long been made into pendants across the viking diaspora, and pierced and mounted dirhams are commonly found in Scandinavian silver hoards rather than graves – the display of silver was an important part of their use in a bullion economy.[17] This is perhaps the key to understanding the use of silver in Viking-age Scotland and beyond.

The other critical feature of the Scottish dirhams is that, where identifiable, they are almost exclusively dated 282–332 AH (*anno Hegirae* in the Islamic calendar, corresponding to AD 895/96–941/42), and were minted by emirs of the Samanid dynasty in Samarkand and al-Shash (Tashkent), both in modern-day Uzbekistan. Samanid dirhams became the dominant type in the west, with an estimated 125 million exported over the course of the 10th century. The Samanid dynasty entered the international stage in AD 892, acquiring key silver-producing mines as they expanded across Central Asia. They ruled a vast territory semi-independently under the Abbasid caliphate based in Baghdad and were ideally placed to access trade routes to the east.[18] So many of their dirhams went north that it is argued the Tashkent mint was producing them for the express

A SILVER AGE

Fig. 6.3: Selection of hacksilver objects from the Galloway Hoard, including hacked and complete arm-rings, ingots and offcuts.

purpose of trade with the Rus'.[19] It is a timely reminder that not all the changes of this period are due solely to the agency of Scandinavian 'explorers' and merchants – but the Rus' were ready when the opportunity for a major trade venture presented itself

USING SILVER

The 9th-century hoards discussed in chapter 4 have been historically treated as separate from the great silver caches of the 10th century largely because of the different character of the silver. While the early hoards contained silver objects, they were mainly of insular objects taken out of their usual function, including Anglo-Saxon coinage and Northumbrian and Pictish dress items. Only with the Galloway Hoard (deposited around AD 900) do we begin to see evidence for large amounts of silver objects purposely made for use in a bullion, or metal-weight, economy (pp 86–7). The varied contents of the lidded vessel in the Galloway Hoard are more like the mixed materials of the 9th-century hoards. But of the more than 5 kilograms of silver ingots and arm-rings deposited outwith the vessel, many were weight-adjusted, or made to standard weight units. These weighed out increments of silver approximate to what we would today call 'money' [6.3].[20] Silver could be supplied in any form, from coins to ingots to hacked-up fragments of other objects, as long as it was of good quality. It was not simpler or more 'primitive' than a coinage economy: it required the building of safeguards, sureties and agreement of weight units to operate smoothly. Coins, however, are based on trust in the mints of a particular ruler; and western rulers up to this point, unlike the caliphs, had a rather spotty record when it came to ensuring a consistent quality of silver in their issues. A bullion economy, on the other hand, was scalable across large distances – good quality silver was easily recast into locally acceptable forms.

The Galloway Hoard shows that parts of Scotland were already participating in a 'common market' that was based on payments in silver bullion by the end of the 9th century.[21] Moreover, standardised forms of distributing silver had been developed for local use, initially in the Irish Sea zone, in the form of weight-adjusted silver arm-rings [6.4]. These were multipurpose objects: they could be worn as dress accessories and were often embellished with stamped decoration, or could be hacked into pieces for small transactions [6.5]. Their design was also not just ornamental; it served as a visual display of access to good-quality silver. Such display was a large component of building trust in a bullion economy.

Arm-rings were just one of several kinds of dress items

CRUCIBLE OF NATIONS

that were used in this way. In chapter 5 [5.34], we saw that new kinds of silver 'bossed' penannular brooches were developed in Ireland from the late 9th century, making use of the new sources of silver that had begun to flow in during the age of raids. Yet these are rarely found in graves, and were instead used in other kinds of deposits, notably hoards.[22] The brooch from the Galloway Hoard was deposited without its pin, near the top of the vessel filled with exquisite and rare objects, almost as though its zoomorphic terminals were 'guarding' the contents [6.6].[23] It is not clear whether such brooches were worn in Scotland, or mainly used for silver storage and exchange. By the time of the large Scandinavian-style hacksilver hoards of the 10th century, such as Cuerdale, Lancashire (deposited in c.906–10), and Storr Rock, Skye (c.AD 935–40), these brooches were routinely reduced to pieces, chopped up for their weight in silver. Exceptions include hoards from Orton Scar and Penrith, both in the northwest of England, where bossed penannular brooches were deposited complete.[24]

The hoard deposited on a rocky shoreline near to the Storr Rock, Isle of Skye, encapsulates this new age of silver [6.7].[25] Gone were the complete objects, glass beads and the mixed materials of the 9th-century hoards. In the 10th and 11th centuries, hoards were predominantly of silver objects, more often than not hacked to pieces. The Storr Rock Hoard consisted mainly of coins: 111 including 19 dirhams, and 23 other pieces of hacksilver. In contrast, there were only two non-Arabic coins from the Skaill Hoard, despite the similar origins of the dirhams stock of both hoards. The hacksilver came from a range of sources including fragments of both Irish and Norse-made brooches. A twisted, spiral silver ring is a rare 'Permian' ring of a kind first used as currency in Baltic Russia, but later copied in Scandinavia. Made from dirham silver and weight-adjusted to an Islamic-derived weight unit, they were first introduced to Britain along with dirham coins by the Great Army. The Storr Rock fragment is currently the only example from Scotland.[26] The Anglo-Saxon coins in the Storr Rock Hoard were largely from southern England, ranging from Plegmund, Archbishop of Canterbury (AD 890–914) to Aethelstan of Wessex (924–39), and were largely undamaged. Overall, the hoard shows the mixture of silver sources being used concurrently in the Irish Sea zone and along the Atlantic seaways, a maelstrom of silver flowing through a trade zone stretching from England and Ireland to Uzbekistan via the Baltic.[27] We are no longer talking about just 'Norse' or 'Danes' here: this 'common market' was

---

Fig. 6.4 (left): A typical example of a broad-band silver arm-ring used in the Irish Sea zone in the late 9th to early 10th centuries, from the Galloway Hoard, length 180 mm, weight 130.6 g; NMS X.2018.12.54.

Fig. 6.5 (middle): Fragment of a stamped broad-band silver arm-ring, hacked at both ends, Largo, Fife, length 25 mm; NMS X.FC 47.

Fig. 6.6 (right): Hoop of a silver bossed penannular brooch from inside the vessel of the Galloway Hoard, width 78 mm; NMS X.2018.12.71.9.

A SILVER AGE

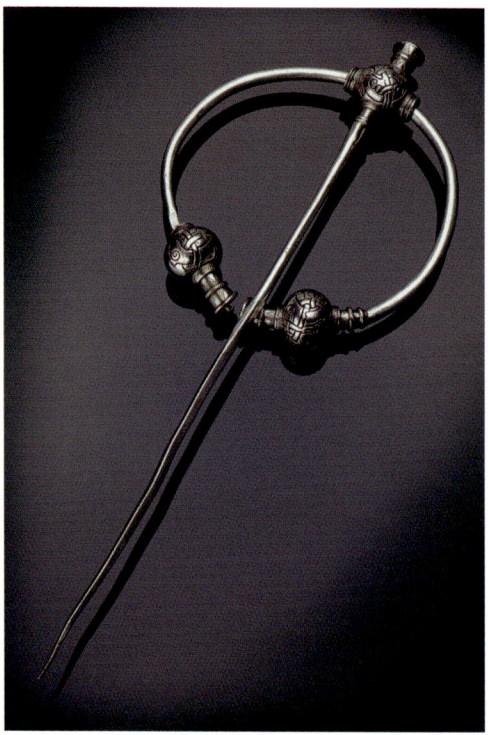

certainly being funnelled through southern and eastern Scandinavia, judging by the objects found alongside insular silver objects.

It is clear that hacksilver and coins circulated together in a sophisticated 'dual economy'.[28] This would allow traders, such as those behind the Storr Hoard, to be flexible: able, using coins, to move between urban centres such as Dublin and York, coin-producing Anglo-Saxon *burh* market towns such as Chester, or rural beach markets using bullion as may be found in Viking-age Scotland. However, there is some debate over the extent to which silver was used for everyday transactions. The evidence would be in the form of stray finds of coins, ingots and other hacksilver – but while finds are growing through metal-detecting practice, they are still rather thin on the ground. What were the larger transactions that required bullion? It may be that silver was reserved for particular kinds of high-value exchanges or highly ritualised social processes – ransoms, tribute payments, treaties, dowries – and this is why we primarily find hoards of silver. In these cases, where the payments were likely made before witnesses, the visual character of the silver was as important as achieving the right weight. Even in hoards with a great amount of hacksilver, there are complete objects which were probably used in the 'public' part of the exchange. It is striking how often these took the form of dress items, recalling how, in the previous century, silver brooches were the most commonly hoarded objects in northern Britain (pp 82–5). Neck- and arm-rings fulfilled a similar role in Norway at the start of the Viking Age.[29] Coins or ingots may seem to us like the most obvious ways to store and transport wealth, but in honour-based power structures with no history of coin-

Fig. 6.7 (left): Hoard of hacksilver, Anglo-Saxon and Arabic coins from Storr Rock, Skye, deposited *c*.935–40.

Fig. 6.8 (right): Silver ball-type brooch, Skaill Hoard, Orkney, diameter 16.1 cm, pin length 37.75 cm, weight 466.5 g; NMS X.IL 1.

Fig. 6.9: Silver thistle brooch terminal fragment with brambling and 'Mammen-style' ornament, Skaill Hoard, Orkney, length 86mm, weight 148.82g; NMS X.IL 5.

Fig. 6.10: Silver pinhead with engraved and brambled ornament from a large ball-type penannular brooch, Skaill Hoard, Orkney, length 86mm, weight 117.7g; NMS X.IL 861.

Fig. 6.11: Silver annular arm-ring of plaited rods united into solid animal-head terminals, Skaill Hoard, Orkney, diameter 110mm, weight 233.53g; NMS X.IL 22.

6.9

6.10

6.11

use, where gift-exchange was the primary expression of power, the influx of silver fuelled the creation of new kinds of arm-rings, neck-rings and brooches as symbols of status, loyalty and lineage.

One new type of brooch was developed during this period in order to showcase large amounts of silver: these are the ball-type, which includes the 'thistle' brooches where the terminals and pin-heads are ball-shaped, in some cases decorated with a brambled texture that gives them their name.[30] Complete examples from Scotland come from the Skaill Hoard, deposited on the west mainland of Orkney in c.960–80 [6.8].[31]

The Skaill Hoard is perhaps the most emblematic of the Viking Age – as well as being more specifically a superlative example of a 10th-century Scandinavian-style silver hoard. It consists of over 115 silver objects and 21 coins, of which 19 are dirhams. At 8.11 kg of silver it is one of the heaviest (and therefore most valuable as bullion) hoards anywhere in Britain or Ireland; indeed it is heavier than most hoards in Norway.[32] The most striking contents are the ball and thistle brooches, which are otherwise rare in Scotland but more common in the Irish Sea zone – there are a minimum of 17 individual brooches of this type either as complete objects or fragments. These have hoops of silver as large as 20.7cm in diameter, with pins over a foot long at 37.75cm, They can weigh nearly half a kilogram of silver apiece [6.9, 6.10].

Other material responses to the flush of new silver reveal the kinds of objects that best communicated status in the 10th century [6.11]. Often overshadowed by the massive brooches are two ringed pins rendered in silver included in the Skaill Hoard [6.12–13]. One is in the form of the polyhedral-headed ringed pin, the most common type in 10th-century Ireland, but with a unique spiral motif engraved on the head. The other is a

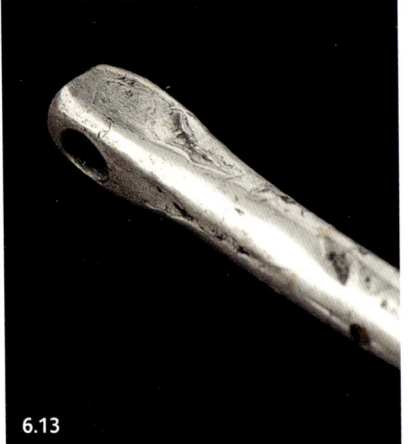

simpler needle-like head missing its ring, but its extreme length (20 cm) puts it in a class of elaborate display items rendered in silver, like the ball brooches. Silver dress-pins are very rare during this period, though notable examples are known from Jarlshof [6.14] and the boat grave at Kiloran Bay, Colonsay [5.36].[33]

An antiquarian record of silver pins and combs in the lost Broch of Burgar (Orkney) Hoard is worth briefly reappraising here. Although Burgar has been considered a 'Pictish' hoard by its description in antiquarian accounts, the Skaill Hoard provides the only 10th-century silver parallels for the description of pins; and similarly the only parallel for silver combs is the single fragment of a silver comb from the Cuerdale Hoard, deposited c.906.[34] The mention of large numbers of amber beads suggests Scandinavian connections, and the only other Scottish hoard with amber beads is the 9th-century Croy hoard discussed in (pp 92–5). The description of the ornate silver vessel in the Broch of Burgar Hoard also deserves a reassessment in light of the unusual decorated vessel in the Galloway Hoard, which is probably of Central Asian origin.

The Skaill brooches, arm-rings and neck-rings show little sign of extensive wear, but a high amount of fragmentation and testing. A telltale sign of the Scandinavian hacksilver economy is the appearance of small nicks where the object has been tested for silver quality with small stabs or slices with a blade. Almost all the objects in the Skaill Hoard bear such nicks. The most nicked objects are often the smallest: a fragment of ingot 27 mm long has been tested 34 times [6.15]. One of the complete ball-type brooches [6.8] is among the few objects with no nicks, and the other well-preserved brooches and neck-rings

Fig. 6.12: Polyhedral-headed ringed pin, Skaill Hoard, Orkney, length 102 mm, weight 21.88 g; NMS X.IL 50.

Fig. 6.13: Silver pin with perforated head, Skaill Hoard, Orkney, length 200 mm, weight 25.79 g; NMS X.IL 517.

Fig. 6.14: Polyhedral-headed silver stick-pin with ring-stamped ornament from the broch at Jarlshof, Shetland, length 154 mm, weight 22.61 g; NMS X.GA 998.

Fig. 6.15: Hacked end of a silver ingot, nicked 34 times, Skaill Hoard, Orkney, length 27 mm, weight 21.5 g; NMS X.IL 51.

tend to have little or no nicking. They were either reserved for display, or their finish communicated the quality of the silver well enough. The fragmentation or preservation of objects was not dictated by how long they had been in circulation, as these hoards were clearly assembled from a variety of sources; there are three separate 'parcels' of hacksilver detectable in the Skaill Hoard, for instance, and at least four different 'donors' of the Galloway Hoard.[35] One of the 'preserved' Skaill brooches is a silver penannular with expanded polygonal terminals of a kind likely made in Norway [7.9]. A hacked terminal of a nearly identical brooch from the Storr Hoard shows they were already circulating as bullion in Scotland, whereas the brooch from the Skaill Hoard had continued in use as a complete object. Nicking did not preclude these objects from being used in non-monetary ways – all four examples of silver dress-pins that are mentioned above were nicked from previous use in bullion transactions, including one from a grave at Kiloran Bay.

The Skaill Hoard dirhams are heavily fragmented with lots of evidence for bending, another way of testing for silver quality, indicating that they had been in active economic use as bullion before being deposited. However, this was still most likely not their primary function in Scotland by this point. Analysis of the silver alloys reveals that only one of the ingots from the earlier Storr Hoard was made from Central Asian silver, which stands to reason as so few of its dirhams showed evidence for fragmentation. In contrast, some ingots and ball-type brooches from the Skaill Hoard had similar alloys to the dirhams.[36] The 42 dirhams that survive from Scotland seem rather insignificant in comparison to the tens of thousands from Gotland, but it is clear that these are only the tip of the iceberg in terms of the silver which passed through here. Most silver was re-made, worn and gifted, but the dirhams taken out of circulation in these hoards saved them from the crucible. The Skaill dirhams capture further fragmentation in progress.

The minuscule weight of a fraction of a silver coin demonstrates that the exchanges these coins represent must have been carried out using sensitive weighing equipment. The Great Army camps of Torksey and Aldwark included hundreds of lead weights: among these were dozens of 'cubo-octahedral' weights, adopted from the Islamic world and used for very fine weight increments of under 4 grams. This matches the heavily fragmented state of the dirham coins, which were almost certainly being used to weigh, for small and frequent transactions. In contrast, there are no cubo-octahedral weights from Scotland as yet, and the lead weights tend to be much heavier (see pp 89–90). Silver bullion does not seem to have been regularly used for smaller transactions in Scotland before the mid-10th century.

The balance scales found in Scotland so far are of variable precision. The earliest balance scales are fixed-beam, non-collapsible types such as those from Kiloran Bay [6.16] and Croy [4.33], both coin-dated to around the late 9th century. These were less precise than later folding balances which, like the cubo-octahedral weights, were introduced to the north from the Islamic world along with Arabic dirhams in the 870s. But then, the weights from Kiloran Bay, which ranged from 12.94g–129.3g, and Gigha, 10.2g–100.3g, were being used for large transactions.[37] It has been noted that weights from graves in viking Dublin, often decorated with insular metalwork like those at Kiloran Bay, tend to be heavier than the simpler, undecorated lead weights from elsewhere in the settlement; the balance scales in the graves were also accordingly much larger and often decorated with zoomorphic detailing. The weights and scales in Dublin graves were invariably in male graves, often well furnished with weapons. Similar patterns exist for the rest of Scotland, where inset lead weights tend to be very heavy, while plain lead weights found in settlement contexts (such as at Barhobble in Wigtonshire), tend to be lighter.[38] The collection of decorated inset lead weights now known from southwest Scotland at Talnotrie (88.18g), Lochmaben (152.55g),

Kirkton (31.22g), and Whithorn (58g), are an indication that considerable wealth was moving through the area [4.22, 4.23]. The English names inscribed into the silver arm-rings of the Galloway Hoard show that it was not only Scandinavians who were benefitting from this new economy, at least in southwest Scotland.

Folding-arm, collapsible balance scales were the most common type from the 10th century onwards [6.17]. They are sometimes found in decorated bronze boxes and were used to measure fine weight increments on a lighter, Islamic-derived weight standard than that used in viking Dublin. In eastern Scandinavia they were used alongside another form of 'regulated' weight from the Islamic world – the 'oblate spheroid' or flattened sphere. Early variants in Scandinavia were even marked with pseudo-Arabic characters to display knowledge of their specialist origins. Only two of these weights have been published from Scotland: one from Orkney, the other from South Uist.[39] A third, plain type was recognised during the course of this research among the assemblage from Jarlshof, Shetland [6.18]. The only scale box from Scotland is a hinged brass example, missing its lid, from a poorly-recorded female-gendered grave from Unst [6.19], along with an oval brooch.[40] Weighing equipment is sometimes found in female graves in Scandinavia, and this is a salutary reminder that the 'domestic' role of women in the Viking Age included the buying of raw material and selling of finished products.[41]

Discussion of trade in the Irish Sea zone is invariably dominated by the finds from Dublin, the largest and most well-documented market town in the region. The proposed 'Dublin ounce' – standard weight unit of 26.6g – is detected in weights and hacksilver objects. However, it is clear that multiple standard units were in use at the same time; in 9th-century Woods-

Fig. 6.16: Set of copper-alloy fixed-beam balance scales from a boat grave at Kiloran Bay, Colonsay: beam, length 196mm, NMS X.IL 774; scale pans, diameter 100mm, NMS X.IL 775–6; and lead weights, weight 12.9–129.6g, NMS X.IL 777–83.

Fig. 6.17 (left): Copper-alloy folding balance beam, missing arm, Jarlshof, Shetland; NMS X.HSA 870.

Fig. 6.18 (right, above): Possible oblate-spheroid copper-alloy weight, Jarlshof, Shetland, maximum diameter 11mm, weight 4.26g; NMS X.HSA 877.

Fig. 6.19 (right, below): Brass box for a set of balance scales, missing its lid, from a woman's grave, Unst, Shetland, diameter 50mm; NMS X.IL 314.

town as in 11th-century Whithorn, there was a lighter unit of 22g–23g proposed.[42] Wherever metrological studies have been carried out in Viking-age Britain, it is clear no single weight standard was used everywhere; even where 'regulated' weights on Islamic models were used, there is large variation.[43] No large-scale metrological analysis has been carried out across Viking-age Scotland, but it is obvious that both the heavier Dublin unit and the lighter Islamic-derived weight units were used, allowing merchants to be nimble and to generate profit moving between trade zones.[44] Weight calibration varied in different markets, but the performance of weighing by individuals with specialist equipment was also important. The larger, more elaborate balances and weights found in graves in Dublin and Kiloran Bay were likely used by officials whose function it was to weigh before witnesses any tribute payments or ransoms, and to divide loot among the warband.[45] To call these the graves of 'merchants' is rather to understate the social and political function of specialist weighing in the Viking Age.

A SILVER AGE

Figs 6.20 a–b: Detail (right) of a fixed-arm balance beam showing back-turned beast-head finial; and (below) vertical and angled markings indicating notches on the beam, from Croy Hoard, near Inverness; NMS X.FC 15.

THE CROY STEELYARD

A balance scale seems a simple tool, but they are deceptively complicated. Each arm needed to be the exact same dimensions to achieve equilibrium, as did the matching scale pans and any strings or chains used to attach them. Roman types of equal-arm balance were used to a limited extent in the Merovingian and Anglo-Saxon contexts, but fell out of use as these societies transitioned to a coin economy.[46] The most common Viking-age folding-balance scales seem to have been introduced directly from the Islamic caliphate, along with dirhams and Islamic-derived weights.[47] Early examples were mainly fixed-beam (non-collapsible) types such as those from Kiloran Bay and from the Croy Hoard [4.33]. It has been argued that Croy and related balances with animal ornament belong to a 'continuing Roman tradition', but there is little evidence for their use before the Viking Age in Britain or Ireland.[48]

However, there is considerable evidence in the animal ornament and the decoration of scale pans (as seen in the examples from Gigha and Dublin) that these were manufactured in an insular context, perhaps even in ecclesiastical workshops given the parallels between the Croy animal heads and the ridge-poles of insular reliquary shrines.[49] However, as discussed previously (pp 94–95), what we now might call the Croy-type of balance was very rare, in that they have notches cut into one side of the beam, rendering the weight of the arms unequal [6.20 a–b]. These required the use of a sliding counterweight, like a steelyard balance, although those devices usually have a single arm. They appear to be an experimental early phase in the insular series of balances, meant to hit target weights in regular increments, such as might be expected for use in weighing objects of standardised weight like coins. It is just possible they were used by insular craftspeople to weigh out specific metal weights for a consistent alloy: the matching example from Haug, Verdal [4.34], was found in a boat grave containing, amongst other things, smithing tools including a small hammer and tongs that are more appropriate for non-ferrous work.[50] Another possibility is that they were used for even more specialist weighing: in Byzantine contexts, steelyards were traditionally retained for specific types of material such as silk and pearls; and in later medieval northern Europe, tradition dictated that certain goods were weighed by different weight units.[51] Regardless, the rarity of these insular 'steelyards' means that their function did not last long.

In the absence of surviving examples, a way to spot them would be to look for pendant weights such as the plumb-bob-like counterweight found with the steelyard from Ronaldsway, Isle of Man [4.35].[52] These are rare, but examples of various types are known from Birka, Kaupang, York and Dublin.[53] Interestingly, pendant weights are some of the objects known to have been manufactured in the post-raid workshop at Portmahomack.

CRUCIBLE OF NATIONS

Fig. 6.21: Hacksilver hoard containing ring-money arm-rings, Anglo-Saxon and Frankish coins, Burray, Orkney, deposited c.997–1010.

A looser approach to weight standards can also be detected in other parts of the Scottish Viking-age silver economy. The Skaill Hoard also had another significant difference from the earlier Storr Rock Hoard: the appearance of arm-rings referred to as 'ring-money'. A variety of ornate dress items had been developed to help store, display and transport silver by the mid-10th century, but the Skaill Hoard represents the first appearance of this new type of 'ring-money' arm-ring in Scotland. The Burray Hoard (c.997–1010) [6.21], the next heaviest silver hoard in Scotland at 2 kg, is almost exclusively made up of this distinctive type of penannular arm-ring.[54] They appear in 15 hoards from Scotland, in contrast to only five each in Ireland and Man, and only one in England, in hoards dated c.950–1060. It seems most likely they were a regional adaptation of the more widespread concept of weight-adjusted dress items, developed specifically for use within a 'Scoto-Scandinavian' context, perhaps within the sphere of influence of the earldom of Orkney.[55]

Ring-money represents another local response to the flow of silver into Scotland in the 10th century. While early 'experimental' and decorative examples of ring-money arm-rings first appeared in the Skaill Hoard, these were higher in silver with indications they were made predominantly of Arabic silver, like other objects of that time.[56] By the turn of the millennium, ring-money hoards such as Burray show they had been standardised to a plainer, more consistent shape and, importantly, their silver content had become very debased. The Burray rings average about 70% silver and the alloys used no longer seem to contain much Arabic silver. Similarly low silver content has been detected across the corpus of ring-money, and this debasement is not specific to Burray.[57] Instead it seems that within the zone using ring-money, these objects fulfilled a specific social or political role as a ritualised form of proto-money. Such roles were just as important as hitting an exact target of silver content or weight standard.[58] We will come back to this when we turn to the changes of the 11th century (chapter 8).

BEYOND THE SILVER ECONOMY

We should pause here to take stock of what these hoards mean for the northern experience of the Viking Age. Most obviously, they tell us about the great quantities of portable wealth available to those who were plugged into what had become a transcontinental silver economy. The silver inexorably draws a great deal of attention because of the amount of data bound up in each fragment of hacked silver. But whether these hoards represent accurate snapshots of normally circulating currency, or are outliers representing singular events such as tribute or other payment, is a question still unanswered.[59] Certainly the hacksilver hoards of the 10th/11th centuries appear almost exclusively in the north and west, corresponding with other evidence of Scandinavian settlement. Even in these areas, they tend to cluster into short bursts of more intense deposition, particularly around the 970s and again around the turn of the millennium.[60] Some of these can be explained by the increased availability of English or Anglo-Scandinavian coinage – and perhaps strategic diplomacy as a way of dealing with northern kings.[61]

A SILVER AGE

Fig. 6.22: Fragment of silver ring-money arm-ring, hacked at both ends, from Kildonan, South Uist, length 39.4mm; NMS X.GS 213.

The absences of hoards are equally informative. There are no hacksilver hoards anywhere in the kingdom of Alba and the wider Gaelic-speaking northeast until the first appearance of coin-hoards in Tayside and Fife in the 11th century (chapter 8). But that is not to say there was no money flowing through these areas in the 10th century. There are numerous finds of imported silver coins, generally of Anglo-Saxon and Anglo-Scandinavian issues, scattered throughout northern Britain.[62] Despite numerous excavations of secular and ecclesiastical sites in recent years, it is remarkable how many of these 10th-century silver coins are from ecclesiastical sites, including Auldhame, East Lothian; Isle of May, Fife; Newark Bay, Orkney; and the nearby Brough of Deerness chapel, to name a few. It shows not only continued use of these sites, but perhaps also their function as meeting-places for carrying out transactions, maybe even seasonal markets. Certainly the early monastic burial ground at Whithorn had by this time been subsumed by a market town, explaining the numerous coins from there. Several coin- and ring-money hoards from around the turn of the millennium are also found in association with earlier monasteries, even in some cases deposited in churchyards, including Cockburnspath near St Helen's Church in East Lothian (c.930–50); Portmahomack (Tarbat), Ross (c.970); Iona, Argyll (c.986); Kirk O' Banks, Caithness (c.1000); Dull, Perthshire (c.1025). This situation is also paralleled in Viking-age Ireland, where a large proportion of Viking-age silver was deposited in churches or on ecclesiastical estates.[63]

We know that ring-money circulated alongside coins in Scotland, as they are found together in hoards such as Burray and Tarbat. There is a growing number of single examples and fragments of ring-money outside of hoards, which might help to support the possibility that they were used singly or even as 'pocket change' in a similar way to coins. The only complete example from outside a hoard comes from the 'House 1' midden at Jarlshof [4.5b].[64] The rest of the single finds were all hacked before deposition, indicating they have been used for economic transactions. One from Whithorn, Wigtonshire, belongs to a rich seam of late Viking-age material displaced by the medieval cemetery; by the 11th century the old monastery had transformed into a trade town which operated in a similar way to viking Dublin, accepting ring-money alongside foreign coinage.[65] Fragments of ring-money terminals have now been found in the Orkney power centres of Orphir and Brough of Birsay, in the latter joining other minuscule chunks of hacked silver, cut coins and a rare hacked gold ingot, a snapshot of the mixed bullion economy in operation by the 10th and 11th centuries.[66] The intensity of the hacking of silver objects at Birsay is indicative of small, perhaps everyday, transactions. It also demonstrates how easy it can be to miss the evidence of early money. A fragment at Kildonan, South Uist [6.22], adds to the growing evidence for Viking-age economic activity there, along with the recent find of a silver dirham mentioned above.[67]

Two final examples come from more unexpected contexts. A metal-detected find of ring-money from Dornoch, Sutherland, adds proof for Viking-age activity there.[68] This gives a wider context for the hoard of silver including hacked arm-rings and coins deposited in the churchyard at Portmahomack, c.970, and may show that patrons of the church were enmeshed in the silver economy by this time, as they were on Iona. Finally, an example of a rare form of silver arm-ring was found near Bankfoot, Perthshire, just off a major overland route following the Tay inland out of Perth [6.23]. The punched decoration appears to be early in the series of ring-money in Scotland,

Fig. 6.23: Fragment of stamped silver ring-money arm-ring, hacked at both ends, from Bankfoot, Perthshire.

with parallels in the Skaill Hoard.[69] This last example, from the heartland of Alba near Dunkeld, is currently the only indication that silver bullion was used in that kingdom.

It has been noted that many of the largest silver hoards in Ireland are deposited on ecclesiastical estates belonging to some of the major royal monasteries.[70] Indeed, there are even cross-marked silver ingots found in hoards such as Cuerdale, Lancashire, which are now known to have been produced in Knowth and Dublin. By the 10th century, Irish kings were receiving tribute payments in weight-adjusted silver ingots – in other words, it is by this time more difficult to discern 'viking' from other economic activity. In the area of Lough Ennell, Co. Westmeath, the heartland of the powerful Clann Cholmáin dynasty, eight hoards contain 50 kg of silver, almost half the weight of all Viking-age silver from Ireland. Royal monasteries like Clonmacnoise were receiving major new investment in massive stone high crosses, inscribed grave-markers and new stone churches at this time, and this boom seems to be, in part, bankrolled by payments of silver tribute from the Hiberno-Norse towns. However, in 10th century Scotland there is less evidence that royal monasteries controlled similar amounts of wealth; and the distribution of ring-money, as with hacked silver ingots, is increasingly shaped by metal-detecting activity from outside known archaeological sites and settlements.

While the silver hoards only show us where money was being accumulated from the 10th century onwards, we have noted in chapters 2 and 4 how frequently the earliest raids sought to appropriate, rather than simply to extract, the wealth of the monasteries. The occupation of ecclesiastical settlements at Portmahomack and Dublin, and possibly Birsay, involved the repurposing of local metalworking capabilities towards the processing of silver into ingots, the manufacture of dress items and other economic material. Stray finds of exotic material such as a clipped Carolingian coin from Hoddom, Dumfriesshire [4.29], and a carnelian bead from Coldingham, Scottish Borders [4.31], show that these ecclesiastical sites could have similar types of material culture connections that are otherwise associated with the movements of Great Army raiding parties (pp 87–97).

These finds are of interest, but it is in the 10th-century Hebrides we can best perceive the transition of monasteries from the targets of the earliest raids to centres of Hiberno-Norse patronage in the following centuries. Barra, Iona and the Clyde island of Inchmarnock all have stone cross memorials bearing Old Norse runic inscriptions dated broadly to the 10th/11th centuries.[71] Iona was famously the site of numerous early viking raids, but by the 10th century the Columban Church had come under the patronage of the king of Dublin, Amlaíb Cuarán. After losing the Battle of Tara in 980 he was 'retired' to Iona and eventually buried there.[72] The runic cross-slab may be broadly contemporary with these events, and uses personal names that seem to be associated with later earls of Orkney.[73] A hoard of silver coins and three fragments of gold and silver were deposited near the core of the monastic site in c.986, the same year there was a raid by rival Norse dynasts [6.24].[74] All together, the royal burial, hoard and the raid of the 980s inform us that there was still wealth and political power to be gained through control of the important monastery of Iona. A series of stray finds of dress items and metalwork suggests that Iona had become a centre of trade as well by the 10th and 11th centuries.[75] There is even a mention, albeit in a later Norse saga, the *Fagrskinna*, of a visit to the *caupstaðenn* or 'market' of Iona, by Magnus Barelegs, king of Norway.[76] The viking raids may have been devastating to many ecclesiastical communities, but in the long term some found a way to survive, even thrive, under new management, subsidised in part by the new silver economy.

A SILVER AGE

Fig. 6.24: Non-numismatic objects from the Iona Hoard, deposited c.986: (left to right) silver ingot, with length 133.4 mm, weight 45 g, NMS X.IL 715; silver finger-ring bezel set with gold filigree and glass, with length 29.2 mm, weight 5.7 g, NMS X.IL 716; fragment of gold wire, with length 38 mm, weight 4.56 g, NMS X.IL 717.

OPTING IN AND OPTING OUT OF THE SILVER AGE: ALBA AND STRATHCLYDE

Not everyone in Scotland benefited from the new silver economy. Evidence from Alba shows little taste either for hacked silver objects or the massive amounts of silver coins that were issued by English kings. This was despite very well-documented engagement with both the kings of Dublin and England from the time of Causantín mac Áeda (anglified as Constantine, son of Áed, r.900–43), who was a key player in the insular politics of the early 10th century.[77]

Causantín ascended the throne in 900 when his predecessor was killed by 'heathens' at the royal fort of Dunottar. He came to fame by defeating the same Dublin-based viking forces in Strathearn in 904, but would go on to ally with the kings of Dublin for a number of fateful battles with King Aethelstan of Wessex. In 927 he was forced publicly to submit to Aethelstan and at this point seems to have baptised his son and future king of Alba with an English name, Hildulf, Gaelicised as Ildulb. In 934 Aethelstan invaded Scotland as far as Dunottar, sending his fleet still further north as far as Caithness. In 937 Causantín was part of an allied force, along with Olaf Guthfrithson of Dublin and Owain of Strathclyde, that confronted Aethel-stan at the unlocated Battle of Brunanburh: one of the decisive moments in the formation of the polities that would become known as England and Scotland. The victorious Aethelstan died not long after in 939, at which point Olaf Guthfrithson took much of Northumbria. Causantín himself would continue to rule in Alba until 943 when he retired to St Andrews as a penitent and died peacefully in 952.

The kings of Alba were well connected, sometimes through alliance or competition, to the users of the silver economy, but we have very little archaeological evidence of these ties from within Alba itself. Apart from a lost silver hoard from Gordon, Scottish Borders, there are no examples closer to the territory of the Scots.[78] There is still less artefactual evidence for the dramatic invasion of Scotland by Aethelstan in 934. Anglo-Saxon swords from Torbeckhill, Dumfriesshire, and Harviestoun, Clackmannanshire, would fit well within an early 10th-century bracket, but while there is always the temptation to link them with historical battles, typological dating is still too loose to do so with great confidence. Similarly, finds of 'Anglo-Scandinavian' type with links to the Danelaw from across Scotland, including zoomorphic strap-ends, polygonal pendant bells and lozenge-headed pins, tell us a story of continued contacts between nations more so than specific historical events such as military campaigns [6.25–6.27].

There is much that is still unknown about the new kingdom of Strathclyde, created in the aftermath of the disastrous siege of Dumbarton Rock in 870 (see p. 74). A burst of stone sculpture, including 'hogback' and cross-marked grave-markers, appears at Govan. Was this the political centre of the new entity, or an interface between the strath (inland valley) and the firth-lands? The Govan sarcophagus, and the dedication to St Constantine, are now thought to be a shrine to the Pictish king Constantín mac Cináeda, martyred by Dublin vikings after

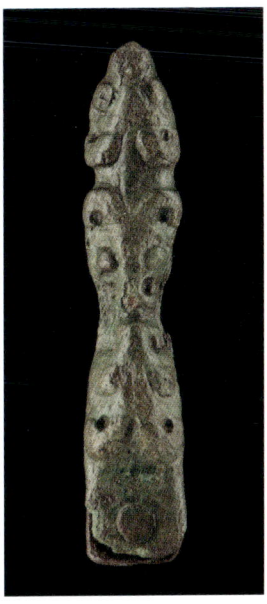

Fig. 6.25 (left): Copper-alloy hexagonal pendant bell of Anglo-Scandinavian type with ring-and-dot decoration, Freswick Sands, Caithness, height 34mm; NMS FB.YT.546.

Fig. 6.26 (middle): Copper-alloy strap-end of Anglo-Scandinavian type with three animal masks, Hurly Hawkin, Angus; NMS X.HHA 30.

Fig. 6.27 (below): Copper-alloy stick-pin with perforated lozenge-shaped head inlaid with silver wire, Brough of Birsay, Orkney, length 120mm; NMS X.HB 428.

the Battle of Dollar in 875, a kingly cult similar to the veneration of St Edmund the Martyr of East Anglia, killed by the Great Army.[79] There was an 'alliance' between Alba and Strathclyde under St Constantine's eponymous successor against the kings of Dublin and York at the Battle of Corbridge, 918.[80] All three joined forces at Brunanburh in 937 against Aethelstan of Wessex, but the evidence still suggests that Strathclyde remained independent of Hiberno-Norse and Scottish rule until as late as the Battle of Carham in 1018.[81]

There are several hints that the kingdom of Strathclyde did not straightforwardly replace the earlier kingdom of Alt Clut. Beginning with Dumbarton Rock itself, it seems that the aftermath of the siege in 870 was a shortlived occupation marked by diagnostic Hiberno-Norse finds including a sword-hilt guard and two lead weights of a kind most commonly found in the viking towns of Ireland.[82] There are Viking-age furnished burials on Arran and Midross near Luss on Loch Lomond, which suggests some land in the wider Firth of Clyde area was ceded to Hiberno-Norse rulers (p.96). Two such graves – on Arran and at Midross – contain Anglo-Saxon coins, in the latter case pierced for suspension. These were also previously linked with the archaeological 'footprint' of the Great Army (pp 87–97). The cemetery at Midross, as yet unpublished, contains 15 furnished and unfurnished burials dated to the 9th and 10th centuries and would appear to relate to a settled community.[83] Inchmarnock's famous 'Hostage Stone' may be a depiction of an otherwise unrecorded viking raid, but by the 10th century a new runic cross from Inchmarnock further demonstrates Norse-speaking Christian rulership in this area [2.15]. Balance scales with inset lead weights of similar kinds appear in the boat grave at Kiloran Bay, Colonsay, and a poorly-recorded find on the Isle of Gigha; and given the Great Army-related 'pegged' weight from the former, it is likely that the occupants of the Inner Hebrides were in close contact with those in the Clyde basin.[84] Therefore the Clyde Firth, and perhaps the province of the Lennox incorporating Luss on Loch Lomond-side, was likely of a separate *Gall-goídil* (foreigner-Gael) lordship.[85]

An increasing number of silver finds from this region help to flesh out the picture. There is only a single hoard from Port Glasgow, located in a distinct location at the mouth of the Clyde, consisting of an uncertain number of English coins and at least two ring-money arm-rings.[86] This was deposited in *c*.970, around the same time as two others of similarly mixed character from the Inner Hebrides at Tiree and Machrie, Islay.[87] There are, however, important instances of stray silver finds from here. A complete but nicked silver ingot from Scalpsie Bay, Bute,[88] and an undated silver dirham from Stevenston Sands, Ayrshire [6.1c], join lost dirhams and hacksilver from the Machrie Hoard, Islay, and may belong to the same pulse of silver in the 970s. Most notably, the Hunterston Brooch, from

A SILVER AGE

the sandy coast of Ayrshire, also fits into this wider context. Although it does not appear to have been used in an economic transaction as it remains largely undamaged, the runic inscription on its reverse [6.28] speaks volumes about the potential *Gall-goídil* context of the Clyde Firth province. The inscription is difficult to date precisely, but it has been ascribed to the 10th century. The commonly attested Gaelic name Máel Brigte, is used, but spelled *Malbriþa*, reflecting a local pronunciation in a Norse- and Gaelic-speaking context. The word used for brooch, *stilk*, presents a 'minor semantic problem' in that it is only rarely used in Old Norse texts and there mainly related to the stalk of a plant.[89] However, as noted in chapter 5, Irish and English terms for brooch used similar plant-based terminology such as thorns and leaves, so this may instead be a genuine Norse rendering of a specific insular term in a bilingual context. Alongside the Norse-language inscription of the Inchmarnock runic cross, and the 'Scoto-Scandinavian' hacksilver economy attested in the hoards, the Clyde Firth area seems to be a true crucible of language and identity, exemplified by the Hunterston Brooch.

Other than these finds, the best archaeological evidence for the 9th–11th centuries in the broader Clyde catchment is largely bound up in the form of carved stones that are difficult to date. Many of these fall within a loosely-defined 'Govan School' which characterises the lower Clyde valley and Renfrewshire, but with outliers on the firth islands of Bute and Great Cumbrae.[90] The important thing here is that by the time of this 'school', a key interface at Govan, with its mix of sculpture including hogback burial monuments, had begun sharing ideas with the *Gall-goídil*, mediated perhaps through the Church. However, historical evidence tells us that the kings of Strathclyde retained British names, and in the early 10th century are still in conflict with Hiberno-Norse rulers. Like Alba, the inland zone of Strathclyde is materially different with none of the western and Scandinavian connections of the wider Firth of Clyde. Perhaps the Strath, the valley of the Clyde, had a similar power basis in land and the agricultural economy as Alba did. Further study of the economic and environmental archaeology of the Clyde Valley may shed some light on this split and the politics of the 10th century.

COMMODITY MONEY

One of the clearest changes of the 9th–12th centuries, in Scotland as elsewhere, is the gradual establishment of the idea of money. While it seems obvious to us today, money is a strange sort of power to communities that do not use it. The ability to acquire goods by deploying an agreed medium of exchange is not obvious to everyone. We tend to associate money with coins, but it can take almost any form – as long as it is agreed upon by all parties and is backed by trustworthy guarantors, bound by law or honour. We tend to see currency as part of the path to 'civilisation' – that is, coins and money feel like mod-

Fig. 6.28 (opposite): Detail of the inscription in Norse runes on the reverse of the Hunterston Brooch, Ayrshire; NMS X.FC 8.

ernity, and their absence feels backward, 'medieval' in the derogatory sense.

Yet only some of the insular realms were coin-using at this time. The kings of Alba, Cumbria, Ireland and Norway ruled without them down to the 11th or 12th centuries, instead extracting their silver and turning it to other purposes. Sometimes this could take the form of proto-currency like weight-adjusted arm-rings, but outside the Scoto-Scandinavian bullion zone there was little apparent reliance on silver at all. This means that there were alternative forms of wealth, generated and mobilised in ways that archaeology is uniquely suited to reveal.

The idea of money is different to 'value'. A herd of cattle will have always held some form of inherent value in the form of food, hide and traction, but it is not until the 8th century or so when the precisely measured value of a cow was set down in Irish legal texts.[91] Even then, they represent an ideal and it is difficult to prove that such laws were rigorously adhered to everywhere. Centuries before the first banks, currency required trust that went beyond the two parties in any single transaction. Such trust needed to be guaranteed by a stable institution – in this era often the king or the Church – whose coins symbolised that backing. But as noted throughout this volume, royal and ecclesiastical institutions were themselves in flux during this period: even when David I issued the first Scottish coinage in the early 12th century, a coin-using economy took time to become established across his realm.[92] It is important to remember that Scotland was not alone in this, and coinage was by no means the only way to assess wealth and value in the early medieval period. Even though evidence exists for the use of standardised weight units, such proof did not presuppose a monetised economy.

This is not because coins were strange or exotic. Hoards across Ireland, Scotland and Man were overflowing with issues from the mints of Edgar and Aethelstan from the burgeoning kingdom of England in the second half of the 10th century. By the 11th century, regulated currencies were being established in a growing number of areas as kingdoms became increasingly powerful and more bureaucratised. But coins remained powerfully symbolic and highly politicised. When early medieval kings began to mint their own, it was often an aspiration to, rather than evidence for, a stable institution.[93] As long as there were trading partners who did not subscribe to a currency-based model, coins always necessarily co-existed with other forms of exchange in kind, other social and economic relationships, and other ways of calculating value.[94] Kingdoms thrived, fleets were paid for, armies were kept fed. They did so through long-established means and by adapting in ways that worked well enough that coins were not needed. The idea of money was certainly around, but no single economy existed and hard currency was only one aspect of a bigger picture.

The reality would have been several overlapping systems of ascribing value and negotiating exchange. We have already seen different regional patterns and weight standards operating together within the silver bullion economy: such systems were connected to areas that were using coins, and those regions which subscribed to neither a coin nor a bullion economy. In short, a coin-based exchange system was not the only way to participate in the wider northern economy in the 9th–12th centuries. We need to find different ways to discuss the economy without 'progress' toward a royal mint as the only logical end goal. Instead, there should be more talk about what was valued, how that changed over time, and what it meant for the people caught up in these epochal changes. In Scotland, as elsewhere in the north, this is largely a story of rural development and the exploitation of natural and human resources.

So much of our attention is hoarded by the silver economy and a few urban centres where we have evidence for it operating. The more regular regional markets could not have been supported by the kinds of high-value elite exchange which brought in the massive hoards of silver. The day-to-day running of an urban centre as a nodal point in an inter-regional economy required a thriving rural sector to provide the necessities of food, materials and other consumables, but also to drive regular trade in tools and other mundane goods.[95] Even without a single recognisable permanent market town, Scotland's islands and maritime zones were thriving, as seen not only in the silver hoards but in the ostentatious furnished burials that represent notable sacrifices of other forms of wealth (chapter 3).

Taking the Orkney earldom as an example, the archaeological evidence reveals a diverse economy of 'pirate fishermen', where raiding and tribute-taking modes were supported by agricultural development increasingly geared toward surplus production.[96] Less quantifiably, wealth could also be generated by virtue of the strategic position of the isles on the major maritime trade routes between Scandinavia, the insular zone and the wider north Atlantic. In a time when long-distance trade by sea was immensely profitable, Scotland's islands were in an ideal nodal position. Ways of assessing the wealth of the northern isles included:

- silver hoards such as Skaill and Burray, two of the largest in Britain
- patronage of the arts, especially Skaldic poetry
- monumental stone architecture such as the churches of Orphir and Egilsay
- evidence for piracy and mercenary activity
- shipping tolls for merchandise passing through
- provisioning and piloting merchant ships
- export goods – especially steatite and dried stockfish.

The major exports from Orkney and Shetland at this time seem to be steatite (soapstone), dried fish, fish-oil and, eventually, mercenaries, all to various extents and at different times critical to the support of a maritime economy. A taste for seafood which exemplified the start of the Viking Age in the north soon grew into a thriving export economy, with sites such as Freswick Links, Caithness and Quoygrew, Westray, building up large middens of fish-bone in quantities which certainly exceeded local consumption. The evidence for fish production and consumption is on a scale never before seen in Scottish prehistory. This is matched by numerous archaeological finds relating to the fishing industry appearing in Viking-age and later medieval contexts, including fish-hooks and any number of sinkers and line weights [6.29, 6.30].

The Shetland steatite trade also seems to have become quite profitable. This relatively soft, easily workable stone lent itself to a wide variety of uses, from moulds for metalworking (p. 33) to vessels for serving and cooking, and weights for fishing [6.30]. Organised quarrying of steatite is one of the earliest detectable 'trades' in Norway from the 8th century, and the movement of steatite across the north reveals trade links from Shetland, the major naturally-occurring source of steatite in Scotland.[97] It has been noted that several Viking-age graves and settlements in Shetland are at or near known steatite quarries: from the female grave at Clibberswick, to the runic-inscribed stones of Cunningsburgh, to the boat grave at Fetlar.[98] And blocks of stone were transported to settlements like Jarlshof, where they were finished and exported to Orkney and beyond.

Like other forms of wealth, steatite [6.31] probably became a marker of a regional identity in the isles of the north. New object types like bake-plates may even have originated in the Scottish isles before becoming staples of Scandinavian production [6.32]. Their spread across the diaspora is well-studied and steatite vessels can be found among the female-gendered grave-goods of Westness, while children played with toy versions of these rounded bowls at Jarlshof [6.33]. A particular form of portable, four-sided steatite ingot mould seems to be a widespread innovation of the early Viking Age, found at Birsay [2.9] and Jarlshof in Scotland, with rare finds from market

Fig. 6.29: Pair of iron fishing-hooks, Jarlshof, Shetland, lengths 51mm and 109mm; NMS X.HSA 923–924.

Fig. 6.30: Selection of steatite and sandstone fishing-line sinkers, Jarlshof, Shetland; NMS X.HSA 589, 595, 596, 605, 610, 621 and 629.

Fig. 6.31: Small square steatite bowl, Shetland; NMS X.AQ 31.

Fig. 6.32: Fragments of a bake-plate of scored steatite, Jarlshof, Shetland, estimated diameter 450mm; NMS X.HSA 729.

Fig. 6.33: Miniature cooking bowl of steatite, hemispherical, probably used as a toy, Jarlshof, Shetland, diameter 58mm; NMS X.HSA 696.

towns further afield including York (Coppergate) and Kaupang.[99] In one notable instance, a steatite mould of this type was found in a male weapon grave from Vik, Grimstad, alongside smithing tools and lead weights inset with coins of Eanred of Northumbria (c.830–41).[100] Steatite objects, even mundane tools, could also act as status symbols in an age of raids.

As noted in chapter 3, one of the major sources of wealth in the Viking Age was the production of textile and cloth. Textiles were probably one of the main products in the economic lifeblood of the settlement of Jarlshof before and after the Viking Age: about half of the loom weights registered in the archaeological collections of National Museums Scotland are from this site alone [6.34]. As mundane as these items may seem, weaving equipment and textile production tools could become intensely personalised items, included as grave-goods, inscribed with runes, or decorated [6.35]. Unfortunately, due

A SILVER AGE

Fig. 6.34 (left): Selection of stone spindle-whorls and loom weights, Jarlshof, Shetland; NMS X.HSA 422, 426, 429, 568, 569, 571, 572, 575, 578.

Fig. 6.35 (middle): Spindle-whorl of steatite, with runic inscription reading 'Gautr carved the runes', Stromness, Orkney; NMS X.BE 360.

Fig. 6.36 (below): Hoard of steatite ladles, Houlland, Unst, Shetland, largest diameter 180 mm; NMS X.AQ 2–5.

to the nature of the excavations at Jarlshof, these objects are certainly of various dates rather than belonging to a single phase of occupation, but this concentration suggests production on more than just domestic scale and over a long period of time. The production of sailcloth is one possibility, a high-investment but high-value output that has been suggested as a major source of wealth on other sites with concentrations of textile production. Sailcloth would be essential on this island group, which was the first landfall in a North Sea crossing and final port on return to Norway.[101] Even everyday woollens carried economic value: in medieval Iceland, taxes and tribute could be paid in lengths of wool, *vaðmál*, a form of currency accepted in markets across the diaspora.[102] In Ireland and England there is evidence for the growing commercialisation of the wool trade and production of goods for the export market by the 12th century, though likely much earlier.[103] This may help us to rethink the frequent inclusion of textile tools in women's graves from personal possessions to symbols of wealth-creation and power.

Such goods could be bought and sold on the open market, but for Scotland more widely it is likely that these products could themselves be used as forms of money. Recent research on different kinds of economic exchange across the viking diaspora has revealed the importance of 'commodity money'.[104] Silver was not the only means of payment, nor the only way of measuring value. Even after Scotland became a coinage economy with market burghs in the 12th century, payment of tithes, taxes and tribute in kind remained important.[105] In medieval Iceland in particular, cloth, butter and other products could be used as commodity money. Butter and dairy production were a staple of western Scotland and Ireland's produce before the Viking Age, and the local means of production in the Hebrides were merely appropriated and developed in the Norse

Fig. 6.37 (above): Wooden trough containing bog-butter, Durness, Sutherland, length 736mm; NMS X.SHC 9–10.

Fig. 6.38 (below): Blue glass bead of fluted or 'melon' shape, from a cache of ten glass and paste beads found in a moss in Hillswick, Northmavine, Shetland; NMS X.FJ 55.

period.[106] 'Bog-butter' deposits of dairy products preserved in and recovered from Scottish bogs were a common occurrence in the Scottish Iron Age, but occasional deposits from north-west Scotland, like a trough of butter from Durness, Sutherland, have been dated to the 9th–12th centuries and may be a sign of local economic produce [6.37].[107] It has likewise been argued that beads served as forms of currency throughout the period, but especially in the 9th century before the influx of Samanid silver.[108] It is worth noting the frequent occurrence of beads in the 9th-century mixed hoards of Scotland (chapter 4); large bead-caches are known from across the viking diaspora and represent accumulations of wealth similar to silver hoards [6.38].[109]

Just like silver, commodity money is characterised by its ability to be stored and accumulated; but unlike silver, it is often more locally produced and consumed. There are numerous examples of hoards and special deposits [6.36] in the 'age of silver' that can be understood as either security caches, or as sacrifices of forms of wealth. Enigmatic deposits of objects in cists without evidence for human remains are often characterised as cremation burials, but collections of beads from the Knowe of Moan, Orkney, or Hillswick, Shetland, and lengths of quality woollen fabric from Greenigoe, Orkney, may be better understood as hoards.[110]

The most famous example of such a commodity hoard may be the Lewis Chess-pieces [6.39a], which could otherwise be thought of as the Lewis Hoard. The hoard is not in fact a single chess set, but is made up of numerous sets of walrus-ivory playing-pieces and even dress objects.[111] Walrus ivory [6.40] was one of the most valuable commodities in medieval Europe, and perhaps one of the major drivers of Norse colonisation of the North Atlantic.[112] North Atlantic ivory was certainly noted in sources from the Islamic caliphates in the 10th century, and may have been traded as far as China.[113] There is scant evidence for the working of walrus ivory in

Scotland, but its arrival in the markets of Dublin and Scandinavia almost certainly passed through the western and northern isles, and may have been a reliable source of tolls and tax and, of course, a desirable commodity.

A SILVER AGE

Figs 6.39a–c: Selection of walrus-ivory and whale-tooth chess-pieces from the Lewis Hoard, deposited *c.*1200; H.NS 19–29.

Fig. 6.40: Walrus-ivory double-sided comb, found in a grave at Jedburgh Abbey, Scottish Borders, 11/12th century, height 50 mm; NMS H.HXB 1.

CRUCIBLE OF NATIONS

152

BLACK JEWELLERY

Among the many insular dress items adopted by Scandinavian settlers were bangles, finger-rings and other jewellery made of black stone. Several deposits of carbon-rich stones in northern Britain can be worked and polished into jewellery, including jet and lignite, and oil shale or cannel coal. Whitby jet was one of the many materials worked and exported from Viking-age York, and workshops particularly in western Scotland had been producing lignite and cannel-coal dress items since prehistory.[114] These became fashionable in the Viking Age, particularly as female-gendered dress items. They can be found in women's graves including Lamba Ness, Sanday [6.41]; Westness, Rousay; Newark Bay, Deerness; and Castletown, Caithness. Beads of black stone were gender-neutral and can be found in a woman's grave from Cruach Mhor, Islay, as well as a male grave from Kildonnan, Isle of Eigg.

The production of black-stone jewellery is one of many crafts continued from pre-Viking to Viking-age Scotland with little discernible change in workshop practices. It can be difficult to distinguish between these materials by eye, but scientific analysis can now trace the movement of these materials. Evidence comes from a number of sites with Viking-age phases, but it is not always closely datable: these range from the monastery of Inchmarnock, Bute, close to local coal measures in the central belt of Scotland, to the settlement of Jarlshof in Shetland, where the raw material was imported from as far as western Scotland to be worked into finished products. The 'Gausel Queen', for example, wore a black finger-ring among many other insular imports.

Jet in particular is rarer in Scotland, but analysis reveals beads from the Isle of Eigg were of both jet and lignite. Jet, like amber, has electrostatic qualities and was often used for amulets. Eventually even Christianity adopted this material. Cruciform pendants likely made in northern England can be found across the north Atlantic, but may be as late as the 12th century [7.1].[115] In the Clyde Firth area, monasteries and other ecclesiastical sites have the best evidence for production in the Viking Age: at Portmahomack the evidence for production, using material imported from Brora on the Sutherland coast, is confined to the Viking Age alone.[116] Black jewellery was one of the first cottage industries to be ramped up for export in Scotland and represents yet another adoption of local fashions in a colonial context.

Fig. 6.41: Lignite bangle from a woman's grave, Lamba Ness, Sanday, Orkney, interior diameter 64mm; NMS X.IL 349.

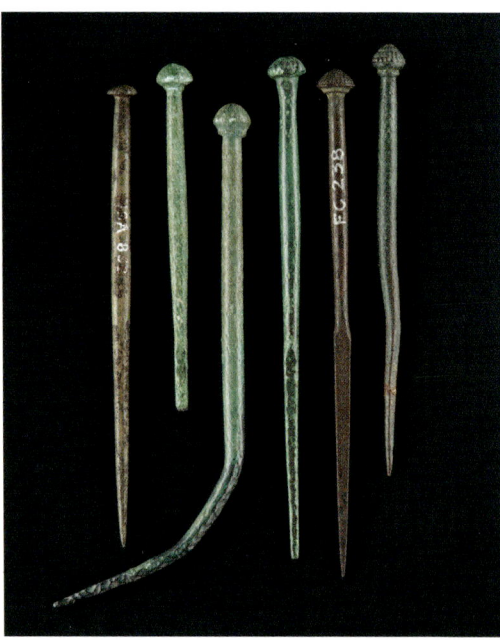

Fig. 6.42: Group of 11th- to 13th-century stick-pins: (from left) Jarlshof, Shetland, NMS X.HSA 852; two from Culbin Sands, Moray (unregistered); Luce Sands, Galloway (unregistered); Ross and Cromarty, length 90mm, NMS X.FC 238; and Tiree, NMS X.FC 306.

Perhaps it would be easier to understand the economy in this period if we had more archaeologically-attested markets, but these are very thin on the ground in Scotland. Other than Viking-age Whithorn, there are no convincing urban centres in Scotland, and it is presumed that external/inter-regional trade occurred mainly at seasonal 'beach markets'.[117] Sand-dune sites such as Luce Sands, Galloway, Stevenston Sands, Ayrshire, and Culbin Sands, Moray, have produced concentrations of coins and Viking-age material suggesting their use for trade. The evidence for a thriving hacksilver economy in the northern and western isles certainly suggests the existence of a merchant class. Other proxy evidence may yet be found in scatters of pins from sand-hill sites across the Hebrides. A recent summary of the evidence from Iona turned up a surprising amount of stick-pins of 11th- to 13th-century date, a supposed 'dark age' for the monastery there, but, as we have seen, with good circumstantial evidence for high-status patronage and a possible market.[118] Stick-pins of these dates were certainly being produced in great numbers in the Irish Viking-age trade-town of Dublin and 'open settlement' of Knowth, presumably for export.[119] A striking amount of these stick-pins are found at sites of known Viking-age settlement and burial in Scotland from Tiree to Shetland, attesting to the success of these 'pioneer' communities in establishing themselves and continuing to trade with the Irish Sea zone long after the age of raids [6.42]. It is also likely some of these were produced locally, given concentrations in the Hebrides.[120]

In addition to the above, there are any number of other natural resources and agricultural products that were traded from northern Britain. It has been argued, for instance, that timber from the Scottish highlands would have been a highly-prized resource for the lords of the sparsely-wooded northern isles, and may have driven the development of the harbours of the Dornoch Firth, near the linguistic boundary between Old Norse- and Gaelic-speakers.[121] From the Roman period onwards, commodities that were most often recorded as exports from Britain and Ireland included leather goods and woollen goods, furs and pelts, dairy products (especially butter), hunting-dogs and slaves.[122] The *Lebor na Cert*, perhaps dating to the 10th century, captures the fascinating range of items used as tribute payments between Irish kings, including drinking-horns, hunting-dogs, female slaves, weapons, gaming-equipment, garments and livestock.[123] Some of these are archaeologically visible, but many are not – and this should serve to remind us how much we are missing from material that does not survive well.

THE COST OF SILVER

The big question remaining is which, if any, of these trade goods might explain the masses of silver flowing into Britain and Ireland by the 10th century. It is important to remember it was not just goods but services that could be enormously profitable, as the case of the Orkney 'pirate fishermen' reminds us. There is certainly evidence for the production and repair of boats from across this period in Scotland. Most well-known are the two prepared curved oak stem-posts for what would have been boats of clinker-built Viking-age type found in a peat-bog

Fig. 6.43 (left): Wooden stem-post of a clinker-built boat, Laig, Isle of Eigg, length 1930mm; NMS X.IN 4.

Fig. 6.44 (below): Carving of a viking ship on a slate, Jarlshof, Shetland, length 400mm; NMS X.HSA 792.

in Laig, Eigg [6.43].[124] More oak boat-timbers have now been dated to the 12th century at the 'shipyard' of Rubh' An Dunain on Skye.[125] Viking-age radiocarbon dates were obtained from Smoo Cave and Glassknappers Cave, near Durness, Sutherland, where there was evidence for the smithing of clench-nails, used in clinker-built boats, suggesting that boat-repair was taking place here.[126] The possibility that sailcloth was being produced at Jarlshof was suggested above. The depiction of longships on a number of slate motif-pieces and graffiti from this site supports the centrality of maritime activity to the community in that area [6.44].

The profitability of the fur trade should also not be underestimated. Recent research into trade items from northern Europe in Islamic sources emphasises the importance of exotic furs in the courtly culture of the caliphate and the high prices that could be commanded.[127] The wild animal-bone assemblage from Viking-age Birka, Sweden, was dominated by squirrel, red fox and pine marten, and other fur-bearing species.[128]

Black and white furs were the most valuable: there is evidence for the hunting of polar bear in Greenland alongside the better-attested walrus-ivory trade.[129] Other less exotic pelts were in high demand for their softness, and one of the big changes in animal-bone assemblages from the Viking Age onwards is the appearance of cat bone. Urban centres such as Whithorn and Dublin were large producers of cat fur for gloves and small items, and cat bones were commonplace in the later medieval burghs.[130] There is some evidence for the exploitation of fur-bearing species such as badgers, otters, stoats and foxes in Scotland, but the evidence remains scant for the Viking Age.[131] The runic bear-tooth pendant from Birsay [7.2] may denote the presence of fur traders, but given the general absence of bear bone in any Viking-age Scottish assemblage, it is likely bears were already extinct from Scotland by then. On current evidence, it seems unlikely that the Scottish fur trade was ever great enough to support the amounts of silver represented in the hoards.

This then leaves the slave trade as the most likely high-value export, and one we know was certainly traded for silver. There has long been a reticence to discuss slave-taking and its consequences. This is partly because of the nature of the evidence.[132] There are plenty of contemporary historical mentions of slaves being taken, but very little information about what happened to them afterwards. We know that some were destined for big slave markets in Dublin, Hedeby and Prague, meaning it was profitable for large numbers of humans to be shipped abroad. Other major harbours and market towns, including Bristol and Chester, certainly flourished from the 10th century partly through their participation in the Irish Sea slave trade as well. The best example is from the audacious, four-month siege of the hillfort of Alt Clut (Dumbarton Rock) by the Dublin-based viking warlords Óláfr and Ívarr (anglicised as Olaf and Ivar) in AD870. After the siege, the Dublin army stayed in Scotland for the winter: by the time they returned to Dublin the following year, they came with '200 ships, bringing away with them in captivity to Ireland a great prey of English, Britons and Picts'.[133]

Viking traders were not simply so barbaric that slavery was their *modus operandi*. They were responding to a huge market demand from the east – not just the Islamic world, but Byzantium too – where slaves were purchased in exchange for silks as well as silver.[134] The Viking Age must be understood in its global context or it will not be understood at all.

Nor did the vikings introduce the slave trade.[135] From as early as the 5th century, St Patrick gives us the first eyewitness accounts of life as a slave and his attempts later in life to denounce the practice. The early Irish legal texts preserve a system of valuation based on the *cumal*, the price of a female slave.[136] We have no such sources from Scotland itself except for the *Life of St Columba*, which describes (in negative terms) the keeping of slaves.[137] Regardless, we know enough from legal texts, annals and other source material that slave-keeping societies were well-established when the vikings arrived in Britain and Ireland.[138] It is unclear to what extent Scandinavian economies relied on slave labour before the Viking Age, but they certainly did during and afterwards.[139]

But, as in west Africa in early modern times, pre-existing indigenous human trafficking practices in Ireland were of a completely different scale when compared to that which followed in the Viking Age.[140] The trade in slaves that came with the Viking Age was enormously scaled up and required a completely new conception of how this practice affected societies in northern Europe.[141]

A glimpse of life as a slave in Viking-age Scotland comes from the *Life of St Findan*.[142] Findan was a 9th-century Irish monk who was captured and enslaved while trying to free his sister from slavery. Although this is a saint's biography and not to be taken as a straightforward historical account, we hear lots of interesting details indicative of the age – notably that Findan was sold down the line three times after being taken in Ireland, eventually ending up on Orkney where he managed to escape. Some of those trades, and certainly the transport of trafficked humans, occurred in what is now Scotland.

At a certain point, slave-taking became a strategy used by insular warlords and kings themselves. As early as 949, Máel Coluim mac Domnaill of Alba undertook raids which resulted in slaves from Northumbria.[143] In the 11th century it has been argued that Irish kings had normalised slave-raiding as a punitive practice against rivals, and we see an apparent rise of captive-taking in the historical annals.[144] In 1079, Malcolm III of Alba is recorded as having raided as far as the Tyne and taken captives, although the increasing mentions of Scottish slave-raiding may be a product of our sources, primarily coming from Norman England.[145]

All the references to raids on Iona (AD 795, 802, 806, 825 and 986) refer to burnings and killings. But in most cases it appears that the 'normal' course of events in a raid on a monastery was to extract movable wealth – and it seems that people were just as, or more, lucrative than the gold and silver treasures held there.[146]

The lack of clear archaeological evidence means that so far we have been able largely to avoid talking about the slave trade in Viking-age Scotland. But as with the legacies of the transatlantic slave trade in early modern Scotland, it is clear there were many ways to be involved and to profit from the slave trade without being an enslaver. Whether it will ever be visible archaeologically, the slave-trading markets of the Viking Age grew into the towns and cities that fuelled the economic expansion of Europe in the second millennium AD.[147] The increased production of all manner of agricultural produce and finished trade goods described above was almost certainly enabled, at least in part, by enslaved labour.

Silver is the clearest proxy evidence for the Viking-age slave trade, which then requires us to recalibrate our view of the silver economy as the currency of people – and perhaps the

Fig. 6.45: Group of silver objects, Skaill Hoard, Orkney: thistle brooch, NMS X.IL 3; thistle brooch terminal, NMS X.IL 5; twisted-rod neck-ring, NMS X.IL 21; and plaited arm-ring; NMS X.IL 22.

massive hoards of silver as a proxy archaeology of slavery, however indirectly [6.45]. We can also refer to the remarkably heavy decorated inset lead weights discussed from Scotland. Did the large amounts of silver being weighed relate to payments for slaves? Was ring-money developed to facilitate silver payments for the slave trade?[148] To what extent was the ostentatious display of silver a direct acknowledgement of participation in slave trade? Was the taking of slaves seen as prestigious? We can begin the process of recalibrating everything we think we know about the silver economy, and especially its ceremonial qualities, in light of these questions.

The evidence discussed above shows us that it was not just vikings who took part in these transactions, nor were they the only ones to profit. Does this help to explain the absences of silver hoards as much as their survival? The luxurious appeal of silver, and all the data bound up in it, means that the focus of study is on the places where it has been found. But, as mentioned earlier, the evidence for the 10th and 11th centuries elsewhere is largely bound up in other metals and other media – particularly the carved stone and other sacred objects relating to Christianity. It is to that evidence – and to those areas – that we need to turn in order to further understand the Scottish experience of the Viking Age.

NOTES

1. Graham-Campbell 2001.
2. Graham-Campbell 1995; Horne 2022.
3. Driscoll 2002; Woolf 2007.
4. Hodges 2006.
5. McCormick 2001.
6. The famous Offa Kufic dinar now in the British Museum (1913,1213.1) was said to have been found in Rome: Naismith 2005, 195–8.
7. Loveluck et al. 2018.
8. Blackburn 2003; Merkel 2018.
9. Mackay 2015, 132.
10. Hadley and Richards 2016.
11. Jarman 2021.
12. Kovalev and Kaelin 2007.
13. Kilger 2008a, 202; Gruszczyński 2018, 171.
14. Graham-Campbell 1995 for all of the Scottish dirhams except one found by metal-detecting in South Uist in 2019, allocated to Museum nan Eilean, Stornoway: TT142/19, information from Ella Paul.
15. Griffiths 2009; Sharples and Parker Pearson 1999; the dirham from South Uist is TT 142/19, 'very likely an Abbasid dirham minted between 251–277h (AD 865–891),' from J Oravisjärvi pers. comm.; with thanks to Jane Kershaw for putting us in touch.
16. Compare Jankowiak 2018.
17. Garipzanov 2005; several examples of pierced dirhams in hoards in Skre (ed.) 2008, e.g. figs 5.7, 7.18, both from relatively early dirham hoards with little or no hacksilver.
18. Kovalev 2003.
19. Kovalev and Kaelin 2007, 567.
20. G Williams 2007; Skre 2011.
21. Goldberg and Davis 2021.
22. Compare Harrison and Ó Floinn 2014, 149.
23. Goldberg and Davis 2021, 80; cf. Kilger 2015.
24. Graham-Campbell 2011a, 10.
25. Graham-Campbell 1995, 28, 144–6.
26. Sheehan 2020, 420.
27. Horne 2022.
28. Horne 2022; Kershaw 2017.

29. Hårdh 2008.
30. Graham-Campbell 1983; 1995, ch. 4.
31. Graham-Campbell 1995, 34–48, 108–27.
32. Graham-Campbell 2011a, 5–7.
33. Another silver ringed pin of this type coming from Adare, Co. Limerick, measured 35 cm: Fanning 1994, 30.
34. Graham-Campbell 1995, 157–8; a lost hoard from the Broch of Burgar, Orkney, was also said to have included silver pins, but of uncertain type and date: Graham-Campbell 1987a, 252–3; 2011a, 129.
35. There are three separate 'parcels' of hacksilver detectable in the Skaill Hoard, for instance, and at least four different 'donors' of the Galloway Hoard have been theorised: Graham-Campbell 1995, 47; Goldberg and Davis 2021.
36. Kruse and Tate 1995.
37. Kilger 2008b, 285–6; Gigha balance and weights: Hunterian Museum GLAHM:A.188/1, 2.
38. Cormack 1995, 75–6.
39. Sharples (ed.) 2021, 106–8; Maleszka 2003.
40. Norstein 2020, 240; NMS X.IL 313.
41. Stalsberg 1991; Kershaw 2019, 134.
42. Hill 1997, 392–3; Russell and Hurley 2014, 228.
43. Kershaw 2019.
44. Kruse 1992; Maleszka 2003.
45. Harrison and Ó Floinn 2014, 171.
46. Kruse 1992.
47. Pedersen 2008.
48. Steuer 1987, 444, fn. 144.
49. Megaw 1940; cf. Harrison and Ó Floinn 2014, 174.
50. Farbregd 1974.
51. Morrisson 2012; Kyhlberg 1975, 160; cf Henning 2007, cat no. 154.
52. Skinner and Bruce Mitford 1940.
53. Kyhlberg 1975; Pedersen 2008, 125; Mainman and Rogers 2002, 2563, illus. 1259; Wallace 1998.
54. Graham-Campbell 1995, 51–2, 131–41.
55. Sheehan and Sikora 2019.
56. Graham-Campbell 1995, 38–40; Kruse and Tate 1995.
57. Critch 2015, 185.
58. Compare Gaimster 1991; Kruse 1993.
59. To be addressed more fully in Horne 2022.
60. Graham-Campbell 1993; Kruse 1993.
61. Naismith 2016; cf. Blackwell et al. 2017.
62. Metcalf 1995; Hill 1997, 332–45; Sharples and Parker Pearson 1999, 54–5; Bateson and Holmes 1998, 2004, 2013.
63. Sheehan 2018.
64. Hamilton 1956, 152; Graham-Campbell 1995, 161.
65. Hill 1997, SR13, 398–400; Hill 1997, 332–45.
66. Graham-Campbell 2009, 196; cf. Sharples (ed.) 2021, 103–9.
67. Morris and Barrowman 2021, 318–9; Graham-Campbell 1995, 162–3.
68. TT84.10; Canmore ID 333881; cf. hacked silver ingot from Clashmore, TT78.13; both allocated to Dornoch Historylinks Museum.
69. TT18.15, now Perth Museum PERGM: 2016.35; identification by J. Graham-Campbell, pers. comm.
70. Sheehan 2018.
71. Barnes and Page 2006.
72. Clancy 2013.
73. Stevenson 1953.
74. Liestøl 1983.
75. Campbell et al. 2019; Maldonado et al. 2021.
76. A. Woolf, pers. comm.
77. For the following, see Woolf 2007 and Downham 2007.
78. Graham-Campbell 1995, 102.
79. Davies 2010.
80. Clarkson 2014, 54–5, 61–3; Edmonds 2018.
81. Edmonds 2018.
82. Alcock and Alcock 1991.
83. Summary of the sequence available at: <https://www.gla.ac.uk/schools/humanities/events/archaeologyevents/conferences/vikings%2020%20years%20on/thecarrickmidrosswestdunbartonshire/> [accessed July 2021]
84. Graham-Campbell and Batey 1998, 144, 152, 228; Hadley and Richards 2018, 15.
85. Graham-Campbell 1995, 95.
86. *Ibid.*, 49.
87. TT03.13; information via Ella Paul.
88. Clancy 2008; with thanks to A. Woolf, pers. comm. for clarification on these matters.

89. Barnes and Page 2006, 219–21.
90. Driscoll et al. 2005.
91. Kelly 2000.
92. Holmes 2004.
93. G. Williams 2007.
94. Kershaw 2017; Kilger 2008b, 270–1; Hadley and Richards 2018.
95. Skre 2017.
96. Barrett 2007.
97. Sindbæk 2013; Schou 2017.
98. Marttila 2016; Forster 2009.
99. Curle 1936, 264, fig. 13; Forster and Jones 2017, 232; Mainman and Rogers 2000, 2477; Pedersen 2008, 167, fig. 6.32.
100. Oslo Kulturhistorisk Museum C7823; Williams 1999, 23–4.
101. Dommasnes and Hommedal 2016, 153–5; cf. Bender Jørgensen 2012.
102. Hayeur Smith 2018.
103. Hudson 1999; Langlands 2020.
104. Skre 2011; Kershaw et al. (eds) 2018.
105. Spearman 1988; Ross 2019.
106. O'Sullivan et al. 2014, 265–6; Graham-Campbell and Batey 1998, 209; Foster 2017.
107. Earwood 1994.
108. Callmer 1977.
109. O'Sullivan 2015, 82.
110. Graham-Campbell and Batey 1998, 59–60, 64.
111. Caldwell, Hall and Wilkinson 2009.
112. Frei et al. 2015; Star et al. 2018.
113. Gillman 2017; Dectot 2018.
114. Hunter 2008b.
115. Pierce 2013; Ó Floinn 2020, 240–1.
116. Carver et al. 2016, Digest 6.3, D85; Hunter 2016.
117. Griffiths 2014.
118. Campbell et al. 2019; Maldonado et al. 2021.
119. O'Rahilly 1998; Barton-Murray and Johnson 2012.
120. For example, Campbell et al. 2019; Close-Brooks and Maxwell 1972; Close-Brooks 1996, 270–3.
121. Barrett 2007, 317; Graham-Campbell and Batey 1998, 220–21; Crawford and Taylor 2003.
122. O'Sullivan et al. 2014, 265–6, 276–7.
123. *Ibid.*, 279–80.
124. Graham-Campbell and Batey 1998, 84, 221; one of these, NMS X.IN 5, has been radiocarbon-dated: Beta-114594, 1060 BP +/- 50, calibrated to AD777–1151 at 95% confidence, IntCal 21.
125. Martin 2009.
126. Pollard 2005.
127. Kovalev and Kaelin 2007, 569–71; Michailidis 2012; Howard-Johnston 2020.
128. Ljungqvist 2005.
129. Wigh 2001, 121.
130. Smith 1999; Hill 1997, 390, 612.
131. Fairnell and Barrett 2007.
132. Fontaine 2017; Raffield 2019; Raffield, Gardeła, and Toplak 2021.
133. Woolf 2007, 109.
134. Jankowiak 2016; 2017; 2020.
135. Rio 2017 for the wider early medieval European context.
136. Eska 2011.
137. Book 2:34, 40; Sharpe 1995.
138. Pelteret 1995.
139. Myhre 2000; Skre 2020.
140. Woolf 2018.
141. Holm 1986.
142. Thomson 1986.
143. Etchingham 2021.
144. Woolf 2007, 180, 188.
145. Holm 1986.
146. McGuigan 2021, 156–8, 282.
147. Raffield 2019; McCormick 2002; Smith 2019.
148. The Scottish arm-rings are eerily similar to the bronze manilla arm-rings used as currency in west Africa during the trans-Atlantic slave trade.

CHAPTER SEVEN
An animated world

The preceding chapters have focused on points of dialogue between the various actors in the drama of the Viking Age. The most consequential of these interactions was the encounter with the Christian faith. Our contemporary sources, written from a Christian point of view, clearly emphasise the 'heathen' nature of the Northmen. Yet the Christian Church was not eradicated even in areas of Scandinavian settlement. Instead, there are numerous examples of Christian material culture re-purposed in 'pagan' grave goods, and even a surprising number of such burials in the vicinity of churches, and eventually evidence for Norse-speaking Christians. Instead of a clash of incompatible worldviews, archaeology reveals that people in the Viking Age engaged with the supernatural in ways which cannot be so neatly boxed into Christian or pagan.

Perhaps the best way to approach religion in this period is to show the power that objects held in both insular and Scandinavian contexts. The location and function of supernatural forces were described with different words, but both Christian and pagan cosmologies were also in the time period we are considering here. Archaeology cannot always reveal belief; but it can, if used with sensitivity, reveal the enchantment of the early medieval material world.

AMULETS

The evidence for amulets in the 9th–12th centuries will show how unsatisfactory it is to have to choose simply between 'Christian' and 'pagan' in the early medieval thoughtworld. Amulets are here defined as objects worn or carried on the body for supernatural protection, although the term is a slippery one. Crosses and crucifix pendants, then as now, can be worn by Christians not just for protection, but to signal religious affiliation in a multicultural context. It is assumed Thor's Hammer pendants had a similar range of meanings in a Norse pagan context. The point is rather moot in a Scottish context, however, as there are so few of either. The only Thor's Hammer pendant comes from a heavily corroded iron neck-ring around the female wearing oval brooches in a cist grave at the Broch of

Opposite: Detail of a stone cross-slab from Invergowrie, Angus, showing confronted horned beasts; NMS X.IB 251.

Fig. 7.1 (right): Pair of jet cross pendants: (left) from Lochspouts Crannog, Ayrshire, diameter 38 mm, NMS X.HW 11; (right) Lauder, Berwickshire, length 23 mm, NMS X.NO 79.

Fig. 7.2 (below): Bear canine perforated for suspension, inscribed with Norse runic inscription reading 'FUTHARK', and a rune-like symbol, Brough of Birsay, Orkney, length 50 mm; NMS X.HB 253.

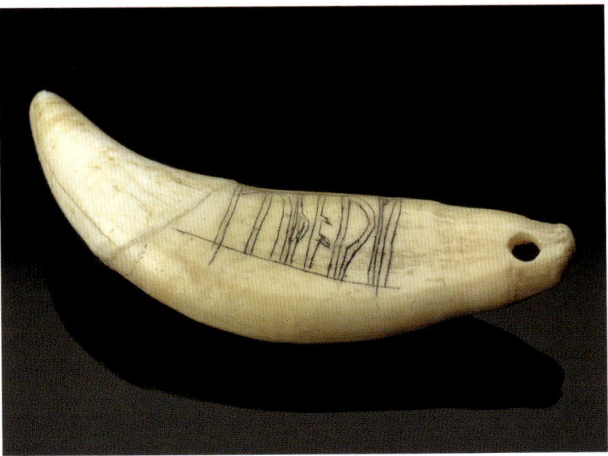

Gurness, although there are a growing number of stone ingot moulds with T-shaped cavities, possibly for casting hammer-shaped pendants.[1]

Cross-shaped pendants are somewhat more common, but tend to be towards the later end of the period. Four cruciform pendants of Whitby jet, which may be as late as the 12th century, have been discovered in Scotland [Fig 7.1].[2] Small cross pendants of lead and bone have now been found from the late 10th- to 12th-century layers of Norse longhouses in Bornais and Cille Pheadair, both South Uist, although they are rare beyond these well-excavated settlements.[3]

The amulets we have are generally not specific to any religious group. A desire for protection by or from supernatural forces is a consequence of living in an animated world. If an object is understood to provide protection, its use may be pragmatic and need not indicate familiarity with scripture or consecration into a religious community. Amulets can also be used to enhance or amplify the chances of certain outcomes: for instance, to increase fertility or virility, or just for luck.

One of the most striking stray finds of this period is a pendant made from a bear's tooth inscribed with Old Norse runes [7.2]. This was found in the rich midden layers of the Brough of Birsay, making it hard to date closely. Even without an inscription, a canine made into a pendant would easily be considered an amulet of some sort. Brown bears might have walked in Scotland as late as the Pictish period, when they are depicted on several carved stones, but are thought to have been extinct by the Viking Age – certainly no other bear bones have been identified in numerous excavation assemblages of the period. As such, this is likely to have come in with a trader from the better-known bear-hunting regions of the Baltic or northern Norway. However, bear-tooth pendants were rare everywhere by the Viking Age, except in the Baltic where the fur trade boomed and bear-cult continued to thrive.[4] The Birsay tooth is unique in being inscribed. Its message is simple: 'FUTHARK', followed by a rune-like pencil-shaped character. These are the first six characters in the runic alphabet and may be an example of a textual amulet, where writing itself was seen as powerful and protective.[5] The final character is either an unfinished rune, or a symbol, perhaps of a spear or even a tooth, representing the kind of protection from harm a runic amulet could provide.[6] Textual amulets occur in various contexts, including an inscribed bone-pin with three A runes from Westness [1.3], and a bronze ring inscribed with 9th- or 10th-century Anglo-Saxon runes, which do not spell any known words, from Cramond near Edinburgh [7.3].[7]

With decorated pins, rings and pendants, it is futile to draw the line between amulets and other accessories in the early medieval context.[8] We have already explored the animated world of dress items, metal objects writhing with serpents which

Fig. 7.3: Finger-ring of leaded bronze inscribed with Anglo-Saxon runes, from Cramond Churchyard, Edinburgh, diameter 19mm; NMS X.NJ 19.

pricked like thorns (chapter 5). Dress items of all kinds could bear some sort of amuletic function, from the protective beast of a zoomorphic pin to the prophylactic function of interlace. In the 10th century the most common type of ringed pin, the polyhedral-headed type, often bore cruciform imagery, as did many of the decorated copper-alloy belt-fittings of the Viking-age Irish Sea.[9] Similarly, the role of oval brooches in signalling or enhancing female fertility has already been discussed (see p. 107–8).

A series of well-made, highly polished bone-pins with cross-shaped heads might at first appear to signal a Christian presence [7.4]. In Scotland, these are only found at two Viking-age sites where the dating is unfortunately not very clear – Skaill, Deerness, and Jarlshof, Shetland.[10] Parallels for these are broadly 10th–12th century across the 'viking diaspora' including Norway, Ireland and Iceland.[11] One example in silver from Hegreberg, Rogaland, came from a male-gendered cremation grave of possible 10th-century date with other insular objects, which is probably not to be understood as a 'Christian' burial.[12] A study of Christian amulets among the Rus' discovered they only appear from the mid-10th century onwards, incorporated into the traditional ostentatious furnishings of wealthy female graves.[13] Christian objects could then be a form of signalling status, like pendants of foreign coins and exotic beads discussed in previous chapters, as much as tokens of faith. Conversely, we can also understand coin-pendants and imported beads as being ascribed other affordances beyond signalling wealth.

The cross-headed bone-pins from Jarlshof are joined by a number of other well-executed 'amuletic' pins. Some were in the shape of miniature weapons, especially axes [7.5]. While these may be dress-pins, other examples of miniature axes in copper-alloy have been found in Dublin, Norway and Denmark, often suspended from rings, and in some cases found at the hip in a burial context, suggesting they were carried like charms and not worn as pins.[14] One of the Jarlshof axe-pins is perforated for use in this way. Other miniature weapon-pins from Scotland include one in the shape of a sword hilt from Jarlshof, and another shaped like a hammer or mallet from the Birsay area of Orkney.[15] Perhaps the most famous amuletic pins from Shetland are those which are rendered with snarling dragons and other beasts [7.5]. Beast-headed pins are not an innovation of the Viking Age, with numerous examples going back to Iron Age and Pictish contexts [5.2]. Unfinished examples of both cross-headed and beast-headed pins from Jarlshof show that they were being produced on site, perhaps in the 11th century according to finds from similar contexts.[16] The bone dragon-headed examples, where the animal head is parallel to the shaft of the pin, are well-known from other Viking-age contexts, particularly in Dublin and Iceland.[17] However, several forms of zoomorphic pin are known in metal, including one from Jarlshof [7.6a–b], so it may be futile to discern between 'amuletic' and 'dress'-pins.[18]

It is also unclear as to what extent lay Christians wore crosses or other obvious tokens of faith in northern Britain. The dress items we have from insular contexts already bear cruciform and Christological motifs, but they are not always readily apparent; brooch-pins with beast-heads confronted across a lozenge, or diamond-shaped, motif can be understood as a cryptic symbol of Christ.[19] Indeed, a number of brooches and pins would be developed from the 8th–12th centuries with lozenge-shaped plates and heads that may be understood as Christian, even if they did not have crosses or crucifixion

AN ANIMATED WORLD

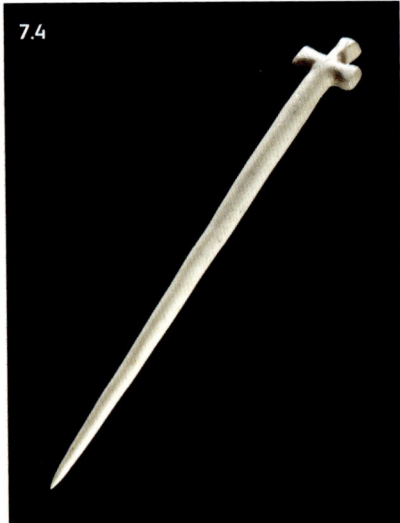

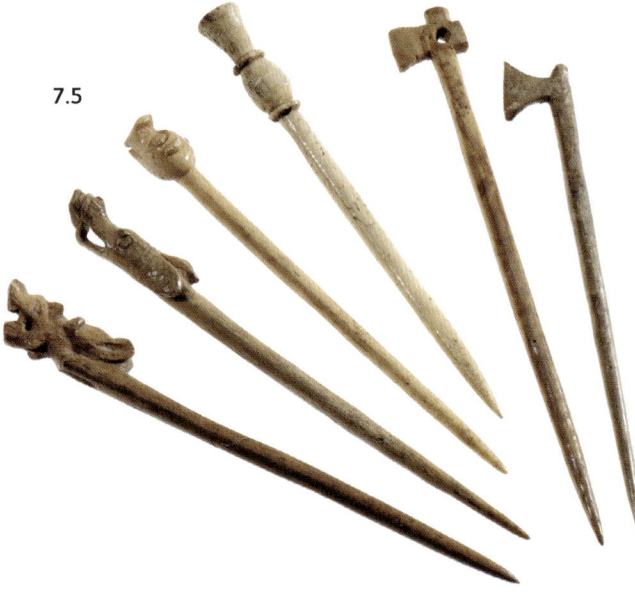

imagery.[20] A series of lozenge-headed pins has been found across the Danelaw, Ireland and Scandinavian parts of Scotland, or largely 11th-century contexts where datable, including in one case the burial of Bishop Wulfstan of Ely in 1023.[21] However, another quite different and robust example in brass comes from a poorly recorded grave of a woman, possibly a cemetery at Cornaigbeg on Tiree [7.7].[22] It is remarkably long at 17.1 cm, with an open lozenge head, beaded corners and a perforation for an attachment at the head. Its brass composition originally would have given it a bright gold colour, and suggests that it was made outside Scotland, perhaps in Dublin or York, but it otherwise has no parallel. Its appropriation as a female dress item is interesting given the depiction of a gold-coloured lozenge-shaped object with beaded corners on a depiction of the Virgin Mary in the Book of Kells (c.800).[23] However, this does not seem to be a faithful representation of a pin, and the perforation at the head of the Tiree example suggests it was used with a chain. Its robustness and unusual form may even indicate an original use in a reliquary context.

Materials themselves, as much as the finished object, could also take on amuletic significance. In addition to their rarity in an insular context, amber and jet also have electrostatic properties that have contributed to their use as gemstones since prehistory.[24] There are relatively few beads or pendants of amber or jet in Viking-age Scotland, although urban centres like Dublin and York were producing amber pendants

Fig. 7.4: Cross-headed bone-pin, Jarlshof, Shetland, length 127mm; NMS X.HSA 124.

Fig. 7.5: Amuletic bone-pins, Jarlshof, Shetland: (from left) NMS X.HSA 3 (length 114mm), 4, 2, 12, 8 (pierced) and 7 (unpierced).

Figs 7.6 a–b: Beast-headed bronze pin (with detail), from Jarlshof, Shetland, length 65mm; NMS X.HSA 843.

Fig. 7.7: Open lozenge-headed brass pin with perforated head, from a woman's grave, possibly Cornaigbeg, Tiree, length 171mm; NMS X.IL 220.

CRUCIBLE OF NATIONS

Fig. 7.8: Composite pendant of silver encasing a damaged glass bead, with suspension loop pierced through a coin of Coenwulf of Mercia (d.821), diameter 28.16mm; NMS X.2018.12.71.5.

in a variety of shapes.[25] Amber beads were rarely discovered in necklaces, but are most often found singly, worn around the neck, indicating they had an amuletic function separate from the usual use of beaded necklaces as dress items.[26] Other exotic beads were highly profitable trade items and even used as currency (p. 151), but their use as pendants blurs the line between economic and spiritual value. The objects placed inside the silver vessel from the Galloway Hoard (pp 86–7) capture the range of symbolic values that could be held by objects.[27] A single, cracked polychrome glass bead had been kept intact by constructing a casing of silver with openings so the bead inside could still be seen [7.8]; it was capped by a perforated coin of Coenwulf of Mercia, minted decades before the hoard was deposited in c.900. The composite pendant was treated as a 'relic' like the string of well-worn heirloom glass beads at the top of the vessel. A black schist-like stone, used as a touchstone for assessing the quality of precious metal, was encased in an elaborate gold-filigree casing to make it a pendant. A naturally rattling stone and rock-crystal ball made into a pendant join two 'dirt balls', likely earth-relics from a holy shrine, showing the range of materials that could be elevated to the status of relics and sacred matter in a Christian context.

TRADE MAGIC

The coin-pendant from the Galloway Hoard is one of many ways in which coins were reused as display items in the 9th and 10th centuries [4.21, 4.26, 6.2]. It is a reminder that what seems to us like cold, hard currency still operated in an animated world in which silver had its own specific cultural significance.[28] When silver did begin to flow into the north, the response was only rarely to transform it into coins. Instead, where we see silver repurposed it is into locally meaningful objects of power – neck-rings and arm-rings in Scandinavia; penannular brooches and elaborate pins in Britain and Ireland. Even that is too neat a division, as we reviewed in the abundant evidence for Scandinavian appropriation of penannular brooches and brooch-pins, as much as the insular adoption of rings. This is perhaps because the underlying ideology is similar – the giving of rings and pinning of objects on the body were ways of performing power in gift-giving societies.[29] As different sources of silver became available, the objects themselves became less culturally specific: instead, the actions – that is, the performance of the exchange itself – grew much more important. The Galloway Hoard, with its inscribed names, clustered arm-rings and separate parcels of objects, looks increasingly like a vow or contract committed to the ground.

Indeed we cannot see hoards of silver as completely 'economic' in significance. Every act of deposition is a 'time capsule' in a sense: either a cache to be retrieved in the future, or a gift, or a sacrifice. Hoards contain clues to their social function in the ways they were assembled and deposited. The top layer of the Galloway Hoard was marked with a pectoral cross and it is possible that crosses, complete rings and other ritually charged ornaments were added to hoards as supernatural protection.[30] The St Ninian's Isle Hoard was placed in a wooden box, under a cross-slab, inside a church, so there is no escaping its religious significance, even if the exact meaning is obscure to us now [4.13]. Even the clearly economic hoards of the later

Fig. 7.9: Silver penannular brooch with stamp-decorated polygonal terminals, with pin bent into a hook-shape, from the Skaill Hoard, Orkney, diameter 136mm, weight 163.6g; NMS X.IL 8.

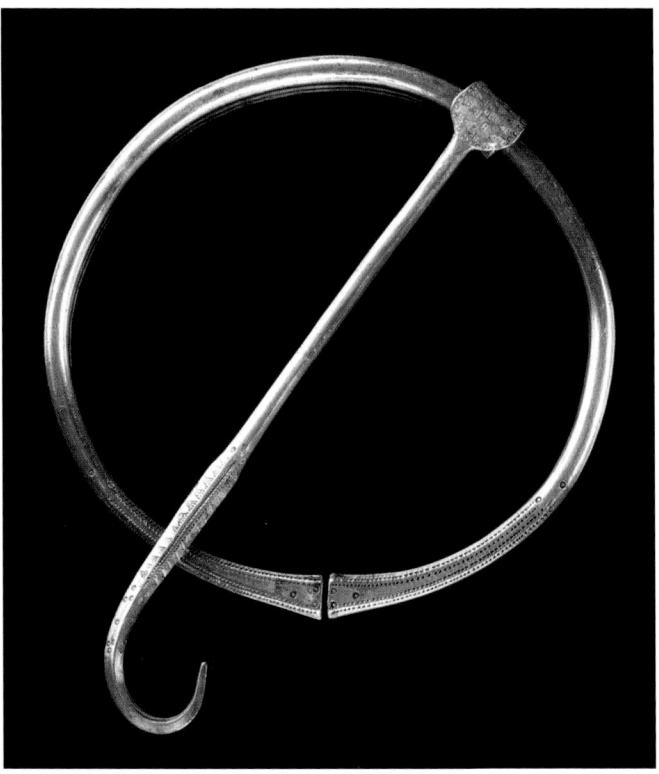

9th–11th centuries have potentially ceremonial, even amuletic aspects to them. The large Skaill Hoard was deposited at or near the initial occupation of what became a thriving settlement on the Bay of Skaill, as if to mark its foundation.[31] Some pins in the hoard were subjected to the same kind of bending, perhaps as a way of testing the quality of silver during the exchange, or as a performative aspect of that exchange [7.9]. The later sagas and legal traditions of Scandinavia preserve stories of silver hoards deposited as land-claims and proof of inheritance.[32] The strong correlation of large silver hoards and royal Irish settlements, especially crannogs or artificial islands, speak to the use of silver in a long-lived practice of deposition of vows, sacrifices and tribute in watery places.[33] In Scotland most of the silver hoards are within sight of water, but this may be to do with the largely maritime nature of most Viking-age settlements. Yet some are far from settlement, and instead may be engaging with other aspects of the natural landscape: the Storr Rock Hoard faced the sea beneath one of the most striking natural rock formations on the Isle of Skye; the Burray Hoard was deposited in an alder bowl, in a raised bog near a spring.[34]

However, the deposition of a hoard was the last act in a potentially long chain of exchanges, peaceful or otherwise. Every act of trade carried with it an element of risk which was mitigated by establishing trust between the two sides of the transaction: testing the quality of the silver by nicking, for instance, or showcasing the reliability of the weighing equipment itself (chapter 6). The rituals of trade and the symbols of 'merchant' status in a time when silver was won as much as earned, were swathed in ceremony. To return to the Galloway Hoard, the touchstone pendant stands at the head of a class of pendant whetstones and touchstones from across the viking diaspora [7.10].[35] Most have no cap or suspension mechanism remaining, but some are mounted with silver or copper-alloy, likely indicating an exotic origin or heirloom status.[36] While whetstones were practical tools to carry along with knives, touchstones had a specialist function reserved for a restricted elite along with decorated balance scales and weights. Dark stones were best for revealing the light coloured streaks of gold and silver, but stones of striking lithology, such as banded layers of contrasting colours, were also used, showing that the display of the touchstone itself was part of the 'performance' of trade in precious metals. These overlap with a class of 'whetstone-shaped' pendants of stone that bear no signs of use as touchstones and were too small for use as whetstones. A pendant of sandstone was found alongside a single amber bead around the neck of a six-year-old child in the Viking-age cemetery of Cnip, Lewis, strongly suggesting use as 'magic for the dead' so often found in association with child burials in medieval contexts before, during and after the Viking Age.[37] A minuscule (44mm) pendant of striking banded lithology was found in a Viking-age settlement mound at Skaill, Orkney.[38] Another example is the pendant 'whetstone' of polished porphyritic green stone from a lost ruined settlement known as 'St Salvador's Chapel' on Shapinsay, Orkney [7.11].[39] At 52mm, this oblong bar is well crafted and highly polished, showing no trace of use-

Fig. 7.10: Touchstone of black schist encased in gold-filigree mount, perforated for suspension, from the Galloway Hoard, length 67.3 mm, NMS X.2018.12.71.22.

Fig. 7.11: Pendant of porphyritic stone, Shapinsay, Orkney, length 52 mm; NMS X.AL 20.

Fig. 7.12: Baltic-type penannular brooch of copper-alloy with traces of silver, with terminals in the shape of knobbed weights or playing-pieces, Harrow, Caithness, diameter 70 mm; NMS X.1992.23.

Fig. 7.13: Baltic-type bronze penannular brooch of copper-alloy, with terminals in the shape of polyhedral weights, found at Gogar Burn, Midlothian, diameter 60 mm; NMS X.FC 153.

wear, and its association with a possible burial ground strongly suggests it was worn as an amulet.

Over time, merchant and military activity became less closely intertwined and there are signs of early 'guilds' of merchants forming across the northern world in the 10th and the 11th centuries.[40] Spaces where market trade occurred could be walled off or enclosed, with different social norms and laws operating within the area. This promoted trust among merchants, regardless of origin, reducing the risk of violence in a field of competitive exchange.[41] A merchant identity could be signalled by items of trade rendered as tokens or amulets.[42] The link between dress and merchant identity is nowhere more explicitly captured than in the series of 10th-century penannular brooches with terminals in the shape of lead weights [7.12–13]. One from Harrow, Caithness, has terminals in the same shape as the castle-shaped weight found among the set from the Kiloran Bay, Colonsay, boat burial, which in an insular context has now been linked to the archaeological 'footprint' of the Great Army [6.16]. The more elaborate example – from Gogar Burn, Midlothian – is an enigmatic findspot for Scandinavian material culture, but joins other outliers from this area.[43] The ornament here is based on the cubo-octahedral weights also imported to Norway and Britain via the trade networks used by members of the Great Army (chapter 6), and this may be a Norse copy of a Baltic-type brooch.[44] It provides more proof that the material culture of trade was also a symbol of status amongst a merchant-warrior class. It was not only religious symbols that could become totemic in this period.

THE POWER OF PLAY

Another aspect of daily life that could become imbued with supernatural significance was that of gaming. Gaming-pieces were first introduced to Scotland – as in Scandinavia – in the Roman period, but they quickly took on an important social function. The competition between two players was seen as more than just a pastime, and sets of gaming-pieces were used as grave-goods from the Iron Age onwards.[45] In the Viking Age, game-pieces could be made of whalebone, walrus ivory, glass and amber, as well as more readily available bone and lead, indicating the high value of a good game board. Outside graves, gaming-pieces are routinely found in hall sites, hillforts and monasteries. The Lewis Chess-pieces, of walrus ivory and whale's teeth, were probably meant as rich gifts used in royal court settings.[46] Gaming was more than just play, but display.

Their inclusion as grave-goods suggests that gaming also had a supernatural aspect. Gaming-pieces could be used in divination practices to predict outcomes, and the skill of a player may have been seen as indicative of skill in battle.[47] Gaming-pieces in Viking-age graves often include only one player's set of pieces, laid out for play, as if in expectation of future games in the ancestral space.[48] They are strongly linked with boat burials and male-gendered assemblages, indicating a link to warrior status.

Game boards were less prestigious than gaming-pieces, though one famous wooden example from Ballinderry Crannog, Co. Westmeath, shows the boards could also be richly ornamented.[49] Examples in stone and whalebone survive from Birsay and Jarlshof, but the majority are known from medieval monasteries. The game boards from Inchmarnock and Portmahomack are amongst the earliest from Scotland, with at least 35 found at Inchmarnock alone.[50] The fine playing-pieces from Coldingham Priory and Birsay [7.14a–b, 7.15] were associated with 11th- to 12th-century ecclesiastical sites. It is worth exploring patterns of deposition to learn more about the ritual significance of gaming in early medieval Scotland.

Figs 7.14a–b (above): Cylindrical chess-piece of ivory, Coldingham Priory, Scottish Borders, height 44 mm; NMS H.NS 30 (profile and overhead views).

Fig. 7.15 (right): Playing-pieces of bone and antler: (from left) Ness Broch, Caithness, NMS X.GA 743; Sandwick Bay, Unst, Shetland, NMS X.HR 849; Brough of Birsay, Orkney, height 37 mm, NMS X.HB 275; Freswick Links, Caithness, diameter 48 mm, NMS X.IL 666.

FRAGMENTS OF THE SACRED

From these ambiguous amulets, we can turn to the sacred objects of the Christian Church. It is ironic perhaps that the best way to investigate the material world of Christian belief in this period is to begin with Viking-age graves and hoards. Several studies of insular material in Scandinavian contexts have demonstrated the frequency in which it was objects of ecclesiastical origin that were most often reused as dress items and the like (pp 79–81). The question remains about whether these were still recognised as 'Christian' or in some way suffused with 'magic' even after they were removed from their ecclesiastical context, with some arguing that Christian objects in Norse graves may represent early missionary activity to Scandinavia.[51] Complete insular reliquary shrines are also found in Scandinavia and, however they got there, they appear to have been incorporated into ritual practices in a 'pagan' context.[52] Most of the fragmented objects seem to be modified into dress items for female graves. This fragmentation has been seen as evidence of 'resistance' to Christianity, but it is more likely the conscious selection of sacred art as exotic jewellery helped to display status and access to wealth in an age of raids.[53]

Some insular shrine fragments were treated with a kind of veneration in a different context once taken to Scandinavia. The bronze finial of a large tomb-shrine was deposited in a box with the 'Gausel Queen', Rogaland, a female burial with a number of insular objects. Similarly, the complete Melhus, Overhalla, house-shaped reliquary appears to have been carried on a leather strap before being deposited in a wooden box in the woman's grave.[54] Other shrine mounts were reused as belt-hangings, showing they could act in an amuletic capacity in a new setting.[55] In each case, these sacred objects acquired a different kind of cultic function that was neither simply pagan nor Christian.

It has been argued that the 'exotic' nature of the insular metalwork looted in the age of raids is what afforded it an aura of power in a Scandinavian context: that a fragment of decorated metalwork in Norway would have been valuable partly because it was obtained from far-off lands. It is striking then that so many fragments of insular metalwork were reused in the same ways in Scottish furnished burials, when these objects came from much nearer. In light of evidence for a substantial insular component to the individuals we call 'vikings' buried in Scotland (chapter 3), we can now return to the use of sacred objects. These are almost invariably found in fragments, making it difficult to reconstruct their original forms, as exemplified by the mount from Westness, Rousay, Orkney [7.16]. This was clearly cut from a larger decorative piece, leaving only the rampant lion, and modified with a pin to act as a brooch. The panel may have come from a depiction of the four evangelists, perhaps on the cover of a gospel book, with the distinctive curled mane identifying it as the symbol of Mark [7.17].[56] Its attitude and open jaws recall the Pictish 'dragons' on brooch terminals, as well as the beast licking the cross from the Portmahomack cross-slab (pp 121–4). It would have been one of the outstanding works of insular Christian metalwork had it survived intact, making us reflect on what else has been lost.

Indeed, many types of ecclesiastical objects from Scotland only survive in Viking-age graves or hoards. For instance, the Ballinaby ladle [4.1] is the only one of its kind from Scotland, the others coming from Ireland or in graves in Norway. These objects were used with highly decorated buckets in an ecclesiastical context, likely to carry and pour out holy water, though similar buckets are also found in secular sites.[57] Another rare object is represented by a sheet of decorated copper-alloy, tinned on its surface to give it a silvery look, cut down to a roundel of no more than 4 cm across for reuse as a pin or belt-mount in a female cist grave in Machrins, Colonsay [7.18].[58] The ornament of interlaced beasts shows that this was once part of a decorated bucket. A similarly minuscule roundel of engraved

Fig. 7.16 (below): Rectangular gilt-bronze mount depicting a lion, reused as a brooch in a woman and infant grave from Westness, Rousay, Orkney (1963), length 66mm; NMS X.IL 730.

Fig. 7.17 (bottom): The lion symbol of Mark the Evangelist from the Echternach Gospels, Paris, MS. lat. 9389, f. 75, Bibliothèque Nationale. (© Bibliothèque Nationale, France)

bronze sheet was found in a woman's grave at Torshov, Akershus, perforated for use as an amulet.[59] There is only one other instance of an insular decorated bucket in Scotland. In the same grave as the elaborate prestige sword hilt from Kildonnan, Eigg [3.7], were the heavily fragmented remains of a bronze-bound bucket of insular type [7.19]. The circular escutcheon with cruciform arrangement of animal heads is closely paralleled by a complete bucket from Birka, Sweden, one of several insular buckets discovered in graves there [7.20].[60] Several fragments of undecorated bronze sheet also survive from the Kildonnan grave, indicating that the bucket was buried complete and, like the sword, damaged upon retrieval. The cruciform arrangement of inward-looking animal heads of both the Kildonnan and Birka buckets is evocative of Pictish metalwork such as the elaborate brooches from Rogart, Sutherland [4.16], and Clunie, Perthshire [4.17], and decorated bronze sheet of similar type has been found at Portmahomack, all of which make it possible that some of these buckets were also made in Scotland.[61]

While the modification of these bronze mounts would have rendered the original objects somewhat unrecognisable, others were more carefully dismantled before being reworked. A frequently recurring type of insular object found in Viking-age graves is the decorated disc mount. These circular objects, often convex in profile, were repurposed as brooches or belt-mounts, though in some occasions left unmodified.[62] The best example from Scotland is from a woman's grave from Bhaltos, Lewis. The grave was not excavated professionally so there are no skeletal remains, nor is there a clear idea of how the grave-goods were arranged, but the presence of a pair of Scandinavian-style brass oval brooches is indicative of a female-gendered costume. Interestingly, other than the oval brooches and single bead of amber, the rest of the surviving items are all likely to be of insular make.[63] The gilt-bronze disc, 70mm in diameter, is one of the most elaborate mounts of its kind, with concentric rows of interlace and beading around a prominent central

Fig. 7.18: Bucket mount, Machrins, Colonsay; NMS X.HR 1561.

Fig. 7.19: Bucket escutcheon, Isle of Eigg; NMS X.IL 159 A.

7.20: Decorated insular bucket from Birka, Sweden, grave Bj 507. (© Ola Myrin, The Swedish History Museum/SHM [CC BY])

setting, perhaps for amber or rock crystal, of 18 mm in diameter. The underside of the disc is concave and the mount rises to 5 mm in height at the edges. The outer edge is incised with a chevron pattern, indicating that it stood proud of the surface it was mounted on. It is not clear how this was used in the grave; occasionally disc mounts in Scandinavian graves were deposited wrapped in textile or in wooden boxes, and not worn as jewellery.[64]

Bosses and disc-shaped mounts such as these are often interpreted as coming from book-shrines on the parallel of an example from Lough Kinale in central Ireland, but larger ones may also have come from altar crosses or other shrines; the diameter of the Bhaltos disc [7.21] matches that of the 'underfoot disc' of the Ardagh Chalice (71.5 mm).[65] There are a number of stone crosses with hollows or insets for central bosses of various sizes, although none matches this one exactly.[66] It is also argued that stone crosses with bossed ornament, such as the high crosses of Iona, may be replicating bossed metalwork crosses such as the reconstructed example from Dumfriesshire (pp 80–1). The disc mount from Bhaltos must have come from a very ornate construction, and its nearly undamaged state (except for the loss of its central setting) indicates that it was dismantled with care.

A similarly elaborate convex mount of gilt copper-alloy is known only as 'west of Scotland' [7.22].[67] This has a large central amber setting framed with a lobed design of the same kind found on several items of insular metalwork.[68] Its heavy construction and concave profile suggest it may have come from a processional cross, but as with the Bhaltos mount it has been removed from its parent object with some care and has only scant traces of secondary use. Like other loose mounts found in unrecorded circumstances in Scotland, this object may have been displaced from a Viking-age grave or hoard.[69] Other disc-shaped mounts may have been used in ways we have lost; the 9th-century Invergowrie cross-slab [7.23] depicts what seems to be clerics holding books wearing disc-shaped brooches at the shoulders, perhaps akin to those found in the Galloway Hoard.[70] The central figure does not wear any, but is holding an enigmatic circular or horseshoe-shaped object; it is possible this is a sacred object or liturgical vestment of a type we do not yet understand. There is much more to be gleaned from identification of the material culture depicted on such stones, as we will see below.

There is no single way to understand individual cases of reuse, but certainly the power and status that these objects represented in an insular context could translate abroad. What we forget when we only look at sacred objects in 'viking' contexts is that there was a similar process of fragmentation and

dispersal of sacred objects in the Christian world. As the Church expanded in reach across the west, new foundations required altar plate, liturgical equipment and the relics of the saints. Famous cult items, such as fragments of the True Cross, circulated widely and were given as gifts from popes to bishops and kings. At one point the Carolingian-era requirement for relics to be placed in every altar led to a boom in the illicit trade in relics, real or forged, from Rome and the near East.[71] In an insular context, the relics of a patron saint were shared among the family of foundations owing allegiance to the keeper of the founder's shrine. In the case of St Columba's relics, their partition between the saint's shrine on Iona and major daughter churches in Kells in Ireland and Dunkeld in the territory of the Picts led to bitter rivalries among factions of his own devotees, spilling into violence over the course of the 10th century.[72]

Fig. 7.21 (left, above): Disc mount of gilt-bronze with chevron ornament incised on outer rim, chip-carved interlace ornament, and large central setting, now missing, from a woman's grave at Bhaltos, Lewis, diameter 70mm; NMS X.IL 378.

Fig. 7.22 (left, below): Circular mount of gilt copper-alloy with lozenge-shaped setting of amber and two triangular projections on circumference, west of Scotland, maximum width 51mm; NMS X.IL 363.

Fig. 7.23 (right): Cross-slab of sandstone showing interlace-ornamented cross carved in relief, Invergowrie, Angus, height 1300mm; NMS X.IB 251.

In both Christian and pagan contexts, then, the idea of *pars pro toto*, a part standing in for the whole, had been internalised in ritual contexts. Bones of the saints were dispersed from the 4th century and there is evidence for the circulation of corporeal relics in Ireland as early as the 7th century.[73] These are the origins of the house-shaped reliquaries, used in an insular context from the 7th–10th centuries specifically for transporting fragments of saint's relics outside the Church. Only one has been provenanced to Scotland – the Monymusk Reliquary, which survived the Viking Age and remained in use throughout the medieval period.[74] Like the Monymusk Reliquary, most surviving examples pre-date the Viking Age, but the number of examples reused in Viking-age graves tells us they were still in active circulation in the 9th century: the Inchmarnock 'Hostage Stone' may even depict the capture of one in the course of a raid [2.15]. Further examples may have been looted from Scotland, while others survive only in fragments, such as the Carn a' Bharraich hinged-straps, reused as brooches for a woman in a boat grave in Oronsay [4.8].[75]

More commonly used in Scotland were the 'secondary' or 'associative' relics, in which an object belonging to the saint or associated with their shrine was used instead of fragments of their bodies. In these cases the objects were not fragmented, but instead carried fragments of the saint's aura within them. Iron and bronze handbells are by far the most numerous sacred objects remaining from early medieval Scotland, indeed of any ecclesiastical metalwork in Britain and Ireland.[76] There are at least 26 extant quadrangular handbells of early medieval type from Scotland, although only 19 are from certain ecclesiastical contexts, and several more are lost but attested in earlier sources [7.24].[77] These objects were made before and during the Viking Age, and in some cases older bells were enshrined in the 11th–12th centuries, showing that a good number of older objects remained in circulation. Their distribution is scattered relatively evenly across Scotland, although they survive in greater numbers in the central highlands, where they remained in use the longest. The earliest form consists of a single sheet of iron hammered to shape, often with an external coating of bronze. Bells of cast bronze were made from the 8th and 9th centuries.

Not all handbells were necessarily sacred objects. One in particular from Perthshire has a flatter profile and a handle that is more suited to swinging from a collar than being rung by hand, possibly a good example of a medieval cowbell [7.26].[78] Size is not a reliable indicator either, with even some very small iron bells used as relics. The early iron bell which is encased in the 12th-century Kilmichael Glassary shrine (p. 210) is among the smallest in Scotland (82mm, without handle); and another example from Dunbar, East Lothian, was brazed externally like larger ecclesiastical examples, despite being the smallest yet found in Scotland (51mm without handle), an expense not likely to be borne for an agricultural tool.[79]

There are two depictions of cowbells from Pictish stones: at Fowlis Wester, Perthshire, and Eassie, Angus. On both, cattle are shown with bells around the neck. Along with the 9th-century Stuttgart Psalter, these are the earliest medieval representations of livestock.[80] However, both of these Pictish examples are on cross-slabs that show processions (in the case of Eassie certainly with clerics involved), possibly relating to cattle being offered to the Church or a related Christian festival. Livestock images also appear on other items of architectural sculpture from Pictish churches, such as the animal beneath the feet of the large figure on the Forteviot Arch [2.2], as well as the 'Calf Stone' shrine panel from Portmahomack [2.7].

Stray finds of bells such as the small iron bell from Minchmoor in the Scottish Borders may be related to rural pastoral activity [7.25c] – the Minchmoor Road was a major cattle drove road from the Ettrick Water to Traquair. But even this need not rule out a liturgical or ritual function. In fact, many of Scotland's surviving handbells, whether by accident or design, are linked

Fig. 7.24: Quadrangular bell of cast bronze, with zoomorphic handle, Strath Fillan, Perthshire, height 290 mm; NMS H.KA 2.

Fig. 7.26: Possible animal bell of iron, Perthshire, height 95 mm; NMS X.KA 7.

Fig. 7.25 a–d: Four handbells: (left to right) (a) Saevar Howe, on Orkney, height 333 mm, NMS X.KA 1; (b) Burrian, Orkney, height 60 mm, NMS X.GB 306; (c) Minchmoor, near Traquair, Scottish Borders, NMS X.KA 26; (d) bronze casing detached from iron bell from Monybuie, Kirkcudbrightshire, NMS X.KA 18.

to long-distance overland routes through secluded glens, including three from Glen Lyon alone, the Strathfillan Bell (specifically used to bless cattle), Struan (at a confluence in Glen Garry, still the main road through Atholl), and others from the highland zone.

Quadrangular handbells, including in iron without brazing, are also frequently found in tool hoards and similar structured deposits; most famously in the Mästermyr tool hoard, Sweden, 11th and 12th century.[81] Similar hoards are recognised from northern England; at least one, from Flixborough, Lincolnshire, with its cross-marked bell and lead tank, shows the blurring between sacred and secular embodied by such deposits.[82] There are also many examples from Scotland that show signs of being carefully deposited in meaningful places. The detached bronze casing of a bell from Monybuie [7.25d], found while cutting peat in an upland area, suggests a placed deposit of a significant object despite not being linked with settlement or ecclesiastical site. Several come from cists and churchyards [7.24]. An enigmatic Viking-age reoccupation of a ruined broch at Saevar Howe, Orkney, involved the deposition of a handbell, upside-down with a stone over its mouth, in a cist alongside burials of unknown date [7.25a]. This episode of reuse is dated only by associated objects including Scandinavian-style combs and a perforated coin of Burgred of Mercia (866–68).[83] Another bell from an Orkney broch is from Burrian, retrieved in very poorly recorded circumstances from a site with other signs of early medieval occupation, including Pictish symbols etched in bone and a cross-slab with an ogham inscription [7.25b].[84] On the Brough of Birsay, another early handbell was deposited in a hearth of a stone structure from the 11th-century bishop's palace, likely as a closing deposit.[85] There is no pattern to these deposits of bells, but they cover the period before, during and after the Viking Age: the broch finds from Orkney are among the largest (Saevar Howe, 333 mm height with its handle) and smallest (Burrian, 60 mm) bells in Scotland. Together they reveal that these metal bells, large and small, had a range of cultic functions not limited to the early Christian liturgy.[86]

There is also evidence that small bells of different types were worn as personal amulets: the so-called 'Anglo-Scandinavian' polygonal bells found mainly in the Danelaw area of England [6.25] of which there are now a small number of stray finds from Scotland.[87] However, on the Isle of Man and Iceland they also appear in graves, showing they were likely worn as pendants. A miniature quadrangular handbell with a ring for suspension was found alongside an 'Anglo-Scandinavian' bell in the Shanmullagh Hoard, River Blackwater, suggesting there was wider 9th- to 10th-century use of such amuletic bells beyond the well-known Danelaw type.[88]

One particular object type captures the interface between institutionalised Christianity, private devotion and commodities traded on the open market. Around the turn of the millennium in Scotland, a new class of object enters the archaeological record of the north and west: the intriguing fragments of green porphyry tiles, often referred to as porphyry or *porfido verde antico*, otherwise known as *lapis lacedaemonius*, from Krokeai in southern Greece. The quarries where *verde antico* was obtained were worked in the 1st–5th centuries AD. As imperial structures were abandoned and reused in the coming centuries, these valuable tiles were salvaged and repurposed into Christian basilicas. In Scotland, however, these are never found set into church pavements or into altars, as this material has been used since the Roman period on the continent. Instead, the chunks we find here have clearly been broken off from larger polished tiles. Nor do we find any other polished stones used in classical antiquity – such as red porphyry, *lapis porphyrites*, or white marble – which indicates a shortlived fashion for this specific material.

There are a dozen fragments that are known from Scotland, joining several examples now scattered across the Scandinavian diaspora from Sweden to Iceland.[89] In previous work

Fig. 7.27 (left): Green porphyry tile, Balmerino, Fife, length 38 mm; NMS X.HX 512.

Fig. 7.28 (right): Green porphyry tile, found in a stone urn, Hunday, Orkney, length 58 mm; NMS X.AL 51.

they have been interpreted as souvenirs from pilgrimages taken to Rome. However, this seems too unpredictable and unstructured an explanation, given the uniformity of the kinds of porphyry chunks we find that are invariably of *verde antico*, with one or two polished faces from former use as decorative tiles. The Gaulish provincial capital of Trier has been argued as a possible 'local' source for the northern porphyry finds.[90]

The Scottish tiles come from a variety of contexts [7.27–28]. Several are strongly associated with an early medieval church, although even those found under controlled excavation conditions were in secondary contexts. Those from St Ninian's Isle, Shetland; Papa Stronsay, Orkney; and Whithorn and Barhobble, Wigtonshire, were found in excavations of 11th–12th century chapel buildings (the latter was in a child's grave). The tiles from Birsay and Kebister were effectively unstratified, but come from sites with both 11th-century chapels and secular settlement. In contrast, the two from Bornais, South Uist, are from a wealthy 11th-century trading settlement.[91] The remaining finds were from poorly recorded circumstances, including one at Hunday, Orkney, perhaps from a cremation burial [7.28], and a tile from Keiss, Caithness, from an enclosed site of unknown date and function.[92]

To understand their use we need to look beyond Scotland. Identical chunks of green porphyry have been found in various contexts in Dublin, which like Bornais seems to indicate their use as trade items, providing a mechanism for their importation into insular Viking-age markets.[93] A recent find in Thorinsstadir, Iceland, comes from the southeast corner of an 11th-century family chapel, echoing the position of the find from Papa Stronsay from the foundations of the church. Both could feasibly be offerings made during the construction of the building.[94] Recent finds from Sigtuna, Sweden, also suggest a blurring of the boundaries between secular and sacred, all coming from the feasting halls of wealthy 11th-century burgage plots. Finds from Sweden and Norway have been discovered set into wooden boards, interpreted as portable altars in which the porphyry tile was a token of consecrated altar table but used outside of the church.[95] In this scenario the chunks of porphyry were still seen as sacred matter, but traded like commodities, as shown by their concentration in trade towns like Sigtuna, Dublin and trade settlements like Bornais. The date of the finds is largely 11th century, just when deluxe portable altars incorporating these very kinds of reused porphyry tiles began to be produced in Germany.[96] Such small fragments of tiles may be the offcuts of workshops that produce these deluxe altars, sold on by enterprising merchants. Their clustering in the 11th century in Scandinavian-affiliated contexts indicates their supply was targeted, perhaps an entrepreneurial opening spotted by a canny merchant in Trier with knowledge of the northern markets. Yet their deposition in several cases as special deposits in church buildings shows they were valued as fragments of altars, 'secondary relics' to be used in domestic contexts, or the family chapel. They were never reworked into jewellery or pendants,[97] but some in Scandinavia were set into wooden tablets, and any of our fragments may likewise have been used. As fragments of the sacred, they retained their supernatural potential through the concept of *pars pro toto*. They show the negotiation of the sacred in everyday life in a context before the parochial model ensured regular access to the sacraments of the Church. And this particular engagement with the faith was mediated through the silver-fuelled market economy. Could Christian faith itself be commoditised?

Fig. 7.29 (right): Sculptured slab of the 'Whithorn School', Craiglemine, Glasserton, height 1180mm; NMS X.IB 121.

Fig. 7.30 (below): Cross-shaft, Mains of Penninghame, Wigtownshire, height 1118mm; NMS X.IB 123.

VARIANTS REVISITED

The example of porphyry tiles, Christian amulets traded in the open market, brings us back to the question of how the concept of money changed various aspects of life in the 9th–12th centuries – even of belief itself. A recurring theme of the preceding chapters is the power of 'copies'. In an age of silver, market towns provided the means for more people to acquire status in exchange for money: foreign blades of fashionable styles, furs, woven cloth, serially produced pins and brooches. As more people became accustomed to concepts of currency, crafted goods were increasingly copied and reproduced in large amounts, in the same way as coins and arm-rings. The relationship between the owner and maker was not as important as it had once been – status symbols were becoming commodified. This accelerated processes which had already been seen in operation by the opening of the Viking Age (chapter 5): brooches could be miniaturised or exploded in size, imitations made in base metals or pure silver. One's status came from the knowledge of, and access to, the worlds of specific object types – these kinds of coin, those types of ringed pin. With every 'copy' produced, an opportunity to change it or tweak it came about, bringing about different regional 'dialects' which then took on lives of their own. It was the age of variants.

This helps us understand patterns of social change both within and outwith the new silver economy. A similar shift can be seen in the production of carved stones across Scotland. At the same time as the profusion of mass-produced dress items allows us to see more individuals (chapter 5), the landscape was likewise beginning to become populated with the spread of early Christian sculpture. New 'schools' of production began to appear, typified by the 'Govan School' of hogbacks and other recumbent stones, or the 'Whithorn School' of disc-headed crosses and the large cross-slabs [7.29, 7.30].[98] The carved stone monuments of these centuries were still handmade and

Fig. 7.31: Reverse of a cross-slab from Tullibole, Kinross-shire, height 1295mm; NMS X.IB 99.

idiosyncratic, but with repetitive, recurring features. Both of these nicknames hide considerable variety and an overall experimental quality to a lot of the sculpture of this period in which earlier motifs were copied, sometimes poorly, and new motifs invented. It captures a moment when more patrons were commissioning stones for their local churches, but not always under the eye of a rigorous ecclesiastical authority. The later medieval parish church model, in which a local church was accessible to each community, was still taking shape and these carved stones may be the archaeological signature of its tenuous early days in Scotland.[99]

One problem with an age of variants is that similarity makes objects difficult to date. We tend to devalue imitation, to demean 'copies'. A stone from Tullibole, Kinross-shire, carries motifs that recall earlier Pictish cross-slabs but executed in a rough new style [7.31]; a late cross-slab from Dunblane, Stirlingshire, may be of similar date.[100] What we are actually seeing is the emergence of new communities and group identities grounded in stone monuments, as well as local responses to wider Church reforms in these centuries. This sense of a community of the saved was expressed through material culture such as carved stones, in which replication was a mark of honour. But how do variants work when they jump from one cultural context to another?

Eastern Scotland north of the Forth is characterised in the early medieval period by hundreds of carved stones of various date. We tend to lump all of these into the category of 'Pictish' sculpture, but the distinctive Pictish symbols fall out of use over the course of the 9th century (chapter 1). The absence of inscriptions makes it difficult to date stones closely, especially in an age of variants, and it is likely that many supposed 'Pictish' stones in fact post-date the transition to the kingdom of Alba in 900. Recent work on the remarkable group of sculpture at St Vigeans, Angus, makes it clear there was significant production of stone sculpture of new forms down to *c.*1100 when investment shifted to the architectural masonry of the church itself.[101]

Another challenge is that many early stone monuments remained standing in their landscapes through the troubles of the Viking Age and beyond. From the high crosses of Iona to the crosses which overlook Forteviot [2.1a], there are prominent examples of monuments that stood sentinel for a thousand years and more. In other cases, we have rare later medieval accounts of standing sculpture which shows these stones continued to inspire stories, myths and new kinds of reuse for centuries.[102] We know that the early medieval stones of St Andrews, Fife, retained some memory of their origins even centuries after they were put up. And the founders of the reformed Augustinian monastery in the 12th century described such ancient crosses as proof of the Pictish origins of the site. These same monks then literally built their new church on these foundations:

CRUCIBLE OF NATIONS

Fig. 7.32: Dunkeld 'Apostles Stone', Dunkeld (canmore.org.uk/collection/397542). (© Crown Copyright: HES)

several of the early cross-slabs were found in the walls of the 12th-century St Andrews Cathedral and adjacent church of St Mary on the Rock.[103] A great number of early medieval carved stones have been discovered this way and it seems that a great period of building stone churches in Scotland in the 11th and 12th centuries often involved the recycling of earlier sculpture.[104] It means that we cannot ignore earlier sculpture simply because it was made before the Viking Age – it characterised the landscape during and after these dramatic centuries.

It tells us that throughout the changes from Pictland to Alba, Moray and the earldoms of Orkney and Caithness, there were monuments that 'moved' through the period by staying in place. In some rare cases we can see how these older monuments continued to inspire new forms of sculpture. One particular case is in the Manx crosses of the 10th and 11th centuries, many bearing runic and ogham inscriptions that allow us to identify their multilingual Gaelic- and Norse-speaking patrons.[105] The form of these cross-slabs appears to have been inspired directly by the relief sculpture of eastern Scotland, in one case even replicating the confronted, enthroned figures of a stone from Fowlis Wester, Perthshire.[106] In a similar way, the 9th-century ogham-inscribed cross-slab from Bressay, Shetland [1.13], has been described as a poor 'copy' of another one from Papil; and a runic cross-slab from Iona is a variant of an earlier Gaelic-inscribed cross but with the inscription moved into the border.[107] This all makes it difficult to be sure of the date of our 'late Pictish' and related sculpture, but it can potentially tell us a great deal about how the kingdom of Alba took shape.[108]

There are certain motifs which have been argued to be late in the series of Pictish sculpture in parallel with better-dated examples outside Scotland. The 7-metre-high 'Sueno's Stone', Forres, has been placed in several possible historical contexts ranging anywhere from the mid-9th century to the start of the 11th.[109] Pictish or not, the consensus is that it is 'late', a cross-slab with no symbols, with legions of soldiers and riders recalling the crowds depicted on Irish high crosses of the 9th and 10th centuries. Its depiction of a mass beheading has been taken as a sign of ethnic strife, whether between Picts and Scots, or Scots and Norse. However, other late sculpture also bears similar multitudes, there more plausibly drawn from biblical imagery. This includes a shaft of what must have been another towering cross at Dunkeld [7.32].[110] Its use of New Testament imagery – the Apostles in this case, and perhaps Christ on one narrow edge – is what sets it apart from earlier Pictish sculpture, where depictions of Christ are exceedingly rare, and biblical figures tend to be of Old Testament stock, particularly the iconography of David. The monastery of Dunkeld appears to have been founded in the early 9th century, allowing us to narrow the date of this to the end of the Pictish period at the earliest.

The Dunkeld 'Apostles Stone' shares features of two fragments of crosses on a much smaller scale than Abernethy,

Fig. 7.33 (right): Fragment of cross-shaft, Abernethy, Perthshire, width 584mm; NMS X.IB 290.

Fig. 7.34 (below): Fragment of cross-shaft with crucifixion scene, Abernethy, Perthshire, height 508mm; NMS X.IB 255.

Perthshire. One depicts two rows of five frontal-facing figures in ankle-length robes, each holding different objects [7.33]. The cross has been ascribed a 9th- to 10th-century date, but on limited evidence, based on a superficial similarity to Irish high crosses.[111] The heads of the lower register appear to be cowled or wearing some sort of headdress, making it possible they are women. Rows of men and women bearing different objects, but seemingly not apostles nor always ecclesiastics, are reminiscent of 11th- and 12th-century metalwork shrines and stone sculpture from Ireland.[112] Other than two figures bearing staffs, the only recognisable attribute is a set of balance scales. This could be a rare insular depiction of psychostasis, weighing the soul before entering heaven, but such a lofty message seems rather out of place here. The earliest balance scales in Scotland are of the later 9th century (chapter 6), but carved stones often copy iconographic motifs from illuminated manuscripts and other exemplars. Depictions of balance scales are also rare in Irish sculpture, and in two cases it is Michael the Archangel who holds them, while also fighting demons with his sword; several depictions of balance scales in the 9th-century Stuttgart Psalter are held by Christ or the hand of God.[113] These are quite different to the imagery of Abernethy. Two figures hold what could be liturgical equipment; the central figure may be swinging a bowl-like censer (for incense) and/or a flail whip or scourge; the figure to the right holds a noose-like object, less feasibly a harp.[114] There is a remote possibility then that all three are figures relating to judgement and punishment. In an extreme sense, the 'Sueno's Stone' beheading scene shares the same intent, but there are several depictions of the Day of Judgment and Christ as judge from the Irish high-cross series as well.[115] Other 10th-century cross-slabs from Angus showing enthroned frontal figures have been interpreted as the figures of the Trinity sitting in judgement.[116] These crosses may then have had multiple roles, marking the sacred precinct, as well as creating spaces for law-giving and the swearing of oaths.[117]

The other stone from Abernethy appears to be a similar cross-shaft – a narrow pillar-like monument which may be the stem of a free-standing cross [7.34]. This one is a rare Scottish depiction of a crucifixion scene, as identified by two spear-bearing figures to either side of a standing figure. Underneath this are the heads of three cowled figures, again recalling scenes from Abernethy and Dunkeld, so these likely form a group of similar date. Another cross-shaft from Monifieth, Angus [7.35] shows the legs of a figure in a tunic: this seems to be another depiction of Christ as judge, given parallels elsewhere, with rows of frontal figures below.[118] These figures hold staffs and drinking-horns, with David the Psalmist at the foot of the shaft; a possible interpretation of this mix of Old and New Testament imagery might be a progression of the precursors of Christ, again with clear parallels in the scriptural crosses of Ireland in the 9th to 12th centuries.[119]

Pillar-like cross-shafts of stone appear across the former Pictish realms, as far north as Reay, Caithness, where a pillar depicting several beasts appears to have been cut back to feature an interlaced cross, perhaps after the shaft had lost its head [7.37a–b]. But unlike the Irish high crosses, the Scottish freestanding ones are generally quite small, person-sized monuments. Larger outliers like Dunkeld, and a monumental cross-head from Brechin which may be as late as the 11th century,[120] are more akin to the Irish high-cross series, but are restricted to powerful monasteries or bishop's seats with substantial royal patronage. Regardless of the Irish parallels, these free-standing crosses join a series of related crosses being produced across northern England at this time, especially in Yorkshire, as well as an important series of crosses in the Scottish Borders and in the Lothians [7.36].[121] Indeed, the late cross-shafts of Alba were once characterised as 'Northumbrian' for their shape.[122] Instead of looking in one direction or another to classify them on such terms, we should instead expect that these monuments were commissioned by a class of landowners whose horizons were broader than we might think.

If the new 'schools' of sculpture of Whithorn and Govan are any indication, it seems that cherry-picking influences to create new, regionally specific forms was the spirit of the age. There may well be other small 'schools' like these spread across Scotland. For instance, a group of carved stones from Reay, Caithness, are each quite odd and may all post-date the 9th century. Even more interesting, they shared the landscape with one of the only Viking-age cemeteries of furnished 'pagan' graves on the Scottish mainland, and it would be worthwhile getting a better handle on the chronology of burial and sculpture here.[123] Cross-slabs of unique forms continued to be erected in this time, so there is a possibility the 'Pictishness' of these late monuments is instead a lingering regional artistic tradition, consciously conservative, sharing the landscape with masterpieces of a previous era like Forteviot, Meigle and Aberlemno (chapter 2), but increasingly open to ideas from neighbouring kingdoms. Indeed, the same can be said of the long 8th-century 'golden age' of Pictish sculpture itself.[124]

Northern outliers notwithstanding, it is notable so many of these 'late' or post-Pictish carved stones cluster in eastern Scotland, largely the region which came to be known as Angus during this period. These crosses share iconography with Irish high crosses and, while they do not consist of anything like a 'school' of sculpture, they speak to the changing organisation of Alba into smaller parcels of land run on behalf of the king by people with new titles – thanes and mormaers.[125] These thanages became the foundation for the later medieval parish system; and this flourishing of artistic expression may be the archaeological signature of the formation of a new ecclesiastical hierarchy supported by local lords.[126] The 'Irishness' of these stones is matched by the construction of round towers at Abernethy and Brechin, two major centres of sculpture production in this period. They are not so much evidence of the takeover of Pictland by Scots from the west, but the shared imagery and ecclesiastical networks of Gaeldom writ large, of which Alba was a key component.[127] The 'late Pictish' series and the stones of Alba are more diverse than has perhaps been recognised, and well worth further research.

Fig. 7.35: Cross-shaft with depiction of Christ and other figures, Monifieth, Angus, height 1219 mm; NMS X.IB 25.

Fig. 7.36: Arm of a cross with a lion on one face, and an arm of the crucified Christ on the other, Lasswade, Midlothian, width 290 mm; NMS X.IB 21.

Figs 7.37a–b: Cross-shaft of reddish sandstone sculptured in flat relief, found in 1947 built into the south wall of Reay Parish Church, Caithness; NMS X.IB 267 (spirals and cross sides).

Fig. 7.38 (right): Panel of sandstone with chamfered edges, surviving as two fragments, carved on one side with a serpent or hippocamp, from Jarlshof, Shetland, maximum length of larger slab 428 mm; NMS X.HSA 782 A–B.

Fig. 7.39 (below): Panel depicting riders and soldiers from Dull, Perthshire, width 810 mm; NMS X.IB 58.

THE GREAT REBUILDING

The cross-shafts and other 'late' sculpture from Angus join other enigmatic evidence of carved stones from across Scotland which seem to relate to stone ecclesiastical architecture. There were clearly stone-built churches from the Pictish period in Scotland: the shrine of St Columba on Iona dates back to the mid-8th century, while the carved fragments from Portmahomack, along with the Forteviot Arch in Perthshire, show the ambition of royal Pictish foundations [2.2]. A series of carved panels, slabs of stone orientated horizontally and carved on one side, seem to relate to tomb-shrines or internal divisions of some complexity, and may hint at lost stone churches.[128] However, not all bear overtly Christian imagery and they may have been used to ornament elaborate outdoor grave monuments, or perhaps secular power centres, as suggested for an enigmatic panel bearing a dragonesque figure from Jarlshof, Shetland [7.38].[129]

However, some of these panels are certainly ecclesiastical and the example from Flotta is most likely to be the frontal panel of a composite table altar. Other panels from known monastic sites – such as Dull [7.39] and Portmahomack [2.7] – also do not depict crosses or explicitly Christian iconography. However, they too can readily be interpreted in an allegorical manner, in terms of salvation from damnation through the Church, in a way that was intelligible to an audience that was not necessarily familiar with scripture.[130]

Fig. 7.40: Sandstone slab, probably the front of an altar or tomb, with a cross of interlaced work in centre, Flotta, Orkney, width 1676mm; NMS X.IB 48.

Fig. 7.41: Possible altar slab from Hoddom, Dumfriesshire, width 660mm; NMS X.1999.29.6.

Fig. 7.42: Stone with an incised cross on rectangular base, probably representing an altar cross, Birsay, Orkney, length 115mm; NMS X.HB 607.

Fig. 7.43: One of two possible stone gable finials, Mid Calder, West Lothian, height 381mm; NMS X.IB 129.

Though difficult to date closely, these fragments of architectural sculpture tell us more about the rich world of Christian monuments that were being commissioned at the start of the Viking Age and which continued to develop in the centuries that followed. Where monasteries have been explored, there is evidence for new structures in timber and increasingly in stone from the 10th century onwards, generally in the same place, making it difficult to see earlier structures without careful excavation of churches that are often still in use. The Flotta altar frontal [7.40] shows the importance of the table altar as the focus of the church, and we should expect this to be archaeologically visible in some way. A square panel of stone with a simple outline cross from the Hoddom excavations was interpreted as an incomplete cross-slab [7.41],[131] but its dimensions would work equally well as a composite altar frontal. Many of the fragmented metal objects from Viking-age graves discussed above may come from altar crosses and other objects that were used in the liturgy, but were lost except for their depictions in stone [7.42].

Moving into the 12th century, we begin to see in Scotland an explosion of evidence for the building and rebuilding of churches in stone, often in forms characteristic of pan-European Romanesque and Gothic styles. The Scottish examples are inflected with other important influences from Ireland and existing local architectural traditions. A cross-shaft from Hoddom, Dumfriesshire, shows gabled buildings, but these may be stock iconographic depictions of saints copied from other crosses or manuscripts [2.6]. One clearly shows a gabled portal surmounted by a ringed cross finial. There is a poorly understood series of disc-headed and wheel-head crosses standing on uncarved shafts from Scotland which have been interpreted as grave-markers, including one from Hoddom itself.[132] These are of varying dates, perhaps as late as the 12th century. One example acquired in 1883 from Mid Calder, West Lothian [7.43], is matched by another of identical size and shape that is still displayed in the church itself.[133] These are a good candidate for a pair of gable finials of the type found in other media. And there is even more to be discovered from items in our own collections at National Museums Scotland.

These and other carved stones help to reveal the biggest change at the end of the period, the 'Europeanisation' of the Church and other aspects of life under increasingly powerful kings, bishops and popes. We can now turn to the material culture of the 11th and 12th centuries to see what is distinctive about the northern experience of these bigger changes.

NOTES

1. Graham-Campbell and Batey 1998, 128, 146–9; Buchanan 2012, 215.
2. Pierce 2013; Ó Floinn 2020, 240–1.
3. Sharples (ed.) 2021, 147–8; Parker Pearson et al. 2018, 324.
4. Asplund 2005; Kivisalo 2008; Kirkinen 2017.
5. Gilchrist 2008, 125; 2020, 116–21.
6. Compare MacLeod and Mees 2006.
7. Blackwell 2018, 158–9.
8. Fuglesang 1989.
9. Fanning 1994; Paterson and Stanford 2020.
10. Buteaux 1997; Hamilton 1956; Curle 1935, fig. 22, 292; another example was identified in the course of this research from an undated assemblage of bone-pins from North Uist: National Museums Scotland (NMS) H.RHL 4, labelled NMS NA 282.
11. Sheehan et al. 2001; Sigurðsson 2019.
12. Arkeologisk Museum, Universitetet i Stavanger, S6782.a.
13. Androshchuk 2011.
14. Harrison and Ó Floinn 2014, 157–9; Pedersen et al. 2014, 284–5.
15. NMS X.HSA 129; NMS X.IL 352.
16. Graham-Campbell 1980, 60.
17. Wallace 2015, 303, fig. 8.41; Sigurðsson 2019, 22–3.
18. Harrison and Ó Floinn 2014, 158–9; Bourke 2010, 34, fig. 39, no. 317; Curle 1935, 305–6, fig. 45, no. 1.

19. Blackwell 2011.
20. Whitfield 1997.
21. Armstrong 1922, pl. XIII, fig. 4, nos 9–11; O'Rahilly 1998, 30; Richards and Haldenby 2018, 341; Ross 1991, 347–50; Curle 1982, 62–3, 84, illus. 39.
22. Anderson 1874, 554–5; Eremin et al. 2002.
23. Trinity College MS 58, folio 7v; cf. Whitfield 1997.
24. Gilchrist 2008, 139.
25. Wallace 2015, 289; Mainman and Rogers 2000, 2589.
26. Batey and Paterson 2013, 652.
27. Goldberg and Davis 2021, 77–83, 108–17.
28. Blackwell et al. 2017, 127–32.
29. Gaimster 1991; Sheehan 2013.
30. Kilger 2015.
31. Griffiths et al. 2019, 311–2.
32. Kilger 2020.
33. Graham-Campbell and Sheehan 2009.
34. Graham-Campbell 1995, 139–41.
35. Ježek 2017.
36. McCarthy et al. 2014, 227–9.
37. Gilchrist 2008, 147–9; Fuglesang 1989, 20–1.
38. Griffiths et al. 2019, 267–8.
39. *PSAS* 1863, 490.
40. Downham 2016; Naismith 2020, 644; Woolf 2018, 121–3.
41. Sheehan 2008; cf. Redknap 2004; Gustin 2017, 244.
42. Compare Harrison and Ó Floinn 2014, 172–4, 502.
43. Graham-Campbell and Batey 1998, 100–2; Buchanan 2012, 230–7.
44. Graham-Campbell 2011b.
45. Hall 2013; Hall and Forsyth 2011; Solberg 2007.
46. Caldwell et al. 2009, 176–8.
47. Solberg 2007; Hall 2016.
48. Rundkvist and Williams 2008, 95–6.
49. Johnson 1999, 47–56.
50. Hall 2015.
51. Mikkelsen 2019.
52. Heen-Pettersen and Murray 2019; Sørheim 2011; Staecker 2009.
53. Sheehan 2013; Heen-Pettersen 2014; Ashby 2015; Aannestad 2018.
54. Gausel: as reconstructed in Sørheim 2011; Melhus: Heen-Pettersen and Murray 2018, 76–7.
55. Heen-Pettersen 2015.
56. Compare Youngs 2020 for other insular parallels.
57. Youngs 1989, nos 119, 120, 123, 126; Graham-Campbell 2001; Heen-Pettersen 2014, 3.5.
58. Ritchie 1982.
59. Wamers 1985, no. 138, *taf.* 9, 5.
60. Arbman 1943, *taf.* 205; Historiska Museet, Stockholm 427330, Bj 557.
61. Henderson and Henderson 2004, 120–1; Carver et al. 2016, 211; Youngs 1989, no. 119.
62. Wamers 1985, *taf.* 12, 13, 16; Youngs 1989, nos 140–4.
63. MacLeod and Curle 1915; Graham-Campbell 1983, 313; Paterson 2001, 126–7.
64. Compare Jåttå, Rogaland, Stavanger, Arkeologisk Museum, Stavanger S14171; Lilleberge, Nord-Trøndelag, British Museum 1891,1021.78.
65. Kelly 2006; Organ 1973.
66. For comparison, the large central recess on the west face of St John's Cross, Iona, is much larger at 280 mm diameter, and the second recess below this is 190 mm; but a central cavity in the cross-head of Cropthorne, Worcestershire, is *c*.80 mm diameter; Fisher 2001, 133; Bryant 2012, 353–6.
67. Stevenson 1985, 235.
68. Wamers 1987.
69. Compare to the Crieff mounts, NMS X.FC3, X.FC 4, discussed in chapter 4, 'Age of raids'.
70. Goldberg and Davis 2021.
71. Geary 2011.
72. Herbert 1988; Clancy 2011; 2013.
73. Ó Floinn 1994; Wycherley 2016.
74. Blackwell 2012, 36–42.
75. Henderson and Henderson 2004, 115–6; Graham-Campbell and Batey 1998, 91, 116–8.
76. Bourke 2020, 5.
77. This figure includes the recently stolen bells of Loch Shiel and Fortingall, as well as the bell-shrine handle from Inchaffray, although it is technically possible that the latter comes from the shrine of one of the other extant bells. The figure excludes

'St Lolan's Bell', now on display at St Mungo's Museum, which is likely a modern copy: Bourke 2020, 501–2; Caldwell et al. 2013, 238–9.
78. However, the peculiarities of the bell's construction mean that it is an outlier in many ways, and may not be early medieval: C. Bourke pers. comm.
79. Kilmichael Glassary: NMS H.KA 4–5; Dunbar: NMS X.2014.22.1; Perry 2000, 127; cf. Willmott and Daubney 2020.
80. Canmore ID 32092 (Eassie) and 26193 (Fowlis Wester); cf. Stuttgart Psalter f. 164 v., Württembergische Landesbibliothek Stuttgart, Bibl. fol. 23.
81. Arwidsson and Berg 1983; Lund 2006.
82. Wilmott and Daubney 2020.
83. Hedges 1983.
84. MacGregor 1975.
85. Curle 1982, 50–2.
86. Compare Bitel 2007; Márkus 2009, 125–6.
87. Schoenfelder and Richards 2011; Batey 1988; Coleman and Photos-Jones 2008.
88. Bourke 2010, 28, 34, fig. 4, nos 38, 39.
89. Lynn 1984; Cormack 1989; Lowe 2002, 92–4.
90. Tesch 2007.
91. Sharples (ed.) 2021, 247–8.
92. Moorland Mound, Keiss: Canmore ID 9355; Hunda: Lynn 1984, 22.
93. Lynn 1984.
94. Kristjánsdóttir 2015.
95. Tesch 2007; Stolt 2001.
96. Okasha and Reilly 1984, 35; Sanjosé i Llongueras 2018; Luginbill 2020.
97. Although the amulet from St Salvador's Chapel, Shapinsay [7.11], is of a very similar porphyritic stone, and while it has not been confirmed petrologically as *verde antico*, may well have been selected for its similar lithology.
98. Driscoll et al. 2005; Craig 1991.
99. Compare to patterns in Craig 1991; Lang 2002; Bailey 2010.
100. Canmore ID 24673; Driscoll 2002.
101. Geddes 2017.
102. Hall 2014, 26–30; Geddes 2017, 18–27; Ritchie 1999, 14; cf. Thompson 2018, 183.
103. Hay Fleming 1931; Taylor 2000, 116.
104. For example, Carver et al. 2016, 130.
105. Kermode 1907.
106. Trench-Jellicoe 2002.
107. Fisher 2001, 14–5.
108. Driscoll 2002.
109. Sellar 1993; Henderson and Henderson 2004, 135–6; Carver et al. 2016, 285–6.
110. Henderson and Henderson 2004, 147.
111. Stevenson 1959, 46.
112. Murray 2014; Overbey 2012, 58.
113. Harbison 1992, 300–1.
114. Stevenson 1959, 45.
115. Harbison 1992, 297–300.
116. Geddes 2017, 132–6.
117. Hall 2014, 190–2.
118. Compare Harbison 1992, figs 568, 578–9, Temple Brecan, Inishmore West and North crosses.
119. Henderson and Henderson 2004, 145.
120. *Ibid.*, 147–8; Canmore ID 35069.
121. Whitworth 2011; Thompson 2018.
122. Curle 1940.
123. Batey 1993, 156–7; Canmore ID 7252, 7351, 7352.
124. Henderson 1998; Goldberg 2012.
125. Driscoll 1998; Taylor 2016.
126. For example, Geddes 2017, 157–62.
127. Compare Hicks 1980; Murray 2007.
128. Henderson and Henderson 2004, 196–213; Foster 2019.
129. Graham-Campbell et al. 2019; cf. Whitworth 2020.
130. Goldberg 2012.
131. Lowe 2006, 126–7, pl. 5.5; 62 cm x 66 cm (broken lower edge), 6 cm thickness.
132. Radford 1953, 160, fig. 2.
133. King n.d. (b).

CHAPTER EIGHT
An experimental age

The 9th–11th centuries have been seen as the darkest bit of the 'Dark Ages',[1] a benighted lull between a Golden Age of insular art interrupted by viking attacks, and a 12th-century 'renaissance' exemplified by Romanesque architecture and other aspects of Europeanisation. The preceding chapters have shown that the problem is not in the material evidence itself, but in how we look at it. There is something rather predetermined about ending this journey in the 12th century, as if everything changes thereafter, but there is nothing inevitable about the changes of this era. For instance, coins had been known about in Scotland for a thousand years when King David I issued the first Scottish coinage; he was only able to issue his own coins when he took Carlisle, with its royal mint using silver from Cumberland mines, in 1136.[2] The Forteviot Arch [2.2], along with other fittings discussed in chapter 7, reveal that stone churches had stood in Scotland for centuries. But neither coins nor Romanesque architecture were adopted everywhere in the 12th century, as there were local alternatives to both already in place by the 11th. There is a sense of the 11th and 12th centuries as distinctly experimental. Perhaps we need to imagine the 12th century not as a break with the past, but in the context of a 'long eleventh century'.

THE FORGOTTEN ELEVENTH CENTURY

For all the epochal historical events that took place in the 11th century, the archaeological evidence from Scotland rarely gets a mention – not that it does not exist, but it is overlooked. Scholarship on medieval Scotland is still too often contained in silos: 'early medieval' Scotland, often meaning pre-Viking; viking and Norse archaeology, focused on the western and northern seaways; and the history, or more rarely the material culture, of later medieval Scotland. The 11th century rather falls into the cracks between these areas.

Why study the 11th century archaeologically? The century is absolutely stuffed with dramatic historical turning-points. The Battle of Clontarf in 1014 is often seen as the beginning of

Opposite: Crutch-headed, stirrup ringed pins of copper-alloy, and crutch-head stick-pins, of mainly 11th-century types; extreme left comes from Culbin Sands, Moray, length 55mm; unregistered.

the end of Norse power in Ireland; the Battle of Carham, 1018, is taken as the moment the Anglo-Scottish border settled on the River Tweed; the rise of King Cnut in that same year in England created an Anglo-Danish empire; the Norman Conquest in 1066 sparked massive changes beyond the language of the royal court; and at the end of the century the First Crusade marks a new era of papal authority over a Christian empire in western Europe. All of these are, of course, gross simplifications of complicated, gradual changes,[3] but together give a sense of great change in the air on a continental scale. Historical events rarely leave archaeological traces of course, but there are echoes of them in Scotland's material culture, if only we are inclined to listen.

Back home, the shape of the Scottish kingdom of the 12th century was largely determined by the political machinations of the 11th. King David I expanded the kingdom's authority from Moray to Dumfriesshire, and his successors continued to check the power of neighbouring realms in Galloway and the *Gall-goídil* territories of the Clyde Firth zone. It is worth remembering that for nearly two decades during the 12th century, Scotland under David I expanded south as far as the Tyne and Ribble, taking control of Newcastle and Carlisle, and with them Northumbria, Cumbria and Westmorland. One can easily imagine an alternate timeline in which these northern realms remained part of 'Scotland', and it has been argued that, in the 11th century at least, the area between the Forth and the Tees stood apart as something separate from either Scottish or English identity.[4] David I so rarely travelled north of the Forth that, in another situation, his kingdom could have been based on the Tyne–Forth zone, with *Scotia*, the realm from the Forth to the Spey, as a tributary.[5] All this is to say that there is nothing predestined or natural to the border on the Tweed, despite the cosmic significance it took on in the coming centuries.[6] Nor does the extent of a political territory determine identity: even when it was under Scottish rule, the lands of Lothian and the Borders were still referred to as 'England' down to the 13th century (chapter 1). Narratives of national destiny collapse in this part of 'middle Britain', and the spectre of the later Wars of Independence should be a constant reminder that the idea of what it meant to be Scottish was in no way complete by the end of the 12th century.[7]

There are also many poorly understood artefact types in this period. A series of zoomorphic (animal-art ornamented) openwork bronze-fittings found across Scotland have been ascribed a variety of dates over the years, from Pictish to 11th or 12th centuries [Figs 8.1–8.3].[8] These are strap-distributors, sometimes with swivelling loops. Parallels are now known from across England, but with a distribution largely south of the Humber, through the Portable Antiquities Scheme.[9] The loops would only be large enough to take a narrow leather strip or cord,

Fig. 8.1 (left): Zoomorphic buckle from Aberlady, East Lothian, length 34mm; NMS K.2001.723.

Fig. 8.2 (right): Zoomorphic strap-distributors of bronze, 12th century: (from left) Dunbeg, Argyll, maximum length 55mm, NMS K.1999.227; from unknown location, NMS X.FC 128; Inverkeithny, Banffshire, NMS X.FC 127.

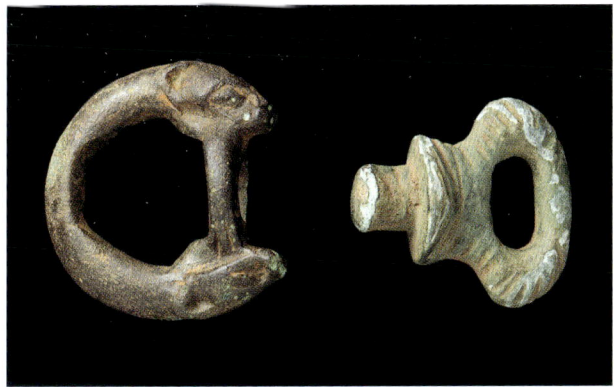

Fig. 8.3: Zoomorphic swivel-mount, diameter 30 mm, NMS K.2004.159, and decorated swivel handle, NMS K.2004.160, both from Cockburnspath, Scottish Borders.

but some are found with metal hoops attached.[10] These appear to be decorative attachments for hunting-dog leashes, but they could have had multiple functions, for instance on horse-harnesses. Their chronology is still unclear and may not all be 11th or 12th century as frequently presumed.[11] Hunting-dogs are often depicted on Pictish sculpture, but very rarely with dog-collars [7.39];[12] and there are no metal collar-fittings on dogs in Viking-age burials in Scotland. They are not likely to date before the 11th century, but may be as late as the 15th: their distribution across Scotland and England shows a shared, possibly 'Romanesque' fashion that transcends political boundaries.

This is why the events of the 11th century are in such need of revision. In a political sense, the land north of the Tweed–Solway line is still a patchwork of regional kingdoms and jurisdictions throughout the medieval period, and there is no fixed 'end' in the project of creating the idea of Scotland. Nor is the creation of Scotland only an issue of Anglo-Scottish relations. We saw in chapter 7 how strong the links between Alba and Ireland had become by the 10th century, and relations with the Norse earldoms to the north and west played a key role, as we will see below. The continued links across the north channel and the North Sea are both critical to understanding the material culture highlighted in this chapter. And that material culture itself has been understudied.

GAELS VERSUS NORMANS?

From a political perspective the most long-lasting effects of the 11th century for the north stem from the protracted dynastic struggles that saw the end of the Alpinid dynasty, descendants of the last kings of the Picts in the 9th century, and the establishment of a new dynasty by Máel Coluim III in 1058 which would eventually define the extent and character of the medieval kingdom of Scotland.[13] Of all the historical changes mentioned so far, it may be this one which has the greatest capacity to spark the imagination, through the semi-mythical and literally Shakespearean character of 'Macbeth' and the rise of 'Malcolm Canmore'.[14] A Moray man and king of Alba from 1040–57, Mac Bethad mac Findlaích is often miscast as the last of the 'Celtic' kings, and this is largely to do with the rewriting of key historical sources after the accession of a new dynasty under Máel Coluim.

The haze surrounding the origins of Mac Bethad serves as a reminder of how much textual evidence has been lost or overwritten. One critical aspect of the material culture of this period, although it is not often seen in this way, is the production and survival of texts, including some of the key histories and king lists of Scotland.[15] The survival of texts produced in Scotland really begins in the 11th century and speaks to a new urgency to reframe the past in this period. This has succeeded in establishing blind spots and biases in Scotland's own view of itself for a millennium.

One of the places where these texts were copied and rewritten was the monastery of Abernethy, Perthshire.[16] In the aftermath of 1066, Máel Coluim III had only recently raided Northumbria himself, sacking Lindisfarne in 1061. Máel Coluim played a supporting role in the events of 1066 by securing safe passage for the northern invasion of Harald Hardrada and harbouring Anglo-Saxon exiles.[17] When William emerged as Conqueror, it was years before he travelled up to Abernethy to meet Máel Coluim in 1072.

The outcome of the meeting was that Máel Coluim's territory would not be invaded, but vows of fealty were taken, often cast as part of a process of what is often called 'Normanisation' in the north. Part of this drama would be played out by architectural display in the form of stone churches and palaces that were built by imported Anglo-French masons.[18] Despite these changes, the major royal monasteries at Abernethy and Brechin, Angus, would continue a shared 'Gaelic' flavour with new Irish-style round towers. There is still debate over the date of Abernethy's round tower, which may or may not have been present by 1072, but certainly Máel Coluim and William would have worked out a treaty in a monastery marked by finely carved, Irish-style scriptural crosses discussed in chapter 7.

At the same time, new royal churches at Dunfermline (c.1072), and later 'St Margaret's Chapel' in Edinburgh Castle, would adopt the fashionable Romanesque style, often associated with incoming Norman lords. Rather than seeing the Romanesque movement in Scotland as an aspect of 'Normanisation', it is clear this was part of a wider change in fashion across Europe, spearheaded architecturally by reformed monastic movements led by the Benedictine order from the 11th century, but visible in other ways through changes in material culture. In fact, much of what is called 'Norman' influence in Scottish histories of the time is part of wider trends across Europe to systematise the collection of tax and provision of military service, but played out across Scotland in ways adapted to local circumstances and at different speeds.[19] Not all of these changes went in a straight line towards more centralised royal power, and new ecclesiastical and aristocratic centres rose and fell as these changes bedded in.

A longer, drawn-out reorganisation of the landscape of power, still poorly understood, is the construction of the first castles and other fortified places across Scotland at this time. In Scotland these are often a mix of old and new, with frequent evidence for reoccupation of ancient power centres. For example, a renewed fashion for occupying crannogs, artificial lake settlements, around the turn of the millennium is now confirmed through targeted radiocarbon-dating of lake timbers.[20] This adds to the scattered evidence of 10th to 12th-century finds at sites with otherwise only Iron Age evidence for occupation, such as the jet cross-pendant from Lochspouts Crannog [7.1]. This fashion for lake settlements pre-dates the Norman period and may be a case of emulating power centres in Ireland, where crannogs continued in use throughout the Viking Age.[21] However, this must be seen in the context of other new forms of power centres and hall sites being built in these centuries, up to and including the first 'mottes' or early castles, which were used by both Normans and Gaels in Scotland.[22] Whatever form they took, these early castles, halls and palisaded settlements also acted as fixed points of assembly of various kinds, whether for the gathering of tax or other tribute. They shared characteristics with existing assembly sites, making it difficult to tell a 'motte' (castle) from a 'moot hill' (open-air law court) or other kind of gathering-place.[23] The 11th and 12th centuries were an experiment with the grammar of power.

RELICS RE-IMAGINED

To call these administrative changes something as targeted as 'Normanisation' would be to miss part of the story of the 11th and 12th centuries as told by our Museum's collection. Sticking with the art of the Church, a new work of art commissioned in the 11th century captures the spirit of the age. Only the richly ornamented crest remains of the bell-shrine from Inchaffray in Perthshire [8.4]. Its zoomorphic ornament depicts writhing beasts which would have grasped the shoulders of a quadrangular handbell of a type discussed in chapter 7. The ornament has clear signs of Scandinavian influence in the form of 'Ringerike-style' details, such as the moustachioed faces of the beasts. However, it is not as simple as imagining it was commissioned for a Norse patron. The Inchaffray shrine was part of a flourishing trend for the re-enshrinement of relics in Ireland and England in the 11th century, and is closely paralleled by sim-

Fig. 8.4 Bronze handle of a bell-shrine inlaid with silver and niello, with 'Ringerike'-style zoomorphic ornament, Inchaffray, Perthshire, length 320mm; NMS X.KA 32 A–B.

ilar openwork shrine crests from Ireland, themselves adopting 'Ringerike' and 'Urnes' styles.[24] For complex political reasons, in the aftermath of Clontarf and the taking back of Dublin by Irish kings in the first half of the 11th century, Dublin and other ecclesiastical workshops started a productive merging of motifs recognisable from insular and Scandinavian objects of a previous age. This was a deliberate appropriation of 'heritage' motifs adopting Scandinavian influences as a triumphalist statement, but also communicating the venerable antiquity of the relics within.[25] A similar mixing of insular and Scandinavian motifs helped to foster other art styles at this time.[26] In other words, these 11th-century objects were part of a creative boom caused by the meeting of different craftspeople working under ecclesiastical patronage.

The Inchaffray Bell may well have been made in Ireland, where there are several examples of handbells that were made into shrines during the 11th century. In contrast, the Scottish bells were only rarely encased in shrines. This shrine would have appeared conspicuously Irish, a mark of prestige in a time when both aristocratic genealogies and saintly hagiographies were being rewritten to create Irish pedigrees.[27] Other styles of reliquary had more of a shared development across Scotland and Ireland. Crosiers, crook-headed staffs used by bishops and abbots as badges of office, mostly survive from the 11th and 12th centuries in Scotland. The *Coigreach* of St Fillan from Glendochart, Perthshire, survives in two parts: an inner crook of the 11th century, and a 15th-century reliquary casing in the same shape. The original crook was stripped of its filigree panels and placed inside the reliquary, which then incorporated the 11th-century filigree into its ornament [8.5, 8.6].[28] Not one but two 'drops', the vertical end of the crook-head of this type of crosier, were found in the churchyard of Hoddom, Dumfriesshire: one of 11th-century work, the other of 12th-century but reproducing the form of the earlier [8.7].[29] In an age of variants where fashions changed quickly, conservatism was a sign of respect for antiquity and the sacred matter of the venerated saints was proudly redisplayed for a new era.[30]

In short, the imagery of the Church in 11th-century Scotland is characterised by revivals and reform movements sweeping Europe at the time, seen through a major reinvestment in churches and their related fittings, including reliquaries and altar plate. Scotland participated in this wider trend, although its reliquaries have a distinctly Irish feel, as seen through the occurrence of 11th-century reliquaries such as the *Coigreach* (literally, 'the foreigner') and the Inchaffray Bell. There is so much overlap between Scottish and Irish sacred metalwork in the 11th century that, like the 'Irish-style' stone crosses discussed in chapter 7, the output of Alba and Ireland should be considered a single artistic zone, with regional variants – in other words, the archaeology of Gaeldom.[31]

There were also material connections that were less regionalised, but cut across the insular context. An example is a rarely studied class of object known as a chrismal or chrismatory: small, pear-shaped bronze vessels with round bottoms and two lugs at the mouth. They could not have rested upright and so were clearly suspended, from a belt or thong. A sub-group known only in Ireland have a footed base so they could be set upright.[32] These have been seen as several different things over

AN EXPERIMENTAL AGE

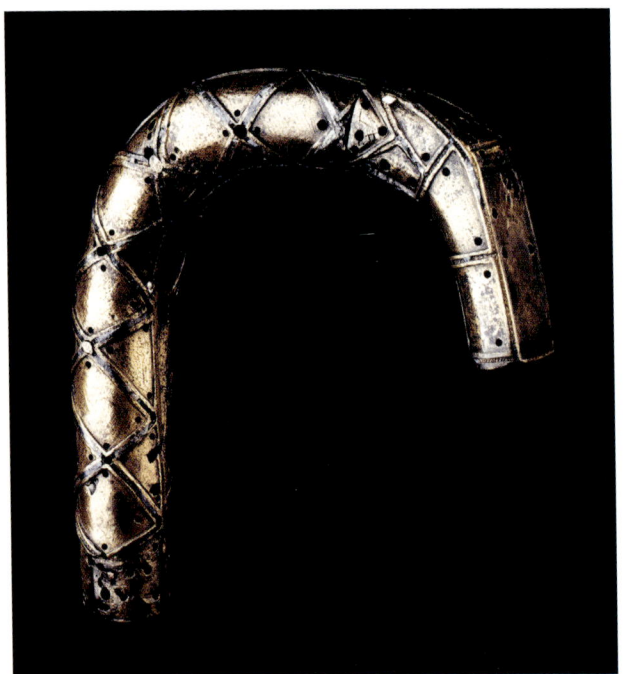

Fig. 8.5 (above, left): Crosier head of St Fillan of Glendochart, Perthshire, bronze with bands ornamented with niello, height 160mm; NMS H.KC 1.

Fig. 8.6 (above, right): Reliquary known as the *Coigreach*, or crosier shrine, of St Fillan of Glendochart, Perthshire, silver-gilt, 15th century, housing the crosier head, NMS H.KC 1; incorporating earlier filigree panels, height 235mm; NMS H.KC 2.

Fig. 8.7 (left): Crosier drop with enamel inlay, Hoddom, Dumfriesshire, length 160mm; NMS X.KC 3.

Fig. 8.8: Three copper-alloy chrismatories, or vessels for sacred oils: (from left) Legerwood, Scottish Borders, height 52mm, NMS X.FT 89; Texa, Isle of Islay, height 61mm, NMS X.2000.16; Fettercairn, Angus, height 41mm, NMS K.2000.198.

the years, from altar vessels to flasks for carrying mercury. Since the inception of the Portable Antiquities Scheme in England and Wales, dozens of examples are now known across the country, and this has led to the recognition of the several examples from Scotland during the course of this research [8.8]. An inscribed example from Surrey reveals their purpose was to carry chrism, a perfumed oil used in Christian sacraments such as ordination and the last rites.[33] Their portable form, and the number of finds from ploughsoil, shows they were actively used in pastoral care in the 11th–13th centuries. Like the swivel-mounts discussed above, they are found right across the country, regardless of political boundaries. This provides evidence for another ongoing process of this period, the establishment of a parish system, in which the Church would be available to ever more communities. These processes of expanding access to the Church, like the 'schools' of sculpture spreading across the landscape discussed in chapter 7, are the underlying mechanics which underpin the artistic spread of the Romanesque.

HALLOWED GROUND

In chapter 3 we considered the evidence for ostentatious, furnished 'viking' burial in Scotland from the perspective of landtaking and establishment of settlements in a time before written charters. Rather than understanding them solely as statements of a 'viking' or 'pagan' identity, they were markers of ownership, repositories of family history and, of course, emotionally laden send-offs for loved ones. But the traditional view of 'viking burial' still clings to another category of evidence: the hogback carved stone grave-markers, often considered to be statements of Norse identity (pp 144–6). However, they are completely absent from Scandinavia, and only rarely appear outside a limited part of northern Britain, which includes the Clyde, Forth and Teviot basins,[34] where there is only tenuous connection to Norse settlement. In northern England, they are associated with churches patronised by an emergent Anglo-Scandinavian merchant class and are derived from insular forms of recumbent grave-marker.[35] In southeast Scotland, they tend to be of later forms than the possibly 10th-century Govan hogbacks, instead overlapping with coped stone burial monuments, which use the same 'roof-tile' tegulation but are straight-backed and may be as late as the 12th and 13th centuries.[36] One such example from Tyninghame, East Lothian [8.9a–b], is heavily damaged from later reuse as a trough and survives at somewhat over half its original length. It is of a type rare in Scotland, which originally had pictorial representations on both faces instead of the typical tegulation, reserved to a narrow end-panel. The almost heraldic lions recall those from nearby St Helen's, Cockburnspath, as well as a coped stone from Ancrum, Scottish Borders, all depicting lions of types more akin to Romanesque ecclesiastical art than Old Norse myth.[37] A similar pairing of lion and tegulation come from a panel of possible architectural sculpture from Lasswade, Midlothian [8.10], introducing the possibility these late pictorial hogbacks overlap in time with the earliest, likely 12th-century, stone churches in this region. An episode of re-cutting at Tyninghame applied a chequerboard pattern, as used in 12th-century architectural detailing in

AN EXPERIMENTAL AGE

Figs 8.9 a–b: Fragment of a hogback grave-marker of sandstone showing chequerboard pattern and lion-like figure; and reverse view showing two lion-like creatures to either side of an orb and a ring-knot at far left, from Tyninghame, East Lothian, width 1100 mm; NMS X.IB 289.

Fig. 8.10: Sculptured sandstone panel bearing lion and scale-like tegulation, Lasswade, Midlothian, width 406 mm; NMS X.IB 20.

Dalmeny, West Lothian; and the tegulation, whether original or a product of re-cutting, also recalls the fishscale-like motif used on column capitals at Tyninghame itself.[38] The hogbacks of southeast Scotland have nothing to do with Norse occupation, and instead correspond remarkably well with the spread of Romanesque sculpture of the 12th century and the newly visible lordly class who commissioned these great re-buildings in stone.[39] They do not all need to be as late as the 12th century, but the cluster in southeast Scotland matches well with the earliest organisation of parishes and shires, reflecting the growing shift of power towards what would become the heart of the kingdom in the Forth basin.[40]

Like furnished burials before them, these later hogbacks likely relate to the establishment of a new settled wealthy warrior class – not vikings, but knights and earls.

The changes of the 12th century appear so dramatic that we often speak of Scotland before and after it. Yet the origins of the parish, the locations of many churches and the retention of saints' cults, show that these changes were well rooted in an early medieval infrastructure.[41] It may be that the coped, tegulated stones appearing from the Forth to the Tweed and lumped together as 'hogbacks', may instead be a late reflex of earlier fashions first popularised in Cumbria and Yorkshire. The same may be said of other monuments in the Govan and Whithorn 'schools' of sculpture (pp177–81). If we can move away from the idea that monuments like these were primarily statements of 'ethnic' or political identity, and see instead what they reveal about local practices of commemoration and investment in 'public' works like consecrated burial grounds and parish churches, we can begin to glimpse a very different process of formation of the archaeological record. On a wider scale, such local concerns are also part of pan-European processes of reform based on the creation of clear hierarchies of power within the Church, ultimately leading to a centralisation of papal authority in Rome. The 11th- and 12th-century hogbacks and early Romanesque sculpture tell us how these processes were articulated locally, through the patrons who shored up their authority by sponsorship of the Church. In this way they do share something with 'viking' burials, in that they are ways of establishing lordship through a shared aesthetic of aristocratic funerary display.

Fig. 8.11 (left): Detail of silver ring-money arm-rings from the Burray Hoard, Orkney, deposited c.997–1010.

Fig. 8.12 (below): Terminals and hacked fragments of a neck-ring of twisted silver strands from the Burray Hoard, length of terminals 65 mm; NMS X.IL 270.

AGE OF GOLD AND SILVER

More concrete evidence for a 'long eleventh century' comes from an economic perspective. The evidence for trade is clear in some ways, but can also be difficult to piece together from scattered fragments. The easiest place to start is with the evidence for coins and hoards of precious metal. By the year 1000, silver hoards were becoming more rare in the north and west, but still provide some key examples. The hoard from Burray in Orkney [8.11, 8.12] (see p.141), is one of the largest caches of silver surviving from Scotland, containing ring-money and coins from England and Normandy (deposited c.997–1010).[42] The Lews Castle, Stornoway, Isle of Lewis Hoard is similar to Burray in that it consisted mainly of ring-money fragments, though the ring-money here is well-hacked in contrast to the many complete rings of Burray (deposited c.990–1040).[43] These examples show a combination of heavy fragmentation, but minimal evidence for testing silver quality by nicking, indicating that the establishment of the ring-money trade zone had increased trust in the hacksilver economy. The concept of ring-money, probably backed by the earls of Orkney, worked in a similar way to minted coins. The spread of ring-money in Scotland describes the limits of the Scandinavian silver economy at its peak, from the linguistic border between Gaelic and Norse on the Dornoch Firth, to the edges of *Gall-goídil* territory on the Clyde at Port Glasgow, and as far as Whithorn in Galloway (pp141–3).

Notably there is a spike in silver hoards deposited in churchyards around the turn of the millennium, including Iona (c.986), Portmahomack (c.990–1000), Dull, Perthshire (c.1025) and Kirk O'Banks, Caithness (late 10th–11th century). Hoards from Inch Kenneth, Mull (c.998–1001), and Jedburgh Bongate, Scottish Borders (c.1000–25) may feasibly be from ecclesiastical estates, or market sites affiliated with the Church. We may instead consider these 'sanctuary hoards', in which money could either be offered to the Church, or was secreted there for safekeeping with added saintly protection. There are good 9th-century parallels for large offerings of silver at or near ecclesiastical sites from St Ninian's Isle, Shetland (p.83), possibly the Galloway Hoard (pp86–7), and a large number of cases from royal Irish foundations in the 9th and 10th centuries.[44] Stray finds may also attest to a continued economic function of church sites. The most northerly coins of William the Conqueror (r.1066–87) are from the monasteries of Auldhame, East Lothian, and the Isle of May, Fife, in both cases from excavations near their churches.[45] Coins from Whithorn certainly attest to their use at a market site associated with an ecclesiastical settlement, and there is other evidence that a market existed on Iona at this time (p.143), but there is no real indication of such from the excavations from the Isle of May or Auldhame.

Other patterns in these late silver hoards include less frequent use of hacked dress items like pins and brooches [8.12], and mixed supplies of coins. Instead of the recurring ball-type and bossed penannular brooches of the 10th-century hoards, the dress items appearing in these hoards are of more singular types; the Iona hoard has a rare lozenge-shaped ring bezel [6.24] and the Inch Kenneth hoard from Mull has a length of woven silver chain, one of only four known from Scotland.[46] The coins in these hoards also tell us about big changes in neighbouring kingdoms: some of the first coins minted by the Hiberno-Norse kings of Dublin appear in the Inch Kenneth hoard, and stray finds of the first issues from Norway would appear in the isles from the late 11th century.[47] These were occasionally fragmented, showing they were circulating as bullion rather than for their face value – but the days of uncoined silver bullion were closing in by 1100.

The Iona, Portmahomack, Inch Kenneth and Stornoway hoards are the first appearance of a fateful new actor into our story. The earliest Norman arrivals in Scotland are coins of King Richard (r.942–96). Richard was the third ruler of Normandy, founded by treaty between Norse warlords and the king of the Franks in 911.[48] The Normans would of course go on to be the future rulers of England after 1066, but at the time these coins were deposited it was the kings of Denmark who were making waves. The first mention of Danes (*Danair*) in the Irish annals is in 986, leading to the so-called 'Christmas Eve Massacre' on Iona.[49] Danish armies would continue to harry the Welsh and English coasts over the following decades, each time carrying off massive amounts of silver payments. The strategy of Aethelred II ('the Unready', r.978–1016) to pay off rather than go to war with the Danish raiders may help to explain why his coins are so frequently encountered in the Scottish hoards of this time. The inclusion of Normandy issues in these hoards from Lewis and Mull makes it possible there was Hebridean involvement in these attacks. The Danish prince Cnut took the English throne briefly in 1014 and then permanently in 1016, eventually also taking the thrones of Denmark and Norway, beginning a period of Danish rule in England that would last until 1042, with numerous consequences for the kings of Alba.[50] There are poorly recorded conflicts between Máel Coluim mac Cináeda (r.1005–34) and Cnut, which concluded with a peace treaty sometime before 1026.[51] On at least one occasion, Cnut came to Scotland for a summit with Máel Coluim, possibly in 1031, attended by future king Mac Bethad mac Findlaích and Echmarcach, king of the isles.[52]

The subsequent relationship between Alba and the Anglo-Danish kings remains largely undocumented,[53] but may also have left its traces in several coin hoards of this time. Indeed, it is only in the reign of Cnut that we get the first silver hoards in Alba. Two separate hoards of Cnut coins are known from Fife. These join another find from Jedburgh in the Scottish Borders (*c*.1000–25), and a massive cache of 300 Cnut coins from Caldale, Orkney (deposited *c*.1032–40).[54]

It is fascinating to note that a hoard of Cnut coins from Parkhill, Lindores, Fife, dated 1025–32, was followed shortly by a second hoard from Fife of Dublin coins dated 1035–55. The latter is one of only three Scottish hoards, along with Inch Kenneth and Dull, which contain Dublin coins. The Dull 'hoard' is in fact a single roulade of silver pennies straight from the Dublin mint.[55] Dublin and Cnut coins are never found in the same hoard, although the Inch Kenneth hoard contains Dublin and Norman coins. It shows eloquently the transactional nature of

Fig. 8.13: Silver penny of David I (1136–53): NMS H.C4116.

the participation of *Fir Alban* in the grand dynastic battles of the early 11th centuries. The Dull hoard strongly suggests a recent payment, perhaps for mercenary activity, which shows links to Ireland via the central highland glens as noted in the 11th-century reliquaries discussed above.[56] Numerous studies have pointed to a rise of soldiers and fleets for hire in the 11th century and mercenary action became lucrative in a way that viking raids were in a previous age.[57] Another possibility is that this burst of early 11th-century hoards represents negotiated diplomatic payments, treaties or bribes to keep the peace, in an echo of a strategy established by Roman generals to deal with northern warbands centuries earlier.[58]

The distribution of these 'payment' hoards do not relate to geographic proximity, with Hiberno-Norse coins making it to eastern Scotland and Cnut issues reaching Orkney: this supports the notion they were targeted payments rather than silver in general circulation. It is also notable how large some of these payments were. The sudden visibility of the eastern lowlands with regards to the distribution of silver coins is also a change from the preceding two centuries where the evidence was heavily weighted toward the northern and western maritime zones. This forecasts the increasing centrality of the Forth and Tay basins as the seats of royal power in the 11th and 12th centuries. However indirectly, these finds speak to the historical events detailed above in interesting ways that require further attention.

David I introduced the first Scottish coinage in the first half of the 12th century, but actual finds of his coins are very rare [8.13]; it is not until the start of the 13th century that we begin to get coin hoards and stray coin finds in any great numbers.[59] The transformation to a monetary economy did not take place overnight, a reminder that the decision to begin issuing coins is always politically motivated in the early medieval period and could often be aspirational.[60] And here we run into another historical and archaeological bias: monetisation has been elevated to a critical stage in the development of the state and 'modernity', but we are getting better at identifying alternative forms of valuation in areas without urban centres and centralised markets, in ways perhaps better suited to the economic capacity of highland and island environments. In chapter 6, we saw that commodity money and payment in kind remained significant in Scotland, even after the establishment of coinage and market towns.

Before moving away from coins, stray finds of money seem to be on the increase in this period, speaking to the growth of 'pocket change' in Scotland for the first time since the Roman period [6.22–23]. Aside from the ring-money and coins discussed previously, there are also three Byzantine folleis (bronze coins) of this period from Scotland, and a lost gold dinar of 1097 from Morocco found in Monymusk, Aberdeenshire.[61] The easiest thing to do with such exotica is to dismiss them as modern losses from collectors. But a search of the Portable Antiquities Scheme database of finds shows that related coins have been found in England.[62] It is more interesting to think through how they may have come here. Foreign gold coins certainly circulated to an extent in 11th- to 12th-century England and were accepted as payment; gold coins were not issued by Scottish kings until the 14th century, so the Moroccan dinar may represent a genuine import, although it need not have been deposited anywhere near its mint date.[63]

We have characterised the 10th and 11th centuries as a 'Silver Age', while noting there were other forms of exchange available. Even in areas which used silver, other commodities such as glass beads, butter, fish products and cloth may have been used for payment. One material, however, blurs the boundaries between hard currency and commodity money. Alongside the evidence for silver hoards there were much rarer caches

of gold rings. These were often single finds or found in very small hoards, but without the associated coins of the silver hoards they are difficult to date. The Galloway Hoard (*c*.900) had a remarkable amount of gold in it; but other than a gold ingot and a simple ring, it was bound up in decorative mounts and other accessories.[64] A stamped gold finger-ring from Tundergarth, Dumfriesshire, shows that the kinds of highly decorated ribbon arm-rings of silver from the Galloway Hoard were also rendered in gold, if only very rarely.[65] Instead, there is a class of twisted or plaited gold finger-rings, arm-rings, and more rarely neck-rings, which begin to appear across Scotland at this time. The particularly fine arm-rings from Oxna, Shetland, and the Sound of Jura. typify the category: stray finds with little context, but from broadly Scandinavian-dominated parts of the country [8.14, 8.16]. Related finds from coin-dated hoards elsewhere suggest that gold rings were in circulation from the start of the Viking Age, but in an insular context belong mainly to the later 10th and 11th centuries.[66] A hoard of finger-rings, some clipped into fragments before deposition, probably from North Uist, shows they circulated as hack-gold in a bullion economy [8.15].

In Scandinavia, gold rings like these were almost always deposited complete and with little or no evidence for testing by nicking. This is either because they come late in the series, when nicking was less frequent, or because gold rings were not used in economic transactions in the same way as silver rings. In Scotland, gold was generally reserved for high-value transactions, such as marriage gifts, ransoms and donations to the Church.[67] The rarity of gold-ring finds in both Norway and Britain indicates that they were not seen as equivalent to silver in either region.[68] However, they certainly took on more of an economic function in an insular context, and the Scottish examples include several nicked and clipped fragments.[69]

There are other differences in how gold rings were used. One recurring pattern is their association with water. It is no

---

Fig. 8.14 (left): Arm-ring of plaited gold rods, from Oxna, Shetland, diameter 75 mm, weight 62.44 g; NMS X.FE 71.

Fig. 8.15 (right, above): Gold-ring hoard, possibly North Uist, NMS X.FE 17–26; plain ring in foreground, diameter 27 mm, weight 6.51 g, NMS X.FE 23.

Fig. 8.16 (right, below): Arm-ring of twisted gold rods merging into a stamp-decorated connecting-plate, Sound of Jura, maximum width 76 mm, weight 112.5 g; NMS X.FE 103.

CRUCIBLE OF NATIONS

Fig. 8.17: Gold fillet decorated by running scrolls in repoussé, found in a small hoard with three silver spoons, under the floor of Iona Nunnery, length 330 mm, weight 8.4 g; NMS H.HX 36.

surprise that most of the Scottish finds are near the sea, given their use in the northern and western isles. But some were clearly thrown into the sea: the Sound of Jura arm-ring was discovered in the seabed by a scuba diver; and one from Eastbourne, Sussex, was dragged up by a fishing boat from the bed of the English Channel some 7 km from shore.[70] It is also peculiar that they appear in areas not otherwise linked to the Scandinavian bullion economy, but again this may be due to their use relatively late in the period, into the 11th and 12th centuries.[71] The latest securely dated examples from Scotland are from two very small hoards on Iona and the Isle of Bute, both at or near important churches known to have been in use at the time. The hoard from Plan Farm near St Blane's Church, Bute, included a plaited gold ring and a plain gold ring, three finely decorated thin gold fillets, a small silver ingot, and coins of the kings David I, Henry I and Stephen, giving a date of deposition in the 1150s.[72] This is currently also the latest dated example of a silver ingot from a hoard in Scotland. The Iona hoard was smaller still, containing only a plaited gold ring, two portions of similar gold fillets to those found at St Blane's, and a fragment of gold wire, found during clearance works at St Ronan's Church.[73] These 12th-century hoards are separated from the last flush of silver hoards by a century or more, but recall an earlier impulse: their association with churches makes them 'sanctuary hoards', or perhaps offerings or sacrifices under the eyes of God. The tiny Iona 'hoard' was actually deposited as a ring, the gold fillets rolled neatly within the circumference of the plaited gold finger-ring and tied in place with the gold wire. The location, at the south-east corner of St Ronan's Chapel, may hint at a foundational deposit or a vow.[74]

The gold fillets in these two 12th-century deposits are fascinating in their own right. They are interpreted as female head-cover ornaments and, made from ribbon-like strips of gold foil with stamped decoration, were extremely delicate to wear.[75] Fillets are increasingly being recognised from trade sites, including clipped fragments from Whithorn, Bornais, and from Cille Pheadair, South Uist, showing they were used in a hack-gold economy similar to silver bullion.[76] It has been noted that their weight in gold also conforms to the Scandinavian *øre* standard, such that they may originate in a Scandinavian context of weight-adjusted dress accessories.[77] The St Ronan's example shows, however, that even a clipped terminal could be used in a votive manner. A complete gold fillet with fine vine-scroll decoration also comes from another Iona hoard, with silver spoons found wrapped in linen underneath the chancel arch of the Benedictine Nunnery church [8.17].[78] Rather than stashes of money, the use of gold fillets linking these three separate Hebridean hoards suggests a coherent phenomenon of utilising gold objects for making vows and offerings, blurring the boundaries between economic and spiritual value. The use of gold rings as watery deposits elsewhere certainly seems to be a variation on this, and their inclusion in modern-day wedding vows may be a distant echo a millennium later.

The source of these gold objects remains understudied, but there must have been new sources opening up in the 11th and 12th centuries that fuelled the increase in their deposition in Scotland; the Moroccan dinar from Monymusk hints at one such origin. Two centuries earlier, the large amount of gold in the Galloway Hoard now looks even more significant in a time with less evidence for gold circulation in Scotland. With its exotic rock crystal, silk and Central Asian silver vessel, the Galloway Hoard tells us that it was not only vikings who had connections with the east; and in this case the role of the Church requires much more emphasis. The establishment of trade routes connecting western Europe to Constantinople and the Islamic caliphates from the 8th century, and strengthened in the Viking Age, is what gradually made long-distance pilgrimage possible.[79] Historical sources reveal an increased capacity

Fig. 8.18: Marvered Islamic glass phial, 12th- to 14th-century date, found in St Andrews, Fife; NMS X.1997.761.

for insular and later Scandinavian individuals to undertake pilgrimages to Rome over the course of the 9th–11th centuries, including kings from Burgred of Mercia to Cnut and Mac Bethad.[80] This is the wider context for the beginning of the Crusades at the end of the 11th century. While there is no direct evidence for much Scottish participation in the First Crusade,[81] the striking appearance of a camel making its way, as a royal gift, through the Scottish and Irish courts in 1105 is very suggestive of a new world of contacts with the east.[82] And a broken glass phial from St Andrews, Fife, has been identified as 12th- to 14th-century Islamic marvered ware, possibly from Syria [8.18].[83] We do not need explicitly to connect all exotica to Crusader activity, but the establishment of these networks meant that there were simply more ways for such items to enter normal channels of trade and exchange, while still retaining the allure of the exotic – as we saw when discussing the circulation of green porphyry tiles in the 11th century (pp 175–6).

BEFORE THE BURGHS

One of the biggest changes of the 12th century was the establishment of towns and cities in Scotland. After the decline of the Roman forts and *vicus* settlements from the 3rd century AD, there was nothing like an urban centre in Scotland for centuries. Among the innovations of the reign of David I was the establishment of royal burghs, urban centres where market-based exchange was protected by royal charter. However, it may be these are only the first documented examples, or the first formal recognition by law, of places which were already in operation without royal supervision. There is evidence for the introduction of Anglo-Danish merchants to Scotland from the 11th century onwards, including bases on the Tay such as Perth and Dundee, which would become major cities.[84] Finds from recent decades of metal-detecting have created clusters of Viking-age economic and trade objects, and early coins from the vicinity of places which would eventually become burghs, especially Roxburgh in the Borders which was heavily favoured by David I in the 12th century.[85] In a previous chapter, we highlighted the Dornoch and Moray firths as early concentrations of imported material, including rare Anglo-Scandinavian bells of likely 10th-century date and a fragment of ring-money arm-ring from Dornoch (p. 142).[86] A convincing case has also been made for the 10th- or 11th-century origins of Perth on the Tay, based on radiocarbon dates and stratified finds from excavations at the High Street, as well as tantalising stray finds of a Viking-age sword and black glass linen-smoother [8.19].[87] The glass linen-smoothers are problematic, as very similar examples were also used in early modern times; two stray finds from another early burgh at Kirkcudbright on the Solway Firth are often linked with the discovery of a 10th-century weapon burial here, but again may be of Viking Age to modern date.[88] Recent metal-detecting finds indicate a boom in activity in and around Kirkcudbright from the 10th century onwards, supporting textual evidence that this was a major power centre of the *Gall-goídil* before the 12th century.[89] Finds include an arm of a Northumbrian-style stone cross of likely 9th-century date, and a lead papal bulla of Pope Clement II, *c.*1040, both from St Cuthbert's Church; a 'Winchester style' strap-end of 10th- or 11th-century date from near Kirkcudbright; and a rare early coin of David I.[90]

The most intriguing new evidence for activity around this time in Kirkcudbright is a small, openwork crucifixion plaque and an openwork copper-alloy object, a book or box-fitting, both of 11th or 12th century date, found on nearby St Mary's

Fig. 8.19 (left): Underside of a black glass linen-smoother, Perth, diameter 87 mm; NMS X.IL 364.

Fig. 8.20 (middle and bottom): Openwork plaque of cast copper-alloy, depicting the crucifixion, width 70 mm; and openwork mount of cast copper-alloy, with zoomorphic motif and perforated loop at one end, length 91 mm; both from St Mary's Isle, Kirkcudbright, NMS X.2015.182–183.

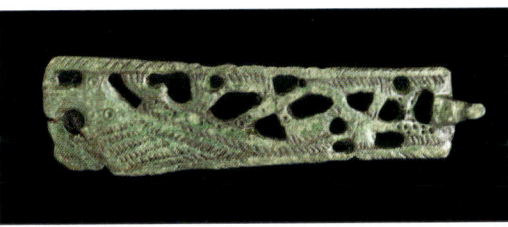

Isle [8.20]. St Mary's is a peninsula that is almost an island in Kirkcudbright Bay just south of the modern town, and was the site of an ecclesiastical settlement associated with Holyrood Priory from at least the late 12th century.[91] This plaque most likely comes from an altar cross, of a type only previously found in Ireland.[92] Its discovery in southwest Scotland is evidence for close links across the Irish Sea as seen most clearly in the finds of this period in Whithorn, and may have been a gift for the foundation of an early priory here.

These examples reveal that the process of urbanisation in Scotland was likely not directed by kings, but by an emerging merchant class. While there are finds of stray coins and ring-money fragments in places that would become burghs later, we find lots of evidence for craftworking and trade in coastal areas far from any urban centres, including several sand-dune sites in the Hebrides (p. 154). Finds eroding from such dunes are often mixed with material from many time periods, and they were regularly donated to museums in Scotland from large private collections without clear provenance. Some of the most frequent finds from such sites are metal pins dating from the Iron Age to the early modern period: with the exception of easily recognisable types like hand-pins and ringed pins, they have not been given much targeted archaeological attention.[93] However, when put together they reveal crucial information about the supposedly 'dark' 11th century and beyond.

In an age of variants, where dress items such as pins were produced in great numbers at market towns like Dublin, certain types of pin were fashionable for discrete periods of time. Excavations at urban sites in Ireland now allow us to date changes in the use of dress-pins with more clarity than before. Certain types of ringed pin are strongly associated with 11th-century layers in Ireland, including variants of the classic Viking-age ringed pin. By the 11th century, the ring on these pins had become more decorative and less functional; the freely swivelling ring became a movable semicircle known as a 'stirrup ring'. Types with crutch-heads (T-shaped) are increasingly found in Scotland (p. 188). At the same time as these late ringed pin variants proliferated, further variants without rings were also fashionable. This indicates the ring had by this time become more an affectation than a functional fastening element [8.21].

These crutch-headed pins are often found in places far from known Scandinavian settlement.[94] One was discovered in a cave in Archerfield, East Lothian, and two in a hillfort at

AN EXPERIMENTAL AGE

Fig. 8.21 (right): Skeuomorphic kidney-ring stick-pin, Garvard, Colonsay, length 96 mm, NMS X.IL 798.

Fig. 8.22 (below): Frustrum-head stick-pins, 11th–13th century: longest pin, 108 mm, Boreray, North Uist; NMS X.GT 244.

Doune of Relugas, Moray.[95] The latter site has four Hiberno-Norse ringed pins of 9th–11th century, a remarkable cluster for this part of Scotland, and recent excavations by the University of Aberdeen have confirmed refortification of the hillfort in the 10th and 11th centuries.[96] Rather than seeing these as evidence for 'viking' raiding parties, an 11th-century reoccupation of hillforts in Moray is more likely to relate to the dynastic struggles between rival kindreds, and challenges to the kings of Alba, which characterised the early 11th century, leading ultimately to the rise of Mac Bethad to the throne.[97]

A related 11th-century type was the 'kidney-ringed' pins, where the earlier polyhedral heads were fitted with a decorated broad ring.[98] Half of all examples known from Scotland are from or near North Uist in the Hebrides. Like the crutch-headed pins, these are now known from eastern Scotland as well.[99] At first kidney-shaped rings were still movable, but soon the ring was cast in place, and some even have the head and ring cast in a solid piece, rendering the head completely decorative. These skeuomorphic types [8.21] give rise to still more variants, reaching into the 12th century and beyond.

The transition to stick-pins, pins without rings, would characterise Irish and Scottish fashions during the 12th and 13th centuries [6.42].[100] While these late ringed pins and their unringed variants were used in both Ireland and Scotland in the 11th century, there are some types that are almost exclusively found in Scotland: these tend to be of the stick-pin variety. The so-called 'frustrum head' pins [8.22] with their expanding conical or box shape have a distribution concentrated largely in the Hebrides, including three on Iona alone, with examples from either end of the Great Glen showing the main avenue of transmission from west to east.[101] These appear to be a Hebridean response to Irish stick-pin fashions in the 11th or 12th century, and probably continue in use for a long period of time.[102]

Such pins and their distribution tell us there was more interaction between the Hebrides and northeastern Scotland in these centuries than typically appreciated. It supports the other evidence above for what we might call an archaeology of Gaeldom, including shared fashions which may ultimately derive from the Viking-age workshops of Dublin, but before long were produced in the Hebrides and exported to Alba. The Hiberno-Norse trade town of Whithorn appears to be a major market for them, and large numbers of stick-pins from the Uists, Lewis, Tiree and Iona may relate to lost beach-market sites.[103]

In another wrinkle, stick-pins are increasingly being recognised in several major 'Late Norse' settlement centres of Orkney and Shetland. In fact, nearly all the metal pins from these settlements fall into the types identified as being produced in Dublin in the 11th–13th centuries, including one

Fig. 8.23: Lyre-headed bronze pin from Jarlshof, Shetland, length 76mm; NMS X.HSA 851.

distinctive 'lyre-headed' type of which the only example known from outside Dublin is from Jarlshof [8.23].[104] The material culture reveals that there is much more overlap between Alba, Moray, the Norse earldoms and Hiberno-Norse western isles in the 11th and the 12th centuries. The appearance of these pins at halls, hillforts and other power centres speaks to a period of shared elite fashion with distinct echoes of the shared 'insular' aesthetic of penannular brooches across these regions at the start of the Viking Age (chapter 5). This material, along with the coins, offers a new dimension to other textual evidence for interaction between the kings of Scots, the kings of the isles and the earls of Orkney, in which the realm of Moray becomes an important linchpin between them all.

A 'LONG ELEVENTH CENTURY'?

There is much more work to be done on the material culture of the 11th and 12th centuries, but we no longer need to cast it as the darkest part of the 'Dark Ages' in Scotland. The period suffers only because so much of the attention is reserved for the remarkable historical characters of the Viking Age before it, and the dynasty founded by Máel Coluim III and Margaret thereafter. It is most often seen as either the end of an era or the start of one, leaving it neglected by comparison.

Much of the evidence traces the ways in which what appears like revolutionary changes of the 12th century are always grounded in processes trickling along for long periods of time, and often in a way that is adapted to local circumstances. The burghs only become formalised by royal charter under David I, but in many cases have a century or more of earlier trade activity. A new lordly class of royal followers commission stone churches in fashionable styles, but on sites already ancient, and in some cases marking their own graves using stones that derive from the venerable 'hogback' form. The sacred matter of these refoundations also derives from ancient relics, bells and crosiers that were either retained intact or encased in fashionable new reliquaries. The lordly classes further north dressed in styles that incorporated stick-pins ultimately derived from the Viking-age workshops of the Irish Sea, now commodified for sale in emergent beach markets from the Hebrides to the Moray Firth. In many cases a connection with Ireland is obvious, where a shared language also fostered shared cultural markers visible in material culture. The connections to England in eastern Scotland have also been explained as growing Norman influence. The archaeology reveals that these connections are grounded in years of interaction with neighbouring polities, and can get us past simple colonial narratives that leave Scotland as the passive recipient of outside forces.

If there is an argument for a 'long eleventh century', it is to emphasise the deeper roots of the changes of the 12th century. Like the 'long eighth century' aspects of the early Viking-age (chapter 2), the point is to give some wider context to the notable historical events which shape our understanding of the medieval past. It emphasises as well the experimental nature of these centuries – in all their messiness and complexity.

NOTES

1. Carver 2008.
2. Allen 2017; Smart 1985.
3. Clarke and Johnson (eds) 2015; Woolf and McGuigan (eds) 2018; Hadley and Dyer (eds) 2017; Frankopan 2012.
4. Molyneaux 2015, 8–9; McGuigan 2015a.
5. Taylor 2016, 11.
6. See chapters in McGuigan and Woolf (eds) 2018.
7. Broun 2010, 2015b.
8. Laing 1975; Caldwell 1982, A5, 9–10; Hinton 2005, 182.
9. For example, HAMP-0557A1, LEIC-BD987A, SF4759.
10. For example, BH-5C6A22, BH-8036D2.
11. Egan 1998; 296; Read 2001, no. 483.
12. For instance, the panel from Dull, National Museums Scotland (NMS) X.IB 58, 8th/9th century; see also Meigle 6, Canmore ID 30866, and an undated incised slate depicting dogs chasing deer from St Blane's, Bute, NMS X.GC 51.
13. McGuigan 2021, 51, 63–7.
14. For example, Watson 2010.
15. Broun 1997b.
16. Clancy 2000.
17. McGuigan 2021, 222–4.
18. Fawcett 1985.
19. Driscoll 1998; Oram 2011, 209–15, 225–32; Broun 2015a, 67–71; Taylor 2016, 452–6.
20. Stratigos and Noble 2018.
21. For example, Johnson 1999.
22. Oram 2008.
23. O'Grady 2014, 113–4, 123.
24. Compare Sheehan 1988.
25. Murray 2020.
26. Ljung 2015; Staecker 2007; cf. Caldwell et al. 2013.
27. Broun 1999.
28. Caldwell 1982, 12; cf. Michelli 1987, 385.
29. Michelli 1987; British Museum 1851,0715.5.
30. Murray 2007, 91–2.
31. Compare Hicks 1980; Murray 2007.
32. Murray 2013b, 165.
33. SUR-FA2ABO; Geake 2004, 244–5; fig. 4a, p. 246.
34. Lang 1974.
35. Stocker 2000; Williams 2016.
36. Barnes 2019.
37. King, n.d. (a).
38. Dalmeny: Canmore ID 50567; Tyninghame St Baldred's: Canmore ID 57713.
39. Compare Cusack 2015.
40. Compare Barrow 2003.
41. For example, Taylor 2014.
42. Graham-Campbell 1995, 52, 141.
43. *Ibid.*, 151.
44. Sheehan 2018.
45. Bateson and Holmes 2013.
46. British Museum 1851,0613.1; the others are from Croy (see chapter 4, NMS X.FC 25, [4.32]), Ballinaby, Islay (NMS X.IL 146) and Skaill (NMS X.IL 101).
47. Coins of Harald Hardrada (r.1044–66) are known from the Udal, North Uist, and Dunrossness, Shetland; coins of Olav Kyrre, or Olaf the Peaceful (r. 1067–93), are known from Birsay and Bornais: Sharples (ed.) 2021, 103–6.
48. Blackburn 1995; Ridel 2007; Metcalf 1995, 24, for the possibility that four unprovenanced Normandy deniers also came from a hoard at Lindores, Fife.
49. Clancy 2013.
50. Woolf 2007, 230–2.
51. *Ibid.*, 239–40.
52. *Ibid.*, 244–8.
53. McGuigan 2021, 82–5, 90–1; Woolf 2007, 244–52.
54. Metcalf 1995.
55. Bateson 1993.
56. Although we should not dismiss direct links between Dull and the Hebrides through the offices of the Columban *familia*: cf. McGuigan 2021, 79–82.
57. Holm 1986; Candon 1988; Barrett 2007; Abels 2008.
58. Blackwell et al. 2017.
59. Holmes 2004.
60. G. Williams 2007.
61. Byzantine coins: Bateson and Holmes 1998, 535; 2013, 256; see now TT 46/19, an AE Class 2 anonymous follis of Basil II or Constantine VIII, *c*.AD976–1028 from the Torosay, Mull,

allocated to Mull Museum, Tobermory; information from Ella Paul. Monymusk: Graham-Campbell 1995, 87.

62. For example, CAM-064213; DOR-0F6596; SUR-5B70C4; NMS-26FAC5; DENO-426C9D; SF-9EB484.
63. Kelleher 2007; Blackburn 2007; Archibald 2014; McGuigan 2021, 424–5; with thanks to Alice Blackwell and Neil McGuigan for discussion.
64. Goldberg and Davis 2021.
65. British Museum AF.466; Graham-Campbell 1995, 157–8.
66. Graham-Campbell 1995, 55.
67. N. McGuigan, pers. comm.
68. List of all insular finds in Graham-Campbell 2011a, 159–60, with additions in Kershaw 2018.
69. For example, Graham-Campbell 1995, 158–9; 2008, 196–7.
70. Kershaw 2018, 243.
71. Graham-Campbell 1995, 165–7.
72. *Ibid.*, 166.
73. *Ibid.*, 166–7.
74. Compare Gilchrist 2020, 124–6.
75. Ó Floinn 1983.
76. Sharples (ed.) 2021, 146–7.
77. Ó Floinn 1983.
78. Curle 1924; Gilchrist 2020, 126.
79. McCormick 2001.
80. Woolf 2007, 77, 245, 259.
81. Parsons 2019.
82. Candon 1988, 407–8.
83. Compare Carboni 2001; information from Professor Julian Henderson and Venetia Porter.
84. Crawford 2002.
85. Shiels and Campbell 2011.
86. See also TT 226/12 for finds from Clarkly Hill near Burghead, Moray, including another polygonal bell; F Hunter pers. comm.
87. Hall et al. 2006; 2007.
88. Scott 1956; 1983.
89. Place-names of Kirkcudbrightshire, n.d.; Edmonds 2019, 112–13; Oram 2000.
90. All finds now in Stewartry Museum, Kirkcudbright: Craig 1992, vol. 2, 345–7; Robison 1927, 9, 38; TT 138/15; TT 112/16.
91. Reid 1959.
92. Murray 2013a; Murray and Maldonado in prep.
93. Stevenson 1955, Laing 1973, Foster 1989.
94. Fanning 1994, 41–6.
95. Archerfield: NMS X.HM 18; Cree 1909. Relugas: NMS X.FC 131: *PSAS* 1863, 378.
96. Noble and Sveinbjarnarson 2017.
97. Woolf 2007, 227–30, 240–2, 246–8.
98. Fanning 1994, 39–41.
99. Sanquhar Park, Forres, Moray: TT 149/99, allocated to Forres Museum. Whitehills, Banffshire: TT89/04, allocated to Marischal Museum, ABDUA:64530.
100. O'Rahilly 1998.
101. Isle of Lismore, NMS X.FC 141, 142, 143, Laing 1973. Urquhart Castle near Inverness, H.HY 19, Batey 1992. Dores, Inverness-shire, Inverness Museum TT.51/02. Dornoch, Historylinks Museum, TT.108/16.
102. Batey 1992; Campbell et al. 2019, 316–8.
103. Hill 1997, 364–8; Close-Brooks and Maxwell 1974; large collections of metal pins in the Hunterian Museum from Ballevullin and elsewhere in Tiree have yet to be assessed, but examples of crutch-headed, frustrum-headed and other types were identified among them as part of this research, e.g. GLAHM:B.1951.2052; information via Cameryn Clark.
104. Hamilton 1956, 128, 235; Griffiths et al. 2019, 239–40.

Envoi

In the 12th century a change was in the air. New mortared stone churches in fashionable architectural styles were springing up across the country. They were more than just landmarks. The first stone church towers in Scotland brought with them a new sound – the peal of church bells. Scotland had joined the soundscape of medieval Christendom.

Bells of various kinds had been used in Europe since the Roman period, but the half-oval bell with splayed lip – what we think of now as 'bell-shaped' – was a development of the later first millennium.[1] Casting-pits for bronze tower bells are known from England dating back to the 10th century, but the earliest surviving hanging bells are of the 12th century.[2]

In Scotland the earliest surviving tower bell was taken to be one discovered in Kersmains Farm, near Roxburgh in the Scottish Borders, dated to the late 12th century.[3] However, a bell from St Olaf's in Cullivoe, Yell, Shetland, is of a type that may be 11th or 12th century.[4] This matches other early evidence for church towers in the Norse earldoms of the northern isles.[5] The northern seaways may have helped to introduce the idea of church towers – and tower bells – to Scotland from the continent before the 12th century.

Before these tower bells, the sound of bells in Scotland was mainly associated with handbells of iron and bronze (chapter 7) – used to mark the hours and to call the brethren of a monastery to prayer. In time, some bells became associated with a charismatic saint and were treated as a form of portable relic. The sound of the bell was likened to the voice of the saint. Its voice would have been used to mark blessings and the saint's sanctuary, but could also curse, punish and cast out demons.[6] Each bell would have had its own distinctive voice depending on its size and material, but they would have made a duller, thunking sound than the sonorous peal of the church bells we are used to.

The sound of the tower bell did not chase away the clang of the earlier handbells – the Dumbarton 'Skellat' or 'Deid Bell' was used for funeral processions as late as the 17th century, and a bell associated with St Columba remains with the parish church of Little Dunkeld, Perthshire, today.[7] In just a handful of cases in Scotland, early handbells were embellished or

Opposite: Detail of bronze reliquary ornamented with figure of the crucified Christ from Kilmichael Glassary, Argyll, late 12th century, NMS H.KA 5.

encased in shrines [8.4]. More than just relics of the saints, they were witnesses to the ancient origins of Christianity in Scotland.

The Kilmichael Glassary bell-shrine literally encapsulates the period covered by this book. Like the *Coigreach* of St Fillan [8.6], it takes the shape of the object it holds within it – a small iron handbell. This is one of the smallest quadrangular bells in Scotland, meaning that it was never meant to ring out across a whole landscape, designed instead for portability and use in close company. Its clapper was missing and the handle had been detached, but it was still treated as an heirloom.[8]

We cannot know how old it was by the 12th century, but in Scotland such iron bells were generally made during the period 700–900. The bell's voice had been definitively silenced by the time it was enshrined. It was once brazed internally and externally, but only the barest traces of bronze remained on the pitted surface. Patches of wool adhering to the iron tell us it was wrapped inside its shrine, 'shrouded' like the venerated dead and their relics.[9] Perhaps it was enshrined at the point it became too corroded for use; perhaps it was commissioned for a newly rebuilt church.

It was one of many such ancient relics of the saints which were venerated in Scotland. While the saint's tomb was still the primary focus of devotion and pilgrimage, objects associated with the saint remained in use throughout the medieval period. By the later medieval period,[10] the title of *deòradh*, anglicised as dewar, was given to lay-men who were the hereditary keepers of such relics. The social importance of these dewars as peacekeepers and trusted officials ensured the survival of several of Scotland's handbells and other relics.[11]

It need not have been made anywhere near where it was deposited, at or close to the striking local prominence known as Torbhlaren – Tòrr a' Bhlàrain, 'the hill of the little level or flat place', which may instead be the residence of its dewar.[12] But its design shows that it comes from a Gaelic-Scandinavian milieu which perfectly describes Argyll and the Hebrides by the 12th century.[13]

Like the Hilton of Cadboll stone with which we began this journey (pp xii–xvi), the Kilmichael bell was an artefact of the

---

Left: The Kilmichael Glassary bell reliquary, Argyll, height 148mm, NMS X.KA 5.

Right: Quadrangular iron bell inside the Kilmichael Glassary reliquary, Argyll, height 82mm, NMS X. KA 4.

pre-Viking Age which continued to 'move' through the centuries by remaining in use. We cannot know more about how either one was used in these centuries, but we do know that they were repurposed in the 12th century, with the cross-slab re-erected alongside a new chapel, and the bell encased in an elaborate shrine. If they were associated with particular saints, they had passed into oral lore.

We can now, at the end of this journey, say more about what happened in the intervening period. The Hebrides and the Fearn peninsula appear to have been at the forefront of the raids of the early Viking Age, although, as we saw in chapter 2, viking raiders did not have a monopoly on violence against the Church. Iona remained a major monastery through these centuries (chapters 4, 6), while at Portmahomack, where the tall cross-slabs of sandstone which encircled the Fearn peninsula were produced, fragments of sculpture cast down in the 9th-century raid were used to build the foundations of humbler parish churches in the 12th and 13th centuries. Iona and Portmahomack both received important silver hoards in the late 10th century, a sign these regions were now within the silver bullion economy spanning Scandinavia to Ireland (chapter 6). The area of Argyll where the Kilmichael Glassary bell was discovered, like Portmahomack itself, was at the frontier between Gaelic and Norse speakers. Both communities had found different ways to manage the changes of the Viking Age. Both had retained precious relics of the past and found them newly relevant in the 12th century.

The sound of church bells soon rang out across all these landscapes, marking the passing of time rather than heralding a new era.[14] But new links with the early medieval past continued to be made. The 13th-century parish church at Portmahomack incorporated the foundations of the earliest, possibly Pictish church, as a crypt. The churchyards nearest to the find-spot of the Kilmichael Glassary bell include early medieval carved stone crosses.[15] The traditional location of St Columba's cell was marked with a cross set into a millstone on Iona, still remembered centuries after he last wrote there.[16] The material witnesses of these dramatic days were not forgotten, but in our crucible of nations were instead recast for a new beginning.

NOTES

1. Arnold and Goodson 2012, 104; Bourke 2020, 258–9.
2. Bayley et al. 1993.
3. Clouston 1978.
4. Shetland Museum REL 65405; Bourke 2020, 260–1.
5. Fernie 1986.
6. Overbey 2012, 127–8; Bitel 2007.
7. Bourke 2020, nos 116, 122.
8. *Ibid.*, no. 66.
9. Caldwell et al. 2013, 207–8.
10. Lucas 1986.
11. Márkus 2009.
12. Caldwell et al. 2013, 201–7.
13. There has long been speculation that a panel of wavy ornament at the crest above the *Manus Dei* (hand of God) is a pseudo-Arabic inscription, but it is now understood as egg-and-dart ornament, perhaps representing the clouds from which the hand emerges: Caldwell et al. 2013, 224; Bourke 2020, 372.
14. A bell-casting pit in the nave of the church at Portmahomack was dated to the 11th–13th centuries: Carver et al. 2016, 290.
15. Fisher 2001, 149–50.
16. Campbell and Maldonado 2020, 18–20, 25.

Bibliography

ABBREVIATIONS USED

PSAS: Proceedings of the Society of Antiquaries of Scotland
TDGNHAS: Transactions of the Dumfriesshire and Galloway Natural History and Antiquarian Society

REFERENCES

Aannestad, H. L. 2014. Kulturmøter i vikingtid. Importgjenstander i gravene på Gulli. In C. Gustavsen (ed.), *Hauglagt – vikingenes gravskikk på Gulli*, 38–45. Sandefjord: Vestfoldmuseene.

Aannestad, H. L. 2018. Charisma, violence and weapons: the broken sword of Vikings. In M. Vedeler, I.M. Røstad, E.S. Kristoffersen and Z.T. Glørstad (eds) 147–66.

Abels, R. 2008. Household men, mercenaries and vikings in Anglo-Saxon England. In J. France (ed.), *Mercenaries and Paid Men: The Mercenary Identity in the Middle Ages* 143–65. Leiden: Brill.

Abrams, L. 2020. The Scandinavian encounter with Christianity overseas: diplomatic conversions in the 9th and 10th centuries. In A. Pedersen and S. M. Sindbæk (eds) 34–46.

Ager, B. 2020. The Carolingian cup from the Vale of York Viking Hoard: origins of its form and decorative features. *The Antiquaries Journal* 100: 86–108.

Alcock, L., and Alcock, E. 1991. Reconnaissance excavations on Early Historic fortifications and other royal sites in Scotland, 1974–84: 4, excavations at Alt Clut, Clyde Rock, Strathclyde, 1974–75. *PSAS* 120: 95–149.

Allen, M. 2017. The first sterling area. *Economic History Review* 70(1): 79–100.

Anderson, J. 1873. Notes on the evidence of spinning and weaving in the brochs or Pictish towers supplied by the stone whorls and the long-handled 'broch combs' found in them. *PSAS* 9: 548–61.

Anderson, J. 1874. Notes on the relics of the Viking period of the Northmen in Scotland, illustrated by specimens in the Museum. *PSAS* 10: 536–94.

Anderson, J. 1876. Notice of a Find of Silver Ornaments, &c., at Croy, Inverness-shire, now presented to the Museum by Rev. Thomas Fraser, minister of Croy. *PSAS* 11: 588–92.

Anderson, J. 1907. Notice of bronze brooches and personal ornaments from a ship-burial of the Viking time in Oronsay, and other bronze ornaments from Colonsay. *PSAS* 41: 437–50.

Androshchuk, F. 2007. The rural Vikings and the Viking Helgö. In U. Fransson, M. Svedin, S. Bergerbrant, and F. Androshchuk (eds) *Cultural Interaction Between East and West: Archaeology, Artefacts and Human Contacts in Northern Europe*. Stockholm Studies in Archaeology 44, 153–63. Stockholm: Stockholms Universitet.

Androshchuk, F. 2011. Symbols of faith or symbols of status? Christian objects in tenth-century Rus'. In I. Garipzanov and O. Tolochko (eds) *Early Christianity on the Way from the Varangian in the Greeks*. Ruthenica Supplementum 4, 70–89. Kiev: Instytut istoriï Ukraïny NAN Ukraïny.

Arbman, H. 1943. *Birka Untersuchungen und Studien I: Die Gräber*. Uppsala: Almqvist and Wiksell.

Archibald, M.M. 2014. Islamic and Christian gold coins from Spanish mints found in England, mid-eleventh to mid-thirteenth centuries. In R. Naismith, M. Allen, and E. Screen (eds) *Early Medieval Monetary History: Studies in Memory of Mark Blackburn*, 377–96. Farnham: Ashgate.

Arcini, C. 2018. The *Viking Age: A Time with Many Faces*. Oxford: Oxbow.

Armstrong, E.C.R. 1922. Irish bronze pins of the Christian period. *Archaeologia* 72: 71–86.

Arnold, J.H., and Goodson, C. 2012. Resounding community: the history and meaning of medieval church bells. *Viator* 43(1): 99–130.

Arwidsson, G., and Berg, G. 1983. *The Mästermyr Find: A Viking Age Tool Chest from Gotland*. Stockholm: Almqvist and Wiksell.

Ashby, S. 2009. Combs, contact and chronology: reconsidering hair combs in early-historic and Viking-age Atlantic Scotland. *Medieval Archaeology* 53: 1–33.

Ashby, S. 2015. What really caused the Viking Age? The social content of raiding and exploration. *Archaeological Dialogues* 22(1): 89–106.

Opposite: Detail of a Trewhiddle-style disc-brooch from the Galloway Hoard.

Asplund, H. 2005. The bear and the female: bear-tooth pendants in late Iron Age Finland. *Suomalaisen Tiedeakatemian Toimituksia. Sarja Humaniora* (336): 13–30.

Bailey, R.N. 2010. *Corpus of Anglo-Saxon Stone Sculpture, Volume IX: Cheshire and Lancashire.* Oxford: Oxford University Press.

Bäcklund, J. 2001. The Picts and the martyrs, or did Vikings kill the native population of Orkney and Shetland?, *Northern Studies* 36: 33–47.

Bakka, E. 1965. Some decorated Anglo-Saxon and Irish metalwork found in Norwegian Viking graves. In A. Small (ed.) *The Fourth Viking Congress, York, August 1961,* 32–40. Edinburgh: Oliver and Boyd.

Balfour, J. 1909. Notice of a Viking Grave-mound, Kingscross, Arran, *PSAS* 43: 371–375.

Barber, J.W. 1981. Excavations on Iona, 1979. *PSAS* 111: 282–380.

Barnes, J. 2019. *Of Warriors and Beasts: The Hogbacks and Hammerhead Crosses of Viking Age Strathclyde and Northumbria.* Ph.D. thesis, University of Glasgow. Available at: <http://theses.gla.ac.uk/75049/> [accessed August 2021]

Barnes, M.P. 1994. *The Runic Inscriptions of Maeshowe, Orkney.* Uppsala: Institutionen för nordiska språk, Uppsala universitet.

Barnes, M.P., Hagland, J.R., and Page, R.I. 1997. *The Runic Inscriptions of Viking Age Dublin.* Dublin: Royal Irish Academy.

Barnes, M.P., and Page, R.I. 2006. *The Scandinavian Runic Inscriptions of Britain.* Uppsala: Institutionen för nordiska språk, Uppsala universitet.

Barrett, J.H. 2007. The pirate fishermen: The political economy of a medieval maritime society. In B. Ballin-Smith, S. Taylor, and G. Williams (eds) *West over Sea: Studies in Scandinavian Sea-borne Expansion and Settlement Before 1300.* The Northern World 31: 299–340. Leiden: Brill.

Barrett, J.H. 2010. Rounding up the usual suspects: causation and the Viking Age diaspora. In A. Anderson, J. H. Barrett, and K. Boyle (eds) *The Global Origins and Development of Seafaring,* 289–302. Cambridge: McDonald Institute.

Barrett, J.H., and Gibbon, S.J. (eds) 2016. *Maritime Societies of the Viking and Medieval World.* Leeds: Maney.

Barrett, J.H. and Richards, M.P. 2004. Identity, gender, religion and economy: new isotope and radiocarbon evidence for marine resource intensification in Early Historic Orkney, Scotland, UK, *European Journal of Archaeology* 7(3): 249–271.

Barrett, J.H. et al. 2000. What was the Viking Age and when did it happen? A view from Orkney. *Norwegian Archaeological Review* 33(1): 1–39.

Barrow, G.W.S. 2003. *Kingship and Unity: Scotland AD 1000–1300.* Edinburgh: Edinburgh University Press.

Barrowman, R. 2011. *The Chapel and Burial Ground on St Ninian's Isle, Shetland: Excavations Past and Present.* London: Society for Medieval Archaeology.

Barton-Murray, R., and Johnson, C. 2012. Metal stick-pins. In G. Eogan (ed.) *Excavations at Knowth 5: The Archaeology of Knowth in the First and Second Millennia AD.* RIA Monographs in Archaeology, 305–27. Dublin: Royal Irish Academy.

Bateson, J.D. 1993. A Hiberno-Norse Hoard from Dull, Perthshire. *Numismatic Chronicle* 153: 211–14.

Bateson, J.D., and Holmes, N. 1998. Roman and medieval coins found in Scotland, 1988–95. *PSAS* 127: 527–61.

Bateson, J.D., and Holmes, N. 2004. Roman and medieval coins found in Scotland, 1996–2000. *PSAS* 133: 245–76.

Bateson, J.D., and Holmes, N. 2013. Roman and medieval coins found in Scotland, 2006–10. *PSAS* 143: 227–64.

Batey, C.E. 1992. A copper alloy pin from Urquhart Castle, Inverness-shire. *PSAS* 122: 351–53.

Batey, C.E. 1988. A viking-age bell from Freswick Links, Caithness. *Medieval Archaeology* 32: 213–16.

Batey, C.E. 1993. The Viking and Late Norse graves of Caithness and Sutherland. In C.E. Batey, J. Jesch, and C.D. Morris (eds), 148–72.

Batey, C.E. 2003. Excavations at the Earl's Bu, Orphir, Orkney, c.1859–1939. *New Orkney Antiquaries Journal* 3: 29–71.

Batey, C.E. 2016. Viking burials in Scotland: two 'new' boat burial finds. In V. Turner, O. Owen, and D.J. Waugh (eds) *Shetland and the Viking World: Papers from the Seventeenth Viking Congress, Lerwick,* 39–45. Lerwick: Shetland Amenity Trust.

Batey, C.E., Jesch, J., and Morris, C.D. eds. 1993. *The Viking Age in Caithness, Orkney and the North Atlantic.* Edinburgh: Edinburgh University Press.

Batey, C.E., and Paterson, C. 2013. A Viking burial at Balnakeil, Sutherland. In A. Reynolds and L. Webster (eds) *Early Medieval Art and Archaeology in the Northern World: studies in honour of James Graham-Campbell.* Northern World 58, 631–62. Leiden: Brill.

Baug, I., Skre, D., Heldal, T., and Jansen, Ø.J. 2019. The beginning of the Viking Age in the west. *Journal of Maritime Archaeology* 14(1): 43–80.

Bayley, J., Bryant, R., McDonnell, G., and Heighway, C. 1993. A tenth-century bell-pit and bell-mound from St. Oswald's Priory, Gloucester. *Medieval Archaeology* 37: 224–36.

Becket, A., and Batey, C.E. 2014. A stranger in the dunes? Rescue excavation of a Viking Age burial at Cnoc nan Gall, Colonsay. *PSAS* 143: 303–18.

Bell, B., Dickson, C., Sellar, T., and Foster, S. 1990. Excavations at Warebeth (Stromness Cemetery) Broch, Orkney. *PSAS* 119: 101–31.

Bender Jørgensen, L. 2012. The introduction of sails to Scandinavia: raw materials, labour and land. In R. Berge, M.E. Jasinski, and K. Sognnes (eds) *N-TAG TEN: Proceedings of the 10th Nordic TAG conference at Stiklestad, Norway.* BAR International Series 2399, 173–81. Oxford: Archaeopress.

Biddle, M., and Kjølbye-Biddle, B. 1992. Repton and the Vikings. *Antiquity* 66(250): 36–51.

Bitel, L.M. 2006. Tools and scripts for cursing in medieval Ireland. *Memoirs of the American Academy in Rome* 51/52: 5–27.

Blackburn, M. 1995. Two Norman deniers from the Stornoway Hoard 1988–90. *Numismatic Chronicle* 155: 334–38.

Blackburn, M. 2000. Danish silver penny ('sceat'). In D.R. Perry (ed.) *Castle Park, Dunbar: Two Thousand Years on a Fortified Headland.* Soc Ant Scot Monograph Series 16, 168–69. Edinburgh: Society of Antiquaries of Scotland.

Blackburn, M. 2003. 'Productive' sites and the pattern of coin loss in

England, 600–1180. In T. Pestell and K. Ulmschneider (eds) *Markets in Early Medieval Europe: Trading and Productive Sites, 650–850*, 20–36. Macclesfield: Windgather.

Blackburn, M. 2007. Gold in England during an 'Age of Silver' (eighth to eleventh centuries). In J. Graham-Campbell and G. Williams (eds), 55–98.

Blackwell, A. 2011. The iconography of the Hunterston brooch and related early medieval material. *PSAS* 141: 231–48.

Blackwell, A. 2012. Individuals. In D.V. Clarke, A. Blackwell, and M. Goldberg (eds), 2–67.

Blackwell, A. 2018. *A Reassessment of the Anglo-Saxon Artefacts from Scotland: Material Interactions and Identities in Early Medieval Northern Britain*. Ph.D. thesis. Glasgow: University of Glasgow. Available at: <http://theses.gla.ac.uk/30708/> [accessed November 2020]

Blackwell, A., Goldberg, M., and Hunter, F. 2017. *Scotland's Early Silver*. Edinburgh: National Museums Scotland.

Bond, J., and Hunter, J. 1988. Flax-growing in Orkney from the Norse period to the 18th century. *PSAS* 117: 175–81.

Bond, J.M., Dockrill, S.J., and Downes, J. 2017. The Knowe of Swandro, excavation. *Discovery and Excavation in Scotland* New Ser., 17: 131–32.

Bourke, C. 2003. Three Early Medieval Mounts from County Armagh. *Ulster Journal of Archaeology* 62: 92–6.

Bourke, C. 2010. Antiquities from the River Blackwater IV: early medieval non-ferrous metalwork. *Ulster Journal of Archaeology* 69: 24–133.

Bourke, C. 2020. *Early Medieval Hand-Bells of Ireland and Britain.* Dublin: Wordwell.

Breay, C., and Story, J. 2018. *Anglo-Saxon Kingdoms: Art, Word, War.* British Library.

Brooks, N., and Graham-Campbell, J. 2000. Reflections on the Viking-Age silver hoard from Croydon, Surrey. In N. P. Brooks (ed.) *Communities and Warfare, 700–1400*, 69–92. London: Hambledon.

Brophy, K., and Noble, G. 2020. *Prehistoric Forteviot: Excavations of a ceremonial complex in eastern Scotland: SERF Monograph 1.* York: Council for British Archaeology.

Broun, D. 1997a. Dunkeld and the origin of Scottish identity. *Innes Review* 48(1): 112–24.

Broun, D. 1997b. The birth of Scottish history, *Scottish Historical Review*, 76(1): 4–22.

Broun, D. 1999. *The Irish Identity of the Kingdom of the Scots in the Twelfth and Thirteenth Centuries*. Woodbridge: Boydell and Brewer.

Broun, D. 2007. *Scottish Independence and the Idea of Britain from the Picts to Alexander III.* Edinburgh: Edinburgh University Press.

Broun, D. 2010. Becoming a nation: Scotland in the twelfth and thirteenth centuries. In H. Tsurushima (ed.) *Nations in Medieval Britain*, 86–103. Donington: Shaun Tyas.

Broun, D. 2015a. Statehood and lordship in 'Scotland' before the mid-twelfth century. *Innes Review* 66(1): 1–71.

Broun, D. 2015b. Britain and the beginning of Scotland. *Journal of the British Academy* 3: 107–37.

Brunning, S. 2019. *The Sword in Early Medieval Northern Europe: Experience, Identity, Representation.* Woodbridge: Boydell.

Brunning, S. 2020. Touching the past: The Breadalbane brooch and its bearers. In C. Thickpenny, K. Forsyth, J. Geddes, and K. Matthis (eds), 99–106.

Bryant, R. 2012. *Corpus of Anglo-Saxon Stone Sculpture,* Volume X: The Western Midlands. Oxford: Oxford University Press.

Bryce, T. 1913. Note on a balance and weights of the Viking period, found in the Island of Gigha. *PSAS* 47: 436–43.

Buchanan, C.H. 2012. *Viking artefacts from southern Scotland and northern England: cultural contacts, interactions, and identities in peripheral areas of Viking settlement*. Ph.D. thesis. University of Glasgow. Available at: <http://theses.gla.ac.uk/3391/> [accessed March 2021]

Buckberry, J., and Cherryson, A.K. (eds) 2010. *Burial in Later Anglo-Saxon England c.650–1100 AD.* Oxford: Oxbow.

Burley, E. 1958. A Catalogue and Survey of the Metal-work from Traprain Law. *PSAS* 89: 118–226.

Burström, N. 2015. Things of quality: possessions and animated objects in the Scandinavian Viking Age. In A. Klevnäs and C. Hedenstierna-Jonson (eds) *Own and be Owned: Archaeological approaches to the concept of possession*, 23–48. Stockholm: Department of Archaeology and Classical Studies, Stockholm University.

Buteaux, S. 1997. *Settlements at Skaill, Deerness, Orkney: Excavations by Peter Gelling of the Prehistoric, Pictish, Viking and Later Periods, 1963–1981.* Oxford: British Archaeological Reports.

Caldwell, D.H. 1982. *Angels, Nobles and Unicorns: Art and Patronage in Medieval Scotland.* Edinburgh: National Museum of Antiquities of Scotland.

Caldwell, D.H., Hall, M.A., and Wilkinson, C.M. 2009. The Lewis Hoard of gaming pieces: a re-examination of their context, meanings, discovery and manufacture. *Medieval Archaeology* 53(1): 155–203.

Caldwell, D., Kirk, S., Márkus, G., Tate, J., and Webb, S. 2013. The Kilmichael Glassary Bell-shrine. PSAS 142, 201–44.

Callmer, J. 1977. *Trade beads and bead trade in Scandinavia, ca. 800–1000 AD.* Lund: Habelt.

Campbell, E. 2007. *Continental and Mediterranean Imports to Atlantic Britain and Ireland, AD 400–800.* York: Council for British Archaeology.

Campbell, E., Batey, C.E., Murray, G., and Thickpenny, C. 2019. Furnishing an early medieval monastery: new evidence from Iona. *Medieval Archaeology* 63(2): 298–337.

Campbell, E., and Driscoll, S. (eds) 2020. *Royal Forteviot: Excavations at a Pictish Power Centre in Eastern Scotland: SERF Monograph 2.* York: Council for British Archaeology.

Campbell, E., and Heald, A. 2007. A Pictish brooch mould from North Uist: implications for the organisation of non-ferrous metalworking in the later 1st Millenium A.D. *Medieval Archaeology* 51: 172–78.

Campbell, E., and Maldonado, A. 2020. A New Jerusalem 'at the ends of the earth': Interpreting Charles Thomas's excavations at Iona abbey 1956–63. *The Antiquaries Journal* 100: 33–85.

Candon, A. 1988. Muirchertach Ua Briain, politics and naval activity in the Irish Sea, 1075 to 1119. In G. MacNiocaill and P.F. Wallace (eds)

Keimelia: Studies in Medieval Archaeology and history in memory of Tom Delaney, 397–416. Galway: Galway University Press.

Carboni, S. 2001. *Glass from Islamic Lands: The al-Sabah Collection at the Kuwait National Museum*. New York: Thames and Hudson.

Cartwright, B. 2014. Making the cloth that binds us: the role of textile production in producing Viking-Age identities. In M. Hem Eriksen, U. Pedersen, B. Rundberget, I. Axelsen, and H.L. Berg (eds) *Viking Worlds: Things, Spaces and Movement*, 160–78. Oxford: Oxbow.

Carver, M. 2008. *Post-Pictish Problems: The Moray Firthlands in the 9–11th centuries*. Rosemarkie: Groam House Museum.

Carver, M. 2019. *Formative Britain: An Archaeology of Britain, Fifth to Eleventh Century AD*. Abingdon: Routledge.

Carver, M.O.H., Garner-Lahire, J., Spall, C., Geddes, F., and Allen, S. 2016. *Portmahomack on Tarbat Ness: changing ideologies in North-east Scotland, sixth to sixteenth century AD*. Edinburgh: Society of Antiquaries of Scotland.

Charles-Edwards, T.M. 2000. *Early Christian Ireland*. Cambridge: Cambridge University Press.

Charles-Edwards, T.M. 2008. Picts and Scots. *Innes Review* 59(2): 168–88.

Charles-Edwards, T.M. 2012. *Wales and the Britons, 350–1064*. Oxford: Oxford University Press.

Church, M.J. et al. 2013. The Vikings were not the first colonizers of the Faroe Islands. *Quaternary science reviews* 77: 228–32.

Clancy, T.O. 2000. Scotland, the 'Nennian' recension of *Historia Brittonum*, and the *Lebor Bretnach*. In S. Taylor (ed.), 87–107.

Clancy, T.O. 2001. The real St Ninian. *Innes Review* 52(1): 1–28.

Clancy, T.O. 2003. Diarmait sapientissimus: the career of Diarmait, dalta Daigre, abbot of Iona. *Peritia* 17-18: 215–32.

Clancy, T.O. 2008. The Gall-Ghàidheil and Galloway. *Journal of Scottish Name Studies* 2: 19–50.

Clancy, T.O. 2010a. Atholl, Banff, Earn and Elgin: 'New Irelands' in the east revisited. In W. McLeod, A. Burnyeat, D.U. Stiubhart, T.O. Clancy, and R.Ó. Maolalaigh (eds) *Bile ós Chrannaibh. A Festschrift for Professor William Gillies*, 79–102. Brig o' Turk: Clann Tuirc.

Clancy, T.O. 2010b. Gaelic in medieval Scotland: advent and expansion. *Proceedings of the British Academy* 167: 349–92.

Clancy, T.O. 2011. Iona v. Kells: succession, jurisdiction and politics in the Columban familia in the later tenth century. In F. Edmonds and P. Russell (eds) *Tome: studies in medieval Celtic history and law in honour of Thomas Charles-Edwards*. Studies in Celtic History 31, 89–102. Woodbridge: Boydell.

Clancy, T.O. 2013. The Christmas Eve massacre, Iona, AD 986. *Innes Review* 64(1): 66–71.

Clancy, T.O. 2017. VIG001 (the Drosten stone): the inscription. In J. Geddes (ed.) *Hunting Picts: Medieval Sculpture at St Vigeans, Angus, 107–118*. Edinburgh: Historic Scotland

Clarke, D.V. 2012. Communities. In D.V. Clarke, A. Blackwell, and M. Goldberg (eds), 68–139.

Clarke, D.V., Blackwell, A., and Goldberg, M. 2012. *Early Medieval Scotland: Individuals, Communities and Ideas*. Edinburgh: National Museums Scotland.

Clarke, H.B., and Johnson, R. 2015. *The Vikings in Ireland and beyond: before and after the Battle of Clontarf*. Dublin: Four Courts.

Clarkson, T. 2014. *Strathclyde: And the Anglo-Saxons in the Viking Age*. Edinburgh: Birlinn.

Close-Brooks, J. 1986. Excavations at Clatchard Craig, Fife. *PSAS* 116: 117–84.

Close-Brooks, J. 1996. Excavation of a cairn at Cnip, Uig, Isle of Lewis. *PSAS* 125: 253–77.

Close-Brooks, J., and Maxwell, S. 1972. The Mackenzie Collection. *PSAS* 105: 287–93.

Clouston, R. 1978. Kersmains bell. *PSAS* 107: 275–78.

Coleman, R., and Photos-Jones, E. 2008. Early medieval settlement and ironworking in Dornoch, Sutherland: excavations at The Meadows Business Park. *Scottish Archaeological Internet Reports* 28. Available at: <http://dx.doi.org/10.5284/1017938> [accessed November 2020]

Cormack, W.F. 1989. Two recent finds of exotic porphyry in Galloway. *TDGNHAS* 64: 43–7.

Cormack, W.F. 1995. Barhobble, Mochrum: excavation of a forgotten medieval church site in Galloway. *TDGNHAS* 70: 5–106.

Coupland, S. 2014. Holy Ground? The Plundering and Burning of Churches by Vikings and Franks in the Ninth Century. *Viator* 45(1): 73–97.

Crabtree, J. 2010. Agricultural innovation and socio-economic change in early medieval Europe: evidence from Britain and France. *World Archaeology* 42(1): 122–36.

Craig, D. 1991. Pre-Norman sculpture in Galloway: some territorial implications. In R.D. Oram and G.P. Stell (eds) *Galloway: Land and Lordship*, 45–62. Edinburgh: Scottish Society for Northern Studies.

Craig, D. 1992. *The Distribution of Pre-Norman Sculpture in South-West Scotland: Provenance, Ornament and Regional Groups*. Ph.D. thesis. Durham: Durham University. Available at: <http://etheses.dur.ac.uk/1553/> [accessed November 2020]

Crawford, B.E. (ed.) 2002. *The Papar in the North Atlantic: Environment and History*. St Andrews: Committee for Dark Age Studies.

Crawford, B.E. 2002. Scandinavian Influence? II: Historical Background. *In Perth and Beyond: Resourcing the Medieval Burgh, an Archaeological Perspective*, Tayside and Fife Archaeological Committee Available at: <https://www.tafac.org.uk/crawford.pdf> [accessed March 2021]

Crawford, B.E. 2013. *The Northern Earldoms: Orkney and Caithness from AD 870 to 1470*. Edinburgh: Birlinn.

Crawford, B.E., and Taylor, S. 2003. The Southern Frontier of Norse Settlement in North Scotland Place-names and History. *Northern Scotland* 23: 1–76.

Cree, J. 1909. Notice of the excavation of two caves, with remains of early Iron Age occupation, on the estate of Archerfield, Dirleton. *PSAS* 43: 243–68.

Critch, A.J. 2015. *'How are princely gifts repaid by your powerful friends?' 'Ring-money' and the appropriation of tradition in insular Viking politics, AD900–1065*. Ph.D. thesis. University of Cambridge.

Crone, A., Hindmarch, E., and Woolf, A. 2016. *Living and dying at Auldhame, East Lothian: the excavation of an Anglican monastic settlement and medieval parish church.* Edinburgh: Society of Antiquaries of Scotland.

Cross, K. 2017. 'But that will not be the end of the calamity': why emphasize Viking disruption? In M.D.J. Bintley, M. Locker, V. Symons, and M. Wellesley (eds) *Stasis in the Medieval West? Questioning Change and Continuity,* 155–78. New York: Palgrave Macmillan.

Curle, A. 1924. A note on four silver spoons and a fillet of gold found in the Nunnery at Iona; and on a finger-ring, part of a fillet, and a fragment of wire, all of gold, found in St Ronan's Chapel, the Nunnery, Iona. *PSAS* 58: 102–11.

Curle, A. 1935. An Account of the Excavation of a Dwelling of the Viking Period at 'Jarlshof,' Sumburgh, Shetland, carried out on behalf of H.M. Office of Works. *PSAS* 69: 265–321.

Curle, A. 1936. An account of the excavation of further buildings of the Viking Period (Viking House No. II), at 'Jarlshof,' Sumburgh, Shetland, carried out on behalf of HM Office of works. *PSAS* 70: 251–70.

Curle, C. 1940. The Chronology of the Early Christian Monuments of Scotland. *PSAS* 74: 60–116.

Curle, C.L. 1982. *Pictish and Norse finds from the Brough of Birsay 1934–74.* Edinburgh: Society of Antiquaries of Scotland.

Cursiter, J. 1887. Notice of the Bronze Weapons of Orkney and Shetland, and of an Iron Age Deposit found in a Cist at Moan, Harray. *PSAS* 21: 339–46.

Cusack, C. 2015. Two Scottish Romanesque parish churches: St Athernase, Leuchars and St Cuthbert, Dalmeny. *Journal of the Sydney Society for Scottish History* 15: 97–122.

Davies, J.R. 2010. *The cult of Saint Constantine.* Glasgow: Society of Friends of Govan Old.

Deckers, P. 2012. 'Productive' sites in the Polders? 'Griffin brooches' and other early medieval metalwork from the Belgian coastal plain. *Medieval and Modern Matters: Archaeology and Material Culture in the Low Countries* 3: 21–43.

Dectot, X. 2018. When ivory came from the seas. On some traits of the trade of raw and carved sea-mammal ivories in the Middle Ages. *Anthropozoologica* 53(1): 159–74.

Dickinson, T.M. 2005. Symbols of protection: the significance of animal-ornamented shields in early Anglo-Saxon England. *Medieval Archaeology* 49: 109–63.

Dobat, A.S. 2015. Viking stranger-kings: the foreign as a source of power in Viking Age Scandinavia, or, why there was a peacock in the Gokstad ship burial? *Early Medieval Europe* 23(2): 161–201.

Dockrill, S.J. et al. 2010. *Excavations at Old Scatness, Shetland volume 1: The Pictish Village and Viking Settlement.* Lerwick: Shetland Heritage.

Dommasnes, L.H. 1991. Women, kinship, and the basis of power in the Norwegian Viking Age. In R. Samson (ed.), 65–74.

Dommasnes, L.H., and Hommedal, A.T. 2016. One thousand years of tradition and change on two West-Norwegian farms AD 200–1200. In L.H. Dommasnes, D. Gutsmiedl-Schümann, and A.T. Hommedal (eds) *The Farm as a Social Arena,* 127–70. Munster: Waxmann Verlag.

Downham, C. 2004. The historical importance of Viking-age Waterford. *The Journal of Celtic Studies* 4: 71–96.

Downham, C. 2007. *Viking Kings of Britain and Ireland: The Dynasty of Ívarr to AD1014.* Edinburgh: Dunedin.

Downham, C. 2009. Hiberno-Norwegians' and 'Anglo-Danes': anachronistic ethnicities and Viking-Age England. *Mediaeval Scandinavia* 19: 139–69.

Downham, C. 2011. Viking identities in Ireland: it's not all black and white. *Medieval Dublin* 11: 185–201.

Downham, C. 2015. The break up of Dól Riata and the rise of *Gallgoídil,* in H.B. Clarke and R. Johnson (eds), 189–205.

Downham, C. 2016. Coastal communities and diaspora identities in Viking Age Ireland. In J.H. Barrett and S.J. Gibbon (eds), 369–83.

Downham, C. 2017. The earliest Viking activity in England? *English Historical Review* 132(554): 1–12.

Driscoll, S.T. 1998. Formalising the mechanisms of state power: early Scottish lordship from the 9th to the 13th centuries. In S. Foster, A. Macinnes, and R. MacInnes (eds) *Scottish Power Centres,* 32–58. Glasgow: Cruithne.

Driscoll, S.T. 2002. *Alba: The Gaelic Kingdom of Scotland, AD800–1124.* Edinburgh: Birlinn.

Driscoll, S.T. 2004a. *Govan from Cradle to Grave.* Glasgow: Friends of Govan Old.

Driscoll, S.T. 2004b. The archaeological context of assembly in early medieval Scotland – Scone and its comparanda. In A. Pantos and S. Semple (eds) *Assembly Places and Practices in Medieval Europe,* 73–94. Dublin: Four Courts.

Driscoll, S.T. 2016. Reading Govan Old: interpretative challenges and aspirations. In F. Hunter and A. Sheridan (eds) *Ancient Lives: Object, People and Place in Early Scotland. Essays for David V. Clarke on his 70th Birthday,* 73–91. Leiden: Sidestone.

Driscoll, S.T., O'Grady, O., and Forsyth, K. 2005. The Govan School revisited: searching for meaning in the early medieval sculpture of Strathclyde. In S. Foster and M. Cross (eds) *Able Minds and Practiced Hands: Scotland's Early Medieval Sculpture in the 21st Century.* SMA Monograph 23, 135–58. Leeds: Maney.

Dumville, D.N. 1997. *The Churches of North Britain in the First Viking-Age.* Whithorn: Friends of the Whithorn Trust.

Dumville, D.N. 2000. The Chronicle of the Kings of Alba. In S. Taylor (ed.), 73–86.

Dumville, D.N. 2002. The North Atlantic monastic thalassocracy: sailing to the desert in early medieval Insular spirituality. In B.E. Crawford (ed.), 121–31.

Dumville, D.N. 2017. Origins of the Kingdom of the English. In D.A. Woodman and R. Naismith (eds) *Writing, Kingship and Power in Anglo-Saxon England,* 71–121. Cambridge University Press.

Dunbar, L., and Paton, K. 2018. Mayback Boat Burial, Papa Westray, excavation. *Discovery and Excavation in Scotland* New Ser., 18: 145.

Dunbar, L., and Roy, M. 2018. A Viking-age inhumation from Crow Taing, Sanday, Orkney. *Scottish Archaeological Journal* 40(1): 83–99.

Earwood, C. 1994. The dating of wooden troughs and dishes. *PSAS* 123: 355–62.

Edmonds, F. 2018. Carham: the western perspective. In N. McGuigan and A. Woolf (eds), 79–94.

Edmonds, F. 2019. *Gaelic Influence in the Northumbrian Kingdom: The Golden Age and the Viking Age.* Woodbridge: Boydell and Brewer.

Eeles, F., and Clouston, R.W.M. 1967. The church and other bells of the Stewartry of Kirkcudbright. *PSAS* 99: 191–210.

Egan, G. 1998. *The Medieval Household: Daily Living c.1150–c.1450.* London: Stationery Office.

Ellis, C. 2021. Remembering the Vikings: ancestry, cultural memory and geographical variation. *History Compass* 19(4). Available at: <https://onlinelibrary.wiley.com/doi/10.1111/hic3.12652> [accessed August 2021].

Eremin, K., Graham-Campbell, J., and Wilthew, P. 2002. Analysis of copper-alloy artefacts from pagan Norse graves in Scotland. In E. Jerem and K.T. Biró (eds) *Archaeometry 98: Proceedings of the 31st Symposium, Budapest, April 26–May 3 1998.* BAR International Series 1043, 343–49. Oxford: Archaeopress.

Eska, C.M. 2011. Women and slavery in the early Irish laws. *Studia Celtica Fennica* 8: 29–39.

Etchingham, C. 1996. *Viking Raids on Irish Church Settlements in the Ninth Century: a Reconsideration of the Annals.* Maynooth: Department of Old and Middle Irish, St Patrick's College.

Etchingham, C. 2014. Names for the Vikings in Irish Annals. In J.V. Sigurdsson and T. Bolton (eds) *Celtic-Norse Relationships in the Irish Sea in the Middle Ages 800–1200.* The Northern World 65, 23–38. Leiden: Brill.

Etchingham, C. 2021. Slavery or ransom? Why Vikings took captives in Ireland and beyond. In M. Toplak, H. Østhus, and R. Simek (eds) *Viking-Age Slavery.* Studia Medievalia Septentrionalia 29, 117–46. Vienna: Fassbaender.

Etchingham, C., and Swift, C. 2004. English and Pictish terms for brooch in an 8th-century Irish law-text. *Medieval Archaeology* 48: 31–49.

Evans, N. 2015. Cultural contacts and ethnic origins in Viking Age Wales and northern Britain: the case of Albanus, Britain's first inhabitant and Scottish ancestor, *Journal of Medieval History* 41(2): 131–154.

Evans, N. 2017. News Recording and Cultural Connections between Early Medieval Ireland and Northern Britain. In C. Cooijmans (ed.) *Traversing the Inner Seas: Contacts and Continuity in and around Scotland, the Hebrides, and the North of Ireland,* 140–69. Edinburgh: Scottish Society for Northern Studies

Ewart, G., Gallagher, D., and Ritchie, A. 2008. The Dupplin Cross: recent investigations. *PSAS* 137: 319–36.

Fairnell, E.H., and Barrett, J.H. 2007. Fur-bearing species and Scottish islands. *Journal of Archaeological Science* 34(3): 463–84.

Fanning, T. 1983. Some aspects of the bronze ringed pin in Scotland. In A. O'Connor and D.V. Clarke (eds) *From the Bronze Age to the 'Forty-five,* 324–42. Edinburgh: John Donald

Fanning, T. 1994. *Viking Age Ringed Pins from Dublin.* Dublin: Royal Irish Academy.

Farbregd, O. 1974. *To nordtrønderske båtgraver: Lø, Steinkjer. Utgraving 1969: Haug, Verdal. Utgraving 1970.* Universitetet i Trondheim.

Fawcett, R. 1985. *Scottish Medieval Churches.* Edinburgh: Her Majesty's Stationery Office.

Fernie, E. 1986. Early church architecture in Scotland. *PSAS* 116: 393–411.

Fisher, I. 2001. *Early Medieval Sculpture in the West Highlands and Islands.* Edinburgh: RCAHMS.

Fisher, I. 2002. Crosses in the ocean: some papar sites and their sculpture. In B.E. Crawford (ed.), 39–57.

Fontaine, J.M. 2017. Early medieval slave-trading in the archaeological record: comparative methodologies. *Early Medieval Europe* 25(4): 466–88.

Forster, A.K. 2009. Viking and Norse steatite use in Shetland. In A. K. Forster and V. E. Turner (eds) *Kleber: Shetland's oldest industry,* 58–69. Lerwick: Shetland Amenity Trust.

Forster, A.K., and Jones, R. 2017. From homeland to home: using soapstone to map migration and settlement in the North Atlantic. In G. Hansen and P. Storemyr (eds) *Soapstone in the North Quarries, Products and People 7000BC–AD1700,* 225–48. Bergen: University of Bergen.

Forsyth, K. 1996a. *The Ogham Inscriptions of Scotland: An Edited Corpus.* Ph.D. thesis. Cambridge, MA: Harvard University.

Forsyth, K. 1996b. The ogham-inscribed spindle whorl from Buckquoy: evidence for the Irish language in pre-Viking Orkney? *PSAS* 125: 677–696.

Forsyth, K. 1997. Some thoughts on Pictish symbols as a formal writing system. In D. Henry (ed.) *The Worm, the Germ, and the Thorn: Pictish and Related Studies Presented to Isabel Henderson,* 85–98. Balgavies: Pinkfoot.

Forsyth, K. 2005. Hic memoria perpetua: the early inscribed stones of southern Scotland in context. In S. Foster and M. Cross (eds) *Able Minds and Practiced Hands: Scotland's Early Medieval Sculpture in the 21st Century.* SMA Monograph 23, 113–34. Leeds: Maney.

Forsyth, K. 2020. Protecting a Pict?: Further thoughts on the inscribed silver chape from St Ninian's Isle, Shetland. *PSAS* 149: 249–76.

Forsyth, K. 2021. Ogham inscriptions from the Brough of Birsay. In C.D. Morris and R.C. Barrowman (eds) *The Birsay Bay Project Volume 3: The Brough of Birsay, Orkney: Investigations 1954–2014,* 374–87. Oxford: Oxbow.

Forsyth, K., and Tedeschi, C. 2008. Text-inscribed slates. In C. Lowe (ed.) *Inchmarnock: An Early Historic Island Monastery and its Archaeological Landscape,* 128–51. Edinburgh: Society of Antiquaries of Scotland.

Foster, R. 2017. The use of the Scandinavian place-name elements –*sætr* and –*Ærgi* in Skye and the Outer Hebrides. In C. Cooijmans (ed.) *Traversing the Inner Seas: Contacts and Continuity in and around Scotland, the Hebrides, and the North of Ireland,* 107–39. Edinburgh: Scottish Society for Northern Studies.

Foster, S.M. 1989. *Aspects of the Late Atlantic Iron Age.* Ph.D. thesis. Glasgow: University of Glasgow. Available at: <http://theses.gla.ac.uk/1051/> [accessed November 2020]

Foster, S.M. (ed.) 1998. *The St Andrews Sarcophagus: a Pictish Masterpiece and its International Connections.* Dublin: Four Courts.

Foster, S.M. 2014. *Picts, Gaels and Scots: Early Historic Scotland.* Birlinn.

Foster, S.M. 2019. 'A bright crowd of chancels': whither early church archaeo-logy in Scotland? In A. E. Blackwell (ed.) *Scotland in Early Medieval Europe*, 35–50. Leiden: Sidestone.

Frankopan, P. 2012. *The First Crusade: The Call from the East.* Cambridge, MA: Harvard University Press.

Fraser, J.E. 2009. *From Caledonia to Pictland: Scotland to 795.* Edinburgh: Edinburgh University Press.

Fraser, J.E. 2013. St Patrick and barbarian northern Britain in the fifth century. In F. Hunter and K. Painter (eds) *Late Roman Silver: The Traprain Treasure in Context,* 15–27. Edinburgh: Society of Antiquaries of Scotland.

Frei, K.M. et al. 2015. Was it for walrus? Viking Age settlement and medieval walrus ivory trade in Iceland and Greenland. *World Archaeology* 47(3): 439–66.

Freund, A. 2020. *Runic Writing in Orkney: Expression of a Norse Identity?* Ph.D. thesis. University of the Highlands and Islands. Available at: <https://pure.uhi.ac.uk/en/studentTheses/runic-writing-in-orkney> [accessed August 2021]

Fuglesang, S.H. 1989. Viking and medieval amulets in Scandinavia. *Fornvännen* 84: 15–27.

Gaimster, M. 1991. Money and media in Viking Age Scandinavia. In R. Samson (ed.), 113–22.

Garipzanov, I.H. 2005. Carolingian coins in ninth-century Scandinavia: a Norwegian perspective. *Viking and Medieval Scandinavia* 1: 43–71.

Garver, V.L. 2018. 'Go humbly dressed as befits servants of God': Alcuin, clerical identity, and sartorial anxieties'. *Early Medieval Europe* 26(2): 203–230.

Geake, H. 2004. Medieval Britain and Ireland in 2003: Portable Antiquities Scheme report. *Medieval Archaeology* 48(1): 232–47.

Geary, P.J. 2011 [1978]. *Furta Sacra: Thefts of Relics in the Central Middle Ages.* Princeton: Princeton University Press.

Geary, P.J. 1994. *Living with the Dead in the Middle Ages.* London: Cornell University Press.

Geddes, J. 2017. *Hunting Picts: Medieval Sculpture at St Vigeans, Angus.* Edinburgh: Historic Scotland.

Gilchrist, R. 2008. Magic for the dead? The archaeology of magic in later medieval burials. *Medieval Archaeology* 52: 119–59.

Gilchrist, R. 2020. *Sacred Heritage: Monastic Archaeology, Identities, Beliefs.* Cambridge University Press.

Gillman, M.E. 2017. A tale of two ivories: elephant and walrus. *Espacio Tiempo y Forma Serie VII: Historia del Arte* 5: 81.

Gleeson, P. 2019. Making provincial kingship in early medieval Ireland: Cashel and the creation of Munster. In J. Carroll, A. Reynolds, and B. Yorke (eds) *Power and place in late Roman and Early Medieval Europe: interdisciplinary perspectives in governance and civil organisation.* Proceedings of the British Academy 224, 346–68. Oxford: British Academy.

Glørstad, Z.T. 2012. Sign of the times? The transfer and transformation of penannular brooches in Viking-Age Norway. *Norwegian Archaeological Review* 45(1): 30–51.

Goldberg, M. 2012. Ideas and ideologies. In D. V. Clarke, A. Blackwell, and M. Goldberg (eds), 140–203.

Goldberg, M. 2015a. At the western edge of the Christian world, *c.*AD 600–900. In J. Farley and F. Hunter (eds) *Celts: Art and Identity*, 173–205. London: British Museum.

Goldberg, M. 2015b. Out of a Roman world, *c.*AD 250–650. In J. Farley and F. Hunter (eds) *Celts: Art and Identity*, 153–71. London: British Museum.

Goldberg, M., and Davis, M. 2021. *The Galloway Hoard: Viking-age Treasure.* Edinburgh: National Museums Scotland.

Gordon, K. 1990. A Norse Viking-age grave from Cruach Mhor, Islay. *PSAS* 120: 151–60.

Graham-Campbell, J. 1973. The 9th-century Anglo-Saxon Horn-mount from Burghead, Morayshire, Scotland. *Medieval Archaeology* 17(1): 43–51.

Graham-Campbell, J. 1980. *Viking Artefacts: A Select Catalogue.* London: British Museum Publications.

Graham-Campbell, J. 1983. Some Viking-age penannular brooches from Scotland and the origins of the 'thistle-brooch'. In A. O'Connor and D.V. Clarke (eds) *From the Bronze Age to the 'Forty-five: Studies presented to R. B. K. Stevenson, Former Keeper, National Museum of Antiquities of Scotland*, 310–23. Edinburgh: John Donald.

Graham-Campbell, J. 1984. Western influences on penannular brooches and ringed pins. In G. Arwidsson (ed.) *Birka Untersuchungen und Studien 2.1: Sytematische Analysen der Gräberfunde*, 31–8. Stockholm: Almqvist and Wiksell.

Graham-Campbell, J. 1987a. A lost Pictish treasure (and two Viking-age gold arm-rings) from the Broch of Burgar, Orkney. *PSAS* 115: 241–61.

Graham-Campbell, J. 1987b. Western penannular brooches and their Viking Age copies in Norway: a new classification. In J.E. Knirk (ed.) *Proceedings of the Tenth Viking Congress, Larkollen, Norway, 1985*, 231–46. Oslo: Universitetets Oldsaksamling.

Graham-Campbell, J. 1993. The northern hoards of Viking-Age Scotland. In C.E. Batey, J. Jesch, and C.D. Morris (eds), 173–86.

Graham-Campbell, J. 1995. *Viking-age Gold and Silver of Scotland, AD850–1100.* Edinburgh: National Museum of Scotland.

Graham-Campbell, J. 2001. National and regional identities: the 'glittering prizes'. In N. Edwards, S. Youngs, A. Lane, and J. Knight (eds) *Pattern and Purpose in Insular Art*, 27–38. Oxford: Oxbow.

Graham-Campbell, J. 2003a. *Pictish Silver: Status and Symbol.* Cambridge: Department of Anglo-Saxon, Norse and Celtic.

Graham-Campbell, J. 2003b. The Vikings in Orkney. In D.J. Waugh (ed.) *The Faces of Orkney: Stones, Skalds and Saints,* 128–37. Edinburgh: Scottish Society for Northern Studies.

Graham-Campbell, J. 2005. 'Danes … in this Country': discovering the Vikings in Scotland. *PSAS* 134: 201–39.

Graham-Campbell, J. 2009. Viking Age and Late Norse Gold and Silver from Scotland: An update. *PSAS* 138: 193–204.

Graham-Campbell, J. 2011a. *The Cuerdale Hoard: and Related Viking-age Silver and Gold from Britain and Ireland in the British Museum.* London: British Museum.

Graham-Campbell, J. 2011b. 'Pins and penannular brooches', in D. Skre (ed.) *Things from the Town: Artefacts and Inhabitants in Viking-Age*

Kaupang. Aarhus: Aarhus University Press (Norske Oldfunn 24), 99–106.

Graham-Campbell, J. 2020. The Galloway Hoard: Viking/Anglo-Saxon Interaction in South-West Scotland. In A. Pedersen and S. M. Sindbæk (eds), 449–64.

Graham-Campbell, J. 2021. Equestrian Burial in Viking-Age Scotland. In A. Pedersen and M. S. Bagge (eds) *Horse and Rider in the Late Viking Age: Equestrian Burial in Perspective*, 271–80. Aarhus: Aarhus University Press.

Graham-Campbell, J., and Batey, C.E. 1998. *Vikings in Scotland*. Edinburgh: Edinburgh University Press.

Graham-Campbell, J., Henderson, I., Ritchie, A., and Scott, I.G. 2019. A Pictish 'serpent' incised slab from Jarlshof, Shetland. *PSAS* 148: 189–208.

Graham-Campbell, J., and Sheehan, J. 2009. Viking Age gold and silver from Irish crannogs and other watery places. *The Journal of Irish Archaeology* 18: 77–93.

Graham-Campbell, J., Sindbæk, S.M., and Williams, G. (eds) 2011. *Silver Economies, Monetisation and Society in Scandinavia, AD800–1100*. Aarhus: Aarhus University Press.

Graham-Campbell, J., and Williams, G. (eds) 2007. *Silver economy in the Viking age*. Walnut Creek, CA: Left Coast.

Grieg, S. 1940. *Viking Antiquities in Scotland*. Oslo: Aschehoug.

Grieve, S. 1914. Note upon Carn nan Bharraich, or Cairn of the Men of Barra, a burial mound of the Viking time on the island of Oronsay, Argyllshire. *PSAS* 48: 272–91.

Griffiths, D. 2009. Sand dunes and stray finds: evidence for pre-Viking trade? In J. Graham-Campbell and M. Ryan (eds) *Anglo-Saxon/Irish Relations Before the Vikings*. Proceedings of the British Academy, 265–80. Oxford: Oxford University Press.

Griffiths, D. 2014. *Early Medieval Whithorn, the Irish Sea Context: the 21st Whithorn Lecture, 2013*. Stranraer: Whithorn Trust.

Griffiths, D. 2019. Rethinking the early Viking Age in the West. *Antiquity* 93(368): 468–77.

Griffiths, D., Harrison, J., Athanson, M., Alldritt, D.M., and Greig, A. 2019. *Beside the Ocean: Coastal Landscapes at the Bay of Skaill, Marwick, and Birsay Bay, Orkney: Archaeological Research 2003–18*. Oxford: Oxbow.

Griffiths, D., Philpotts, R., and Egan, G. 2007. *Meols: The Archaeology of the North Wirral Coast: Discoveries and Observations in the 19th and 20th Centuries, with a Catalogue of Collections*. Oxford: Oxford University School of Archaeology.

Gruszczyński, J. 2018. The importance of containers for the deposition and non-retrieval of silver hoards: a comparison between Gotland and Pomerania. In J. Kershaw, G. Williams, S. Sindbæk, and J. Graham-Campbell (eds), 169–88.

Gruszczyński, J., Jankowiak, M., and Shepard, J. (eds) 2020. *Viking-Age Trade: Silver, Slaves and Gotland*. London: Routledge.

Guido, M. 1978. *The Glass Beads of the Prehistoric and Roman Periods in Britain and Ireland*. Society of Antiquaries of London.

Gustin, I. 2017. Contacts, identity and Hybridity: Objects from South-western Finland in the Birka graves. In J. Callmer, I. Gustin, and M. Roslund (eds) *Identity Formation and Diversity in the Early Medieval Baltic and Beyond*, 205–58. Leiden: Brill.

Hadley, D.M. 2002. Viking and native: re-thinking identity in the Danelaw. *Early Medieval Europe* 11(1): 45–70.

Hadley, D.M. 2008. Warriors, heroes and companions: negotiating masculinity in Viking-Age England. *Anglo-Saxon Studies in Archaeology and History* 15: 270–84.

Hadley, D.M., and Dyer, C. 2017. *The Archaeology of the 11th Century: Continuities and Transformations*. London: Routledge.

Hadley, D.M., and Hemer, K.A. 2011. Microcosms of Migration: Children and Early Medieval Population Movement. *Childhood in the Past* 4(1): 63–78.

Hadley, D.M., and Richards, J.D. 2016. The winter camp of the Viking Great Army, AD 872–3, Torksey, Lincolnshire. *The Antiquaries Journal* 96: 23–67.

Hadley, D.M., and Richards, J.D. 2018. In search of the Viking Great Army: beyond the winter camps. *Medieval Settlement Research* 33: 1–17.

Hadley, D.M., and Richards, J.D. 2021. *The Viking Great Army and the Making of England*. London: Thames and Hudson.

Haldenby, D., and Kershaw, J. 2014. Viking-Age Lead Weights from Cottam. *Yorkshire Archaeological Journal* 86(1): 106–23.

Haldenby, D., and Richards, J.D. 2009. Settlement shift at Cottam, East Riding of Yorkshire, and the chronology of Anglo-Saxon copper-alloy pins. *Medieval Archaeology* 53: 309–14.

Hall, A. 2010. Interlinguistic communication In Bede's *Historia Ecclesiastica Gentis Anglorum*. In A. Hall, O. Timofeeva, A. Kirisci, and B. Fox (eds) *Interfaces between Language and Culture in Medieval England*. 37–80. Leiden: Brill.

Hall, D., and Bowler, D. 1998. North Berwick, East Lothian: its archaeology revisited. *PSAS* 127: 659–75.

Hall, D.W.; Cook, G.T.; Hall, M.A.; Muir, G.K.P.; Hamilton, D.; Scott, E.M. 2007. The early medieval origin of Perth, Scotland. *Radiocarbon* 49(2): 639–44.

Hall, M. 2007. Context and meaning: finding a place for some fragments of Early Medieval metalwork from Perthshire, Scotland. In R. Moss (ed.) *Making and Meaning in Insular Art*, 70–8. Dublin: Four Courts.

Hall, M. 2013. Board of the kings: the material culture of playtime in Scotland AD 1–1600. In M. Teichert (ed.) *Sport und Spiel bei den Germanen*, 163–96. Berlin: De Gruyter. Reprinted in Gilchrist, R. and Watson, G., eds. (2016) *Medieval Archaeology vol. 3: Medieval Life. Critical Concepts in Archaeology*. Abingdon: Routledge.

Hall, M. 2014. The Meigle stones: a biographical overview. *Northern Studies* 46: 15–46.

Hall, M. 2015. Ecclesia ludens: board and dice games in a Scottish monastic context. *PSAS* 145: 283–98.

Hall, M. 2016. Board games in boat burials: play in the performance of migration and Viking Age mortuary practice. *European Journal of Archaeology* 19(3): 439–55.

Hall, M. and Forsyth, K. 2011. Roman rules? The introduction of board games to Britain and Ireland. *Antiquity* 85(330): 1325–38.

Hall, M., Hall, D., and Cook, G. 2006. What's cooking? New radiocarbon dates from the earliest phases of the Perth High Street excavations and the question of Perth's early medieval origin. *PSAS* 135: 273–85.

Hall, M., Henderson, I., and Taylor, S. 1998. A sculptured fragment from Pittensorn Farm, Gellyburn, Perthshire. *Tayside and Fife Archaeological Journal* 4: 129–44.

Hallén, Y. 1995. The use of bone and antler at Foshigarry and Bac Mhic Connain, two Iron Age sites on North Uist, Western Isles. *PSAS* 124: 189–231.

Halsall, G. 2000. The Viking presence in England? The burial evidence reconsidered. In D.M. Hadley and J.D. Richards (eds) *Cultures in Contact: Scandinavian Settlement in England in the Ninth and Tenth Centuries*. Studies in the Early Middle Ages 2, 259–76. Turnhout: Brepols.

Halsall, G. 2010. *Cemeteries and Society in Merovingian Gaul: Selected Studies in History and Archaeology, 1992–2009*. Leiden: Brill.

Hamilton, J.R.C. 1956. *Excavations at Jarlshof, Shetland*. Edinburgh: Her Majesty's Stationery Office.

Harbison, P. 1992. *The High Crosses of Ireland*. Bonn: Habelt.

Hårdh, B. 2008. Hacksilver and ingots. In D. Skre (ed.), 95–118.

Harris, O.J.T.; Cobb, H.; Batey, C.E.; Montgomery, J.; Beaumont, J.; Gray, H.; Murtagh, P.; Richardson, P. 2017. Assembling places and persons: a tenth-century Viking boat burial from Swordle Bay on the Ardnamurchan peninsula, western Scotland. *Antiquity* 91(355): 191–206.

Harrison, S.H. 2000. The Millhill burial in context. *Acta Archaeologica* 71(1): 65–78.

Harrison, S.H. 2007. Separated from the Foaming Maelstrom: Landscapes of Insular 'Viking' Burial. In S. Semple and H. Williams (eds) *Early Medieval Mortuary Practices.* Anglo-Saxon Studies in Archaeology and History 14, 173–82.

Harrison, S.H. 2008. *Furnished Insular Scandinavian Burial: Artefacts and Landscape in the Early Viking Age*. Ph.D. thesis. Dublin: Trinity College. Available at: <http://hdl.handle.net/2262/76942> [accessed August 2021]

Harrison, S.H. 2016. 'Warrior graves'? The weapon burial rite in Viking Age Britain and Ireland. In J.H. Barrett and S.J. Gibbon (eds), 299–319.

Harrison, S.H., and Ó Floinn, R. 2014. *Viking Graves and Grave-Goods in Ireland*. Dublin: National Museum of Ireland Dublin.

Hay Fleming, D. 1931. *St Andrews Cathedral Museum*. Edinburgh: Oliver and Boyd.

Hayeur Smith, M. 2004. *Draupnir's Sweat and Mardöll's Tears: An Archaeology of Jewellery, Gender and Identity in Viking Age Iceland.* Oxford: John and Erica Hedges.

Hayeur Smith, M. 2018. Vaðmál and cloth currency in Viking and medieval Iceland. In J. Kershaw, G. Williams, S. Sindbæk, and J. Graham-Campbell (eds), 251–77.

Hayeur Smith, M., Smith, K.P., and Frei, K.M. 2019. 'Tangled up in blue': the death, dress and identity of an early Viking-age female settler from Ketilsstaðir, Iceland. *Medieval Archaeology* 63(1): 95–127.

Heald, A. 2005. *Non-ferrous metalworking in Iron Age Scotland c.700BC to AD800*. University of Edinburgh. Available at: https://era.ed.ac.uk/handle/1842/6916 [accessed 30 March 2021]

Heald, A. 2011. The interpretation of non-ferrous metalworking in Early Historic Scotland. In S. T. Driscoll, J. Geddes, and M. Hall (eds) *Pictish Progress: New Studies on Northern Britain in the Early Middle Ages*. The Northern World 50, 221–42. Leiden: Brill

Hedges, J. 1980. A long cist at Sandside, Graemsay, Orkney. *PSAS* 109: 374–78.

Hedges, J.W. 1983. Trial excavations on Pictish and Viking settlements at Saevar Howe, Birsay, Orkney. *Glasgow Archaeological Journal* 10(1): 73–124.

Hedges, J.W. 1987. *Bu, Gurness, and the Brochs of Orkney, Part II: Gurness.* Oxford: British Archaeological Reports.

Heen-Pettersen, A.M. 2014. Insular artefacts from Viking-Age burials from mid-Norway. A review of contact between Trøndelag and Britain and Ireland. *Internet archaeology* (38). Available at: http://intarch.ac.uk/journal/issue38/heenpettersen_index.html.

Heen-Pettersen, A.M. 2015. Insulære beslag fra vikingtidsgraver i Trøndelag: En undersøkelse av gjenstandenes bruk og funksjon. *Primitive Tider* 17: 1–14.

Heen-Pettersen, A.M. 2019. The Earliest Wave of Viking Activity? The Norwegian Evidence Revisited. *European Journal of Archaeology* 22(4): 523–41.

Heen-Pettersen, A.M., and Murray, G. 2018. An Insular reliquary from Melhus: the significance of Insular ecclesiastical material in early Viking-age Norway. *Medieval Archaeology* 62(1): 53–82.

Heisey, D.J. 2011. Bede's Pepper, Napkins, and Incense. *The Downside Review* 129(454): 16–30.

Henderson, I. 1996. *Pictish Monsters: Symbol, Text and Image.* Cambridge: University of Cambridge.

Henderson, I. 1998. Primus Inter Pares: the St Andrews Sarcophagus and Pictish Sculpture. In S. Foster (ed.) *The St Andrews Sarcophagus: a Pictish Masterpiece and its International Connections*, 97–167. Dublin: Four Courts.

Henderson, I., and Henderson, G. 2004. *Art of the Picts*. London: Thames and Hudson.

Henning, J. 2007. Catalogue of archaeological finds from Pliska with Introduction. In J. Henning (ed.) *Post-Roman Towns, Trade and Settlement in Europe and Byzantium, vol. 2: Byzantium, Pliska, and the Balkans.* Millennium-Studien zu Kultur und Geschichte des ersten Jahrtausends n.Chr., 661–704. Berlin: De Gruyter.

Herbert, M. 1988. *Iona, Kells, and Derry*. Oxford: Clarendon.

Herbert, M. 2000. Rí Éirenn, Rí Alban, kingship and identity in the ninth and tenth centuries. In S. Taylor (ed.), 62–72.

Hickey, M. 2014. *Perler fra vikingtiden (Beads of the Viking-Age): A study of the social and economic patterns in the appearance of beads from Viking-Age sites in Britain.* MA thesis. University of York. Available at: <http://etheses.whiterose.ac.uk/8571/> [accessed February 2021]

Hicks, C. 1980. A Clonmacnois Workshop in Stone. *Journal of the Royal Society of Antiquaries of Ireland.* Royal Society of Antiquaries of Ireland 110: 5–35.

Higgitt, J. 1995. The comb, pendant and buckle. In J. Lewis and G. Ewart (eds) Jedburgh Abbey: *The Archaeology and Architecture of a Border Abbey*. Soc Antiq Scot Monograph Series 10, 83–4. Edinburgh: Society of Antiquaries of Scotland

Hill, P. 1997. *Whithorn and St Ninian: the Excavation of a Monastic Town, 1984–91*. Stroud: Sutton.

Hinton, D.A. 2005. *Gold and Gilt, Pots and Pins: Possessions and People in Medieval Britain*. Oxford: Oxford University Press.

Hodges, R. 2006. *Goodbye to the Vikings? Re-reading Early Medieval Archaeology*. London: Duckworth.

Holm, P. 1986. The slave trade of Dublin, ninth to twelfth centuries. *Peritia* 5: 317–45.

Holmes, N. 2004. The evidence of finds for the circulation and use of coins in medieval Scotland. *PSAS* 134: 241–80.

Holmquist Olausson, L., and Petrovski, S. 2007. Curious Birds – two Helmet(?) Mounts with a Christian Motif from Birka's Garrison. In U. Fransson, M. Svedin, S. Bergerbrant, and F. Androshchuk (eds) *Cultural Interaction Between East and West: Archaeology, Artefacts and Human Contacts in Northern Europe*. Stockholm Studies in Archaeology 44, 231–37. Stockholm: Stockholms Universitet

Horne, T. 2022. *A Viking Market Kingdom in Ireland and Britain: Trade networks and the importation of a Southern Scandinavian bullion economy*. London: Routledge.

Howard-Johnston, J. 2020. The fur trade in the early middle ages. In J. Gruszczyński, M. Jankowiak, and J. Shepard (eds), 57–74.

Howlett, D. 2000. The structure of *De Situ Albaniae*. In S. Taylor (ed.), 124–45.

Hudson, B.T. 1999. The changing economy of the Irish Sea province: AD 900–1300. In B. Smith (ed.) *Britain and Ireland, 900–1300: Insular Responses to Medieval European Change*, 39–66. Cambridge: Cambridge University Press.

Hunter, F. 2008a. The oil shale artefacts and related material. In C. Lowe (ed.) *Inchmarnock: An Early Historic Island Monastery and its Archaeological Landscape*, 193–202. Edinburgh: Society of Antiquaries of Scotland

Hunter, F. 2008b. Jet and Related Materials in Viking Scotland. *Medieval Archaeology* 52(1): 103–18.

Hunter, F. 2016. 'Coal money' from Portpatrick (south-west Scotland): reconstructing an early medieval craft centre from antiquarian finds. In F. Hunter and A. Sheridan (eds) *Ancient Lives: Object, People and Place in Early Scotland. Essays for David V. Clarke on his 70th Birthday*, 281–302. Leiden: Sidestone.

Hunter, J., Bond, J.M., Smith, A.M., and Historic, S. 2007. *Investigations in Sanday, Orkney: Excavations at Pool, Sanday: a multi-period settlement from Neolithic to late Norse times*. Kirkwall: The Orcadian/Historic Scotland.

IJssennagger, N.L. 2017. *Central because Liminal: Frisia in a Viking Age North Sea World*. Ph.D. thesis. University of Groningen. Available at: <https://research.rug.nl/en/publications/central-because-liminal-frisia-in-a-viking-age-north-sea-world> [accessed August 2021]

Isaac, G.R. 2005. A note on Cormac's Pictish brooch. *Journal of Celtic Linguistics* 9(1): 73–82.

Isaksen, E. 2012. *Hvalbeinsplater fra yngre jernalder: en analyse av hvalbeinsplatenes kontekst og funksjon*. Masters thesis. University of Tromsø. Available at: <https://munin.uit.no/handle/10037/4308> [accessed March 2021]

James, H.F., Henderson, I., Foster, S., and Jones, S. (eds) 2008. *A Fragmented Masterpiece: Recovering the Biography of the Hilton of Cadboll Pictish Cross-slab*. Edinburgh: Society of Antiquaries of Scotland.

Jankowiak, M. 2016. Byzantine coins in Viking-Age northern lands. *Byzantium and the Viking World*, 117–39.

Jankowiak, M. 2017. What Does the Slave Trade in the Saqaliba Tell Us about Early Islamic Slavery? *International journal of Middle East studies* 49(1): 169–72.

Jankowiak, M. 2018. Silver fragmentation: reinterpreting the evidence of the hoards. In J. Kershaw, G. Williams, S. Sindbæk, and J. Graham-Campbell (eds), 15–31.

Jankowiak, M. 2020. Dirham flows into northern and eastern Europe and the rhythms of the slave trade with the Islamic world. In J. Gruszczyński, M. Jankowiak, and J. Shepard (eds), 105–31.

Jarman, C. 2021. *River Kings: A New History of Vikings from Scandinavia to the Silk Road*. London: William Collins.

Jarman, C.L., Biddle, M., Higham, T., and Ramsey, C.B. 2018. The Viking Great Army in England: new dates from the Repton charnel. *Antiquity* 92(361): 183–99.

Jennings, A. 1998. Iona and the Vikings: survival and continuity. *Northern Studies* 33: 37–54.

Jennings, A. and Kruse, A. 2009. One coast - three peoples: names and ethnicity in the Scottish west during the early Viking period, in A. Woolf (ed.) *Scandinavian Scotland – Twenty Years After*. St John's House Papers No 12. St Andrews: University of St Andrews, Committee for Dark Age Studies, 75–102.

Jesch, J. 2001. *Ships and Men in the Late Viking Age: The Vocabulary of Runic Inscriptions and Skaldic Verse*. Boydell and Brewer.

Jesch, J. 2005. Literature in medieval Orkney. In O. Owen (ed.) *The World of the Orkneyinga Saga: The Broad-cloth Viking Trip*, 11–24. Kirkwall: The Orcadian.

Jesch, J. 2015. *The Viking Diaspora*. London: Routledge.

Ježek, M. 2017. *Archaeology of Touchstones: An Introduction Based on Finds from Birka, Sweden*. Leiden: Sidestone.

Johnson, C.E. 2020. *A comparative study of portable inscribed objects from Britain and Ireland, c.400–1100 AD*. Ph.D. thesis. University of Glasgow. Available at: http://theses.gla.ac.uk/81499/ [accessed August 2021]

Johnson, R. 1999. Ballinderry Crannóg no. 1: a reinterpretation. *Proceedings of the Royal Irish Academy. Section C. Archaeology, Celtic studies, history, linguistics and literature* 99C(2): 23–71.

Kaland, S.H.H. 1973. Westnessutgravningene på Rousay, Orknøyene. *Viking* 37: 77–102.

Kaland, S.H.H. 1993. The settlement of Westness, Rousay. In C.E. Batey, J. Jesch, and C.D. Morris (eds), 308–17.

Kalmring, S. 2014. A conical bronze boss and Hedeby's Eastern connection. *Fornvännen* 109: 1–11.

Kalmring, S. 2017. Excavations in Hedeby's Flat-Grave Burial Ground. A

Preliminary Report. *Jahresbericht Zentrum für Baltische und Skandinavische Archäologie*: 72–6.

Kalmring, S., and Holmquist, L. 2018. 'The gleaming mane of the serpent': the Birka dragonhead from Black Earth Harbour. *Antiquity* 92(363): 742–57.

Kelleher, R. 2007. 'Gold is the strength, the sinnewes of the world': continental gold and Tudor England. *British Numismatic Journal* 77: 210–25.

Kelly, E. 2006. Security and sanctity: the ecclesiastical metalwork of Lough Kinale. *Irish Arts Review* 23(1): 106–109.

Kelly, F. 2000. *Early Irish Farming: A Study Based Mainly on the Law-Texts of the 7th and 8th centuries AD*. Dublin: School of Celtic Studies, Dublin Institute for Advanced Studies.

Kermode, M.C. 1907. *Manx Crosses*. London: Bemrose.

Kershaw, J. 2013. *Viking Identities: Scandinavian Jewellery in England*. Oxford: Oxford University Press.

Kershaw, J. 2017. An early medieval dual-currency economy: bullion and coin in the Danelaw. *Antiquity* 91(355): 173–90.

Kershaw, J. 2018. Gold as a means of exchange in Scandinavian England (c.AD 850–1050). In J. Kershaw, G. Williams, S. Sindbæk, and J. Graham-Campbell (eds), 227–50.

Kershaw, J. 2019. Metrology and beyond: New approaches to Viking-Age regulated weights. In L. Rahmstorf and E. Stratford (eds) *Weights and Marketplaces from the Bronze Age to the Early Modern Period*. Weight and Value 1, 127–38. Göttingen: Wachholtz Verlag Kiel.

Kershaw, J., Williams, G., Sindbæk, S., and Graham-Campbell, J. 2018. *Silver, Butter, Cloth: Monetary and Social Economies in the Viking Age*. Oxford: Oxford University Press.

Kilbride-Jones, H.E. 1980. *Zoomorphic Penannular Brooches*. London: Society of Antiquaries of London.

Kilger, C. 2008a. Kaupang from afar: aspects of the interpretation of dirham finds in northern and eastern Europe between the late 8th and early 10th centuries. In D. Skre (ed.), 199–252.

Kilger, C. 2008b. Wholeness and holiness: counting, weighing and valuing silver in the early Viking period. In D. Skre (ed.), 253–325.

Kilger, C. 2015. Hoards and sinuous snakes. Significance and meaning of ring ornaments in Early Viking Age hoards from Gotland. In L. Larsson, F. Ekengren, B. Helgesson, and B. Söderberg (eds) *Small Things, Wide Horizons: Studies in honour of Birgitta Hårdh*, 35–42. Oxford: Archaeopress.

Kilger, C. 2020. Silver hoards and society on Viking-Age Gotland: some thoughts on the relationship between silver, long-distance trade and local communities. In J. Gruszczyński, M. Jankowiak, and J. Shepard (eds), 242–54.

King, J. (n.d.)a. Ancrum, Roxburghshire. *Corpus of Romanesque Sculpture in Britain and Ireland*. Available at: <https://www.crsbi.ac.uk/view-item?i=2480> [accessed August 2021a]

King, J. (n.d.)b. Kirk of Calder, Mid Calder, Midlothian. *Corpus of Romanesque Sculpture in Britain and Ireland*. Available at: <https://www.crsbi.ac.uk/ view-item?i=3139> [accessed August 2021b]

Kirkinen, T. 2017. 'Burning pelts': brown bear skins in the Iron Age and early medieval (1–1300 AD) burials in south-eastern Fennoscandia. *Eesti Arheoloogia Ajakiri* 21(1): 3–29.

Kivisalo, N. 2008. The Late Iron Age bear-tooth pendants in Finland: symbolic mediators between women, bears, and wilderness? *Temenos-Nordic Journal of Comparative Religion* 44(2): 263–91.

Klevnäs, A.M. 2016. 'Imbued with the essence of the owner': personhood and possessions in the reopening and reworking of Viking-age burials', *European Journal of Archaeology* 19(3): 456–476.

Kovalev, R.K. 2002–2003. The mint of al-Shāsh: the vehicle for the origins and continuation of trade relations between Viking-Age Northern Europe and Sāmānid Central Asia. *Archivum Eurasiae Medii* Aevi 12: 47–79.

Kovalev, R.K., and Kaelin, A.C. 2007. Circulation of Arab silver in medieval Afro-Eurasia: preliminary observations. *History Compass* 5(2): 560–80.

Kristjánsdóttir, S. 2015. Becoming Christian: a matter of everyday resistance and negotiation', *Norwegian Archaeological Review* 48(1): 27–45.

Kruse, A. 2013. Columba and Jonah – a motif in the dispersed art of Iona. *Northern Studies* 45: 1–26.

Kruse, S.E. 1992. Late Saxon balances and weights from England, *Medieval Archaeology* 36(1): 67–95.

Kruse, S.E. 1993. Silver storage and circulation in Viking-Age Scotland: the evidence of silver ingots. In C.E. Batey, J. Jesch, and C.D. Morris (eds), 187–203.

Kruse, S.E., and Tate, J. 1995. XRF analysis of Viking-age silver from Scotland. In J. Graham-Campbell (ed.), 73–9.

Kyhlberg, O. 1975. Vågar och viktlod: Diskussion kring frågor om precision och noggrannhet, *Fornvännen* 70: 156–165.

Lacey, B. 2008. Fahan, Tory, Cenél nÉogain and the Picts. *Peritia* 20: 331–45.

Laing, L. 1973. People and pins in Dark Age Scotland. *Transactions of the Dumfriesshire and Galloway Natural History and Antiquaries Society* [*TDGNHAS*], 50: 53–71.

Laing, L. 1975. Picts, Saxons and Celtic metalwork. *PSAS* 105: 189–99.

Lane, A., and Campbell, E. (eds) 2000. *Dunadd: an Early Dalriadic Capital*. Oxford: Oxbow.

Lang, J.T. 1974. Hogback monuments in Scotland. *PSAS* 105: 206–35.

Lang, J.T. 2002. *Corpus of Anglo-Saxon Stone Sculpture, Volume VI: Northern Yorkshire*. Oxford: Oxford University Press.

Langlands, A. 2020. *Ceapmenn* and *portmenn*: trade, exchange and the landscape of early medieval Wessex. In A. Langlands and R. Lavelle (eds) *The Land of the English Kin*, 294–311. Leiden: Brill.

Lapidge, M. 1982. The cult of St Indract at Glastonbury. In D. Whitelock, R. McKitterick, and D. Dumville (eds) *Ireland in Early Mediaeval Europe, Studies in Memory of Kathleen Hughes*, 179–212. Cambridge: Cambridge University Press.

Larsson, G. 2007. *Ship and Society: Maritime Ideology in Late Iron Age Sweden*. Uppsala: Uppsala Universitet.

Lasko, P. 1956. The Comb of St. Cuthbert. In C.F. Battiscombe (ed.) *The Relics of Saint Cuthbert*, 336–55. Oxford: Oxford University Press.

Leahy, K. 2003. *Anglo-Saxon Crafts*. Stroud: Tempus.

Lee, R., Jonathan, P., and Ziman, P. 2010. Pictish symbols revealed as a written language through application of Shannon entropy. *Proceedings of the Royal Society A: Mathematical, Physical and Engineering Sciences* 466(2121): 2545–60.

Liestøl, A. 1983. An Iona rune stone and the world of Man and the Isles. In C. Fell, P. Foote, J. Graham-Campbell, and R. Thomson (eds) *The Viking Age in the Isle of Man,* 85–93. London: University College London.

Lindow, J., and Andrén, A. 2020. Worlds of the Dead. In J.P. Schjødt, J. Lindow, and A. Andrén (eds) *The Pre-Christian Religions of the North Volume II: History and Structures,* 897–926. Turnhout: Brepols

Ljung, C. 2015. Early Christian grave monuments and the eleventh-century context of the monument descriptor *hvalf*. *Futhark* 5: 151.

Ljungqvist, F.C. 2005. The significance of remote resource regions for Norse Greenland. *Scripta Islandica* 56: 13–54.

Loe, L., Boyle, A., Webb, H., and Score, D. 2014. *'Given to the Ground': A Viking Age Mass Grave on Ridgeway Hill, Weymouth*. Dorchester: Dorset Natural History and Archaeological Society.

Loveluck, C. et al. 2018. Alpine ice-core evidence for the transformation of the European monetary system, AD 640–670. *Antiquity* 92(366): 1571–85.

Lowe, C. 2002. The papar and Papa Stronsay: 8th-century reality or 12th-century myth? In B.E. Crawford (ed.), 83–95.

Lowe, C. 2006. *Excavations at Hoddom, Dumfriesshire.* Edinburgh: Society of Antiquaries of Scotland.

Lucas, A.T. 1967. The plundering and burning of churches in Ireland, 7th to 16th century. *North Munster Studies*: 172–229.

Lucas, A.T. 1986. The social role of relics and reliquaries in ancient Ireland. *Journal of the Royal Society of Antiquaries of Ireland* 116: 5–37.

Lucas, A.T., Raftery, J., Prendergast, E., Ríordáin, B.Ó., and Rynne, E. 1960. National Museum of Ireland Archaeological Acquisitions in the Year 1958. *Journal of the Royal Society of Antiquaries of Ireland* 90(1): 1–40.

Luginbill, S. 2020. The Medieval Portable Altar Database. *Material Religion* 16(5): 683–85.

Lund, J. 2006. Vikingetidens værktøjskister i landskab og mytologi. *Fornvännen* 101: 323–41.

Lund, N. 1989. Allies of God or Man? The Viking Expansion in a European Perspective. *Viator* 20: 45–60.

Lynn, C.J. 1984. Some Fragments of Exotic Porphyry Found in Ireland. *The Journal of Irish Archaeology* 2: 19–32.

Lyons, A.W., and MacKay, W.A. 2008. The Lunettes coinage of Alfred the Great. *British Numismatic Journal* 78: 38–110.

MacDonald, A. 2002. The papar and some problems; a brief review. In B.E. Crawford (ed.), 13–30.

MacGregor, A. 1975. The Broch of Burrian, North Ronaldsay, Orkney. *PSAS* 105: 63–118.

MacKay, W.A. 2015. The coinage of Burgred of Mercia 852–74. *British Numismatic Journal* 85: 101–237.

Macleod, D., Gibson, W., and Curle, J. 1915. An account of a find of ornaments of the Viking Time for Valtos, Uig, in the island of Lewis. *PSAS* 50: 181–89.

Macleod, M., and Mees, B. 2006. *Runic Amulets and Magic Objects.* Woodbridge: Boydell.

Maddicott, J.R. 2005. London and Droitwich, *c.*650–750: trade, industry and the rise of Mercia. *Anglo-Saxon England* 34: 7–58.

Mainman, A.J., and Rogers, N.S.H. 2000. *Craft, Industry and Everyday Life: Finds from Anglo-Scandinavian York.* York: York Archaeological Trust.

Maldonado, A. 2011. *Christianity and Burial in Late Iron Age Scotland, AD 400–650.* Ph.D. Glasgow: University of Glasgow. Available at: <http://theses.gla.ac.uk/2700/> [accessed November 2020]

Maldonado, A. 2013. Burial in early medieval Scotland: new questions. *Medieval Archaeology* 57: 1–34.

Maldonado, A. 2016. Death and the formation of the Christian landscape. In T. Ó Carragáin and S. Turner (eds) *Making Christian Landscapes in Atlantic Europe: Conversion and Consolidation in the Early Middle Ages,* 225–45. Cork: Cork University Press.

Maldonado, A., Kitzler Åhfeldt, L., Sanmark, A., and Zedig, H. in prep. Early medieval literacy and language change in northern Scotland.

Maldonado, A., Campbell, E., Clancy, T.O., and Forsyth, K. 2021. Iona in the Viking Age. *Current Archaeology* (381).

Maleszka, M. 2004. A Viking Age weight from Cleat, Westray, Orkney. *PSAS* 133: 283–91.

Margaryan, A. et al. 2020. Population genomics of the Viking world. *Nature* 585(7825): 390–96.

Márkus, G. 2009. Dewars and relics in Scotland: some clarifications and questions. *Innes Review* 60(2): 95–144.

Martin, C. 2009. Rubh' an Dunain, Highland (Bracadale parish), field survey. *Discovery and Excavation in Scotland* New Ser., 10: 92–3.

Martin, T.F. 2015. *The Cruciform Brooch and Anglo-Saxon England.* Woodbridge: Boydell and Brewer.

Marttila, J. 2016. Resources, Production, and Trade in the Norse Shetland. *Journal of the North Atlantic* 2016(29): 1–20.

Maxwell, H. 1913. Notes on a hoard of personal ornaments, implements, and Anglo-Saxon and Northumbrian coins from Talnotrie, Kirkcudbrightshire. *PSAS* 47: 12–16.

Maxwell, M., Gray, J., and Goldberg, M. 2014. Design Archaeology: bringing a Pictish inspired drinking horn fitting to life. In *All Makers Now? Craft Values in 21st Century Production: Conference Proceedings,* 97–103. Falmouth University.

Maxwell, S. 1956. Paddles from Horizontal Mills. *PSAS* 88: 231–32.

McCarthy, M. et al. 2014. A Post-Roman Sequence at Carlisle Cathedral. *Archaeological Journal* 171(1): 185–257.

McCormick, M. 2001. *Origins of the European Economy: Communications and Commerce AD 300–900.* Cambridge: Cambridge University Press.

McCormick, M. 2002. New light on the 'dark ages': how the slave trade fuelled the Carolingian economy. *Past and Present* (177): 17–54.

McGuigan, N. 2015a. *Neither Scotland nor England: Middle Britain, c.850–1150.* Ph.D. thesis. St Andrews University. Available at: <http://hdl.handle.net/10023/7829> [accessed November 2020]

McGuigan, N. 2015b. Ælla and the descendants of Ivar: politics and legend in the Viking Age. *Northern History* 52(1): 20–34.

McGuigan, N. 2021. *Máel Coluim III, 'Canmore': The World of an Eleventh-Century King*. Edinburgh: Birlinn.

McGuigan, N., and Woolf, A. (eds) 2018. *The Battle of Carham: A Thousand Years On*. Edinburgh: Birlinn.

McGuire, E.H. 2009. *Manifestations of identity in burial: evidence from Viking-Age graves in the North Atlantic diaspora*. Ph.D thesis. University of Glasgow. Available at: <http://theses.gla.ac.uk/1736/> [accessed August 2021].

McGuire, E.H. 2019. 'Whim rules the child': the archaeology of childhood in Scandinavian Scotland. *Journal of the North Atlantic* 11(1): 13 27.

McKerracher, M. 2018. *Farming Transformed in Anglo-Saxon England: Agriculture in the Long Eighth Century*. Oxford: Windgather.

McLeod, S. 2011. Warriors and women: the sex ratio of Norse migrants to eastern England up to 900 AD. *Early Medieval Europe* 19(3): 332–53.

McLeod, S. 2015a. Legitimation Through Association? Scandinavian Accompanied Burials and Pre-Historic Monuments in Orkney. *Journal of the North Atlantic* 2015(28): 1–15.

McLeod, S. 2015b. The dubh gall in southern Scotland: the politics of Northumbria, Dublin, and the Community of St Cuthbert in the Viking Age, *c*.870–950 CE, *Limina* 20(3): 1–21.

Megaw, B.R.S. 1940. The balance-beam from Ronaldsway, Isle of Man. *The Antiquaries Journal* 20(3): 382–85.

Merkel, S. 2018. Provenancing Viking Age silver: methodological and theoretical considerations and a case study. In J. Kershaw, G. Williams, S. Sindbæk, and J. Graham-Campbell (eds), 206–26.

Metcalf, D.M. 1995. The monetary significance of Scottish Viking-age coin hoards. In J. Graham-Campbell (ed.), 16–25.

Metcalf, D.M. 2007. Regions around the North Sea with a monetised economy in the pre-Viking and Viking Ages. In J. Graham-Campbell and G. Williams (eds), 1–11.

Metcalf, P., and Huntington, R. 1991. *Celebrations of Death: The Anthropology of Mortuary Ritual* 2nd (ed.) Cambridge: Cambridge University Press.

Michailidis, M. 2012. Samanid silver and trade along the Fur Route. *Medieval Encounters* 18(4-5): 315–38.

Michelli, P. 1987. Four Scottish crosiers and their relation to the Irish tradition. *PSAS* 116: 375–92.

Mikkelsen, E. 2019. *Looting or Missioning: Insular and Continental Sacred Objects in Viking Age Contexts in Norway*. Oxford: Oxbow.

Molyneaux, G. 2009. The Old English Bede: English ideology or Christian instruction? *English Historical Review* 124(511): 1289–1323.

Molyneaux, G. 2015. *The Formation of the English Kingdom in the Tenth Century*. Oxford: Oxford University Press.

Montgomery, J. et al. 2014. Finding Vikings with isotope analysis: The view from wet and windy islands. *Journal of the North Atlantic* Sp7: 54–70.

Moreland, J. 2000. The significance of production in eighth-century England. In I.L. Hansen and C. Wickham (eds) *The Long Eighth Century. The Transformation of the Roman World* 11, 69–104. Leiden: Brill.

Morris, C.D., and Barrowman, R. 2021. *The Birsay Bay Project Vol. 3: The Brough of Birsay, Orkney: Investigations 1954–2014*. Oxford: Oxbow.

Morrisson, C. 2012. Weighing, measuring, paying: exchanges in the market and the marketplace. In C. Morrisson (ed.) *Trade and Markets in Byzantium*, 379–98. Washington, D.C.: Dumbarton Oaks.

Müldner, G. 2016. Marine fish consumption in medieval Britain: the isotope perspective from human skeletal remains. In J.H. Barrett and D.C. Orton (eds) *Cod and Herring: The Archaeology and History of Medieval Sea Fishing*, 239–49. Oxford: Oxbow.

Murray, G. 2007. Insular-type crosiers: their construction and characteristics. In R. Moss (ed.) *Making and Meaning in Insular Art*, 79–94. Dublin: Four Courts.

Murray, G. 2013a. Irish crucifixion plaques: a reassessment. In J. Mullins, J. Ní Ghrádaigh, and R. Hawtree (eds) *Envisioning Christ on the Cross: Ireland and the Early Medieval West*, 286–317. Dublin: Four Courts.

Murray, G. 2013b. The makers of church metalwork in early medieval Ireland: their identity and status. In J. Hawkes (ed.) *Making Histories: Proceedings of the Sixth International Insular Art Conference, York 2011*, 201–14. Donington: Shaun Tyas.

Murray, G. 2014. The Breac Maodhóg: a unique medieval Irish reliquary. In J. Cherry and B. Scott (eds) *Cavan: History and Society: Interdisciplinary Essays on the History of an Irish Country*, 83–125. Dublin: Geography.

Murray, G. 2015. Insular crosiers from Viking-Age Scandinavia. *Acta Archaeologica* 86(2): 95–121.

Murray, G. 2020. Changing attitudes to Viking art in medieval Ireland. In A. Pedersen and S. M. Sindbæk (eds), 426–34.

Murray, G., and Maldonado, A. in prep. An early Irish crucifixion plaque from Scotland.

Myhre, B. 2000. The Early Viking Age in Norway. *Acta Archaeologica* 71(1): 35–47.

Naismith, R. 2005. Islamic coins from early medieval England. *Numismatic Chronicle* 165: 193–222.

Naismith, R. 2016. The coinage of Æthelred II: a new evaluation. *English Studies* 97(2): 117–39.

Naismith, R. 2020. Gilds, states and societies in the early Middle Ages. *Early Medieval Europe* 28(4): 627–62.

Newman, C. 2007. Procession and symbolism at Tara: analysis of Tech Midchuarta (the Banqueting Hall) in the context of the sacral campus. *Oxford Journal of Archaeology* 26(4): 415–38.

Newman, C. and Burke, S. 2013. The symbolism of zoomorphic penannular brooches. In J. Hawkes (ed.) *Making Histories: Proceedings of the Sixth International Insular Art Conference, York 2011*, 201–14. Donington: Shaun Tyas.

Nicolay, J. 2007. *Armed Batavians: Use and Significance of Weaponry and Horse Gear from Non-military Contexts in the Rhine Delta (50BC to AD450)*. Amsterdam: Amsterdam University Press.

Nieke, M.R. 1993. Penannular and related brooches: secular ornament or symbol in action? In R.M. Spearman and Higgitt, J. (eds), 128–34.

Noble, G. and Evans, N. 2019. *The King in the North: The Pictish Realms of Fortriu and Ce*. Edinburgh: Birlinn.

Noble, G., Goldberg, M., and Hamilton, D. 2018. The development of the Pictish symbol system: inscribing identity beyond the edges of Empire. *Antiquity* 92(365): 1329–48.

Noble, G. and Sveinbjarnarson, O. 2017. Doune of Relugas, excavation. *Discovery and Excavation in Scotland* New Ser., 17: 121–22.

Noble, G. and Sveinbjarnarson, O. 2018. Burghead Fort, excavation. *Discovery and Excavation in Scotland* New Ser., 18: 134–35.

Nordeide, S.W. 2016. Late Iron Age boat rituals and ritual boats in Norway. In J.H. Barrett and S.J. Gibbon (eds), 171–81.

Norstein, F.E. 2020. *Processing death: Oval brooches and Viking graves in Britain, Ireland and Iceland*. Ph.D. thesis. University of Gothenburg. Available at: <https://gupea.ub.gu.se/handle/2077/64094> [accessed August 2021]

Ó Carragáin, T. 2014. The archaeology of ecclesiastical estates in early medieval Ireland: a case study of the kingdom of Fir Maige. *Peritia* 24-25: 266–312.

Ó Floinn, R. 1983. A gold band found near Rathkeale, Co. Limerick. *North Munster Antiquarian Journal* 25: 3–8.

Ó Floinn, R. 1994. *Irish Shrines and Reliquaries of the Middle Ages*. Dublin: National Museum of Ireland.

Ó Floinn, R. 2020. Personal belief in Hiberno-Norse Dublin. In A. Pedersen and S. M. Sindbæk (eds), 235–48.

O'Brien, E. 2021. *Mapping Death: Burial in Late Iron Age and Early Medieval Ireland*. Dublin: Four Courts.

O'Grady, O. 2008. *The Setting and Practice of Open-air Judicial Assemblies in Medieval Scotland: a Multidisciplinary Study*. PhD thesis, University of Glasgow. Available <https://theses.gla.ac.uk/506/> [accessed 1 October 2021]

O'Grady, O.J.T. 2014. Judicial assembly sites in Scotland: archaeological and place-name evidence of the Scottish court hill. *Medieval Archaeology* 58(1): 104–35.

O'Meadhra, U. 1993. Viking-Age sketches and motif-pieces from the Northern Earldoms. In C.E. Batey, J. Jesch, and C.D. Morris (eds), 423–40.

O'Rahilly, C. 1998. A classification of bronze stick-pins from the Dublin excavations 1962–72. In C. Manning (ed.) *Dublin and Beyond the Pale: studies in honour of Patrick Healy*, 23–33. Dublin: Wordwell.

O'Sullivan, A., McCormick, F., Kerr, T., and Harney, L. 2014. *Early medieval Ireland, AD400–1100: The evidence from archaeological excavations*. Dublin: Royal Irish Academy.

O'Sullivan, J. 2015. Strung along: re-evaluating gendered views of Viking-Age beads. *Medieval Archaeology* 59(1): 73–86.

Okasha, E., and O'Reilly, J. 1984. An Anglo-Saxon portable altar: inscription and iconography. *Journal of the Warburg and Courtauld Institutes* 47: 32–51.

Oma, K.A. 2018. Transformative theft of past and present: the human–horse bond reflected in the biography of the Viking Period Gausel bridle. In M. Vedeler, I.M. Røstad, E.S. Kristoffersen, and Z. T. Glørstad (eds), 125–45.

Oram, R.D. 2000. *The Lordship of Galloway*. Edinburgh: John Donald.

Oram, R.D. 2008. Royal and lordly residence in Scotland c 1050 to c 1250: an historiographical review and critical revision. *The Antiquaries Journal* 88: 165–89.

Oram, R.D. 2011. *Domination and Lordship: Scotland, 1070–1230*. Edinburgh: Edinburgh University Press.

Organ, R.M. 1973. Examination of the Ardagh Chalice – a case history. In W.J. Young (ed.) *Application of Science in Examination of Works of Art*, 238–71. Boston: Museum of Fine Arts.

Overbey, K.E. 2012. *Sacral Geographies: Saints, Shrines and Territory in Medieval Ireland*. Turnhout: Brepols.

Owen, O., and Dalland, M. 1999. *Scar: A Viking Boat Burial on Sanday, Orkney*. East Linton: Tuckwell/Historic Scotland.

Owen, O., and Welander, R. 1995. A traveller's end? An associated group of Early Historic artefacts from Carronbridge, Dumfries and Galloway. *PSAS* 125: 753–70.

Øye, I. 2015. Production, quality and social status in Viking Age dress: three cases from western Norway. In R. Netherton and G.R. Owen-Crocker (eds) *Medieval Clothing and Textiles*, volume 11, 1–28. Woodbridge: Boydell and Brewer.

Parker, M. 2012. An eighth-century reference to the monastery at Hoddom. *Journal of Scottish Name Studies* 6: 51–80.

Parker Pearson, M., Brennand, M. Mulville, J., and Smith, H. 2018. *Cille Pheadair: a Norse Farmstead and Pictish Burial Cairn in South Uist*. Oxford: Oxbow.

Parsons, S.T. 2019. The inhabitants of the British Isles on the First Crusade: medieval perceptions and the invention of a Pan-Angevin Crusading heritage. *English Historical Review* 134(567): 273–301.

Paterson, C. 1997. The Viking-Age trefoil mount from Jarlshof: a reappraisal in the light of two new discoveries. *PSAS* 127: 649–57.

Paterson, C. 2001. Insular belt-fittings from the Pagan Norse graves of Scotland: a reappraisal in the light of scientific and stylistic analysis. In N. Edwards, S. Youngs, A. Lane, and J. Knight (eds) *Pattern and Purpose in Insular Art*, 125–32. Oxford: Oxbow

Paterson, C., Parsons, A.J., Newman, R.M., Johnson, N., and Howard-Davis, C. 2014. *Shadows in the Sand: Excavation of a Viking-age cemetery at Cumwhitton, Cumbria*. Lancaster: Lancaster Imprints.

Paterson, C., and Stanford, C. 2020. Power dressing in the Irish Sea area: An interesting group of Hiberno-Scandinavian strap-fittings. In C. Thickpenny, K. Forsyth, J. Geddes, and K. Matthis (editors), 87–98.

Pedersen, U. 2008. Weights and balances, in D. Skre (ed.), 119–195

Pedersen, A., Roesdahl, E., and Graham-Campbell, J. 2014. Dress accessories and personal ornaments of metal: amulets. In E. Roesdahl, S.M. Sindbæk, A. Pedersen, and D.M. Wilson (eds) *Aggersborg: the Viking-Age Settlement and Fortress*, 279–89. Højbjerg: Jutland Archaeological Society.

Pedersen A. and Sindbæk, S. M. (eds) 2020. *Viking Encounters. Proceedings of the Eighteenth Viking Congress, Denmark, August 6–12, 2017*. Aarhus: Aarhus Universitetsforlag.

Peirce, I. 2002. *Swords of the Viking Age*. Woodbridge: Boydell.

Pelteret, D.A.E. 1995. *Slavery in Early Mediaeval England: From the Reign of Alfred until the Twelfth Century*. Woodbridge: Boydell.

Perry, D.R. 2000. *Castle Park, Dunbar: Two Thousand Years on a Fortified*

Petersen, J. 1919. *De norske vikingesverd*. Kristiania: J. Dybwad.

Petts, D. 2017. 'A place more venerable than all in Britain': the archaeology of Anglo-Saxon Lindisfarne. In R. Gameson (ed.) *The Lindisfarne Gospels: New Perspectives*. Library of the Written Word 57, 1–18. Leiden: Brill.

Pickles, T. 2020. Review article: Why should we write about Anglo-Saxon farms and farming? *Early Medieval Europe* 28(3): 466–82.

Pierce, E. 2013. Jet cross pendants from the British Isles and beyond: forms, distribution and use. *Medieval Archaeology* 57(1): 198–211.

Place-names of Kirkcudbrightshire. Kirkcudbrightshire place-name 38: 'Desnes'. *Place-names of Kirkcudbrightshire*. Available at: <https://kcb-placenames.glasgow.ac.uk/place-names/?p=recordandid=38> [accessed August 2021]

Pollard, T. 2005. The excavation of four caves in the Geodha Smoo near Durness, Sutherland. *Scottish Archaeological Internet Reports* 18. Available at: <http://journals.socantscot.org/index.php/sair/article/view/924> [accessed September 2021]

Price, T.D., Peets, J., Allmäe, R., Maldre, L., and Oras, E. 2016. Isotopic provenancing of the Salme ship burials in Pre-Viking Age Estonia. *Antiquity* 90(352): 1022–37.

Price, N. 2010. Passing into poetry: Viking-age mortuary drama and the origins of Norse mythology. *Medieval Archaeology* 54(1): 123–56.

Price, N. 2020. *The Children of Ash and Elm: A History of the Vikings*. London: Allen Lane.

Price, N. et al. 2019. Viking warrior women? Reassessing Birka chamber grave Bj.581. *Antiquity* 93(367): 181–98.

Pryce, H. 2001. British or Welsh? National Identity in Twelfth-Century Wales. *English Historical Review* 116(468): 775–801.

PSAS. 1863. Donations. *PSAS* 4: 489–92.

Radford, C.A.R. 1953. Hoddom, *Antiquity* 27(107): 153–160.

Raffield, B. 2016. Bands of brothers: a re-appraisal of the Viking Great Army and its implications for the Scandinavian colonization of England. *Early Medieval Europe* 24(3): 308–37.

Raffield, B. 2019. The slave markets of the Viking world: comparative perspectives on an 'invisible archaeology'. *Slavery & Abolition* 40(4): 682–705.

Raffield, B., Gardeła, L., and Toplak, M. 2021. Slavery in Viking Age Scandinavia: a review of the archaeological evidence. In M. Toplak, H. Østhus, and R. Simek (eds) *Viking-Age Slavery*. Studia Medievalia Septentrionalia 29, 7–58. Vienna: Fassbaender.

Raffield, B., Price, N., and Collard, M. 2017. Male-biased operational sex ratios and the Viking phenomenon: an evolutionary anthropological perspective on Late Iron Age Scandinavian raiding. *Evolution and Human Behavior* 38(3): 315–24.

Rambaran-Olm, M., and Wade, E. 2021. The Many Myths of the Term 'Anglo-Saxon'. *Smithsonian Magazine*. Available at: <https://www.smithsonianmag.com/history/many-myths-term-anglo-saxon-180978169/> [accessed August 2021]

RCAHMS. 1946. *Royal Commission on the Ancient and Historical Monuments of Scotland: Twelfth Report with an Inventory of the Ancient Monuments of Orkney and Shetland: Inventory of Orkney*. Edinburgh: H.M. Stationery Office.

Read, B. 2001. *Metal Artefacts of Antiquity: A Catalogue of Small Finds from Specific Areas of the United Kingdom*. Langport: Portcullis.

Redknap, M. 2004. Viking-age settlement in Wales and the evidence from Llanbedrgoch. In J. Hines, A. Lane, and M. Redknap (eds) *Land, Sea and Home: Proceedings of a Conference on Viking-period Settlement at Cardiff, July 2001*. SMA Monographs 20, 138–75. Leeds: Maney.

Reece, R. 1981. *Excavations in Iona 1964 to 1974*. London: University College London.

Reid, R.C. 1959. The Priory of St Mary's Isle. *TDGNHAS* 36: 9–26.

Richards, J.D. 2004. Excavations at the Viking barrow cemetery at Heath Wood, Ingleby, Derbyshire. *The Antiquaries Journal* 84: 23–116.

Ridel, É. 2007. From Scotland to Normandy: the Celtic sea route of the Vikings. In B. Ballin-Smith, S. Taylor, and G. Williams (eds) *West over Sea: Studies in Scandinavian Sea-borne Expansion and Settlement Before 1300*. The Northern World 31, 81–94. Leiden: Brill.

Rio, A. 2017. *Slavery After Rome, 500–1100*. Oxford University Press.

Ritchie, A. 1979. Excavation of Pictish and Viking-age farmsteads at Buckquoy, Orkney. *PSAS* 108: 174–227.

Ritchie, A. 1999. *Govan and its Carved Stones*. Balgavies, Angus: Friends of Govan Old/Pinkfoot Press.

Ritchie, A. 2005. Clothing Among the Picts. *Costume* 39(1): 28–42.

Ritchie, J.N.G. 1982. Excavations at Machrins, Colonsay. *PSAS* 111: 263–81.

Robison, J. 1927. *Kirkcudbright (St Cuthbert's Town): Its Mote, Castle, Monastery and Parish Churches*. Dumfries: Robert Dinwiddie.

Rollason, D.W. 2003. Northumbria, 500–1100: Creation and Destruction of a Kingdom. Cambridge: Cambridge University Press.

Ross, A. 1886. Notice of the discovery of portions of two penannular brooches of silver, with beads of glass and amber, and a silver coin of Coenwulf, King of Mercia (A.D. 795–818), at Mains of Croy, Inverness-shire. *PSAS* 20: 91–96.

Ross, A. 2019. Medieval European land assessment, Fortriu, and the *dabhach*. In A. E. Blackwell (ed.) *Scotland in Early Medieval Europe*, 135–48. Leiden: Sidestone.

Ross, S. 1991. *Dress pins from Anglo-Saxon England: their production and typo-chronological development*. University of Oxford. Available at: <https://ora.ox.ac.uk/objects/uuid:3976b772-fccd-41fe-b8c7-f4ae08ac0295> [accessed November 2020]

Rundkvist, M., and Williams, H. 2008. A Viking boat grave with amber gaming pieces excavated at Skamby, Östergötland, Sweden. *Medieval Archaeology* 52(1): 69–102.

Russell, I., and Hurley, M.F. 2014. *Woodstown: A Viking Settlement in Co. Waterford*. Dublin: Four Courts.

Ryan, M. 2004. The Loughan brooch. In C. Hourihane (ed.) *Irish Art Historical Studies in Honour of Peter Harbison*, 109–23. Dublin: Four Courts.

Ryan, M. 2011. Metalwork in Ireland from the later 7th to the 9th Century: a review. In C. Hourihane (ed.) *Insular and Anglo-Saxon Art and Thought in the Early Medieval Period*, 43–58. Princeton: Princeton University.

Samson, R. 1991a. *Social Approaches to Viking Studies*. Glasgow: Cruithne.

Samson, R. 1991b. Fighting with silver: rethinking trading, raiding and hoarding. In R. Samson (ed.), 123–33.

Samson, R. 1992. The reinterpretation of the Pictish symbols, *Journal of the British Archaeological Association* 145(1): 29–65.

Sanjosé i Llongueras, L. de. 2018. L'ara portàtil de Sant Pere de Rodes. Hipòtesi de filiació longobarda. *Miscel·lània Litúrgica Catalana* 26: 13–50.

Sanmark, A. 2017. *Viking Law and Order: Places and Rituals of Assembly in the Medieval North*. Edinburgh: Edinburgh University Press.

Sayer, D., Sebo, E., and Hughes, K. 2019. A double-edged sword: swords, bodies, and personhood in early medieval archaeology and literature. *European Journal of Archaeology* 22(4): 542–66.

Schoenfelder, M. and Richards, J.D. 2011. Norse bells: a Scandinavian colonial artefact. *Anglo-Saxon Studies in Archaeology and History* 17(1): 151–68.

Schou, T. 2017. Trade and hierarchy: the Viking Age soapstone vessel production and trade of Agder, Norway. In G. Hansen and P. Storemyr (eds) *Soapstone in the North Quarries, Products and People 7000BC–AD1700*, 133–52. Bergen: University of Bergen.

Scott, J. 1956. A glass linen smoother from Kirkcudbright. *PSAS* 88: 226–27.

Scott, J.G. 1983. A note on Viking settlement in Galloway. *TDGNHAS* 3rd ser., 58: 52–55.

Sellar, D. 1993. Sueno's Stone and its interpreters, in D. Sellar (ed.) *Moray: Province and People*. Edinburgh: Scottish Society for Northern Studies, 96–116.

Sellevold, B.J. 1999. *Picts and Vikings at Westness: Anthropological Investigations of the Skeletal Material from the Cemetery at Westness, Rousay, Orkney Islands*. Oslo: Norsk Institutt for Kulturminneforskning.

Semple, S. 2013. *Perceptions of the Prehistoric in Anglo-Saxon England: Religion, Ritual, and Rulership in the Landscape*. Oxford: Oxford University Press.

Semple, S., and Sanmark, A. 2013. Assembly in north west Europe: collective concerns for early societies? *European Journal of Archaeology* 16(3): 518–42.

Sharpe, R. (ed.) 1995. *Adomnán of Iona: Life of St Columba*. London: Penguin.

Sharpe, R. 2000. The thriving of Dalriada. In S. Taylor (ed.), 47–61.

Sharples, N.M. (ed.) 2021. *The Economy of a Norse Settlement in the Outer Hebrides: Excavations at Mounds 2 and 2A Bornais, South Uist*. Oxford: Oxbow.

Sharples, N.M., and Parker Pearson, M. 1999. Norse settlement in the Outer Hebrides. *Norwegian Archaeological Review* 32(1): 41–62.

Sheehan, J. 1988. A bronze bell-crest from the Rock of Cashel, Co Tipperary. *North Munster Antiquarian Journal* 30: 3–13.

Sheehan, J. 2008. The longphort in Viking Age Ireland. *Acta Archaeologica* 79(1): 282–95.

Sheehan, J. 2013. Viking raiding, gift-exchange and Insular metalwork in Norway. In A. Reynolds and L. Webster (eds) *Early Medieval Art and Archaeology in the Northern World: studies in honour of James Graham-Campbell*. Northern World 58, 809–23. Leiden: Brill.

Sheehan, J. 2018. Reflections on kingship, the Church, and Viking Age silver in Ireland. In J. Kershaw, G. Williams, S. Sindbæk, and J. Graham-Campbell (eds), 104–122.

Sheehan, J. 2020. Viking-Age bullion from southern Scandinavia and the Baltic region in Ireland. In J. Gruszczyński, M. Jankowiak, and J. Shepard (eds), 415–33.

Sheehan, J., and Sikora, M. 2019. Lurgabrack, Co. Donegal: a Viking Age hoard of Scoto-Scandinavian silver. *The Journal of Irish Archaeology* 28: 103–118.

Sheehan, J., Stummann Hansen, S., and Ó Corráin, D. 2001. A Viking Age maritime haven: a reassessment of the island settlement at Beginish, Co. Kerry. *The Journal of Irish Archaeology* 10: 93–119.

Shiels, J. and Campbell, S. 2011. Sacred and banal: the discovery of everyday medieval material culture. In E. J. Cowan and L. Henderson (eds) *A History of Everyday Life in Medieval Scotland, 1000 to 1600*, 67–88. Edinburgh: Edinburgh University Press.

Sigurðsson, B.M. 2019. *Rannsókn á beinprjónum á Íslandi frá víkingaöld*. Ph.D thesis. Háskóli Íslands. Available at: <http://hdl.handle.net/1946/32850> [accessed August 2021]

Sindbæk, S.M. 2011a. Silver economies and social ties: long-distance interaction, long-term investments – and why the Viking Age happened. In J. Graham-Campbell, S. M. Sindbæk, and G. Williams (eds), 41–65.

Sindbæk, S.M. 2011b. Urban crafts and oval brooches: style, innovation and social networks in Viking age towns. In S. Sigmundsson (ed.) *Viking Settlements and Viking Society: Papers from the Proceedings of the 16th Viking Congress*, 409–23. Reykjavik: University of Iceland Press.

Sindbæk, S.M. 2013. Broken links and black boxes: material affiliations and contextual network synthesis in the Viking world. In C. Knappett (ed.) *Network Analysis in Archaeology: New Approaches to Regional Interaction*, 71–94. Oxford: Oxford University Press.

Sindbæk, S.M. 2014. Crossbreeding beasts: Christian and non-Christian imagery in oval brooches. In I. Garipzanov (ed.) *Conversion and Identity in the Viking Age*. Medieval Identities: Socio-Cultural Spaces 5, 167–93. Turnhout: Brepols.

Skinner, F.G. and Bruce-Mitford, R.L.S. 1940. A Celtic balance-beam of the Christian period. *The Antiquaries Journal* 20(1): 87–102.

Skre, D. 2001. The social context of settlement in Norway in the first millennium AD. *Norwegian Archaeological Review* 34(1): 1–12.

Skre, D. (ed.) 2008. *Means of Exchange: Dealing with Silver in the Viking Age*. Aarhus: Aarhus University Press.

Skre, D. 2011. Commodity money, silver and coinage in *Viking-Age Scandinavia*. In J. Graham-Campbell, S.M. Sindbæk, and G. Williams (eds), 67–92.

Skre, D. 2017. Viking-Age economic transformations: the west-Scandinavian case. In Z. T. Glørstad and K. Loftsgarden (eds) *Viking-Age Transformations: Trade, Craft and Resources in Western Scandinavia*, 1–27. London: Routledge.

Skre, D. 2020. Some reflections on Gotland: slavery, slave-traders and slave-takers. In J. Gruszczyński, M. Jankowiak, and J. Shepard (eds), 437–49.

Small, A., Thomas, C., and Wilson, D.M. 1973. *St Ninian's Isle and its Treasure*. Oxford: Oxford University Press.

Smart, V. 1985. The penny in the pennylands: Coinage in Scotland in the early Middle Ages. *Northern Studies* 22: 65–70.

Smith, B. 2001. The Picts and the martyrs, or did Vikings kill the native population of Orkney and Shetland?, *Northern Studies* 36: 7–32.

Smith, C. 1999. *Dogs, cats and horses in the Scottish medieval town. PSAS* 128: 859–85.

Smith, J.M.H. 2012. Portable Christianity: relics in the medieval west (*c*.700–1200). *Proceedings of the British Academy* 181: 143–68.

Smith, J.M.H. 2013. Writing in Britain and Ireland, *c*.400 to *c*.800. In C. A. Lees (ed.) *The Cambridge History of Early Medieval English Literature.* The New Cambridge History of English Literature, 19–49. Cambridge: Cambridge University Press.

Smith, R.D. 2019. The business of human trafficking: slaves and money between Western Italy and the House of Islam before the Crusades (*c*.900–*c*.1100). *Journal of Medieval History* 45(5): 523–52.

Smyth, A. 1999. The effect of Scandinavian raiders on the English and Irish churches: A preliminary reassessment. In B. Smith (ed.) *Britain and Ireland, 900–1300: Insular Responses to Medieval European Change*, 1–38. Cambridge: Cambridge University Press.

Solberg, B. 1991. Weapon export from the Continent to the Nordic countries in the Carolingian period, *Studien zur Sachsenforschung* 7: 241–259.

Solberg, B. 2007. Pastimes or serious business? Norwegian graves with gaming objects *c*.200–1000 AD. In K. Jennbert, B. Hårdh, and D. Olausson (eds) *On the Road: studies in honour of Lars Larsson*, 265–69. Stockholm: Almqvist and Wiksell.

Sørheim, H. 2011. Three prominent Norwegian ladies. *Acta Archaeologica* 2011(1): 17–54.

Spearman, R.M. 1988. Early Scottish towns: their origins and economy. In S.T. Driscoll and M.R. Nieke (eds) *Power and Politics in Early Medieval Britain and Ireland*, 96–110. Edinburgh: Edinburgh University Press.

Spearman, M. 1993. The mounts from Crieff, Perthshire, and their wider context. In R.M. Spearman and Higgitt, J. (eds), 135–42.

Spearman, R.M., and Higgitt, J. (eds) 1993. *The Age of Migrating Ideas: Early Medieval Art in Northern Britain and Ireland*. Edinburgh: National Museums of Scotland/Alan Sutton.

Speed, G., and Walton Rogers, P. 2004. A burial of a Viking woman at Adwick-le-Street, South Yorkshire. *Medieval Archaeology* 48(1): 51–90.

Staecker, J. 2007. Decoding Viking art: the Christian iconography of the Bamberg Shrine. In K. Jennbert, B. Hårdh, and D. Olausson (eds) *On the Road: studies in honour of Lars Larsson*, 301–306. Stockholm: Almqvist and Wiksell

Staecker, J. 2009. The 9th-century Christian mission to the North. In A. Englert, Trakadas, and Athena (eds) *Wulfstan's Voyage: The Baltic Sea Region in the early Viking Age as seen from shipboard*. Maritime Culture of the North 2, 309–329. Roskilde: Viking Ship Museum.

Stalsberg, A. 1991. Women as actors in North European Viking trade. In R. Samson (ed.), 75–83.

Star, B., Barrett, J.H., Gondek, A.T., and Boessenkool, S. 2018. Ancient DNA reveals the chronology of walrus ivory trade from Norse Greenland. *Proceedings of the Royal Society B: Biological sciences* 285(1884). Available at: <http://dx.doi.org/10.1098/rspb.2018.0978> [accessed November 2020]

Steinforth, D.H. 2018. 'That stepping-stone in the middle of the Irish Sea' the Dublin Vikings and the Isle of Man in the late ninth century. *The Journal of Irish Archaeology* 27: 81–98.

Steuer, H. 1987. Gewichtsgeldwirtschaften im frühgeschichtlichen Europa: feinwaagen und gewichte als Quellen zur Währungsgeschichte, in K. Düwel et al. (eds) *Untersuchungen zu Handel und Verkehr der vor-und frühgeschichtlichen Zeit in Mittel- und Nordeuropa, teil 4: Der Handel der Karolinger- und Wikingerzeit*. Göttingen: Vandenhoeck & Ruprecht, 405–527.

Stevenson, R. 1953. A hoard of Anglo-Saxon coins found at Iona Abbey. *PSAS* 85: 170–75.

Stevenson, R.B.K. 1955. Pins and the chronology of brochs. *Proceedings of the Prehistoric Society* 21: 282–94.

Stevenson, R.B.K. 1959. The Inchyra stone and some other unpublished early Christian monuments. *PSAS* 92: 33–55.

Stevenson, R.B.K. 1966. *National Sylloge of Coins of the British Isles. Pt. 1, Anglo-Saxon coins (with associated foreign coins)*. Oxford: Oxford University Press.

Stevenson, R.B.K. 1985. The Pictish brooch from Aldclune, Blair Atholl, Perthshire. *PSAS* 115: 233–39.

Stevenson, R.B.K. 1989. The Celtic brooch from Westness, Orkney, and hinged-pins. *PSAS* 119: 239–69.

Stifter, D. 2020. Insular Celtic: Ogam. *Palaeohispanica. Revista sobre lenguas y culturas de la Hispania Antigua* (20): 855–85.

Stirling, L., and Milek, K. 2015. Woven cultures: new insights into Pictish and Viking culture contact using the implements of textile production. *Medieval Archaeology* 59(1): 47–72.

Stocker, D. 2000. Monuments and merchants: irregularities in the distribution of stone sculpture in Lincolnshire and Yorkshire in the tenth century. In D. M. Hadley and J. D. Richards (eds) *Cultures in Contact: Scandinavian Settlement in England in the Ninth and Tenth Centuries.* Studies in the Early Middle Ages 2, 179–212. Turnhout: Brepols.

Stolt, B. 2001. Boktyngder och bärbara altarskivor. In *Kyrkliga sällsyntheter på Gotland och annorstädes*, 25–39. Visby: Ödins Förlag.

Stout, M. 2017. *Early Medieval Ireland*: 431–1169. Dublin: Wordwell.

Strachan, D., Sneddon, D., and Tipping, R. 2019. *Early Medieval Settlement in Upland Perthshire: Excavations at Lair, Glen Shee 2012–17*. Oxford: Archaeopress.

Stratigos, M.J., and Noble, G. 2018. A new chronology for crannogs in north-east Scotland. *PSAS* 147: 147–73.

Stuart, J. 1867. *The Sculptured Stones of Scotland, Vol. 2*. Edinburgh: Spalding Club.

Stummann Hansen, S. 2000. Viking settlement in Shetland: chronological and regional contexts. *Acta Archaeologica* 71: 87–103.

Svanberg, F. 2003. *Decolonizing the Viking Age 1*. Stockholm: Almqvist and Wiksell.

Swift, C. 1997. *Ogam Stones and the Earliest Irish Christians.* Maynooth: St Patrick's College, Maynooth.

Swift, C. 2013. *Pictish Brooches and Pictish Hens: Status and Currency in Early Scotland*. Rosemarkie: Groam House Museum.

Taylor, A. 2016. *The Shape of the State in Medieval Scotland, 1124–1290*. Oxford: Oxford University Press.

Taylor, S. (ed.) 2000. *Kings, Clerics and Chronicles in Scotland 500–1297*. Dublin: Four Courts.

Taylor, S. 2000. The coming of the Augustinians to St Andrews and version B of the St Andrews Foundation Legend. In S. Taylor (ed.), 115–23.

Taylor, S. 2002. Reading the map: understanding Scottish place-names. *History Scotland* 2(1). Available at: <https://eprints.gla.ac.uk/7770> [accessed September 2021]

Taylor, S. 2014. The medieval parish in Scotland. *Journal of Scottish Name Studies* 8: 93.

Tesch, S. 2007. Tidigmedeltida sepulkralstenar i Sigtuna. *Situne Dei: Årsskrift för Sigtunaforskning utgiven av Sigtuna Museum* 2007: 45–68.

Thickpenny, C., Forsyth, K., Geddes, J., and Matthis, K. (eds) 2020. *Peopling Insular Art: Practice, Performance, Perception*. Oxford: Oxbow.

Thomas, C. 1967. An early Christian cemetery and chapel on Ardwall Isle, Kirkcudbright. *Medieval Archaeology* 11: 127–88.

Thomas, G. 2000. *A survey of late Anglo-Saxon and Viking-age strap-ends from Britain*. Ph.D. thesis. University College London. Available at: <https://discovery.ucl.ac.uk/id/eprint/1317562/> [access. August 2021]

Thompson, V. 2004. *Dying and Death in Later Anglo-Saxon England*. Woodbridge: Boydell and Brewer.

Thompson, V. 2018. A new reading of Late Anglo-Saxon Sculpture in and around the Tweed Valley: Carham, Lindisfarne, Norham and Jedburgh. In N. McGuigan and A. Woolf (eds), 174–201.

Thomson, W.L. 1986. St Findan and the Pictish-Norse transition. In R. J. Berry and H. N. Firth (eds) *The People of Orkney*, 279–83. Kirkwall: The Orkney Press.

Thorsteinsson, A. 1965. The viking burial place at Pierowall, Westray, Orkney. In B. Niclasen (ed.) *The Fifth Viking Congress, Tórshavn*, 150–73. Tórshavn: Føroya Landsstyri.

Tilghman, B.C. 2011. Writing in tongues: mixed scripts and style in Insular Art. In C. Hourihane (ed.) *Insular and Anglo-Saxon: Art and Thought in the Early Middle Ages*, 92–108. Princeton: Penn State University Press.

Trench-Jellicoe, R. 2000. A missing figure on slab fragment no 2 from Monifieth, Angus, the a'Chill Cross, Canna, and some implications of the development of a variant form of the Virgin's hairstyle and dress in early medieval Scotland. *PSAS* 129: 597–647.

Trench-Jellicoe, R. 2002. Manx sculptured monuments and the early Viking Age. In P. Davey and D. Finlayson (eds) *Mannin Revisited: Twelve Essays on Manx Culture and Environment*, 10–34. Edinburgh: Scottish Society for Northern Studies.

Valante, M. 2013. Castrating monks: Vikings, slave trade, and the value of eunuchs. In L. Tracy (ed.) *Castration and Culture in the Middle Ages*, 174–87. Cambridge: D.S. Brewer.

Vedeler, M. 2018. The charismatic power of objects. In M. Vedeler, I. Røstad, E. Kristoffersen, and Z. Glørstad (eds), 9–29.

Vedeler, M., Røstad, I.M., Kristoffersen, E.S., and Glørstad, Z.T. (eds) 2018. *Charismatic Objects: From Roman Times to the Middle Ages*. Oslo: Cappelen Damm Akademisk.

Wallace, P.F. 1998. Line fishing in Viking Dublin: a contemporary explanation for archaeological evidence. In C. Manning (ed.) *Dublin and Beyond the Pale: studies in honour of Patrick Healy*, 4–18. Dublin: Wordwell.

Wallace, P.F. 2015. *Viking Dublin: the Wood Quay excavations*. Dublin: Irish Academic Press.

Wamers, E. 1983. Some ecclesiastical and secular Insular metalwork found in Norwegian Viking graves. *Peritia* 2: 277–306.

Wamers, E. 1985. *Insularer Metallschmuck in wikingerzeitlichen Gräbern Nordeuropas: Untersuchungen zur skandinavischen Westexpansion*. Neumünster: Karl Wachholtz.

Wamers, E. 1987. Egg-and-dart derivatives in insular art. In M. Ryan (ed.) *Ireland and Insular Art A.D. 500–1200*, 96–104. Dublin: Royal Irish Academy.

Warner, R. 2004. Notes on the inception and early development of the royal mound in Ireland. In A. Pantos and S. Semple (eds) *Assembly Places and Practices in Medieval Europe*, 27–43. Dublin: Four Courts.

Watson, F.J. 2010. *Macbeth: a true story*. London: Quercus.

Watt, T. 1993. Mail churchyard extension (Dunrossness parish): Viking antler comb, *Discovery and Excavation in Scotland*, 106.

Webster, L., and Backhouse, J. 1991. *The Making of England: Anglo-Saxon Art and Culture AD 600–900*. London: British Museum.

Wegner, T. 2006. The Dumfriesshire mounts reconsidered. *TDGNHAS* 80: 59–80.

Welander, R., Batey, C.E. and Cowie, T.G. 1987. A Viking burial from Kneep, Uig, Isle of Lewis, *PSAS* 117: 149–174.

Westerdahl, C. 2008. Boats apart. Building and equipping an Iron-Age and Early-Medieval ship in Northern Europe. *International Journal of Nautical Archaeology* 37(1): 17–31.

Westerdahl, C. 2016. Sails and the cognitive roles of Viking Age ships. In J.H. Barrett and S.J. Gibbon (eds), 14–24.

Whitfield, N. 1997. The Waterford kite-brooch and its place in Irish metalwork. In M. F. Hurley and Ó. Scully (eds) *Late Viking Age and Medieval Waterford: Excavations 1986–1992*, 490–517. Waterford: Waterford Corporation.

Whitfield, N. 2001. The 'Tara' Brooch: an Irish emblem of status in its European context. In C. Hourihane (ed.) *From Ireland Coming: Irish Art from the Early Christian to the Late Gothic Period and its European Context*, 211–47. Princeton: Princeton University Press.

Whitfield, N. 2014. 'Embedded animal heads' on the Hunterston, 'Tara' and Dunbeath brooches: a reconsideration. *Journal of the Royal Society of Antiquaries of Ireland* 144/145: 60–76.

Whitworth, V. 2011. A cross-head from St Mary Castlegate, York, and its affiliations. In *New Voices on Early Medieval Sculpture in Britain and Ireland*. BAR British Series 542, 42–47. Oxford: Archaeopress.

Whitworth, V.T. 2020. Uncanny monsters and telling absences: Ways of reading the Meigle recumbents. In C. Thickpenny, K. Forsyth, J. Geddes, and K. Matthis (eds), 161–66.

Wigh, B. 2001. *Animal Husbandry in the Viking Age Town of Birka and* its Hinterland: Excavations in the Black Earth 1990–95. Stockholm: Riksantikvarieämbetet.

Willemsen, A. 2021. Mixed Emotions: The swords from Dorestad. In A. Willemsen and H. Kik (eds) *Dorestad and Its Networks: Communities, Contact and Conflict in Early Medieval Europe*, 101–115. Leiden: Sidestone.

Williams, G. 1999. Anglo-Saxon and Viking coin weights. *British Numismatic Journal* 69: 19–36.

Williams, G. 2007. Kingship, Christianity and coinage: monetary and political perspectives on silver economy in the Viking Age. In J. Graham-Campbell and G. Williams (eds), 177–214.

Williams, G. 2011. Silver economies, monetisation and society: an overview. In J. Graham-Campbell, S. M. Sindbæk, and G. Williams (eds), 337–72.

Williams, H. 2006. *Death and Memory in Early Medieval Britain*. Cambridge: Cambridge University Press.

Williams, H. 2007a. The emotive force of early medieval mortuary practices. *Archaeological Review from Cambridge* 22(1): 107–123.

Williams, H. 2007b. Transforming body and soul: toilet implements in early Anglo-Saxon graves. In S. Semple and H. Williams (eds) *Early Medieval Mortuary Practices. Anglo-Saxon Studies in Archaeology and History* 14, 66–91.

Williams, H. 2016. Citations in stone: the material world of hogbacks. *European Journal of Archaeology* 19(3): 497–518.

Willmott, H., and Daubney, A. 2020. Of saints, sows or smiths? Copper-brazed iron handbells in Early Medieval England. *Archaeological Journal* 177(1): 336–55.

Wilson, D.M. 2008. *The Vikings in the Isle of Man*. Aarhus Universitetsforlag.

Winterbottom, M. 1978. *The Ruin of Britain, and Other Works*. London: Phillimore.

Wood, I. 2001. *The Missionary Life: Saints and the Evangelisation of Europe, 400–1050*. London: Longman.

Wood, M. 2019. As a racism row rumbles on, is it time to retire the term 'Anglo-Saxon'? BBC History Extra. Available at: <https://www.historyextra.com/period/anglo-saxon/professor-michael-wood-anglo-saxon-name-debate-is-term-racist/> [accessed July 2021]

Woolf, A. 2001. The Verturian hegemony: a mirror in the north. In M.P. Brown and C.A. Farr (eds) *Mercia: an Anglo-Saxon Kingdom in Europe*, 106–111. Leicester: Leicester University Press.

Woolf, A. 2002. The 'when, why and wherefore' of Scotland. *History Scotland* 2 (March/April): 12–16.

Woolf, A. 2007. *From Pictland to Alba, 789–1070*. Edinburgh: Edinburgh University Press.

Woolf, A. 2017. On the nature of the Picts. *Scottish Historical Review* 96(2): 214–17.

Woolf, A. 2018. The Scandinavian intervention. In B. Smith (ed.) *The Cambridge History of Ireland*, 107–130. Cambridge: Cambridge University Press.

Woolf, A. 2020. British ethnogenesis: a Late Antique story. In F. Kaminski-Jones and R. Kaminski-Jones (eds) *Celts, Romans, Britons: Classical and Celtic Influence in the Construction of British identities*, 19–30. Oxford: Oxford University Press.

Woolliscroft, D.J. 2002. *The Roman Frontier on the Gask Ridge Perth and Kinross: An Interim Report in the Roman Gask Project 1995–2000*. Oxford: Archaeopress.

Wycherley, N. 2016. *The Cult of Relics in Early Medieval Ireland*. Turnhout: Brepols.

Youngs, S. (ed.) 1989. *'The Work of Angels': Masterpieces of Celtic Metalwork, 6–9th Centuries AD*. London: British Museum.

Youngs, S. 2001. From Ireland coming: fine Irish metalwork from the Medway, Kent, England. In C. Hourihane (ed.) *From Ireland Coming: Irish Art from the Early Christian to the Late Gothic Period and its European Context*, 249–60. Princeton: Princeton University Press.

Youngs, S. 2020. Lions on Iona. In C. Thickpenny, K. Forsyth, J. Geddes, and K. Matthis (eds), 59–70.

Żabiński, G. 2007. Viking Age Swords from Scotland. *Acta Militaria Mediaevalia* 3.

Index

Abernethy, Perthshire 179–80, 181, 191; *180*
Aberlady, East Lothian 70 n.41; *190*
Abington, South Lanarkshire 70 n.41
Adomnán, abbot of Iona (679–704) 42
Adwick-le-Street, Yorkshire 61
Aethelred I, king of Northumbria (774–9, 790–6) 36–7, 42
Aethelred II 'the Unready', king of England (*c*.966–1016) 198
Aethelstan, king of Wessex (924–39) 133, 144, 147
Alba 3, 7, 9–10, 38, 50, 74, 87, 129, 142–7, 178–9, 181, 191, 193, 198–9, 204, 205
Alcuin of York 34, 36–8, 41, 104
Aldclune, Perthshire 84
Aldwark, Yorkshire 137
Alfred, king of Wessex (871–99) 7–8, 74, 96, 130
altars 36, 41, 73, 80, 83, 185, 193; *184*, *203*
– cross 80, 170, 202–3; *203*
– plate and furnishings 35, 41, 193
– portable 36, 176
Alt Clut (Dumbarton, kingdom and hillfort) 7, 10, 74–5, 87, 144, 155, 209
– siege of 74–5, 87, 117, 144, 155
amber 24, 32–33, 63, 85, 94, 110, 115, 116, 136, 153, 164–5, 166, 168, 170; *93*, *110*
Amlaíb Cuarán, king of Dublin 143
amulets (*see also* bell-pendant, cross pendants, Thor's Hammer) 81, 108, 121, 153, 161–5, 167, 169, 170, 175–6
Anderson, Joseph 106
Angles 7–8
Anglo-Saxon (*see also* coins; historical sources; language; swords; writing)

– material culture 31, 54, 56, 63, 95–6; *63*, *64*, *78*
– terminology 8
Anglo-Scandinavian material culture 90, 144, 198–99, 202; *145*
Annan, River 89
Archerfield, East Lothian 203
Ardagh Chalice 171
Ardnamurchan, Argyll 49, 52–3
Ardwall, Kirkcudbrightshire 16
Armagh, Ireland 80
arm-rings (*see also* ring-money) 17, 86, 89, 103, 127 n.67, 132, 135–6, 147, 153, 165, 177, 200–1; *128*, *132*, *133*, *135*, *141*, *142*, *143*, *153*, *157*, *197*
– broad-band 17, 86, 89, 132; *89*, *128*, *132*, *133*, *200*
Arran, Isle of 58, 96, 145
arrows 51
Ashaig, Skye 67–8
Atholl (*see* Perthshire)
Auldhame, East Lothian 67–8, 121, 142, 198; *67*
axes 51, 54; *52*
Ayrshire 146

Baghdad 130–1; *130*
balance scales 34, 94–6, 137–8, 140, 166, 180; *93*, *96*, *138*, *139*, *140*
– boxes for 138; *139*
– steelyards 94–6, 140; *93*, *140*
Ballinaby, Isle of Islay 58, 90, 106, 169; *58*, *74*, *105*, *106*
Ballinderry Crannog, Co. Westmeath, Ireland 168
Balmaghie, Kirkcudbrightshire 86

Balmerino, Fife *176*
Balnakeil, Sutherland 56–7, 59–60, 66; *59*, *60*, *117*
Baltic Sea 33, 37, 94, 106, 124, 131, 133, 162, 167
Banchory Ternan, Aberdeenshire 114
Bankfoot, Perthshire 142; *143*
baptism 75
Barhobble, Wigtownshire 67, 137, 176
Barra, Isle of 17, 20, 38, 143
battles
– Brunanburh (937) 144–5
– Carham (1018) 145, 190
– Clontarf (1014) 189, 193
– Corbridge (918) 145
– Dollar (875) 87, 91–2, 145
– Milvian Bridge (312) 26
– Tara (980) 143
– unlocated, Pictland (839) 75
Bay of Skaill, Orkney 166
beach markets (*see* markets)
beads 37, 63, 65, 85–87, 90, 92, 95–7, 121, 136, 143, 151, 153, 163, 166, 170, 199; *61*, *63*, *65*, *72*, *87*, *92*, *93*, *105*, *151*, *165*
Beadwulf, bishop of Whithorn 38
bears 16, 155, 162; *162*
beasts (art motif; *see also* lions, drinking birds motif) 28, 30, 63, 94–5, 103, 111, 116, 121–4, 127 n.113, 190, 192; *30*, *32*, *35*, *95*, *102*, *110*, *128*, *133*, *135*, *138*, *140*, *145*, *190*, *193*
Bede 6–8, 34, 36–7
bell/bells 209–11
– handbells 5, 90, 173, 175, 192–93, 205, 209–11; *174*
– -pendants 144, 202, 207 n.86; *145*

CRUCIBLE OF NATIONS

232

– -shrines 192–3, 209–11; *193*, *208*, *210*
– towers and tower bells 209, 211
belts (*see also* strap ends) 36, 40, 67, 81, 101, 105, 108, 120–1, 163, 169, 170; *67*, *121*
Benedictine Order 192, 201
Bernicia 7–8, 10
Bhaltos, Lewis 170–1; *172*
Bible 27, 29, 104, 179
Birka, Sweden 58, 90, 106, 120, 124, 140, 155, 170; *171*
Blackerne, Kirkcudbrightshire 89; *89*
Blackwater (*see* Shanmullagh Hoard)
Blathmacc son of Flann 40
boats and ships (*see also* burial, sails, sea travel) 31, 36, 41, 69, 74, 81, 109, 148, 154–55, 199; *76*, *125*, *155*
– fleets 41, 74, 199
– repair 155
Bonchester Bridge, Scottish Borders 70 n.41
books (*see* manuscripts and books)
book-shrines 63, 80–1, 83, 123, 171, 202; *63*, *82*, *203*
border, Anglo-Scottish xv, 191
Bornais, South Uist 162, 176, 201
Børøyna, Rogaland, Norway 114; *115*
Borre-style, 113, 121; *100*, *113*
Braidwood, Midlothian 92
'Breadalbane' Brooch, 110, 115
Brechin, Angus 181, 192
Branxholme, Scottish Borders 34
brass 62, 116, 138, 164, 170; *62*, *63*, *105*, *106*, *107*, *108*, *117*, *139*, *164*
Bressay, Shetland 13, 17–18, 20, 179; *19*
Bristol 155
Britons 6–7, 9, 30, 43, 74–5, 156
Broch of Burgar, Orkney 85, 136
Broch of Gurness, Orkney 11, 49–50, 161–2; *11*, *50*
brochs 11, 14, 49–50, 85, 96, 107, 175; *11*, *50*, *145*
Bronze Age 28, 33, 85, 88; *88*
brooches (*see also* brooch-pins) 50, 63, 65, 79, 81–2, 101–103, 105–25, 163, 169, 173, 177
– ball/thistle type 125, 135–6, 198; *125*, *134*, *135*, *157*
brooch-pins 59, 64–6, 92, 103, 113, 115–8, 121, 123–5, 146, 165; *23*, *57*, *63*, *64*, *102*, *116*, *117*, *118*

– bossed penannular 86, 125, 133, 198; *87*, *125*, *133*, *134*
– copper-alloy 111, 114, 122; *112*, *122*
– disc/quatrefoil 86, 171; *87*
– oval 61–3, 106–9, 113, 116–8, 121, 125, 138, 161, 170; *50*, *61*, *62*, *63*, *105*, *106*, *107*, *108*, *139*
– penannular 24, 30, 32–3, 61, 84, 85, 92, 94, 103, 109–12, 114, 116, 118, 121–5, 137, 165–7, 205; *34*, *83*, *85*, *93*, *110*, *111*, *112*, *114*, *115*, *122*, *123*, *125*, *134*, *166*, *167*
– production 111, 114, 122, 124
– pseudo-penannular 17, 110–1, 114–6, 118, 145–6; *2*, *102*, *110*, *112*, *115*, *146*
– trefoil 113; *100*, *113*
Brora, Sutherland 153
Brough of Birsay, Orkney 14–17, 33, 58, 77–8, 104, 111, 114, 122–4, 142–3, 148, 155, 162, 163, 168, 175, 176; *4*, *14*, *18*, *33*, *78*, *145*, *162*, *168*, *184*
Brough of Deerness, Orkney 142
buckets 169–71; *171*
buckle 190
Buckquoy, Orkney 14, 16, 20, 61, 78, 104
bullion (*see* hacksilver)
Burghead, Moray 92, 96; *97*
burghs 155, 202–3, 205
Burgred, king of Mercia (852–74) 91, 96, 175, 202; *90*
burial
– as evidence for settlement 49–51, 53, 65–6, 68–9, 76, 106–7, 145, 195–6
– boat 37, 48, 49, 51–3, 56–7, 62, 65–6, 69, 79, 91, 94, 96–7, 120–1, 136–8, 140, 148, 167, 173; *79*, *116*, *119*, *125*
– cremation 28, 85, 96, 151, 163
– furnished 47–69, 74, 76, 78, 80–2, 90, 104–9, 111–6, 118, 120–3, 125, 139, 145, 153, 161–4, 166, 169, 170–1, 173, 175, 176, 185, 195–6; *74*, *78*, *100*, *102*, *105*, *113*, *120*, *123*, *125*, *139*, *148*, *153*
– in cemeteries 30, 40, 43, 49, 69, 115, 145, 166, 167
– long cist 50, 53, 66, 69, 104, 169, 175
– shroud 57–8, 109, 210
– square barrow 28, 48, 50
– weapon, 49, 51, 65, 67, 69, 78, 106, 120, 137, 149, 202; *52*

Burray Hoard, Orkney 141–2, 148, 166, 197; *141*, *197*
Burrian, Orkney 175; *174*
Burness, Orkney 76
Bute, Isle of 145–6, 201
butter 31, 151, 154, 199; *151*
Byzantium 26, 37, 131, 140, 156, 201

Caithness 49, 144, 179
Caldale, Orkney 198
camel 202
cannel coal (*see also* lignite) 31, 153; *153*
Caputh, Perthshire 92; *92*
Carlisle 68, 189–90
Carn a' Bharraich, Oronsay 53, 79, 116, 121, 173; *79*, *116*, *119*
carnelian 92, 143; *92*
Carronbridge, Dumfriesshire 89, 111–2
carved stones (*see also* writing) xiii–xiv, xvi, 4, 10–11, 13, 16–17, 25–31, 40–1, 47–8, 68, 74, 82, 83, 104, 109, 113, 120, 122, 143, 144–6, 157, 161, 171, 173, 177–85, 191–2, 195–6, 202; xii, *4*, *12*, *14*, *15*, *18*, *19*, *26*, *27*, *30*, *32*, *35*, *39*, *41*, *68*, *76*, *160*, *172*, *177*, *178*, *179*, *180*, *182*, *183*, *184*, *196*
Cashel, Co. Tipperary 28
Castletown, Caithness 106, 153
cats 155
Cat Stane, Midlothian 11
cattle 27–8, 31–2, 41, 147, 154; *32*
Causantín mac Áeda, king of Alba (900–43) 9, 144
Central Asia 37, 86–7, 131, 136–7, 201; *86*, *130*, *131*
Charlemagne, king of Franks, 768–814 26, 36, 41
Chester, Cheshire 134, 155
Chester-le-Street, County Durham 38
children 41, 53, 56–57, 59–60, 63, 66, 109, 166, 176
chrism (*see* oils)
chrismatories 193, 195; *195*
Christianity 20, 26, 28, 29, 34, 37, 41, 48, 66, 68, 110–11, 143, 153, 157
Church (institution) 11, 20, 27–9, 48, 68, 116, 121, 146–7, 172, 195–7, 200–1
churches xiv, 14, 27–8, 35, 42, 82–3, 87, 142–143, 148, 201, 209–11, 165, 176

– architecture xiv, 27–8, 183, 185, 189, 191–2, 195–6, 205, 209; *27*, *184*, *196*
Cille Pheadair, South Uist 162, 201
Cináed mac Ailpín, king of Picts (842–58) 27, 29, 75, 84
Clarkly Hill, Moray 31, 207 n.86
Clatchard Craig, Fife 33; *33*
Clement II, Pope 202
Clibberswick, Unst, Shetland 113, 148; *110*, *113*
Clonmacnoise, Co. Meath 143
clothing 27, 63–4, 108, 118, 120
Clunie, Perthshire 34, 75, 84, 92, 111, 170; *85*
Clyde, River and Firth 3, 17, 96, 143–6, 153, 190, 195, 197
Cnip cemetery, Lewis 166
Cnip, Lewis 61, 108, 121; *61*, *120*
Cnoc nan Gall, Colonsay (*see* Machrins, Colonsay)
Cnut, king of England (1016–35) 190, 198, 202
Cockburnspath, Scottish Borders 142, 195; *191*
Coenwulf, king of Mercia (796–821) 26, 86, 94–5, 165; *93*, *165*
Coigreach of St Fillan *194*
coins (*see also* gold) xv, 34, 77, 87–8, 131–2, 134, 137, 140–1, 146–7, 177, 189, 197–203, 205; *88*, *134*
– Anglo-Saxon/English 52, 77–8, 86, 88, 90, 92, 94–7, 132–3, 142–5, 149, 165, 175, 197–8, 201; *72*, *88*, *90*, *93*, *134*, *141*, *165*
– Byzantine 199
– Carolingian/Frankish 88–9, 96, 143; *88*, *92*, *141*
– dinars 130, 199, 201
– dirhams 10, 88–9, 92, 95, 130–33, 136–7, 140–1, 145, 155–6; *88*, *130*, *131*, *134*
– Dublin 198–9
– Norman 197–8, 206 n.48
– Norway 198
– pierced 86–7, 90–91, 94–97, 131, 145; *72*, *88*, *90*, *93*, *131*
– sceattas 31, 37
– Scottish 147, 189, 199, 201, 202
Colonsay, Isle of 58, 107; *204*
Coldingham, Scottish Borders 92, 168; *92*, *168*

combs (*see also* hair) 36, 65, 104, 136, 175; *52*, *63*, *78*, *104*, *152*
'Conan Stone', Easter Ross 127 n.113
Constantín mac Cináeda, king of Picts (862–75) 75, 92, 144–5
Constantín, adopted as royal Pictish name (*see* Causantín mac Áeda, Causantín mac Cináeda, Custantín mac Fergusa) 26, 130
Constantine I, emperor (306–37) 26
Constantine V, emperor (741–75) 26
Constantinople 26, 201
coordinate (artwork) 5; *5*
copper 32–3, 80
Coptic ladle 80
Cornaigbeg, Tiree 164; *164*
Cornwall 74, 94
Corrie Loch, Dumfriesshire 80–1, 90
Cottam, Yorkshire 88–9, 92
Cowie, Stirlingshire 92
Craiglemine, Glasserton *177*
Cramond, Edinburgh 162; *163*
crannogs 84, 109, 115, 118, 162, 166, 192; *162*
Crieff, Perthshire
– mounts 83; *84*
crosiers 79, 193, 205; *80*, *194*
cross pendants 35, 86, 88, 153, 165, 192; *88*
Crow Taing, Sanday, Orkney 59–60
Croydon Hoard, London 89, 130
Croy Hoard, Inverness-shire 84–5, 87, 92–7, 122, 124, 136–7, 140; *93*, *95*, *96*, *140*
Cruach Mhor, Isle of Islay 153
crucifixion, iconography (*see also* Jesus Christ) 180, 202–3; *180*, *203*, *208*
Crusades 190, 202
Cuerdale Hoard, Lancashire 90, 133, 136, 143
Culbin Sands, Moray 31, 154; *154*, *188*
Cullivoe, Yell, Shetland 209
Cul na Muice, Vallay, North Uist *117*
Cumbria 3, 189–90, 147, 196
Cunningsburgh, Shetland 13–15, 17, 67, 148; *15*, *18*
Custantín's Cross, Forteviot 11, 25–9, 43, 104, 178; *26*
Custantín mac Fergusa, king of Picts (789–820) 11, 25–9, 42–3, 75
Cymry (*see* Britons)

Dalmeny, West Lothian 196
Dál Riata 7, 10, 16, 25–7, 42, 43, 75
Dalswinton, Dumfriesshire 31; *31*
Danelaw 75, 87, 92, 144, 164, 175
Danes 8, 36, 41, 74–5, 92, 133, 198, 202
David (Old Testament) 27, 179
David I, king of Scotland (1124–53) 10, 147, 189, 199, 201–2, 205; *199*
Deira 7–8
Denmark 31, 37, 55, 81, 106, 113, 163, 190, 198
dewars (keepers of relics) 210
disc mounts 31, 170–1; *78*, *172*
dogs 154, 190–91, 206 n.12
Donemutha 41
Dorestad, Netherlands 90
Dornoch, Sutherland 9, 31, 96, 142, 154, 197, 202
Doune of Relugas, Moray 204
drinking-bird motif 84–5, 111; *85*, *111*
drinking-horns 5, 31, 96, 154; *97*
Druimalban 16
Dublin, Ireland 9, 49, 57–8, 90, 94, 97, 106, 114, 118, 123, 124, 134, 137–40, 142–5, 151, 154–5, 163, 164, 176, 193, 198, 203; *123*
Dull, Perthshire 142, 183, 197–9; *183*
Dumbarton (*see* Alt Clut)
Dumfriesshire 80–1, 88–90, 170, 190; *89*
Dunadd, Argyll 33
Dunbar, East Lothian 31, 37, 75, 173
Dunbeath, Caithness *24*
Dunblane, Stirlingshire 75, 178
Dundee 202
Dunfallandy, Perthshire 127 n.113
Dunfermline, Fife 192
Dunipace, Falkirk 92, 116–7; *117*
Dunkeld, Perthshire 9, 11, 28, 33, 38, 43, 75, 84, 92, 143, 172, 209, 179, 181; *179*
Dunning, Perthshire 25
Dunnottar, Aberdeenshire 144
Dupplin Cross, Forteviot (*see* Custantín's Cross)
Durham 38
Durness, Sutherland 151, 155; *117*, *151*
dyes 30, 108

Ead, king of Picts 9
Earn, River 25

Eassie, Angus 173
East Anglia 74
Eastbourne, Sussex 201
Echternach, Luxembourg 35
Edinburgh 192, 203
Egilsay, Orkney 148
Eigg, Isle of 42, 153
Elgin, Moray 96
England xv, 6–8, 10, 31, 35–7, 50, 55, 68, 74–6, 79, 81, 87, 106, 113, 129–30, 133, 141, 144–5, 147, 153, 156, 190–1, 196, 198–9, 205, 209
English Channel 36–7, 201
Ervey, Co. Meath 115
Evangelist symbol 169; *170*
Eynhallow Sound 50

Faroe Islands 37
Fetlar, Shetland 52–3, 148
Fife 123, 198
finger-rings 36, 52, 89, 153, 162, 198, 200–1; *52*, *144*, *163*
– gold 89, 91; *91*
– silver 52; *52*
fish and fishing 61, 67, 69, 148, 154, 199; *149*
Flax (*see also* textiles, linen) 65, 105, 108
Flixborough, Lincolnshire 175
Flotta, Orkney 185; *184*
Fords of Frew, Stirling 91–2
Forres, Moray 179–80, 207 n.99
Forteviot (*see* Custantín's Cross) 11, 16, 25–9, 31, 42–3, 48, 50, 75, 91, 122, 178, 181; *26*
– Arch 27–8, 104, 173, 189; *27*
– Palace 27–9, 75
Forth, River and Firth 3, 7, 16, 29, 91, 190, 195–6, 199
Fortriu 6–7, 9, 26, 30–1, 40, 75, 87, 92, 96
Fowlis Wester, Perthshire 173, 179
Frankia 7, 26–7, 29–30, 36–7, 55, 63, 74, 81, 87, 130, 140, 198
Freswick Links, Caithness 121–4; *120*, *122*, *168*
Frisia (*see also* Low Countries) 35, 41, 63, 74–5, 81
furs 37, 154–5, 177

Gaelic (*see* Language)
Gall-goídil 8–9, 17, 75, 145–6, 190, 197, 202

Galloway (kingdom) 9–10, 190, 202
Galloway Hoard 17, 85, 86–7, 90, 95–71, 132–3, 136–8, 165, 166, 171, 197, 200–1; *72*, *86*, *87*, *128*, *132*, *133*, *165*, *167*
gaming
– boards 60, 168
– chess 151, 168; *152*, *168*
– *hnefatafl*
– pieces 60, 154, 168; *52*, *60*, *168*
– toys 148; *149*
Gask Ridge 25, 27
'Gausel Queen' (burial), Rogaland, Norway 80, 120, 153, 169
gender
– female 17, 20, 42, 50, 53, 58, 60, 61, 62–66, 79, 81, 105–9, 113–8, 120–1, 125, 138, 148, 153, 156, 201; *50*, *58*, *61*, *62*, *63*, *64*, *65*, *74*, *78*, *100*, *102*, *105*, *113*, *120*, *124*, *139*, *152*, *153*
– male 17, 20, 27, 51, 53, 56–7, 59–61, 65, 78, 81, 109, 113, 116, 120–2, 125, 137; *12*, *18*, *46*, *52*, *65*, *123*, *125*, *138*, *152*, *199*
Germany 35, 55, 176
gift-giving 30, 34, 36, 81, 108, 134–5, 200
Gigha, Isle of 94, 137, 140
Gildas 6
Glasgow 117; *117*
Glasgow School of Art 5
glass (*see also* beads) 31–3, 35, 40, 85–6, 111, 202–3; *87*, *111*, *202*
Glastonbury, Somerset 73
Glendochart, Perthshire *194*
Glen Lyon, Perthshire 175
Glenmorangie Research Project xv, 5
Gogar, Midlothian 167; *167*
gold 5, 33–4, 55, 73, 84, 86–9, 91–2, 96–7, 109–10, 114–5, 130, 142–44, 156, 164, 165, 166, 197, 199, 200, 201; *2*, *23*, *24*, *29*, *55*, *64*, *79*, *82*, *84*, *85*, *87*, *88*, *91*, *93*, *100*, *110*, *111*, *112*, *113*, *114*, *115*, *118*, *122*, *144*, *167*, *201*
– arm-rings 200; *200*
– coins 96, 130, 157 n.6, 199
– finger-rings 200–1; *200*
– hack-gold and ingots 33, 88, 142–44, 200–1; *88*, *144*, *200*
– hair fillets 201; *201*
– neck-rings 92
Gordon, Scottish Borders 144

Gorton, Strathspey 55, 70 n.41; *56*
Gotland 131, 137
Govan, Glasgow 117, 144, 146
– 'Govan school' sculpture 144, 146, 177, 181, 195–6
grain 28–9, 31–2, 35, 65
– milling 31, 35; *31*
Great Army 38, 68, 74–5, 81, 87–88, 91–2, 96–7, 117, 129–30, 133, 137, 143, 145, 167
Great Cumbrae 146
Great Glen 30, 204
Greenigoe, Orkney 151
Greenland 106
Gretna, Dumfriesshire 89
Gulli, Vestfold, Norway 121
Guthrum, king of the Danelaw (878–90) 74

hack-gold (*see* gold)
hacksilver xv, 5, 33, 86–8, 90, 92, 94, 123, 129–48, 154–7, 197–8, 201; *34*, *88*, *89*, *130*, *132*, *133*, *134*, *135*, *136*, *141*, *142*, *143*, *144*, *197*
hair (*see also* combs) 27, 36–7, 80, 104; *76*
Hålen, Sogndal, Norway 114
handbells (*see* bells)
Harald Hardrada, king of Norway (1046–66) 191
Harris, Isle of 50
Harrow, Caithness 167; *167*
Harviestoun, Clackmannanshire 70 n.41, 144
Haug, Verdal, Norway 94, 140; *95*
Healfdane, leader of Great Army warband 88, 91–2
Hebrides 3, 9, 13, 37, 50, 58, 73–6, 79–80, 94, 107, 143, 145, 154, 204, 210, 211; *74*, *79*, *105*
– settlement of 37, 50, 76
Hedeby, Germany 58, 90, 106, 113, 124, 155
Hegreberg, Rogaland, Norway 163
Helgö, Uppland, Sweden 37, 79; *80*
Hillesøy, Tromsø, Norway *78*
hillforts 11, 27, 30, 33–4, 74, 92, 96–7, 109, 144, 204, 205; *33*, *97*
Hillswick, Shetland 85, 151; *151*
Hilton of Cadboll stone, Easter Ross XIII–XVI; *XII*
historical sources
– Anglo-Saxon/English 6, 8–9, 26, 156
– British/Welsh 6

INDEX

235

– Frankish 31
– Irish 6, 8–9, 26, 38, 40, 42, 50, 109, 198
– Norse/Icelandic 6, 143
– Scottish xiv, 6, 9
hnefatafl (*see* gaming)
hoards and hoarding 5, 16–17, 20, 34, 56, 74, 80, 82–97, 105, 110–1, 114–5, 121–2, 130–7, 140–8, 151, 155–7, 165, 166, 171, 175, 197–201; *83, 89, 128, 130, 131, 132, 133, 134, 135, 136, 140, 141, 150, 152*
Hoddom, Dumfriesshire 31–2, 35, 38, 89, 143, 185; *32, 92, 184, 194*
hogback stones 144–6, 195–6, 205; *196*
Holyrood, Edinburgh 203
horses
– harness gear 77, 80–1, 84, 92, 120–21; *77, 82, 84, 120*
hostage-taking 41–2, 79, 134, 200
– 'Hostage Stone' *41*
Humber, River 8, 190
Hunday Orkney 176; *176*
Hunterston Brooch, Ayrshire 17, 110–1, 115–6, 145–6; *2, 110, 146*
Hurly Hawkin, Angus 145
Hygbald, bishop of Lindisfarne 36, 41
Hyrt, Hordaland, Norway 108

Iceland 37, 61, 105–6, 108, 129, 163, 175
Ildulb, king of Alba 144
incense 34, 36–7
Inchaffray, Perthshire 192–3; *193*
Inch Kenneth, Mull 197–8
Inchmarnock, Bute 13, 20, 31, 41, 68, 79, 143, 145–6, 153, 168; *41, 68*
– 'Hostage Stone' 41, 145, 173; *41*
Indrechtach, abbot of Iona 73
ingots 33–4, 86, 132, 134, 136, 137, 142, 143, 200; *33, 34, 87, 132, 134, 136, 141, 144*
– moulds 33, 40, 148–9, 162; *40*
Invergowrie, Angus 161, 171; *160, 172*
Inverness 92
Iona, Isle of xvi, 25–9, 31, 35, 37–8, 40–2, 67–8, 73, 79–80, 142–3, 154, 156, 171, 172, 178, 179, 197–8, 201, 204–5, 211; *67, 144*
Ireland 3, 7, 9, 13, 25, 28, 34–5, 37–8, 40–2, 48, 50, 55, 63, 68, 73–6, 79–80, 86–7, 90, 92, 104–6, 109–110, 112, 114–6, 118, 123–5, 130, 133, 135, 140–2, 145–7, 154, 156, 163, 164, 165, 166, 169, 172, 173, 180, 181, 185, 190–3, 197–9, 202–5; *117, 123*
Irish Sea 13, 17, 37, 58, 86, 89–90, 95, 125, 132–33, 135, 138, 154–5, 163, 203, 205
Iron Age xiii–xv, 4, 28, 50, 109, 123, 151, 163, 192
iron, production 32
Islamic caliphates 37, 88, 130–4, 136–41, 151, 155–6, 201–2; *130, 131, 202*
Islay, Isle of 107; *74*
Italy 92
Ívarr, king of Dublin (*c*.857–73) 75, 155
ivory
– elephant 36
– walrus 151, 168; *152*

Jarlshof, Shetland 77, 122, 136, 138, 142, 148, 150, 153, 155, 163, 168; *76, 77, 136, 139, 150, 154, 164, 183*
– incised slates from *76*
Jarrow, Tyne and Wear 6, 34
Jedburgh, Scottish Borders 197–8; *152*
Jerusalem 27
Jesus Christ 109, 202–3; *12, 182, 203, 208*
– as *Agnus Dei* 28
jet (*see also* cannel coal, lignite) 153, 162, 164; *152, 162*

Kaupang, Vestfold, Norway 70 n.30, 106, 140, 149
Kebister, Shetland 176
Keiss, Caithness 176
Kells, Co. Meath, Ireland 172
Kenneth McAlpine (*see* Cináed mac Ailpín, king of the Picts [842–58])
Kersmains, Scottish Borders 209
Kilbar, Barra 17, 20, 68; *68*
Kildonnan, Eigg 54, 67, 121, 125, 170; *55, 125*
Killaloe, Co. Clare 13
Kilmichael Glassary, Argyll 173, 209–11; *208, 210*
Kiloran Bay, Colonsay 49, 52, 57, 58, 91, 94, 96, 120–1, 136–7, 139, 167; *59, 125, 138*
Kingscross Point, Arran 96
Kirkcudbright 67, 202–3
Kirkcudbrightshire 67, 86–91, 202–3; *88, 89*
Kirkmadrine, Wigtonshire 11
Kirk O' Banks, Caithness 142, 197

Kirkton, Dumfriesshire 89, 138; *89*
Kitzler Åhfeldt, Laila 15; *15*
knives 11, 50, 59, 65; *11, 63*
Knowe of Moan, Orkney 84, 151
Knowth, Co. Meath 143, 154

L'Anse aux Meadows, Newfoundland 121
La Tène (art style) xiv–xv; *35, 39*
ladles 80; *74, 104*
Laig, Eigg 155; *155*
Lamba Ness, Sanday, Orkney 153; *153*
language (*see also* writing) xvi, 6–7, 20–1
– British/Welsh 6–7, 16, 20
– English/Anglo-Saxon 6–7, 16
– Gaelic 6–9, 11, 13, 16–17, 20, 38, 75, 142, 146, 154, 179, 197, 211
– Latin xiii, xv, 6–7, 10–11, 17
– Norse/Old Norse 6, 16, 20, 38, 68, 146, 154, 162, 179, 197, 211
– Pictish 7, 9, 11, 13, 16–17, 20, 35
Largo, Fife *133*
Lasswade, Midlothian 195; *182, 196*
Lauder, Berwickshire 162; *162*
law 42, 50, 109, 147, 156, 192, 202
lead tanks 175
leather xvi, 5, 27, 31, 105, 120–1, 154, 190
Legerwood, Scottish Borders *195*
Lethnott, Angus 16; *12*
Lewis Chessmen (*see* Lewis Hoard)
Lewis Hoard (of ivory) 151, 168; *152*
Lewis, Isle of 50, 204
Lews Castle, Stornoway, Lewis 197–8
lions 20, 63, 122–23, 195; *19, 32, 63, 123, 196*
lignite (*see also* cannel coal) 88; *88*
Lindisfarne, Northumberland xvi, 36–8, 40–2, 76, 104, 191
Lindores, Fife 198
Lochar Moss, Dumfriesshire 88, 90
Loch Awe 25
Lochmaben, Dumfriesshire 89, 137; *89*
Lochnaw, Wigtownshire 13
Loch Seaforth 50; *51*
Lochspouts Crannog, Ayrshire 162, 192; *162*
Logierait, Perthshire 92
Loire 31
Long eighth century 29–35
Long eleventh century 205
longhouses 52, 77–8

looting 41, 73, 79–82, 84, 116, 118, 125, 139
Lordship of the Isles 3, 198, 205
Lothians 75, 92, 190
Loughan, Co. Derry 114
Lough Ennell, Co. Westmeath 143
Lough Kinale, Ireland 171
Low Countries (*see also* Frisia) 77
Luce Sands, Wigtonshire 154; *154*
Lunnasting, Shetland 13, 17; *18*

Macbeth (*see* Mac Bethad mac Findlaích)
Mac Bethad mac Findlaích, king of Alba (1040–57) 191, 198, 202, 204
Machrie, Islay 131, 145
Machrins, Colonsay 49, 53, 56, 58, 111–2, 114, 169; *58*, *112*
Máel Coluim mac Domnaill, king of Alba (943–54) 156
Máel Coluim mac Donnchada, king of Scotland (1058–93) 156, 191, 205
Máel Sechnaill, king of Ireland (*c*.846–62) 75
Maes Howe, Orkney 17
Magnus Barelegs, king of Norway 143
Mail, Cunningsburgh (*see* Cunningsburgh, Shetland)
Mains of Penninghame, Wigtownshire 177
Malcolm III of Scotland (*see* Máel Coluim mac Donnchada, king of Scotland (1058–93)
Man, Isle of 3, 20, 68, 175, 179
manuscripts and books xiii–xv, 6–10, 17, 27, 31, 35–6, 40, 113; *170*
– Anglo-Saxon Chronicle 8, 36
– Book of Kells xiii, 164
– Chronicle of the Kings of Alba 9
– *Chronicum Scottorum* 9
– *Codex Amiatinus* 34
– Echternach Gospels *170*
– *Historia Brittonum* 7
– *Historia ecclesiastica gentis Anglorum* 6
– *Lebor Bretnach* 7
– *Lebor na Cert* 154
– *Life of St Findan* 156
– Lindisfarne Gospels xiii
– Stuttgart Psalter 173, 180
– vellum/parchment 27, 31, 40
– *Vita Columbae* 156
markets (*see also* trade) 31, 36, 81, 90, 101, 113, 124, 131, 134, 138, 142, 147–9, 154–6, 167, 197–9, 202–3, 204, 205
Mästermyr, Sweden 175
May, Isle of 142, 198
Mayback, Papa Westray, Orkney 53
Meigle, Perthshire 11, 181
Melhus, Trøndelag, Norway 79, 169
Melle, France 130
Melrose, Scottish Borders 75
Meols, Wirral 94
mercenaries 148, 199
Mercia 7–8, 26, 29, 30, 74, 88, 90, 92, 94; *88*, *90*
metalworking (*see also* ingots) 5, 21, 33–4, 40, 78–81, 95, 110–11, 114, 118, 124, 140, 143, 148–9
– tools 95
Mid Calder, West Lothian 185; *184*
Midross, Loch Lomond 96, 145
migration 53, 69, 104, 106–8, 129
Minchmoor, Scottish Borders 173; *174*
missionaries 34–5
monasteries xiii–xiv, 10–11, 13, 16, 25–6, 29–31, 33, 35–8, 40–3, 73–6, 79–80, 104, 142–3, 153–4, 156, 191–2, 201, 209
money (*see also* ring-money; trade) 31–2, 86, 103, 132, 141–3, 145–51, 189, 197–203, 205
Monifieth, Angus 14, 180–1; *182*
Monkhouse Green, Stromness, Orkney *82*
Monybuie, Kirkcudbrightshire 90, 175; *174*
Monymusk, Aberdeenshire 114, 173, 199
Moray 3, 6, 9–10, 30–1, 74, 92–7, 179, 190–1, 202, 204, 205
mormaers 10
Morocco 199, 201
mottes 84, 192
mounts 31, 83, 87, 169, 170–1; *78*, *84*, *170*, *171*
Mull, Isle of 115; *115*

neck-rings 50, 92, 135–6, 165, 200; *50*, *157*, *197*
Neolithic 17, 28, 52
Ness Broch, Caithness *168*
Newark Bay, Orkney 61, 67, 142
Newcastle 190
Newstead, Scottish Borders 33
Nith 89
Normandy 197–8, 206 n.48
Normans 156, 190–2, 197–8, 205
North Atlantic 37, 61, 79, 105–6, 108, 121, 129, 148, 150–1, 163
North Berwick, East Lothian 67
North Sea xv–xvi, 29–31, 36, 37, 43, 54, 76, 81, 90, 104–6, 150, 191
North Uist 44 n.41, 200, 204; *200*
Northumbria 3, 7–8, 10, 13, 17, 25, 29–30, 34, 36, 42, 43, 52, 64–5, 74–6, 81, 84, 86, 88, 91–2, 96, 104, 132, 144, 190; *63*, *64*
Norway xv, 3, 37, 53–55, 61, 65, 76, 79–81, 83, 106, 108, 112–3, 121, 123–5, 135, 137, 147–8, 150, 153, 162, 163, 167, 169, 176, 198, 200; *78*

Offa, king of Mercia (757–96) 26, 130, 157 n.6
ogham (*see* writing)
oils 30, 34, 195
Olaf Guthfrithson, king of Dublin (934–41) 144
Óláfr (Olaf, Amlaíb), brother of Ívarr 75, 155
Old English (*see* language)
Old Norse (*see* language)
Old Scatness, Shetland 78
Onuist map Vurguist, king of Picts (729–61) 26–7
Orkney 5–6, 13, 49, 73, 76–9, 84, 107, 138, 148, 154, 156, 162, 163, 166, 179; *23*, *76*, *82*, *166*, *167*
– earls and earldom of 3, 9, 141, 143, 148, 191, 197, 205, 209
Oronsay 79; *79*
Orphir, Orkney 14, 17, 142, 148
Orton Scar, Cumbria 133
Owain of Strathclyde 144
Oxna, Shetland 200; *200*
Oxtro Broch, Orkney 14

paganism 20, 28, 36–7, 41, 42, 48–9, 50, 54, 56, 61, 68–9, 104, 121, 161, 169, 173, 181, 195
papar- (place-name) 38
Papa Stronsay, Orkney 176
Papa Westray, Orkney 38, 53
Papil, Unst, Shetland 38
Papil, West Burra, Shetland 13, 17, 38, 179
parishes 195–6

pearls 140
pectoral cross (*see* cross pendants)
pendants
 – amber 164–5
 – bear teeth 162; *162*
 – coin 163, 165; *165*
 – jet 162, 165; *162*
 – touchstone 165, 166; *167*
Penrith, Cumbria 133
'Permian' rings 133; *134*
Perth 202
Perthshire 7, 9, 29, 75, 83–4, 91–2; *84*, *92*
Petersen, Jan 54
Pictish symbols xiii–xiv, 11, 14–16, 74, 122, 175; *xii*, *4*
Picts and Pictland (*see also* language, Pictish, Pictish symbols) xiii–xiv, 5–6, 10, 13, 16, 17–18, 25–31, 42, 43, 48, 53, 58, 61, 69, 74–6, 79, 82, 87–88, 91–2, 92–7, 104, 109–11, 114, 120–5, 130, 132, 136, 144, 156, 163, 169, 170, 173, 178, 179, 181, 190–1
 – disappearance of xiv–xv, 75–6
Pierowall, Westray, Orkney 49, 53, 62, 107–9, 114; *52*, *112*
pilgrimage 73, 201–2
pins (*see also* ringed pins, brooch-pins) 50, 81, 101, 103, 105, 108–9, 124, 177, 198, 203
 – bone 77, 162–3; *77*, *102*, *164*
 – cross-head *164*
 – frustrum-head 204; *204*
 – globular 90; *88*, *90*, *105*
 – knobbed 118; *119*
 – linked 91; *88*
 – lozenge-head 164; *145*, *164*
 – lyre-headed 205; *205*
 – racquet-head *92*
 – stick 136, 144, 154, 190, 203, 204–5; *77*, *92*, *136*, *145*, *154*, *204*
 – zoomorphic 77, 103, 163; *77*, *102*, *164*
plough 65; *65*
Pool, Sanday, Orkney 78
porphyry 166, 175–7, 202; *167*, *176*
Port Glasgow, Inverclyde 145, 197
Portmahomack, Easter Ross xiv, xvi, 30, 33, 35, 37–8, 42–3, 122–3, 140, 142–3, 153, 168, 170, 173, 197–8; *32*, *35*, *39*
Prague 155
processional cross 80–1, 171

raids and raiding xvi, 8–9, 30, 36–8, 40, 41–3, 65, 73–80, 82, 86–8, 92, 112, 117, 122, 129, 133, 140, 143, 145, 148–9, 154, 156, 189, 191–2, 198, 204, 211; *39*
Reay, Caithness 49, 181; *182*
regime change 74–5, 129
relics xiii, 34–5, 38, 73, 80–1, 87, 121, 165, 172–3, 176, 193, 205, 209–11; *194*
reliquaries and shrines 29, 34–5, 41, 76, 79–83, 94, 114, 121, 123, 140, 169, 173, 193, 199, 205, 209–11; *79*, *82*, *194*
Renfrewshire 146
Repton, Derbyshire 68
Rhynie, Aberdeenshire 30
Ribble, River 190
Ribe, Denmark 37, 62, 106
Ridgeway Hill, Dorset 57
ringed pins 118, 125, 135, 177, 203–4; *119*
 – crutch-headed 77, 203; *77*, *188*
 – kidney-ringed 118, 204; *204*
 – polyhedral 118, 121, 135, 163, 204; *119*, *120*, *136*
 – Vestfold-type 121; *125*
Ringerike style 192
ringforts 84
ring-money 77, 141–3, 145–51, 153, 157, 197, 199, 202, 203; *77*, *142*, *143*, *197*
rock crystal 83, 86, 165, 201; *84*
Rogart, Sutherland 84, 91–2, 111, 170; *85*, *111*
Rome xiv, 34, 73, 172, 176, 202
Romanesque 185, 189, 191, 195, 196, 204
Romans/Roman Empire 5–7, 11, 25–6, 28–9, 33, 95, 103, 123, 130, 140, 154, 199, 202
Ronaldsway, Isle of Man 94, 140; *95*
Roslin, Midlothian *119*
round towers 192
Roxburgh, Scottish Borders 202, 209
Rubh' An Dunain, Skye 155
runes (*see* writing)
Rus' 131–2, 163
Russia 106, 131, 133

Saevar Howe, Orkney 78, 91, 96, 175; *174*
sails 65, 150, 155
St Andrews, Fife 11, 27, 178, 179, 202; *202*
St Blanes, Kingarth, Bute 201
St Columba 25, 28, 38, 40–1, 43, 73, 80, 143, 156, 209, 211, 172

St Cuthbert 36, 38
St Donnan of Eigg 42
St Edmund the Martyr 145
St Fillan *194*
St Findan 156
St Germain-en-Laye, Paris 80
St Margaret, queen consort of Scotland (1070–93) 192, 205
St Mary's Isle, Kirkcudbright 202–3, 203
St Ninian 36
St Ninian's Isle, Shetland 16, 20, 34, 56, 66, 82–4, 110–2, 114–5, 121–4, 165, 176, 197; *35*, *83*, *110*, *114*, *122*
St Patrick 6, 156
St Vigeans, Angus 11, 16, 20, 178
Salme, Estonia 37
Samarkand, Uzbekistan 131; *131*
Sandwick Bay, Unst, Shetland *168*
Saxons 7–8, 73
Scar, Sanday, Orkney 49, 53, 65, 123–4; *124*
Scotland/*Scotia*, medieval kingdom xvi, 3, 7, 10, 189–92, 199, 205
Scots xvi, 6–7, 9, 27, 30, 38, 74, 129, 144, 205
Scott, Walter 77
Scottish Borders (region) 44 n.41, 75, 91–2, 190, 209; *91*, *92*
Scottus Eriugena, John 7
sculpture (*see* carved stones)
sea travel xv, 30, 36–7, 81, 125
Selkirk, Scottish Borders 91–2; *91*
Shanmullagh Hoard, Co Armagh 80–1, 116, 175
Shapinsay, Orkney 166; *167*
Shetland 13, 49, 6674, 76–9, 82–5, 107, 209, 163; *76*, *77*, *83*
shields 50–1, 54, 57–60; *52*, *58*, *105*
shrines (*see* relics; reliquaries)
Sicga of Northumbria 42
sickles 50, 61, 65; *50*, *52*, *63*
Sigtuna, Sweden 176
silk 36–7, 87, 108, 130–1, 140, 156, 201
silver chain 86, 94, 116, 198; *93*, *105*
Skaill, Orkney
 – hoard 5, 131, 133, 135–7, 141, 143, 148, 166; *134*, *136*, *157*, *166*
 – settlement 163, 166
slavery and slave trade (*see* hostage-taking) 35–6, 41–2, 73, 89, 125, 129, 154–7

Solway Firth 191, 202
Sound of Jura 200–1
spears 51, 57; *52*
spices 30, 36–7, 130
spindle-whorls (*see also* textiles, tools for production) 16, 20, 61, 149–50; *88*, *150*
spoon 85, 111; *83*
stable isotope analysis 37, 43, 53, 61–2, 66
Stanley, Perthshire 92
steatite 33, 148–9, 151; *149*, *150*
steelyards (*see* balance scales)
Stevenston Sands, Ayrshire 89
Stidriggs Hoard, Dumfriesshire 90
Storr Rock Hoard, Isle of Skye 131, 133, 134, 141, 166; *130*, *131*, *134*
strap-ends (*see also* belts) 65, 84, 91, 92, 144, 202; *63*, *64*, *88*, *91*, *145*
Strathclyde 88, 91, 118, 144–6
Strathearn 25, 74, 144
Strath Fillan, Perthshire 25, 175; *174*
Stromness, Orkney *150*
Struan, Perthshire 175
'Sueno's Stone', Forres, Moray 179–80
Swandro and Westness settlement, Rousay, Orkney 52, 54, 62, 78; *11*, *52*
Sweden 37, 79, 90, 106, 175, 176; *80*
swivel-ringed strap-fittings 190; *190*, *191*
swords 16, 34, 40, 51, 53–60, 62, 101, 123, 145, 170, 177; *46*, *55*, *59*, *83*
– Anglo-Saxon 54, 56, 144
– Frankish 54–5, 81, 113
– weaving 65, 105; *63*
Synod of Birr (697) 42
Syria 202; *202*

Talnotrie Hoard, Kirkcudbrightshire 87–92, 94, 130–1, 137; *88*, *89*, *90*, *91*
'Tara Brooch', Bettystown, Co. Meath 110, 115–6
Tarbat (*see* Portmahomack, Easter Ross)
Tashkent, Uzbekistan 131; *131*
tattooing 104
tax (*see also* tribute) 192
Tay, River and Firth 9, 28, 142, 199, 202
Tees, River 190
ten Hompel, Simone 5, 21
Teviot, River 195
Texa, Islay *195*

textiles (*see also* clothing, sails, silk) xvi, 57–8, 65, 86, 105, 108, 148, 150–1, 177, 210
– linen 65, 105, 108, 201–2
– tools and production (*see also* spindle-whorls) 60, 65, 148–50, 154, 199, 202; *52*, *63*, *105*, *150*, *203*
Thorinsstadir, Iceland 176
Thor's Hammer 50, 161–2; *50*
Thurso, Caithness 20
timber 31, 154, 185
Tiree, 145, 154, 204; *154*
Torbeckhill, Dumfriesshire 70 n.41, 144
Torbhlaren, Argyll 210
Torksey, Lincolnshire 81, 88, 92, 96, 130–1, 137
Torshov, Akershus, Norway 170
touchstone 165, 166; *87*, *167*
trade (*see also* burghs; markets) 30–36, 54, 81, 89–90, 95, 106, 129–57, 167
Traprain Law, East Lothian 11, 33
Trewhiddle, Cornwall 94
Trewhiddle-style art 31, 86, 90–1, 96; *91*, *97*
tribute 34, 41, 75, 130, 134, 139, 141, 143, 148, 154, 192, 199
Trier, Germany 176
Tullibole, Kinross-shire 178; *178*
Tundergarth, Dumfriesshire 89, 200
Tweed, River 3, 190–1, 196
tweezers 104; *104*
Tyne, River 7, 10, 156, 190
Tyninghame, East Lothian 195–6; *196*

Ukraine 131
Unst, Shetland 107
Urnes style 193
Uzbekistan 131; *131*

Vallay, North Uist 116; *117*
Vendel (art style) 50; *51*
verde antico (*see* porphyry)
Vik, Grimstad, Norway 149
'viking panic' 40–1, 82–3
vikings (terminology) 8, 59, 69, 73, 82
Vinjum, Sogn og Fjordane 65
Volga, River 131

Walcheren 74
Wales 7, 76, 114, 198

Wamphray, Dumfriesshire 89
weapons, killing of 57, 59, 65
weight units 89–90, 92, 129, 132–3, 138–41, 147, 201
weights, scale 40, 80–1, 88–9, 91, 94–6, 137–8, 140, 145, 149, 157, 166, 167; *88*, *89*, *138*, *139*
– cubo-octahedral 92, 137
– oblate-spheroid 138; *139*
Wessex 7–8, 36, 74, 94, 96, 130
Westerseat, Caithness *107*
Westness, Rousay, Orkney (*see also* Westness Brooch; Swandro and Westness settlement) 16, 49, 51–4, 57, 60–66, 68–9, 111–2, 114–8, 123, 148, 153, 162, 169; *23*, *46*, *52*, *55*, *63*, *64*, *65*, *117*, *170*
Westness Brooch 64–6; 115–18; *23*, *63*, *64*
'west of Scotland' mount 171; *172*
whalebone 65, 124, 168; *124*, *152*
whetstones 37, 166
Whithorn, Wigtonshire 30, 33, 36–8, 67, 89, 138–9, 142, 154–5, 176, 196, 198, 201, 203, 205
'Whithorn school' of sculpture 177, 181
Whitmuirhaugh, Scottish Borders 34
William I, king of England 191, 198
wine xiii, 30, 34
wooden containers 165, 166, 169
Woodstown, Co. Waterford 57–8, 138–9
Workington, Cumbria 68
writing (*see also* Pictish symbols) 10–17, 20
– Greek 10
– Kufic (Arabic) 10
– Latin 10–11, 16–17, 25, 34; *12*, *35*
– ogham 10, 14–16, 20, 175, 179; *11*, *14*, *18*
– runes, Anglo-Saxon 8, 10, 13, 17, 86, 95, 138, 162; *96*, *163*
– runes, Norse 8, 10, 13–17, 20, 68, 143, 146, 148, 162, 179; *2*, *11*, *14*, *15*, *18*, *68*, *146*, *150*, *162*
Wulfheard, abbot of Hoddom (*c*.789–96) 38
Wulfstan, bishop of Ely 164

York 90, 114, 134, 140, 145, 149, 153, 164, 165

Zedig, Henrik 15; *15*

Acknowledgements

The publisher is grateful to the following sources for permission to use their objects, images or text within this publication. No reproduction of material in copyright is permitted without prior contact with the publisher or the original sources.

The author extends grateful thanks to the curators, conservators, critical friends, photographers, picture library and publishing staff, collections services and administrative staff who have contributed to the making of this book. Thanks go especially to Hamish Torrie and the Glenmorangie Company for supporting this critical new research, and to Martin Goldberg and Alice Blackwell for their contributions to the text. Fraser Hunter, Katherine Forsyth, Ewan Campbell, Caroline Paterson and James Graham-Campbell all wrestled with early drafts and I am indebted to them. Andrea Freund, Victoria Thompson and Alex Sanmark were early collaborators. Tom Horne and Colleen Batey have been sounding boards from the start, and the work of Courtney Buchanan, Erin McGuire and Elizabeth Pierce paved the way. Neil McGuigan, Alex Woolf and Stephen Driscoll helped to guide the final chapters. Particular gratitude is also extended to the staff of NMS Photography, Neil Maclean and Amy Fokinther. The input of many others is acknowledged throughout.

IMAGE CREDITS

NATIONAL MUSEUMS SCOTLAND
Image © National Museums Scotland

All images included in this book are © National Museums Scotland, except for the following:

THE BIBLIOTHÈQUE NATIONALE DE FRANCE
© Biliothèque Nationale, France for Figure 7.17

THE BRITISH MUSEUM
© The Trustees of the British Museum for Figure 5.34

DOUG SIMPSON
© Doug Simpson/Still Print for Figure 2.1b

DUMFRIES MUSEUM
Courtesy of Dumfries and Galloway Council Museum Service for Figure 4.22

E. CAMPBELL
For Figure 3.25

HEATHER CHRISTIE
For Figure 3.24

HISTORIC ENVIRONMENT SCOTLAND
AOC Archaeology © Historic Environment Scotland for Fig 4.18
© Crown Copyright: HES For Figure 7.32

MANX MUSEUM
© Manx Museum for Figure 4.35

MUSEUM OF ARCHAEOLOGY, UNIVERSITY OF STAVANGER, NORWAY
© Terje Tveit – Museum of Archaeology, University of Stavanger for Figures 5.17, 5.32

NATIONAL MUSEUM IRELAND
Reproduced by kind permission of the National Museum of Ireland for Figure 5.31

NEIL HANNA
For Figure 1.9

NORGES ARKTISKE UNIVERSITETSMUSEUM
For Ts4052 in Figure 4.6

NTNU VITENSKAPSMUSEET, NORWAY
Photo: Åge Hojem, NTNU University Museum. CC BY-SA 4.0 for Figure 4.34

ORKNEY MUSEUM
Courtesy of Orkney Museum for Figure 5.33

PROFESSOR STEPHEN DRISCOLL
For Figure 2.1a

THE SWEDISH HISTORY MUSEUM
© Ola Myrin, The Swedish History Museum/SHM (CC BY) For Figures 4.9, 7.20